# AFRICAN WOMEN PLAYWRIGHTS

Edited and with an
Introduction by
Kathy A. Perkins

Foreword by
Amandina Lihamba

# AFRICAN WOMEN PLAYWRIGHTS

University of
Illinois Press

Urbana
and
Chicago

∞ This book is printed on acid-free paper.

Library of Congress Cataloging-in-Publication Data

African women playwrights / edited and
with an introduction by Kathy A. Perkins ;
foreword by Amandina Lihamba.
p. cm.
Includes bibliographical references and index.
ISBN-13 978-0-252-03387-2 (cloth : alk. paper)
ISBN-10 0-252-03387-6
ISBN-13 978-0-252-07573-5 (pbk. : alk. paper)
ISBN-10 0-252-07573-0
1. African drama (English—Women authors.
2. African drama (English)—20th century.
3. Women—Africa—Drama.
I. Perkins, Kathy A.
PR9347.A385 2008
822'.9140809287—dc22 2008027197

**Dedicated to**

*Rose Mbowa (1943–1999)*

(Professor in the Department of Music, Dance, and Drama at Makerere University in Uganda. Her contributions to theatre not only in East Africa but also the continent were enormous. At the time of her death, she was in the process of translating her renowned play *Mother Uganda* [1987], which looks at the resilience of the people in her warring homeland.)

# CONTENTS

# FOREWORD

> An attendant solitude, silence or even darkness in the act of literary creation sooner or later comes to an end. That becomes the moment for another kind of revelation. Where the dream of lives, of delights and sorrows and infinities in the world—vividly dreamt in the luminous dark chambers of the mind eventually enters the light of day.
>
> **Hasif Amini, *Prince Claus Fund Journal,* April 2006, 12**

Creative impulses might arise from a number of sources both public and private, individual or collective, but, for the most part, they germinate and flower guided by the individual imagination. Two of the arguments for women's poor representation in the literary output of Africa are their lack of time to dream and indulge their imagination for creative works. Given women's many roles and socioeconomic tasks, that argument might bear credence. Throughout history, however, women have surmounted all society-imposed obstacles to create space for themselves to dream, fertilize their imagination, and participate in the production of culture.

Using a variety of forms, women have been tellers of tales through dance, song, music, drama, and a variety of narrative forms. The women writers whose works are collected in this volume are part of a long tradition of storytellers, but they also bear witness to women's creative powers that have demanded to enter the light of day.

The publication of this volume is cause for celebration. We celebrate women's creative output as inspired by the cultural milieu of Africa with its socioeconomic restlessness, energies, and the synergy of its people's hopes and aspirations. As a result, the women writers and those works that they present are shown to be part of multiple communities within the socially, aesthetically, and politically complicated and diverse Africa.

The celebration, though, is tinged with regret because of those many other works that have not been given the light of day through publication. Complaints that African writers generally and African women writers specifically are not well represented in published literary works are not new.

During the mid-1980s, I made a couple of visits to the world-renowned writer Ayi Kwei Armah, who was living some few miles outside Dakar, Senegal. He had a very interesting building project, which has since come to fruition, that would give him, on one hand, a family home that he needed as a social and literary base and, on the other, a refuge for African writers who wanted to give themselves space and time to write. The growing use of computers and information and communications technology (ICT) added to the belief that voices of African writers, including those of women writers, would increase in volume and variety. With the exception of a few initiatives, including the current volume, gaps await to be filled. The gaps are especially glaring in African women's writing for the theatre.

Although many art and literary forms are conceived, executed, and consumed individually, theatre forms are public and private, collective and individual. The play might be engendered through ideas, imagery, issues, or personages—in the privacy and solitude of one's imagination; however, it demands to be collectively executed with input from other relevant artists and publicly exhibited as performance. Instead of seeing those aspects as a challenge, publishers have taken them for limitations and have published either very few or no works by African writers, especially women writers. Because of the complex skills and factors needed for theatre's success, publishers have found it easier to take their chances with the men rather than with the women writers, most of whom are literary unknowns.

The publication of this volume, however, will make more African women writers known. Our knowledge of them will be either because we are meeting them and their works for the first time or because we know them from their other output or because we have known them literarily and personally for a long time and are being reacquainted with them. In any case, this volume offers us different perspectives on realities and issues depicted and interrogated in such a way that our belief in theatre as something that matters in life is strengthened and deepened. Even when the depiction and interrogation portray despair or bleakness, the writers urge us toward change, the companion of hope.

Amandina Lihamba, Dar es Salaam, Tanzania

# ACKNOWLEDGMENTS

I am extremely grateful to the many people who helped make this collection a reality. To Sandra L. Richards, who guided me to such wonderful people as the late Rose Mbowa in Uganda and provided overall advice. I am also indebted to those who led me to plays, festivals, writers, and other research sources: Pearl Robinson, Tinashe Kajese, Gabriel Kiiza, Praise Zenenga, Ismail Mahomed, Kris Kelley, Vernita Fort, and the ladies at Femrite in Kampala, Uganda.

Special thanks to those individuals who assisted with research, editing, and manuscript preparation: Gloria Bigelow, Ashley Walls, Diana Jaher, Frederic C. Jaher, and Bernard Tabaire.

My various trips to Africa would not have been possible without support from the University of Illinois (UIUC) Research Board, the UIUC College of Fine and Applied Arts Office of the Dean, the African Studies Program, the United States Information Service (USIS), and the Hewlett Foundation.

As always, I wish to thank my family for their personal support: the late Marion and Minerva Perkins, Linda Perkins, and Alphonse Perkins.

Finally, I am most grateful to the remarkable writers who made this collection possible. Thank you for sharing your wonderful stories!

# AFRICAN WOMEN PLAYWRIGHTS

# INTRODUCTION

> Our problem is that we have listened so rarely to women's voices, the noises of men having drowned us out in every sphere of life, including the arts. Yet women too are artists, and are endowed with a special sensitivity and compassion, necessary to creativity.
>
> **Adeola James,**
> ***In Their Own Voices: African Women Writers Talk* (1990)**

In the mid-1980s, a friend gave me a copy of Ama Ata Aidoo's play *The Dilemma of a Ghost,* introducing me to the little-known work of African female playwrights. These women's anonymity was particularly troubling because their male counterparts were comparatively well known. In the early 1970s when I attended Howard, a historically black university, the works of Wole Soyinka, a Nigerian, and Ghana's Chinua Achebe were regularly taught. South African male playwrights, in particular, were popular at this time: Mbongeni Ngema, Athol Fugard, Welcome Msomi, and Duma Ndlovu had plays performed in the United States in the 1970s and 1980s. As a lighting designer, I have had the opportunity to work with a number of visiting African theatre companies on productions written and directed by African men. The marginalization of African female playwrights impacts negatively on many fields, including African history, sociology, women's studies, literature, and theatre studies. In addition, directors, performers, and audiences receive no exposure to plays by African women.

Convinced that African women were not as silent as they appeared, I wanted to find out why African female playwrights were ignored. As a result of my association with various South African exile artists, I made my first trip to Africa in 1995, determined to track down as many African women writers as I could. When I arrived in South Africa, I found that women on the continent had much to say but that their pieces were not regularly published or produced. I encountered such a wealth of dramatic material that my first collection of African plays focused entirely on South Africa women: *Black South African Women: An Anthology of Plays* (1998).

During the past twelve years, I located African female playwrights in nearly a dozen countries. I spoke with South African artists Gcina Mhlope, Fatima Dike, Muthal Naidoo, Malika Ndlovu, Sindiwe Magona, and Magi Williams. Nigerian writers include Stella Oyedepo, Onyema Onyekuba, Juliana (Julie) Okoh, Amanda Chimamanda, Tess Onwueme, and the late Zulu Sofola. Uganda claims Mary Karooro Okurut, Violet Barungi, Mercy Ntangaare, the late Rose Mbowa, and Elvania Zirimu. Ama Ata Aidoo and the late Efua Sutherland are Ghanaians. Zimbabwean female playwrights include Tsitsi Dangarembga and the late Tisa Chifunyise. Werewere Liking works in the Ivory Coast. Two writers, Micere Mugo and Andiah Kisia, are Kenyan. Amandina Lihamba and Penina Mlama are Tanzanians. There are many more, all working on a wide variety of theatrical productions, including radio dramas; staged prose; performance pieces utilizing text, dance, and music; and collective creations (group improvisational projects).

When I ask African male and female artists why so few African women publish, they offer several explanations, not all gender based. A few argue that Africa has a stronger oral, rather than written, cultural tradition. Others associate traditional literary forms with the colonizing Western countries that subjugated Africans to centuries of bigotry and exploitation: Written drama, for example, was taught by missionaries during the colonial period.

Discrimination, however, plays the greatest role. African women experience huge inequities in education. Boys, far more than girls, are encouraged to attend school. Consequently, African women have a lower literacy rate. The 2007 Education for All Global Monitoring Report (EFAGMR) notes that "disparities in education detrimental to girls remain pervasive in sub-Sahara Africa. . . . Disparities between the sexes are even worse at higher levels. . . . More than 60% of the adult illiterates in sub-Saharan Africa are women."[1] South African writer Sindiwe Magona elaborates: "[T]o dream of being a writer, you need to have grown up around people who read and write and to hear of people and see people who look like you do this thing. And if you don't ever come across books written by women who look like you, it doesn't occur to you, even if you like writing, that I could write. How will you ever begin to think? Do you know I was 32 before I held a book in my hand written by a black woman? 32 years old! It was Maya Angelou's *I Know Why the Caged Bird Sings*."[2]

Female playwrights face additional challenges. Theatre is a time-consuming medium, demanding large amounts of rehearsal and production time, and most African women are expected to stay home tending their families. In some cultures, women who work in the theatre are considered immoral or "loose." In my 1998 interview with the late Tisa Chinfunyise of Zimbabwe, she explained, "We wanted . . . to change the attitude of the community towards theatre workers. Our families must know that when we are at work, we are at work like any other person. We are not going out to be a prostitute or anything like that."[3]

Finally, many women engage in a theatrical practice known as collective creation or playmaking (the term varies by country), which is difficult to publish. Ethel Dhlamini, a former staff development fellow (SDF) in the Department of Theatre Arts at the University of Zimbabwe, explains the concept of playmaking/collective creation as practiced in her area:

> Playmaking is when you get all these ideas. . . . [Y]ou start with improvisations and then you agree that, all right, we like this scene—you improvise it, or you should change it like this, and somebody is taking notes, and in the end you will try to make it into a script. So in the end, everybody takes part in the writing of the script. . . . You improvise the first scene the way you have agreed that you want the first scene—to feature this man, this wife, in this house, etc. And usually an assistant director . . . will be jotting down all the blocking and the lines and everything. Then we will go into groups of threes or fours and try to write down the rest using the assistant director. And in the end, this group brings together the script and puts it together, and then you all agree that this is how it went.[4]

A collective creation text, adapted to specific audiences and performed in a variety of local languages, is constantly in flux, making publication and translation a challenge.

Publications by African women are rarely fictional and almost never plays. According to Ghanaian Ama Ata Aidoo, "They will publish us if they can tell themselves that the book will be a textbook, and that's the same orientation that local publishers have. They are not interested unless they think they can get a textbook. . . . But so far there haven't been too many publishers who would publish us, just to publish us."[5]

Most of the playwrights I spoke with feel that publishers are not receptive to creative work. The little fiction that is published is generally written by well-known authors, leaving minimal opportunity for new voices. As playwright Juliana (Julie) Okoh explains, "It is very difficult to publish in Nigeria. Novels are easier and have a larger market. Plays are seen [as having] a smaller audience. . . . It's difficult to publish anything in Nigeria except [by] names such as Soyinka and already-established authors."[6] Aidoo agrees, "It's a vicious cycle. People are not really going to invite you to a conference unless you are published. I mean once you are published, you may get invited, and you may get your next book a lot more easily done, but otherwise, no."[7]

Some writers blame the small fiction market for the African people's lack of interest. Goretti Kyomuhendo, one of the founding members of Femrite, Uganda's only female publishing company, sees the issue as primarily economic: "Creative work doesn't sell. Publishing houses don't have enough capital to invest in creative work. So they have been investing mainly in textbooks—nonfiction. So it's not easy, and we don't blame the publishers because it involves a lot of money and very few people walk into a bookshop to buy a book. The reading culture is really poor, and it's a matter of priority. Buying a book is seen as a luxury—something you can put off until you get enough money."[8] Goretti admits, however, that "lack of interest coupled with low purchasing power are the primary reasons why creative work doesn't sell in Uganda, or Africa for that matter. For example, some people who can afford to buy a book . . . businessmen and women, have no interest in buying them (or are simply ignorant about the value of a book and reading), and those who would love to read, like students and teachers, cannot afford them. So, yes, the two issues go hand in hand."[9]

Many artists I interviewed agree that few people could afford books when items such as food, shelter, and school fees take priority. Most think that the demand for fiction would be greater if Africans had more discretionary income. As Nathalie Etoké points out: "I met Cameroonian students at the university. They were eager to learn, to study, but they just don't have access to books. . . . [P]eople want to learn, but I think money and poverty . . . how can you buy books for ten bucks when if you have ten bucks you can eat for like ten weeks? . . . Yes . . . you have other countries, of course, where people don't read, but I am going to speak for Cameroon—people read. Young people read."[10]

### The Dawn of a New Day

Since beginning this project in the mid-1990s, I have seen African women receive greater exposure, largely through their own efforts. Whether attending African arts festivals (particularly the annual Grahamstown Festival in South Africa, one of the largest arts festivals in the world), book fairs, and readings or participating in theatrical productions, African female playwrights have gained increased visibility, particularly on college campuses.

Though all black female writers are underrepresented in college literature classes, African women are especially neglected. Increasingly, scholars, activists, and artists are addressing this problem. In the United States, for example, during the Yari Yari (the Future) Conference held in 1997 and 2004 at New York University, women writers from Africa and the diaspora met to discuss ways to increase African women's presence in college syllabi. The attendees expressed frustration that the academic world gives short shrift to the literature of black women, particularly women from Africa. Similar events took place in Africa. In

1999, the Zimbabwe International Book Fair (the largest event of its kind on the continent) featured pieces by African women. And in 2005, African writers met in Uganda to address the country's neglect of its female writers. Yet African women writers still have a long way to go. During the 2002 Zimbabwe International Book Fair, when a list of "Africa's 100 Best Books of the 20th Century" was announced, only eighteen were written by women. Three of the authors are represented in this collection: Ama Ata Aidoo (*Anowa*), Sindiwe Magona (*Living, Loving and Lying Awake at Night*), and Tsitsi Dangarembga (*Nervous Conditions*). *Anowa* was the only play on the list.

Since the turn of the twenty-first century, African female writers have seen a small increase in the number of published novels and poems (dramatic works, however, still lag behind). This is largely the result of their own efforts. Frustrated by the indifference of the established presses, African women increasingly turn to self-publication. Weave, a South African women writers' group, published *ink@ boiling point: A Selection of 21st Century Women's Writing from the Southern Tip of Africa* (2000). Zimbabwe Women Writers in Harare, now more than a decade old, offers a variety of publication opportunities and workshops.

Perhaps no women's press on the continent has had more impact than Femrite. Organized in 1996 in Kampala, Uganda, the company publishes journals and novels. In addition, members mentor other African women interested in starting their own publishing companies. (I am fortunate to have a member of Femrite contribute to this anthology.) According to Goretti:

> So people start saying there's nothing coming from Uganda. The writers there are dead. We said, "But we're writing. The manuscripts are here." So we came together and said our ultimate goal is have our works published. . . . We got small funding to start an office, to buy equipment, and to sponsor our plan for the next two years. . . . For us here in Uganda, we're lucky in that we have NGOs [nongovernmental organizations] which fund specifically women's projects. . . . We came as a group. Somebody came and said, "I have a manuscript here." We did it all by ourselves. People brought in stories . . . one would edit; this one proofread; and this one would put it on the computer. That's how we did it—on a voluntary basis.[11]

Publishing houses in the United States are increasingly receptive to African women authors. The Feminist Press, located at the City University of New York, has released three volumes of the four-volume *Women Writing Africa: The Southern Region* (2003), *West Africa and the Sahel* (2005), and *The Eastern Region* (2007). In 2002, Indiana University Press published *African Theatre Women,* a collection of essays, plays, and book reviews edited by Jane Plastow (possibly the first book to focus exclusively on women in African theatre). Random House released Chimamanda Adichie's novel *Half of a Yellow Sun* in 2006. And Nigerian playwright Tess Onuewe, who currently resides in the United States, has had several plays published by the African Heritage Series and Wayne State University Press.

To my knowledge, however, this is the first collection—at least in English—of plays devoted exclusively to those written by African women. Selecting material for this volume proved difficult: There was so much to choose from. To preserve the playwright's original voice, I opted for a representational group of writers from the English-speaking African countries (with the exception of Nathalie Etoké, who writes in French). To counter the stereotype of the primitive African exotic, I focused on plays that depict women living primarily in urban areas and the special problems they face. Finally, because African women writers who live and work abroad stand a better chance of publication, I selected (with one exception) pieces by women who spend most or all of their time in Africa.

I have met all the writers included in this collection. They are a diverse lot, ranging in age from their twenties to early sixties and representing South Africa, Zimbabwe, Uganda, Cameroon, Nigeria, Kenya, and Ghana. Some are emerging writers; others have received national and international recognition. Ironically, the majority of these women consider themselves writers as opposed to playwrights: Five have published novels, six write poetry, two self-identify as spoken-word artists, and two are filmmakers. Many of them have met through conferences, festivals, or women writers' groups. (Until recently, it was difficult for women across the continent to get to know one another. With increased access to the Internet, female artists are now able to communicate and exchange ideas.)

Because African women playwrights work in a variety of genres, I wanted to represent a range of performance styles. Theatre in Africa is as diverse as the people who inhabit the continent: "African theatre is likely to contain and bring together diverse elements of entertainment and communication, including dance, music mime, masquerade, song, etc. Its language can be verbal, musical or physical, and all at the same time."[12] Seven of these pieces were written for the stage, one for radio, and one is an excerpt from a novel. Not all the plays included here contain conventional Western dramatic elements. Traditionally, African women are storytellers, so some of these plays originated as stories. Many African women perform excerpts from novels or short stories, including works by Bessie Head of South Africa or Mariama Ba of Senegal. (This tradition is common throughout the African diaspora; women regularly adapt Toni Morrison, Alice Walker, and Zora Neal Hurston.) With the exception of Violet Barungi's *Over My Dead Body* (Uganda), all the plays in this collection have been performed, some in major theatre complexes, others in universities or community centers. In the accompanying biographies, each writer shares her experiences of working in the theatre of her particular country.

Most of the plays in this volume educate and/or heal. For many African women playwrights, theatre is an opportunity to increase awareness of the country's sociopolitical problems. As traditional African theatre, unlike European theatre, encourages audience participation, playwrights hope to persuade audiences to take action on specific issues or, at the very least, to gain knowledge of them. The plays in this volume examine a wide variety of controversial subjects: cultural differences, HIV/AIDS, female circumcision, land rights, women's right to higher education, racial/color identity, and the prostitution of indigent young girls.

Any anthology of African female playwrights would be incomplete without Ama Ata Aidoo's classic piece, *The Dilemma of a Ghost,* which explores cultural differences and misunderstandings between Africans and African Americans that still resonate more than four decades after the play's original publication. Another earlier published play is *She No Longer Weeps,* by Tsitsi Dangarembga, an internationally known novelist and filmmaker. Written while the writer was a student at the University of Zimbabwe, the play critiques the traditional role women play in a patriarchal society.

Newer plays include one by Nigerian author Juliana (Julie) Okoh, who explores female circumcision in *Edewede* and questions the meaning and relevance of traditional culture. Nathalie Etoké dramatizes the plight of poverty-stricken young women forced into prostitution in *Better Days Come in Bitter Ways.* (Etoké, the only Francophone writer in the collection, graciously translated the monologue excerpt from her book in order to retain its original voice.) Andiah Kisia has written a radio drama, *Homecoming,* which examines corruption and family loyalty. And former Femrite editor and Ugandan novelist Violet Barungi comically treats a serious theme—the importance of women's education—in *Over My Dead Body.*

I feel privileged to publish once again Malika Ndluvo (Lueen Conning) and Sindiwe Magona. Both writers appeared in my anthology of plays on South African women. Malika's *A Coloured Place,* which first appeared in 1996 and has been updated for this volume, outlines the problems Coloureds have experienced in past and present South Africa. Sindiwe's first play, *Vukani!,* looks at the current AIDS crisis in South Africa through the eyes of one middle-class family. Given the AIDS pandemic that is currently ravaging Africa, many female dramatists focus on this particular problem. Two emerging actresses/playwrights, Dania Gurira, from Zimbabwe, and Nikkole Salter, from the United States, have cowritten a play exploring the devastating parallels between AIDS-stricken African and North American black women in *In the Continuum,* which has toured throughout the United States, South Africa, Zimbabwe, and the United Kingdom and received extensive media coverage. (According to the Centers for Disease Control and Prevention [CDC], in 2005, 64 percent of the 127,150 women living with HIV/AIDS in the United States were African American. The 2004 statistics list AIDS as the leading cause of death for African American women aged 25 to 34 years.[13] In 2005, the Joint United Nations Program on AIDS [UNAIDS] reported that "women comprise an estimated 13.2 million—or 59% of adults living with HIV in Africa south of the Sahara."[14])

I hope these plays destroy the accepted—and erroneous—myths currently surrounding African women. Binyavanga Wainaina, playwright and founder of the Kenyan literary magazine *Kwani?* (*So What?*), mentions some of the racist stereotypes often used to describe African women in his satirical article "Oh Africa: Simple Rules in Writing about the Dark Zulu":

> Always include the starving African, who wanders the refugee camp nearly naked and waits for the benevolence of the West. Her children have flies on their eyelids and pot bellies, and her breasts are flat and empty. She must look utterly helpless. She can have no past, no history; such diversions ruin the dramatic moment. . . . Avoid having the African characters laugh, or struggle to educate their kids, or just make do in mundane circumstances. Have them illuminate something about Europe or America in Africa. African characters should be colourful, exotic, larger than life—but empty inside, with no dialogue, no conflicts or resolutions in their stories, no depth or quirks to confuse the cause.[15]

Readers and audience members will meet a variety of African women through these plays. It is time for African women playwrights to shed their anonymity and share their creativity and experience with the world. In the past few years, African women working in other areas enjoy increasing visibility. Wangari Maathia, for example, a trained biologist and environmental activist from Kenya, recently became the first African woman to win a Nobel Peace Prize. In 2006, sixty-seven-year-old economist Ellen Johnson-Sirleaf was elected president of Liberia—the first woman to head an African country. Aloysie Cyanzayire presides over the Rwandan Supreme Court (nearly half of all parliament members are women—the largest percentage of any country in the world). And Dora Akunyili, trained as a pharmacologist, heads the National Agency for Food and Drug Administration Control (NAFDAC) in Nigeria. As African women move into positions of power, they are changing the face of the political landscape. African countries now address such previously ignored social issues as education, land rights for women, female circumcision, spousal abuse, child custody, rape, and disease.

As African women achieve greater recognition in various socioeconomic fields, the world pays more attention to their creative work. I hope that this book will increase the visibility of and appreciation for the works of African female artists, in their own countries and around the world. Vernita Fort, former deputy director for Southern African Affairs with the United States Agency for International Development (USAID), stated:

> In our current global context of economics, culture and politics, we see instances wherein western markets and consumers "validate" and "legitimate" African artistic creations through purchasing their works before African markets and consumers do. The phenomenon of Paul Simon and the South African ensemble Ladysmith Black Mambazo [a cappella singing group] is an example of this in the arena of music. The same might be said of some artistic creations in other parts largely populated by recent African descendents. In Jamaica for example, Chris Blackwell produced and invested in the legendary Bob Marley. Many Jamaicans suggest that Bob Marley's international acclaim preceded and influenced Jamaica's full embrace and support of his music.[16]

African women in all professions play increasingly important roles in their respective countries. I believe in the statement made by dramatist Zulu Sofola during the Women in Africa and the African Diaspora (WAAD) 1992 conference in Nigeria: "Something like a whirlwind is sweeping across our planet and this time it is feminine. But it does not bear a female name like those given to hurricanes and tornadoes in the West. It is curious indeed that when the real thing began to happen, minds that used to christen such natural eruptions and turbulence with female names failed to identify this one as a real female turbulence. Just the same, there is no doubt that a wind of change is blowing strong across our human landscape and it is female."[17]

**Notes**

1. United Nations Educational, Scientific, and Cultural Organization (UNESCO), United Nations Education for All Global Monitoring Report (EFAGMR) Regional Overview: Sub-Saharan Africa, 2006, http://unesdoc.unesco.org/images/0014/001485/148550E.pdf, 6.
2. Sindiwe Magona, personal interview, July 23, 1993.
3. Tisa Chinfunyise, personal interview, June 21, 1998.
4. Ethel Dhlamini, personal interview, June 21, 1998.
5. Ama Ata Aidoo, personal interview, August 2005.
6. Juliana Okoh, personal interview, June 30, 2001.
7. Ama Ata Aidoo, personal interview, August 2005.
8. Goretti Kyomuhendo, personal interview, June 10, 1998.
9. Goretti Kyomuhendo, personal letter, August 25, 2006.
10. Nathalie Etoké, personal interview, October 8, 2005.
11. Goretti Kyomuhendo, personal interview, June 10, 1998.
12. Martin Banham, African Theatre Today, with Clive Wake (London: Pitman, 1976).

13. Centers for Disease Control and Prevention, "HIV/AIDS among Women," June 2007, http://www.cdc.gov/hiv/topics/women/resources/factsheets/pdf/women.pdf.

14. UNAIDS, "2006 Report on the Global AIDS Epidemic," http://www.unaids.org/en/HIV_data/2006GlobalReport/default.asp.

15. Binyavanga Wainaina, "Oh Africa: Simple Rules in Writing about the Dark Zulu," Ode Magazine, April 2006, 49.

16. Vernita Fort, personal letter, May 10, 2007.

17. Zulu Sofola, Sisterhood: Feminism and Power—From Africa to the Diaspora (Trenton, NJ: Africa World, 1998), 49.

*Pause.*

# THE DILEMMA OF A GHOST

*Ama Ata Aidoo*

The purpose of theatre is to entertain people and inform them, and if possible inspire them, by bringing societal issues upwards. It is immediate in a way that nothing else is.

**Ama Ata Aidoo, Ghana**

One of Africa's best-known female writers, Ama Ata Aidoo is a poet, novelist, playwright, short-story writer, and educator. Born Christina Ama Ata Aidoo in 1942 in the village of Abeadze Kyiakor in Ghana, Ama Ata grew up in a royal Fanti household. Her family encouraged education, and she began writing at an early age. When she was just sixteen, her short story "To Us a Child is Born" won a prize given by the national newspaper, *The Daily Graphic.*

In 1961, Ama Ata attended the University of Ghana, where she majored in English. She continued to write, winning a prize organized by Ibadan's Mbari Club—a renowned cultural workshop in Nigeria—for her story "No Sweetness Here." While still a student, Ama Ata wrote her first play, *The Dilemma of a Ghost,* in 1964. Published the following year, *The Dilemma of a Ghost* was one of the first plays published in English by an African woman. Her second play, *Anowa,* was published in 1969.

Ama Ata's extensive list of publications include: *No Sweetness Here,* a collection of short stories (1970); *Our Sister Killjoy,* a novel (1977); two collections of poetry, *Some One Talking to Sometime* (1985) and *An Angry Letter in January* (1992); a second novel, *Changes* (1991); and another collection of short stories, *The Girl Who Can and Other Stories* (1997). She has also written numerous essays and articles. Much of her work focuses on the tensions between disparate African and African American viewpoints.

For many years, Ama Ata taught in the United States and Ghana. In 1982 and 1983, she was Ghana's minister of education. Later, while living in Harare, Zimbabwe, she consulted for the Curriculum Development Unit of the Ministry of Education and was the first chair with the Zimbabwe Women Writers. In the mid-1990s, Ama Ata returned to Ghana permanently, and co-founded Mbaasem (Women's Affairs), a support group for women writers. Ama Ata is a visiting professor in Africana studies at Brown University in the United States.

### Excerpts from Our Interviews

*On her early ambitions to write:*

I was writing before I was eight. . . . you know, kind of scribbling. But it was at age fifteen, that I articulated to myself and to other people . . . that I wanted to be a poet.

*On the conception of* The Dilemma of a Ghost:

I didn't have any idea—I was all of 23, and all I knew was that I wanted to write a play. . . . I had no conception of an audience. I had no idea that I wanted to say anything to anybody. . . . All I remember was that I had wanted to explore the dynamics of marriage between people from different backgrounds. When the idea came to me, I had wondered what I would write about [perhaps] a white boy and a black girl. And I dismissed that immediately because it seemed to me too easy. . . . I mean, there are bound to be problems when black people marry white people. So, I wasn't interested at all. I also thought of writing [about] two Ghanaians from different backgrounds—like with different ethnic backgrounds or something—and I thought, that didn't interest me. So . . . I knew right from the beginning that a marriage between an African American and a Ghanaian would present my imagination with the biggest challenge.

***On some of the controversy surrounding the play:***

A number of African American women have talked to me about the play. In fact, I've met African American American women who say that, you know, the play speaks to them a lot. . . . I think that African American women who are actually married to African men and who have lived in Africa seem to appreciate the play. . . . While other African American women who have never been to Africa and who have had nothing to do with African men seem to resent the play. . . . I've known for a long time that it was a controversial play. But I also know that at the time I was writing it, I didn't tell myself, oh, I'm going to write myself a controversial a play, so I've learned to accept all these diverse reactions to the play.

***On the play's publication:***

As soon as the play got produced, the representative for Longman Publishers actually came to my dormitory on campus and asked me for permission . . . to publish *Dilemma.*

***On why so few African works are published:***

Right now there is a lot more writing [in Africa] going on. . . . [T]he more writers we seem to produce, the less anybody wants to publish us. . . . [S]o far there haven't been too many publishers who would publish us, just to publish us. . . . Unless they can prove to themselves that it will be a good textbook. And that is a problem that all African writers have. And not exclusively women—but all African writers. But of course in any environment, including the U.S., an editor is more likely to pick a book and manuscript bearing a male writer's name than a woman's. . . . The fact that a lot of African American women and white women, too, have been publishing fantastic work and making money might be helping the situation.

***On what African women are writing:***

Well, the normal things—life. People have explored marital . . . life and death, polygamy, oppression, class confusion, marginalization of women and girls, . . . women and careers, and maintaining relationships—heterosexual relationships . . . all those things, like anywhere else.

*The Dilemma of a Ghost* was first presented by the Students' Theatre, Legon, on March 12, 13, and 14, 1964, at the Open-Air Theatre, Commonwealth Hall, University of Ghana, Legon.

Interview December 18, 1995, via telephone from Providence, Rhode Island, and August 2, 2005, in Accra, Ghana.

# THE DILEMMA OF A GHOST

*Ama Ata Aidoo*

### Characters

Ato Yawson (Ebow): A young Ghanaian graduate
Eulalie Yawson (née Rush): Afro-American graduate
Esi Kom (Maami): Ato's mother
Monka: His sister
Nana: His grandmother
Akyere: His elder aunt
Mansa: His younger aunt
Petu: His elder uncle
Akroma: His younger uncle
1st Woman and 2nd Woman: Neighbours
Boy and Girl: Two children in a dream; the boy being the ghost of Ato's former self
The Bird of the Wayside

### Prelude

The action takes place in the courtyard of the newest wing of the Odumna Clan house. It is enclosed on the right by a wall of the old building and both at the centre and on the left by the walls of the new wing. At the right-hand corner a door links the courtyard with a passage that leads into the much bigger courtyard of the old house. In the middle of the left wall there is a door leading into the new rooms. A terrace runs round the two sides of the new sector.

In the foreground is the path which links the roads leading to the river, the farm and the market.

I am the Bird of the Wayside
—The sudden scampering in the undergrowth,
Or the trunkless head
Of the shadow in the corner.
I am an asthmatic old hag

Eternally breaking the nuts
Whose soup, alas,
Nourished a bundle of whitened bones—
Or a pair of women, your neighbours
Chattering their lives away.
I can furnish you with reasons why
This and that and other things
Happened. But stranger,
What would you have me say
About the Odumna Clan? . . .
Look around you,
For the mouth must not tell everything.
Sometimes the eye can see
And the ear should hear.
Yonder house is larger than
Any in the town
—Old as the names Oburumankuma, Odapadjan, Osun.
They multiply faster than fowls
And they acquire gold
As if it were corn grains—
But if in the making of
One Scholar Much is gone
You stranger do not know.
Just you listen to their horn-blower:
"We came from left
We came from right
We came from left
We came from right
The twig shall not pierce our eyes
Nor the rivers prevail o'er us.
We are of the vanguard
We are running forward, forward, forward . . . "

Thus, it is only to be expected that they should reserve the new addition to the house for the exclusive use of the One Scholar. Not that they expect him to make his home there. No . . . he will certainly have to live and work in the city when he arrives from the white man's land. But they all expect him to come down, now and then, at the weekend and on festive occasions like Christmas. And certainly, he must come home for blessings when the new yam has been harvested and the Stools are sprinkled. The ghosts of the dead ancestors are invoked and there is no discord, only harmony and a restoration of that which needs to be restored. But the Day of Planning is different from the Day of Battle. And when the One Scholar came . . . I cannot tell you what happened. You shall see that anon. But it all began on a University Campus; never mind where. The evening was cool as evenings are. Darkness was approaching when I heard the voices of a man and woman speaking . . .

**EULALIE**: Graduation! Ah well, that too isn't bad. But who's a graduate? What sort of creature is it? Why should I have supposed that mere graduation is a passport to happiness?

**ATO**: [*Harshly*] If you must know, woman, I think you do get on my nerves. Since you do not think much of a degree, why for heaven's sake did you go in for it?

**EULALIE**: Don't shout at me, if you please.

**ATO**: Do keep your mouth shut, if you please.

**EULALIE**: I suppose African women don't talk?

**ATO**: How often do you want to drag in about African women? Leave them alone, will you . . . Ah yes they talk. But Christ, they don't run on in this way. This running-tap drawl gets on my nerves.

**EULALIE**: What do you mean?

**ATO**: I mean exactly what I said.

**EULALIE**: Look here, I don't think that I'll stand by and have you say I am not as good as your folks.

**ATO**: But what have I said, for goodness sake?

**EULALIE**: Well, what did you mean by running-tap drawl? I only speak like I was born to speak—like an American!

**ATO**: [*Contrite*] Nonsense, darling . . . But Sweetie Pie, can't we ever talk, but we must drag in the differences between your people and mine? Darling, we'll be happy, won't we?

**EULALIE**: [*Relaxing*] I'm optimistic, Native Boy. To belong to somewhere again . . . Sure, this must be bliss.

**ATO**: Poor Sweetie Pie.

**EULALIE**: But I will not be poor again, will I? I'll just be "Sweetie Pie." Waw! The palm trees, the azure sea, the sun and golden beaches . . .

**ATO**: Steady, woman. Where did you get hold of a tourist brochure? There are no palms where we will live. There are coconut trees . . . coconut palms, though. Unless of course if I take you to see my folks at home. There are real palm trees there.

**EULALIE**: Ah well, I don't know the difference, and I don't care neither. Coconut palms, palm-palms, aren't they all the same? And anyway, why should I not go and see your folks?

**ATO**: You may not be impressed.

**EULALIE**: Silly darling. Who wants to be impressed? Fine folks Eulalie Rush has herself, eh? Could I even point to you a beggar in the streets as my father or mother? Ato, can't your Ma be sort of my Ma too?

**ATO**: [*Slowly and uncertainly*] Sure she can.

**EULALIE**: And your Pa mine?

**ATO**: Sure.

[*Following lines solemn, like a prayer*] And all my people your people . . .

**EULALIE**: And your gods my gods?

**ATO**: Yes.

**EULALIE**: Shall I die where you will die?

**ATO**: Yes . . . And if you want to, you shall be buried there also.

**[PAUSE.]**

**EULALIE**: [*Anxiously*] But darling, I really hope it won't matter at all?

**ATO**: What?

**EULALIE**: You know what, Native Boy.

**ATO**: 'Lalie, don't you believe me when I tell you it's O.K.? I love you, Eulalie, and that's what matters. Your own sweet self should be O.K. for any guy. And how can a first-born child be difficult to please? Children, who wants them? In fact, they will make me jealous. I couldn't bear seeing you love someone else better than you do me. Not yet, darling, and not even my own children.

**EULALIE**: You really sure?

**ATO**: Aren't you the sweetest and loveliest things in Africa and America rolled together? My darling, we are going to create a paradise, with or without children.

**EULALIE**: Darling, some men do mind a lot.

**ATO**: [*Vehemently*] Look at me, we shall postpone having children for as long you would want.

**EULALIE**: But still, I understand in Africa . . .

**ATO**: . . . Eulalie Rush and Ato Yawson shall be free to love each other, eh? This is all that you understand or should understand about Africa.

**EULALIE**: [*Delighted*] Silly, I wasn't going to say that.

**ATO**: Then forget about what you were going to say.

**EULALIE**: [*Persistently*] I only hope it's O.K.

**ATO**: It shall be O.K.

**EULALIE**: Ato!

## ACT 1

[*Evening. The two village women are returning from the river with their water pots on their heads.*]

**1ST WOMAN**: Ah! And yet I thought I was alone in this . . .
The lonely woman who must toil
From morn till eve,
Before a morsel hits her teeth
Or a drop of water cools her throat.

**2ND WOMAN**: My sister, you are not alone.
But who would have thought that I,
Whose house is teeming with children,
My own, my husband's, my sister's . . .
But this is my curse.
"Shall I do this when
This and that have nothing to do?"
No. And they all sit
With their hands between their knees.
If the courtyard must be swept,
It is Aba's job.
If the *ampesi* must be cooked,
It is Aba's job.
And since the common slave was away all day
There was no drop in the pot
To cool the parched throat.
I am telling you, my sister,

Sometimes we feel you are luckier
Who are childless.

**1ST WOMAN**: But at the very last
You are luckiest who have them.
Take Esi Kom, I say.

[*Esi Kom enters from the door on the right with two stools which she puts on the centre of the stage. For the rest of the scene, she moves stealthily but swiftly in and out of the stage arranging six stools in preparation for the next scene.*]

**2ND WOMAN**: What has happened?

**1ST WOMAN**: You know her son
That was away beyond the seas
Is now come back?

**2ND WOMAN**: So, that explains the new paint. When?

**1ST WOMAN**: Yesternight.

**2ND WOMAN**: Is he here?

**1ST WOMAN**: I do not know.

**2ND WOMAN**: I heard her younger children
Crying for eggs.

**1ST WOMAN**: Which means that those of us
Who are in this neighbourhood
Are going to have our mouths watering
With aroma of the fryings and stewings.

**2ND WOMAN**: Of course, that is what she always does.
And meanwhile the debts pile up.

**1ST WOMAN**: Yes, but the arrival of the son
May mean the paying of all the debts at last.
Her soul is a good one.

**2ND WOMAN**: Hmm. For my part, I would be ashamed
To live in a Clan house for
As long as she has done.
But let us hurry, my sister
For my food is getting cold.

[*They go out. After a minute or so, Esi Kom goes out too, having finished arranging the stools.*]

[*Later. It is quite dark now. The old woman totters in supported by her stick. In her youth, she had been a short, dark, petite femme with a will like iron. Now, though she is weak, her tongue is as sharp if not sharper for her eighty plus. She sits on one of the stools in the centre of the stage. She props her chin on her stick. Presently Ato enters from the door on the left. For a few seconds the old woman continues sitting motionless as she has not seen him, then suddenly she speaks.*]

**NANA**: I am glad you came and found me alive.

**ATO**: I am glad too.

**NANA**: And what is on your mind, my grandson.

**ATO**: There is nothing else on my mind, Nana.

**NANA**: Were you not thinking, nay hoping, you will come and find me dead?

**ATO**: Oh!

**NANA**: Do not be pained my grand-child. I just wanted to trouble you a little. But go and tell your mother that if she and the others do not come early, I will be angry.

[*Ato leaves by the door on the right.*] Already, naughty slumber is stealing over my senses.

[*A clanging noise from within.*] Yes, someone has tripped in the doorway, eh. One day the people in this house will commit murder. Do they not know that if the heavens withdraw their light, man must light his own way? But no. They will let us all lie in darkness. How will he find his way around this dark place should the ghost of one of our forebearers pay us a visit? But this is something one should not speak about. They say they buy *kresin* and pay for it with money . . . as, as if the penny will shine and light our way when it is tied in a cloth . . . But of course, they will say I talk too much . . . Are they not coming? They are now removing their pans, tchia! Are these women? I shit upon such women. When we were young a woman cleared her eating place after the last morsel had hardly touched her tongue. But now, they will allow their noise-making pans to lie around for people to trip over. But it is not their fault. If they had to use earthenware pots which broke more easily than eggs, they would have learnt their lessons long ago.

**ATO**: [*From within*] Maami, why do not you and my Uncles hurry? Nana is getting impatient.

[*He re-enters.*]

**NANA**: Have your Uncles Petu and Akroma come?

**ATO**: Yes, Nana.

[*Voices from within.*]

**MANSA**: [*From within*] Oh, the old woman again!

**NANA**: But what are they doing there?

[*Several voices. Petu and Akroma come in. The two men sit down.*]

**PETU**: Old woman, we greet you.

**NANA**: I respond, my Royal Ones. And how are you?

**PETU**: We are all well, Old One.

[*Ato slips into his room, left.*]

**NANA**: Akroma, how is your wife's stomach?

**AKROMA**: It is a bit better.

**NANA**: I notice you do not feel clear in your own inside. You people always say I talk too much. So I try not to put my tongue in your affairs. But I hope you would think of what I always say. Have we not had enough of the white man's medicines? Since they do not seem to do anything for your wife, why do you not take her to Kofikrom? The herbalist there is famous . . .

**AKROMA**: I have heard you, Old One. I would put it to her people and hear what they have got to say too.

**NANA**: [*With her eyes turned towards the entrance*] I say, what are you doing there? Why are you doing this thing to me?

**FEMALE VOICES**: Ah, here we are.

[*Esi Kom, Akyere and Mansa enter. The stage is well-lit now. The women sit around on the terrace.*]

**NANA**: Ah, your characters are not pleasing. What were you really doing by the hearth. I thought you knew that I must not sit here until the dew falls on me.

**MANSA**: Old One, it is all right. We won't do this again.

**AKROMA**: But where is our master, the white man himself?

**ATO**: [*From within*] I am coming, Uncle.

[*He comes out.*]

**PETU**: But where are you sitting? . . .

**ESI**: [*Overlapping Petu and directing her voice to the old sector*] Monka, are you not bringing your brother a chair?

**MONKA**: [*From within*] *Hei* Ebow!

**ALL**: What is it?

**MONKA**: [*Coming back with a chair*] The way some people became scholars is fearful.

**ATO**: What is the matter?

**MONKA**: The master scholar was sitting on the chair studying, so he could not move off!

[*Ato laughs.*] After all, what is he learning? Is it the knowledge of the leopard skin?

[*Sucks her teeth.*]

**ESI**: If it had been in any other home, he, Ebow, would have seen to it that we were all seated.

**AKROMA**: But I do now know what he has done for all of you to pick on him in this way.

**ESI**: Let us say what we cannot keep in us any longer, for the day Ebow becomes like you, he will kick us all around as if we were his footballs.

**NANA**: Esi Kom, leave that child alone, for no one knows what the man of fame and honour was like when he was a child.

**AKROMA**: But Old One, we can soon know the bird which will not do well, for his nest hangs by the wayside.

**ATO**: Let us give him, too, some time.

**MONKA**: I always say that one can always know the man who is civilised.

**NANA**: I think you should all know that Ato was always a humble one.

**PETU**: Of course, he is a first born. Our eldest hold that first borns are always humble. Our white master, we welcome you.

**ATO**: I thank you, Uncle.

**PETU**: Ah, we have been here at home but you . . .

**AKYERE**: I say . . .

**PETU**: What is it?

**AKYERE**: I say, Esi. For a long time I have not been seeing that sheep which you were rearing in Ato's name.

**AKROMA**: As for you women.

**ESI**: Ho, I have sold it.

**MANSA AND AKYERE**: Sold it!

**ESI**: But yes.

**AKYERE**: What did you do with the money?

**ESI**: [*Indirectly addressing Ato*] I have not done anything with it. It had a good market and I thought I would find some more money and add to it to give to Ato's father to pay for the bride price for its owner.

**AKYERE**: That is very good.

**PETU**: But women, can you not wait for us to finish what we came here to say? The child has just come from a journey. You have not welcomed him but already you want to marry for him.

**ATO**: [*As if just awake from sleep*] *Ei,* Uncle, are you talking of marriage?

**ESI**: It is nothing. I was only telling your aunt that I have sold your sheep to pay the bride price for you when you make up your mind to marry . . .

**ATO**: [*Casually*] But I am already married, Maami.

**ALL**: You are married? Married! Married!

**ESI**: [*Overlapping*] Who is your wife?

**AKYERE**: [*Overlapping*] When did you marry?

**MANSA**: Who is your wife?

**MONKA**: [*Overlapping*] What is her name?

**ESI**: Where does she come from?

[*Everyone repeats her words to create confusion.*]

**PETU**: You must all be quiet. One must take time to dissect an ant in order to discover its entrails.

**MONKA**: [*Laughing wickedly*] *Ei,* so I have a sister-in-law whom I do not know?

**AKROMA**: *Ei,* Monka, keep quiet.

**NANA**: [*Who has been sleeping since she last spoke*] What is all this noise about? Have you asked the child news from his journey?

[*Silence while everyone stares at Ato.*]

**PETU**: Ato, when did you marry?

**ATO**: That is what I was going to tell you. One week ago.

**NANA**: [*Spitting*] My grand-child, so you have married? Why did you never write to tell us.

**ESI**: Ato my son, who is your wife?

**ATO**: [*Quite embarrassed*] Eulalie.

**ALL**: Eh!

**ATO**: I said "Eulalie."

[*By now all the women are standing.*]

**MONKA**: Hurere!

**ESI**: Petu! Akyere! What does he say?

**THE WOMEN**: Hurere!

**MONKA**: Oh, let us say, let us say that some of the names that are coming into the world are fearful.

**ESI**: Ato, you know that some of us did not hear the school bell when it rang. Therefore we will not be able to say this name. This Uhu-hu . . . I want her real name, my son.

**ATO**: But Maami, this is her only name.

**MANSA**: Our master, isn't your wife . . . eh . . . Fanti?

**ATO**: No, aunt.

**AKYERE**: [*Contemptuously*] If so, what is her tribe?

**ATO**: She has no tribe. She does not come from . . .

**NANA**: [*Looking up at him*] She has no tribe? The story you are telling us is too sweet, my grand-child. Since I was born, I have not heard of a human being born out of the womb of a woman who has no tribe. Are there trees which never have any roots?

**PETU**: Ato, where does your wife come from?

[*A short silence. All look at Ato.*]

**ATO**: But no one is prepared to listen to me. My wife comes from . . . America.

**ESI**: [*Putting her hands on her head*] Oh Esi! You have an unkind soul. We always hear of other women's sons going to the white man's country. Why should my own go and marry a white woman?

**MONKA**: Amrika! My brother, you have arrived indeed.

**AKYERE**: But we thought that we too have found a treasure at last for our house. What have you done to us, my son? We do not know the ways of the white people. Will not people laugh at us?

**ATO**: [*Very nervously*] But who says I have married a white woman? Is everyone in America white? In that country there are white men and black men.

**AKROMA**: Nephew, you must tell us properly. We do not know.

**ATO**: But you will not listen to me.

[*All quiet. Eyes are focused on Ato.*] I say my wife is as black as we all are. [*Sighs of relaxation.*]

**ESI**: But how is it, my child, that she comes from Amrika and she has this strange name?

[*The old woman spits significantly.*]

**NANA**: Is that what people call their children in the white man's country?

**ATO**: [*Irritably*] It is not the white man's country.

**ALL**: O . . . O . . . Oh!

**ATO**: Please, I beg you all, listen. Eulalie's ancestors were of our ancestors. But [*warming up*] as you all know, the white people came and took some away in ships to be slaves . . .

**NANA**: [*Calmly*] And so, my grand-child, all you want to tell us is that your wife is a slave?

[*At this point even the men get up with shock from their seats. All the women break into violent weeping. Esi Kom is beside herself with grief. She walks round in all attitudes of mourning.*]

**ATO**: [*Wildly*] But she is not a slave. It was her grandfathers and her grandmothers who were slaves.

**NANA**: Ato. do not talk with the foolishness of your generation.

[*The two village women come into the path.*]

**1ST WOMAN**: My sister, what can be the meaning of this?

**2ND WOMAN**: That is what I cannot see.

**1ST WOMAN**: Probably the old woman is dead.

**2ND WOMAN**: She has not been very well lately.

**1ST WOMAN**: This is life.
Some are going
While others are coming.
That is the road to the life hereafter.

**2ND WOMAN**: Then let us start weeping, my sister.

[*They begin to weep and walk up stage, then they notice Nana.*]

**1ST WOMAN**: Ah, but look, she is sitting there.

**NANA**: [*Hobbles towards the women*] Yes, I am sitting here. So you thought I was dead? No, I am not. Go home good neighbours and save your tears for my funeral. It cannot be long now . . . Go.

[*The women turn back.*] No, do not go yet, I still need your tears.

[*All eyes turned on the women.*] My grand-child has gone and brought home the offspring of slaves.

[*Women's faces indicate horror.*] A slave, I say.

[*Esi Kom enacts horror and great distress.*] Hear what has befallen our house.

**ATO**: [*Moving to the front of the stage*] Heavens! Is there any reason why you should make so much fuss? All because I have married an African-American? If you only know how sweet Eulalie is!

[*He looks at the women and whistles.*] Now all this racket you are putting on will bring the whole town here.

[*He turns back abruptly, goes to his door, enters and closes it on the scene. All eyes are turned to the closed door now.*]

**NANA**: My spirit Mother ought to have come for me earlier. Now what shall I tell them who are gone? The daughter of slaves who come from the white man's land.
Someone should advise me on how to tell my story.
My children, I am dreading my arrival there

Where they will ask me news of home.
Shall I tell them or shall I not?
Someone should lend me a tongue
Light enough with which to tell
My Royal Dead
That one of their stock
Has gone away and brought to their sacred precincts
The wayfarer!

[*Everyone except Nana starts leaving the stage.*] They will ask me where I was
When such things were happening.
O mighty God!
Even when the Unmentionable
Came and carried off the children of the house
In shoals like fish,
Nana Kum kept his feet steadfast on the ground
And refused to let any of his nephews
Take a wife from a doubtful stock.

[*She turns to leave, and walks towards the door on the right.*] If it is true that the last gets the best of everything
[T]hen what is this
[W]hich my soul has drawn out for me?

[*Lights go out.*]

## ACT 2

[*A fortnight later. Afternoon. The two village women are returning from the woods where they have gathered some faggots.*]

**2ND WOMAN**: *Ei,* Esi Kom. Some child bearing is profitable.

**1ST WOMAN**: What has happened now?

**2ND WOMAN**: Nothing. It is only that I remember
Her and her affairs when we pass their house.

**1ST WOMAN**: Child bearing is always profitable
For were not our fathers wise
Who looked upon the motion of our lives
And said,
They ask for the people of the house
And not the money in it?
There is nothing that can compare with
Being a parent, my sister.

**2ND WOMAN**: Not always, my sister
If you perchance hear on a silent afternoon
The sound of a pestle hitting a mortar,
Go get out your mortar too
For they are only pounding cassava.

**1ST WOMAN**: Perchance they are pounding yam.

**2ND WOMAN**: Have you forgotten the daughter of this same Esi Kom? Have you not heard it whispered? Have you not heard it sung
From the end of the East road
To the beginning of the West
That Monka never marries well?

**1ST WOMAN**: But if Esi Kom bears a daughter
And the daughter finds no good man
Shall we say
It is Esi Kom's fate in childbirth,
Or shall we say it is her daughter's trouble?
Is not Monka the sauciest girl
Born here for many years?
Has she not the hardest mouth in this town?

**2ND WOMAN**: That is as it may
But Esi Kom suffers for it.

**1ST WOMAN**: My sister, even from bad marriages
Are born good sons and daughters.

**2ND WOMAN**: Who shall look after them?

**1ST WOMAN**: Do you ask that of me
When everybody knows
A son is back from the land beyond the seas?
Shall he not help to look after his nephews
And nieces when it was somebody else who
Looked after him in the days of his childhood?
You talk, my sister,
As if the days are gone
When the left hand washed the right
And the right hand washed the left.

**2ND WOMAN**: Perhaps they are not, my sister.
But those days are over
When it was expedient for two deer

To walk together,
Since anyone can see and remove
The beam in his eye with a mirror.

**1ST WOMAN**: These are sad sayings, my sister.
But where is his wife?

**2ND WOMAN**: I do not know, my sister.
But I heard them say that his mother
Had gone to knock the door of Yaw Mensa
To ask for the hand of his daughter for him.

**1ST WOMAN**: Oh, he would have had a good woman.
I saw that girl when she came home last Christmas.
School has not spoilt her, I think.

**2ND WOMAN**: And that is the sad part of it, my sister.
He has not taken this girl
Whom we all know and like,
But has gone for this Black-white woman.
A stranger and a slave—
But that is his and Esi Kom's affair.
I hear in the distance the cry of a child
That cry is meant for my ear.
Let us hurry home, my sister.

[*She takes the lead.*]

**1ST WOMAN**: Oh, Eternal Mother Nature,
Queen Mother of childbirth,
How was it you went past my house
Without a pause
Without a rest?
Mighty God, when shall the cry of an infant
Come into my ear;
For the sun has journeyed far
In my sky.

[*Lights out.*]

[*Late afternoon of the next day. Everywhere is quiet. Ato is asleep in the inner room. Eulalie comes in with a packet of cigarettes, a lighter, an ash tray and a bottle of Coca-Cola. She sits on the terrace facing the audience. She begins sipping the Coca-Cola and soon the voice of her mind comes across the courtyard. Later her mother's voice is also heard. As the voices speak on, her body relaxes except for her mouth which breaks into a light smile or draws up tightly; and her eyes, which stare in front of her or dart left and right generally expressing the emotions that her thoughts arouse in her.*] [*On the other hand the passage could be spoken as a soliloquy with the mother's voice interrupting from back stage.*]

**VOICE**: So at last here am I in Africa . . . Joseph and Mary! I hope I've done the right thing. What good fun I'm going to have here!

[*Smiles.*] Just reckon, I hear the cottons are exactly the thing! You hold on until I go to the shops . . .

[*She starts as she hears a rumble of drums*] . . . And anyway, supposing this is just an ugly mess I've let myself into, what am I going to do? You got a heart, Eulalie Rush? No. Now it's over to you Eulalie Yawson . . . Yawson. That surely is a name.

[*Smiles.*] Life can be funny at times, that's what Fiona used to say. Now, I must sort of confess that I am finding all this rather cute. Ato says there will be two boys in the house. Fiona, if you could only see me now.

[*Mouth grim.*] Or is it rather if I could only see you now? Sometimes a girl would just like to have someone she loves and knows to tell things to laugh with. But there is no one for me here who would have understood like you would, Fiona. There is no one even back in the States . . . Christ, Fiona, Pa and Ma! There was no one left was there?

[*Bends her head.*] And how can one make a family out of Harlem? Ma . . . with her hands chapped with washing to keep me in College . . . I say, [*smiles*] I never knew there is Coke in these parts.

[*Holding the Coca-Cola bottle affectionately.*] Fiona would have been shocked to hear it. How we used to talk of the jungle and the wild life . . . And I haven't seen a lion yet! As for his folks, they are cute. I adore the old one . . . His mother gives me a feeling, though.

[*She starts and stares as she hears the drums again.*] Ma, I've come to the very source. I've come to Africa and I hope that where're you are, you sort of know and approve. "'Lalie, you shall not stop. Chicken, you must have it all." And I had it all, Ma, even graduation. "You'll be swank enough to look a white trash in the eye and tell him to go to hell." Ma, ain't I telling the whole of the States to go swing! Congress, Jew and white trash, from Manhattan to Harlem . . . "Sugar, don't let them do you in." Ma, I didn't. "Sugar, don't sort of curse me and your Pa every morning you look your face in the mirror and see yourself black. Kill the sort of dreams silly girls dream that they are going to wake up one morning and find their skins milk white and their hairs soft blonde like them Hollywood tarts. Sugar, the dear God made you just that black and you canna do nothing about it." Ma, it was hard not to dream but I tried . . . only I wish you were not dead . . . I wish you were right here, not even in the States, but here in this country where there will be no washing for you no more and where . . . where . . . Oh Ma! But I know you would pat me on the back and say, "Sugar, you sure done fine." Native Boy is the blackest you ever saw . . .

[*Suddenly the drums just roll and roll. Eulalie throws away her cigarette, her eyes pop out. She is really scared. She mutters "Christ, Christ," like a caged animal. She rushed towards the room and crashes into Ato's arms.*]

**ATO**: Hullo, my sweet.

[*Then he notices her frightened look.*] What is the matter?

**EULALIE**: Can't you hear?

**ATO**: Ah, what is it?

**EULALIE**: Can't you hear the drums?

**ATO**: [*Cocks his ears*] Oh, those!

**EULALIE**: Aren't you afraid? I am.

**ATO**: Don't be absurd, darling.

[*Holds her close.*] But I thought that one thing which attracted you about Africa was that there is a lot of drumming here.

**EULALIE**: [*Relaxes and thinks*] Y—e—s. But, you know, I didn't guess they'll be sort of like this.

**ATO**: You thought they would sound like jazz?

**EULALIE**: Sure. Or rather like, you know, sort of Spanish mambo.

**ATO**: I see.

[*Chuckles.*] But there is nothing specially frightening about this, is there?

**EULALIE**: I don't know. I only thought it was witch-hunting.

**ATO**: What?

**EULALIE**: Witch-hunting.

**ATO**: Witch . . .

[*He bursts out laughing till he is quite breathless.*] Witch-hunting? O mine, who put that idea into your head?

**EULALIE**: But I understand there is always witch-hunting out here in Africa.

**ATO**: But still, why were you so scared? You aren't a witch yourself, are you?

**EULALIE**: Don't tease.

**ATO**: I'm not teasing. For after all, only a witch should be afraid of witch-hunting. For the rest of the community, it is a delightful sport.

**EULALIE**: [*Curious*] How quaint? Tell me more.

**ATO**: I will, but first, you tell me: how were Hiawatha and Minnehaha when last you met them?

**EULALIE**: Now you are really teasing, Native Boy. But I thought I would learn about all these things.

**ATO**: [*Chuckles*] Especially witch-hunting?

[*He takes her arm.*] Sorry, I don't know much about them myself. Those were only funeral drums. But I think you must have a siesta. If you don't, you'll have a nervous breakdown before you've learnt enough to graduate in primitive cultures . . .

**EULALIE**: [*Looking up accusingly*] Native Boy.

[*Ato turns to look at her and sees the Coca-Cola bottle.*]

**ATO**: Have you been drinking Coke?

**EULALIE**: Mm . . . Yes.

**ATO**: Excellent of you. I can't bear it warm.

**EULALIE**: And of course you carried a refrigerator down here.

**ATO**: I am sorry.

**EULALIE**: Christ, what are you apologising for? After all, I was only feeling a little homesick and I drank it for sentimental reasons. I could have had a much cooler, sweeter and more nourishing substitute in coconuts, couldn't I?

**ATO**: [*Confused and unable to say anything for some time*] I am thirsty too but I'll have a gin and water.

[*Eulalie's eyes follow him as he goes back to the room and she is still looking in his direction when he returns some minutes later with the bottle of gin, water and a glass. He catches the look in her eyes and sits on the terrace facing her.*]

**ATO**: [*Mixing the drink*] Darling, what is it?

**EULALIE**: What is what?

**ATO**: Well, there was such a look on your face. Were you going to say something?

**EULALIE**: [*Gets up and moves closer to him*] Yes.

**ATO**: [*Lightly*] Box on then.

**EULALIE**: Ato . . .

**ATO**: [*Interrupting*] By the way, are you interested?

[*Indicating the gin and water.*]

**EULALIE**: Yes.

**ATO**: Oh, I beg your pardon then.

[*He gives her the mixture, and forgets about one for himself.*]

**ATO**: Aha—a.

**EULALIE**: Ato, isn't it time we started a family?

**ATO**: [*Surprised*] Why? I thought . . .

**EULALIE**: Ya, I remember I bought the idea, but I got the feeling . . .

**ATO**: Heavens, women! They are always getting feelings. First you got the feeling you needed a couple of years to settle down and now you are obviously getting a contradictory feeling.

**EULALIE**: [*Her turn to look confused*] I hope you aren't taking it so . . . badly?

**ATO**: [*Boldly*] Not at all. It's only that I think we better stick to our original plans.

**EULALIE**: [*Tiredly*] Okay!

[*Long pause*] I'd better go and rest now.

[*She turns towards the door and the drink is entirely forgotten. Ato follows her into the room.*]

## ACT 3

[*Six months later. Saturday afternoon. Ato and Eulalie have come to spend a week-end. Her sunhat is lying on a chair in the courtyard. Two village children run in.*]

**BOY**: What shall we do now?

**GIRL**: *Kwaakwaa.*

**BOY**: All right. I will hide, you find me.

**GIRL**: No, I will not find you, I will hide.

**BOY**: I say, I will hide.

**GIRL**: No, I will.

**BOY**: I will not allow you.

**GIRL**: Then I will not play.

**BOY**: If you do not, I will beat you.

[*Hits her.*]

**GIRL**: [*Crying*] Beast!

**BOY**: Oh, I did not mean to hurt you. But you too! I have told you I want to hide . . . Let us play another game then. What shall we do?

**GIRL**: Let us sing "The Ghost."

**BOY**: Ghost . . . Ghost . . . ah, yes!

[*They hold hands and skip about in circles as they sing.*] "One early morning,
When the moon was up
Shining as the sun,
I went to Elmina Junction
And there and there,
I saw a wretched ghost
Going up and down
Singing to himself
'Shall I go to Cape Coast,
Or to Elmina
I don't know,
I can't tell.
I don't know,
I can't tell.'"

[*They repeat, but halfway through the lights go out. When the lights come up a few seconds later, the children have vanished. Ato bursts in immediately. His hair is disheveled, his trousers creased and his face is looking sleepy-eyed and haggard.*]

**ATO**: [*Looking right and left and searching with great agitation*] Where are they? Where are those two urchins? Heavens! Those scruffy urchins and the racket of noise they were making. Why should they come here? But . . . Where are they? Or was it a dream?

[*Panting*] Ugh! That's why I hate siesta. Afternoon sleep always brings me afternoon dreams, horrid, disgusting, enigmatic dreams. Damn this ghost at the junction. I loved to sing that song. Oh yes, I did. But it is all so long ago. I used to wonder what the ghost was doing there at the junction. And I used to wonder too what it did finally . . . Did it go to Elmina or to Cape Coast? And I used to wonder, oh, I used to wonder about so many things then. But why should I dream about all these things now?

[*Petu enters. He is in an old pair of trousers and a smock which make up his farm clothes.*] Probably I am going mad?

**PETU**: Oh—o!

**ATO**: *Ei,* Uncle.

**PETU**: I heard you are come and that is why I am coming to greet you.

**ATO**: You went to the farm?

**PETU**: My master, where else have I to go?

[*He sits on the terrace while Ato still stands.*] Since the morning has found us, we must eat. And as you know, some of us are not lucky enough to be paid only to sit in an office doing nothing. And that is why I have to relieve the wayside herbs of their dew every morning.

**ATO**: But my Uncle, we too work hard.

**PETU**: [*Sarcastic*] You believe that . . . But nephew, why were you talking so hard to yourself when I came in?

**ATO**: [*Uneasily*] I had had a queer dream.

**PETU**: Is that long ago?

**ATO**: No. It was only this afternoon when I lay down to rest.

**PETU**: An afternoon dream?

[*His face shows he is not terribly pleased even about the idea of it.*] What was the dream?

**ATO**: I dreamt that there were two children in this courtyard singing that song about the ghost who did not know whether to go to Elmina or to Cape Coast.

**PETU**: Ah.

[*He laughs.*] How funny!

**ATO**: But Uncle, the boy looked like me when I was a child.

**PETU**: [*Serious*] *Ei,* this needs thinking about. Do not be disturbed, although I do not like afternoon dreams myself. I will tell your grandmother and hear what she has to say about it.

[*He rises to go and sees Eulalie's hat.*] Did you bring your wife?

**ATO**: Yes. She too is resting.

**PETU**: [*Turns towards the door on the right*] Yo—o. I am going now. When your wife wakes up, tell her I give her welcome. I have brought some cocoyams from the farm and I will be sending her some by and by. Do not think too much about the dream.

**ATO**: Thank you, my Uncle. When you go, tell my mothers that we will be coming to see them this evening.

[*Petu goes away. Ato stands confused. Eulalie comes in.*]

**ATO**: Hullo, 'Lalie.

**EULALIE**: Hullo.

[*They kiss each other on the cheeks.*] I heard talking here, didn't I?

**ATO**: My Uncle came to give us welcome.

**EULALIE**: [*Anxious*] Oh, this means the whole lot of them will be coming to see us.

**ATO**: Would you rather we went to see the new Methodist School?

**EULALIE**: Lovely.

[*She kisses him on the cheek again, and takes her lovely sunhat. She puts it on and cocks her head for admiration. Ato says "Exquisite" and hand in hand they come down the courtyard following the path leading to the left.*]

[*Lights go off.*]

[*Two hours later. Esi Kom enters from the door on the right carrying two bundles wrapped in sack cloth. She opens the door to Ato's apartment. She puts the bundles in the outer room, comes out and is closing the door when Ato and Eulalie enter the courtyard from the path.*]

**EULALIE**: [*Sees the woman*] I say!

[*She glares at Esi Kom for a second or two and then turns on Ato*] Ato, would you care to ask your mother what she wants in our room?

**ATO**: Eh . . . Maami, were you looking for us?

**ESI**: Hmm . . . They told us when we arrived from the farm that you and your wife have come to spend today and tomorrow with us. So I thought I would bring you one or two things for I hear food is almost unbuyable in the city these days. And your nephews are so naughty that I knew if I did not bring them here they would steal the snails and roast them all in an hour's time.

**EULALIE**: What is she saying?

**ATO**: Oh, she only brought us food to take back with us.

**EULALIE**: What kind of food?

**ATO**: Maami, what did you bring?

**ESI**: Can not your wife herself go and see? After all, these are all women's affairs. Or do our masters, the Scholars, know what goes on in their wives' kitchen?

**ATO**: [*Persuasively*] Darling, will you go and check up, please?

[*Eulalie walks rather puzzled into the room. As she enters, she exclaims "Sweet Jesus" and rushes out closing the door behind her.*]

**ATO**: Darling, what is it?

**EULALIE**: Eh . . . some crawling things!

[*Composing herself.*] Anyway, tell your mother we are very grateful.

**ATO**: Maami, my wife says she thanks you a lot for the things.

**ESI**: Tell her I am glad she likes them . . . Now, I think I will go and prepare the evening meal. Monka will cook you and your wife some rice and stew. If you need anything, you come and tell us or just shout for any of the children.

[*She turns off. Then turns back.*]

[*To Eulalie*] "My lady," I am saying goodbye.

[*Accompanied by a wave of the hand. Eulalie waves back. The moment she is through the door on the right, Eulalie rushes to close it. Then she rushes into their room and brings out the sack bundle. She is crossing towards the path when Ato stops her.*]

**ATO**: What's all this?

**EULALIE**: Those horrid creatures of course!

**ATO**: Where are you taking them?

**EULALIE**: Throwing them away, of course.

**ATO**: What rubbish.

**EULALIE**: What do you mean? What rubbish? If you think I am going to sleep with those creatures, then you are kidding yourself.

**ATO**: But how can you throw them away just like that? Haven't you seen snails before?

**EULALIE**: My dear, did you see a single snail crawling on the streets of New York all the time you were in the States? And anyway, seeing snails and eating them are entirely different things!

[*She turns off as if to go on. Ato reaches her in two strides. He grabs a part of the sack.*]

**ATO**: But at least, I could give them to my mother to cook for me alone.

**EULALIE**: And give them the opportunity to accuse me of unadaptability. No, thank you.

[*She wrenches the bundle from Ato and as she turns off, Monka opens the door on the right door. Her eyes take in the scene. Eulalie hurries down and dumps the sack near the path. At the same time, Monka disappears closing the door on the right behind her. Eulalie and Ato just stare at each other.*]

**MONKA**: [*From within*] Maami, Maami, Ato's Morning Sunshine has thrown away the snails you gave them.

[*Ato and Eulalie are still staring at each other when Esi Kom enters.*]

**ESI**: [*Addressing Ato*] Is it true that your wife has thrown away the snails I brought?

**ATO**: Who informed you?

**ESI**: That is not important, but is it true?

**ATO**: [*Defensively*] She does not know how to eat them . . . and . . .

**ESI**: And what, my son? Do you not know how to eat them now? What kind of man are you growing into? Are your wife's taboos yours? Rather your taboos should be hers.

[*Monka re-enters and stands watching. Ato turns to her.*]

**ATO**: Yes, you went and told Maami, eh?

**MONKA**: *Ei,* take your troubles off me. Have you seen me here this afternoon?

**ESI**: These days, the rains are scarce and so are snails. But the one or two I get for you, you throw away.

[*Eulalie goes into their room.*]

**ATO**: But Eulalie . . .

**MONKA**: [*Derisively*] That's the golden name . . .

**ESI**: Yes, Hureri, Hureri . . . What does my lady say today . . . ?

[*Eulalie comes back, sits on the terrace and starts puffing her cigarette.*]

**MONKA**: She reminds me of the words in the song: "She is strange,
She is unusual.
She would have done murder
Had she been a man.
But to prevent
Such an outrage
They made her a woman!"
Look at a female!

[*Eulalie ignores Monka although her face shows she guesses at what is going on.*]

**ESI**: Hureri. Hmm. All the time I have been quiet as if I were a tortoise. But I have been watching, hoping that things would be different, at least, in this house.

**ATO**: [*Moving towards his mother*] Maami, this is only a small affair, what are you trying to say now?

**ESI**: What am I trying to say now?

**MONKA**: If nothing scratched at the palm fibre, it certainly would not have creaked.

**ESI**: If you listen, you will hear what I want to say. This is not the first time I have fallen into disgrace for bringing you things. Only it is my own fault. I should have learnt my lesson. The same thing happened the day I came to visit you at Accra . . .

**ATO**: Ah, are you still harbouring this grievance?

**ESI**: Do not annoy me, please. How can I forget it? I had traveled miles to come and visit you and your wife. And if you threw my gifts into my face and drove me out of your house, how can I forget it?

**ATO**: [*In desperation*] Maami, you make me too unhappy.

**ESI**: Listen to what he is saying.

**ATO**: We asked you and Monka to stay but you insisted on coming back.

**MONKA**: There are two kinds of offers. One which comes right from the bowels and the other which falls from the lips only. My brother, yours fell from your lips.

**ESI**: I had thought I would do as other women do—spend one or two days with my daughter-in-law, teach her how to cook your favourite meals. But as if I was not noticing it, neither you nor your wife bothered to give us seats to sit on or water to cool our parched throats . . .

**ATO**: I remember that Monka drank water.

**MONKA**: I begged for it!

**ESI**: . . . How can I then sleep in a house where I am not welcome? . . . Where did you throw the snails?

[*Ato looks left and right uncertain of what to do. Monka rushes to where Eulalie dumped the bundle and retrieves it.*]

**MONKA**: [*Coming back*] Here they are . . .

**ESI**: Bring them; at least we shall find a beggar to give them to.

[*Eulalie makes as if to stand and speak but sits down again and continues puffing at her cigarette.*] Oh, Esi, of the luckless soul. It is true,
Living a life of failure is like taking snuff
At the Beach. Just consider the troubles I
Have had—the school fees, the uniforms . . .

**MONKA**: As for the balls of *kenkey*, they are uncountable.

**ESI**: The tears I have shed . . .

**ATO**: Must you go on in that way, Maami?

**ESI**: Keep quiet, my son and let me speak now, for something has pricked my wound. My knees are callous with bending before the rich . . . How my friends must be laughing behind me now. "After all the fuss, she is poorer than ever before."

**MONKA**: Even I should not be such a pitiable creature now, after all, my brother is now a great man.

**ESI**: [*Overlapping*] Apart from the lonely journeys I made to the unsympathetic rich, how often did I weep before your Uncles and great Uncles while everyone complained that my one son's education was ruining our home.

**MONKA**: [*To herself*] I remember the time he was preparing to go to the white man's land where he went to take up [*indicating Eulalie*] this "Wonder"! The money . . . the money . . . This is something which no one should hear anything about. A great part of the land was sold and even that was sufficient for nothing . . . Finally, the oldest and most valuable of the family heirlooms, *kentes* and golden ornaments, which none of us younger generation had ever seen before, were all pawned. They never brought them into daylight . . . not even to celebrate the puberty or marriage of a single girl in this house. But since our master must buy coats and trousers, they brought them out on this occasion. They were pawned, I say. And have they been redeemed? When, and with what? Ask that again.

**ESI**: For what do I still trouble myself, giving unacceptable gifts? . . . I cannot get a penny to pay the smallest debt I owe. Hureri must have eh . . . what do they call it?

**ATO**: Maami, is it not enough now? Give me time to work.

**ESI**: No, my son, I shall speak. You have been back a long time yet. The vulture, right from the beginning wallows in the soup he will eat. Have your Hureri got all her machines now? Hureri must have a *sutof.* Hureri must have something in which to put her water to cool. Hureri, Hureri. Oh, the name keeps buzzing in my head like the sting of a witch-bee!

[*And with that she turns quickly off. Monka turns to follow up, taking the sack with her.*]

**MONKA**: We are going. Ato, we wish you and your "Morning Sun" a prosperous marriage.

[*She too goes away, banging the door behind her. The couple are silent, Ato with a bowed head and Eulalie still puffing at a cigarette. Presently Ato speaks.*]

**ATO**: [*Quietly*] Now you have succeeded in making trouble for me. Won't you congratulate yourself?

[*Eulalie continues to puff her cigarette. After what seems to be a long time, she puts the cigarette down, stamps on it, cries "Blast" and gets up to go into the room. Ato comes out of the courtyard, and following the path on the left, walks ever so slowly into the night.*]

## ACT 4

[*Another six months later. The door to Ato's room is open. A great deal of noise comes over from the old sector of the house. The two women are on their way from the market where they have bought fish, pig's feet, seasoned beef, etc., for their evening* fufu.]

**2ND WOMAN**: My sister, do not say it loudly,
Even fish is too dear to eat these days.

**1ST WOMAN**: If I think I have spent
So much on fish . . .

**2ND WOMAN**: And what shall I say?

**1ST WOMAN**: Why is there so much noise from that house today?

**2ND WOMAN**: Do you not know
Tomorrow is their "Sprinkling of the Stools"?
The son has come from the city.

**1ST WOMAN**: This reminds me of something
I had wanted to ask these many days.
If her son gets a goodly bag by the month
Why has Esi Kom still not . . .

**2ND WOMAN**: I crave pardon
For snatching the word from your mouth.
But my sister, roll your tobacco and stuff your pipe.
It has not been good going,
[T]he roof leaks more than ever before.

**1ST WOMAN**: But how can it be?

**2ND WOMAN**: If Nakedness promises you clothes, Ask his name.

**1ST WOMAN**: But I ask, how can it be?

**2ND WOMAN**: You ask me?

**1ST WOMAN**: But you know, my sister,
That my name is Lonesome.
I have no one to go and listen
To come back and tell me.

**2ND WOMAN**: Then scoop your ears of all their wax
And bring them here.
Esi Kom is not better than she was.

**1ST WOMAN**: Why?

**2ND WOMAN**: They never ask "Why."
Is it not the young man's wife?

**1ST WOMAN**: What has she done now?

**2ND WOMAN**: Listen, I hear she swallows money
As a hen does corn.

**1ST WOMAN**: Oh, Esi Kom!

**2ND WOMAN**: One must sit down
If one wants to talk of her affairs.
They say that the young man gets
No penny to buy himself a shirt . . .
But the strangest thing is that
She too works.

**1ST WOMAN**: Then how does she spend all that money?

**2ND WOMAN**: By buying cigarettes, drinks, clothes and machines.

**1ST WOMAN**: Machines?

**2ND WOMAN**: Yes, machines.
Her water must be colder than hailstone.
I heard it said in the market place
Monka's teeth were set on edge
For drinking water in her house.
And her food never knows wood fire.

**1ST WOMAN**: Does she tear at it uncooked?

**2ND WOMAN**: As for you, my sister!
She uses machines.
This woman uses machines for doing everything.

**1ST WOMAN**: Is that why their money
Never stays in their palms?

**2ND WOMAN**: But yes.

**1ST WOMAN**: This is very hard to understand.
Before God-up-there
My breasts have never given suck to a child,
But if what I hear mothers say are true,

Then the young people of the coming days
Are strange . . . very strange.

**2ND WOMAN**: Fear them, my sister.
If you meet them, jump to the wayside.
Have I not born eleven from the womb here?
I know what I am talking about.

**1ST WOMAN**: But this is too large for my head
Or is the wife pregnant with a machine child?

**2ND WOMAN**: Pregnant, with a machine child?
How can she be?
Does she know what it is to be pregnant
Even with a child of flesh and blood?

**1ST WOMAN**: Has she not given birth to a child since they married?

**2ND WOMAN**: No, my sister,
It seems as if the stranger-woman is barren.

**1ST WOMAN**: Barren?

**2ND WOMAN**: As an orange which has been scooped of all fruit?
But it is enough, my sister.

**1ST WOMAN**: Barren?

**2ND WOMAN**: One should not tell too much of a tale
And we must eat tonight.

**1ST WOMAN**: Barren! . . .

**2ND WOMAN**: The mouth will twist that says too much of them.
And as for her son's marriage,
The ear will break that hears too much of it.

**1ST WOMAN**: Barren!

**2ND WOMAN**: I must leave you then.
You know Esi Kom's troubles are many . . .

**1ST WOMAN**: Barren! . . .

**2ND WOMAN**: I say let us go.

[*She takes the lead.*]

**1ST WOMAN**: Barren! . . .
If it is real barrenness,
Then, oh stranger-girl,
Whom I do not know,
I weep for you.
For I know what it is
To start a marriage with barrenness.
You ought to have kept quiet
And crouched by your mother's hearth
Wherever that is—
Yes. With your machines that cook
And your machines that sweep.
They want people.
My people have a lusty desire
To see the tender skin
On top of a child's scalp
Rise and fall with human life.
Your machines, my stranger-girl,
Cannot go on an errand
They have no hands to dress you when you are dead . . .
But you have one machine to buy now
That which will weep for you, stranger-girl
You need that most.
For my world
Which you have run to enter
Is most unkind to the barren.
And for you—
Who shall talk for the stranger?
My daughter or my sister,
Whom I have never set eyes upon,
You will cry until your throat is dry
And your eyes are blind with tears.
Yes, my young woman,
I shall remember you.
I shall remember you in the hours of the night—
In my sleep,
In my sleepless sleep.

[*Lights go out.*]

[*Next morning. Petu enters with a wooden bowl full of white and oiled* Oto *(mashed yam), Akroma comes behind him carrying a brass tray containing a herbal concoction and a kind of sprinkling broom. They go round the courtyard sprinkling the walls and the floor first with* Oto, *then with the potion. The gong man beats the gong behind them. They circle thrice round the courtyard and are just leaving when Petu calls to Ato.*]

**PETU**: Nephew!

**ATO**: [*Comes from the room and for the first time in cloth.*] Here I am, my Uncle.

**PETU**: We have killed the goats and chickens. The women will send you and your wife some of the *Oto* and then you can eat a proper breakfast. But do you not think you and your wife should come near the Stool Rooms?

**ATO**: *Yoo,* Uncle, We are coming.

**PETU**: But you are a man. So you must come and drink with the men first.

**ATO**: Then I am coming with you now.

[*He goes into the room and returns in a minute. They all leave the courtyard by the door on the right.*]

[*Lights go out.*]

[*Several hours later, Eulalie enters from the door on the right. She surveys the courtyard with disgust.*]

**EULALIE**: What a blasted mess! Well . . .

[*She shrugs her shoulders.*] I suppose folks must have their customs. Though if you ask me, I think there has been enough messing round for one day.

[*She goes into the room and returns with a glass of whisky and, as usual, a packet of cigarettes and a lighter. She lights her cigarette and moving to the door on the right, peeps out into the old apartment. She makes a face. Ato enters from that direction.*]

**EULALIE**: [*Moving to him*] Native Boy, I have missed you dreadfully.

**ATO**: But you left us barely five minutes ago.

**EULALIE**: That shows you that after a year of marriage I am still in love with my husband which, incidentally, is a wonderful achievement.

**ATO**: By what standards? Because I am still in love with my wife.

[*They burst out laughing. Ato looks down at the glass in her hand.*] Sweetie Pie, don't drink too much.

**EULALIE**: But I have not been drinking at all.

**ATO**: This looks too strong.

**EULALIE**: I needed it so badly. I was getting rather nervy when I came back.

**ATO**: Well, now that I am back I don't think you need it, do you, Sweetie Pie?

**EULALIE**: Just let me finish this.

[*Voices behind the door to the right.*]

**ATO**: I think some of my people are coming.

[*Anxiously*] Let me put your drink in the room for you.

**EULALIE**: Why?

**ATO**: I don't think they'll approve.

**EULALIE**: [*Taking a sip*] Nonsense.

[*Voices draw nearer.*]

**ATO**: [*Trying to take the glass from her*] But 'Lalie, don't let them find you in the very act.

**EULALIE**: [*Sarcastically*] Is this a taboo?

[*She laughs and goes into the room. Just then, Petu and Akroma enter followed by Monka carrying the brass bowl containing the herbal concoction. Close behind her enter Esi Kom, Mansa, Akyere and Nana.*]

**ATO**: *Ei!*

[*He gives the two chairs in front of the door to the two men who sit down. Everyone cries cheerfully to him "Afenhyiapa." Monka puts her bowl down between the two men. The women sit round on the terrace.*]

**ATO**: [*Addressing Petu*] How is it I found you here, my elders.

**NANA**: [*From her corner*] Young man, one does not stand in ant-trail to pick off ants. You find somewhere to sit and then ask us for the purpose of the visit.

[*Ato hurries off into the room, returning with a chair on which he sits.*]

**ATO**: What brings you here this afternoon?

**AKROMA**: Aha, now you are moving in the right path, young man. If I am not putting my mouth into an affair which does not concern me, may I ask you where your wife is?

**NANA**: Who says it is not your affair? It's his affair, isn't it?

[*Addressing this to Petu.*]

**MANSA**: If this isn't your affair, whose affair is it? It's everybody's affair isn't it?

[*Addressing Akyere.*]

**ESI**: *Ei,* these days, one's son's marriage affair cannot always be one's affair.

[*Ato enters the room.*]

**NANA**: It may be so in many homes. Things have not changed here.

[*Knocking the ground with her stick. Ato returns with Eulalie who shows great surprise at seeing so many people around.*]

**EULALIE**: But why so many people?

[*Ato does not say anything. Everyone just stares at her. She looks round for somewhere to sit. Ato notices that and jumps to give her his chair.*]

**PETU**: And where shall you sit?

**ATO**: Oh, there.

[*Indicating a place on the terrace. Cries of "Ei, Odo" from the gathering.*]

**PETU**: Our master, we are going to talk to you and you must be near enough to hear without our having to shout.

[*Ato looks with consternation at Eulalie. Their eyes meet and they withdraw to aside where they have a tête-à-tête which is inaudible to the audience. At the end, Eulalie walks away into their room.*]

**AKROMA**: What has happened now?

**ATO**: Nothing Uncle.

**PETU**: Ah, is she going away?

**ATO**: Eh . . . eh . . . eh . . .

**AKROMA**: But what we are going to say concerns her.

**ATO**: Eh . . . since she will not understand it, you tell me and I will tell her everything.

**NANA**: I have not heard the like of this before. Is the woman for whom stalwart men have assembled herself leaving the place of assembly?

**ESI**: Yet, this is something which must not be mentioned.

**PETU**: And if she leaves now, whose stomach shall we wash with this medicine?

**MONKA**: Let us say!

[*Followed by meaningful looks from the women folk.*]

**ATO**: Uncle, did you say you are going to use the medicine to wash my wife's stomach?

**PETU**: Yes.

**ATO**: Why?

**AKROMA**: Have patience, our master.

**PETU**: [*Looking round*] I hope I can deliver my message now.

**ALL**: Go on.

**PETU**: It was a couple of days ago that we met. What came out of the meeting is that we must come and ask you and your wife what is preventing you from giving your grandmother a great-grandchild before she leaves us.

[*Everybody nods his/her head. Nana more violently than the other.*]

**ATO**: Oh!

**PETU**: We were to choose this day because, as you know, on this day we try to drive away all evil spirits, ill luck and unkind feelings which might have invaded our house during the past year. You know also, that we invoke our sacred dead to bring us blessings. Therefore, we are asking you to tell us what is wrong with you and your wife so that first we will wash her stomach with this, then pour the libation to ask the dead to come and remove the spirit of the evil around you and pray them bring you a child.

**ATO**: [*Gripping his chair*] Good Heavens!

**PETU**: So my nephew, this is what we bring you.

[*All eyes on Ato.*]

**ATO**: Oh!

**AKROMA**: Ato, they sent us to bring you a message and they asked us to take words from your own mouth to them. And I do not hope that you think we can go and tell them you only said "Oh!" What has been the cause?

**ATO**: Nothing . . . oh!

**PETU**: Haven't you got anything more to say? When two people marry, everyone expects them to have children. For men and women marry because they want children. Or I am lying, Akroma?

**AKROMA**: How can you be lying? It is very true.

**PETU**: Therefore, my nephew, if they do not have children then there is something wrong. You cannot tell us it is nothing. There is no disease in this world but it has a cure. It may cost a great deal, but money is worthless if it is not used to seek for people. If it is your wife . . .

**ATO**: [*Aggressively*] Why do you say it is my wife's fault?

**PETU**: Oh, my witness is your Uncle Akroma here.

[*To Akroma.*] Akroma, you heard me. Did I say it is his wife? All the words which came out of my mouth were "If it is your wife . . . " How can I say it is your wife?

**AKROMA**: Petu could not have said that. Does he know what is in your marriage?

**AKYERE**: What sin would you have committed even if you said that?

**ESI**: I am very quiet.

**AKYERE**: Who does not know that she smokes cigarettes? And who has not heard that she can cut a drink as well as any man?

[*Cries of assent from all.*]

**ATO**: Heavens!

**PETU**: Nephew, we are still waiting.

**AKROMA**: He will say it is nothing.

**PETU**: What is wrong?

**ATO**: Nothing.

**AKROMA**: I told you so.

**PETU**: [*Angrily*] Monka, come carry the medicine.

[*The women are too shocked. They stare vacantly. Monka carries the brass bowl. They all stand up.*] Nephew, we will go our own way. I cannot be angry with you. I was only a messenger. Now, I remember your dream. I was going to ask the dead to come and take away the evil spirit which is haunting you. Now I know it is not a foreign evil spirit, my nephew.

[*He strides out, followed by Akroma, Monka and the other women. Esi Kom turns back and, standing akimbo, stares at Ato for a long time. She only moves when the old woman turns back too and urges her to move, with her stick. But then she herself spits, before hobbling away. Eulalie peeps out and, discovering that the people are gone, comes out. She paces round for some time and then walks up to Ato. He does not stir.*]

**EULALIE**: Native Boy, what did they say?

[*Silence.*] Ato what's the matter?

**ATO**: They came to ask why we haven't started a family.

**EULALIE**: And what did you tell them?

**ATO**: Nothing.

**EULALIE**: What do you mean by "nothing"? I should have thought the answer to that question is very simple.

**ATO**: They would say we are displeasing the spirits of our dead ancestors and the Almighty God for controlling birth . . .

**EULALIE**: [*Bitterly*] You knew all this, didn't you, my gallant black knight? Now you dare not confess it before them, can you?

[*She yawns*] Oh God! What an awful mess!

[*The lights go out.*]

## ACT 5

[*The next morning. Church bells are ringing in the distance. It is Sunday. Ato comes in wearing a mourning cloth. He is attending the Thanksgiving Service of a cousin, fourth removed, who had died the previous year. He walks up and down, obviously irritated.*]

**ATO**: [*Going to the door that leads to their room*] Eulalie, how long does it take you to put on a dress?

[*There is no reply. He paces up and down*] I say Eulalie am I to wait here for ever?

[*Eulalie comes in wearing a house coat. She looks very excited.*]

**EULALIE**: If you must know, darling Moses, I am not coming along.

**ATO**: What do you mean?

**EULALIE**: You know what I mean, or don't you understand English neither?

**ATO**: [*Turning his back to her*] I am waiting for you. If we aren't there by nine, the place will be full up and I wouldn't care to stand through a whole Thanksgiving Service.

**EULALIE**: Of course, you'd only have to come back here to sleep.

[*She giggles.*] I would, only I repeat "I ain't coming" eh. Or you are too British you canna hear me Yankee lingo?

**ATO**: [*Miserably*] Eulalie, you've been drinking!

**EULALIE**: Sure, Moses.

**ATO**: Again?

[*In a horrified voice*] And on a Sunday morning?

**EULALIE**: Poor darling Moses. Sure, I have been drinking and on a Sunday morning: How dreadful? But surely Moses, it ain't matters on which God's day a girl gets soaked, eh?

**ATO**: [*Anguished*] Eulalie!

**EULALIE**: Yeah . . . That jus whar yar beautiful wife as com teh, Soaking on God's holy day . . . My lord, whar a morning!

[*Hums "My Lord What a Morning."*]

**ATO**: [*Looking tenderly at her*] Sweetie Pie.

**EULALIE**: [*Laughing again*] Ain't you going teh say Poor Sweetie Pie? Ain't I poorer here as I would ave been in New York City?

[*In pathetic imitation of Ato*] "Eulalie, my people say it is not good for a woman to take alcohol. Eulalie, my people say they are not pleased to see you smoke . . . Eulalie, my people say . . . My people . . . My people . . . " Damned rotten coward of a Moses.

[*Ato winces.*] I have been drinking in spite of what your people say.

[*She sits on the terrace facing the audience.*] Who married me, you or your goddam people?

[*She stands and moves closer to Ato.*] Why don't you tell them you promised me we would start having kids when I wanted them?

**ATO**: They won't understand.

**EULALIE**: Ha! And so you make them think I am incapable of having kids to save your own face?

**ATO**: It isn't that.

**EULALIE**: Then what is it?

**ATO**: They simply won't understand that one should begin having children only when one is prepared for them.

**EULALIE**: Sure not. What else would they understand but their own savage customs and standards?

**ATO**: Eulalie!

**EULALIE**: And of course, you should have known that. Have they appreciation for anything but their own prehistoric existence? More savage than dinosaurs. With their snails and their potions! You afterwards told me, didn't you, that they wanted me to strip before them and have my belly washed? Washed in the filth!

[*She laughs mirthlessly.*] What did you tell them I was before you picked me, a strip-tease? . . .

[*She sits down again.*] Go and weep at the funeral of a guy you never knew. These are the things they know and think are worthwhile.

[*At this point, she is certainly very sober.*]

**ATO**: Look here. I won't have you insult . . .

**EULALIE**: . . . "My people." Add it, Moses. I shall say anything I like. I am right tired. I must always do things to please you and your folks . . . What about the sort of things I like? Aren't they gotten any meaning on this rotten land?

**ATO**: [*With false forcefulness*] When in Rome, do as the Romans do.

**EULALIE**: [*Contemptuously*] I thought you could do better than cliches. Since you can preach so well, can't you preach to your people to try and have just a little bit of understanding for the things they don't know anything about yet?

**ATO**: Shut up! How much does the American Negro know?

**EULALIE**: Do you compare these bastards, these stupid narrow-minded savages with us? Do you dare . . . ?

[*Like the action of lightning, Ato smacks her on the cheek and goes out of the house going by the path on the left. Eulalie, stunned, holds her cheeks in her hands for several seconds. She tries to speak but the words do not come. She crumples, her body shaking violently with silent tears, into the nearest chair. This goes on for a while and then the lights go out.*]

*[It is midnight of the same day. Ato stumbles from the path into the courtyard. He can barely see his way because it is very dark. As he comes along, he cries, "Maami, Maami," and goes to stand behind the door on the right. The two village women, each wrapped only in a bed cloth, run into the path. They are carrying little tin lamps.]*

**1ST WOMAN**: My sister, what is it?

**2ND WOMAN**: Oh, are you awake too?

**1ST WOMAN**: Is this noise not enough to wake the dead?
Why so much noise at midnight?

**2ND WOMAN**: It is very dark.
I cannot make out the figure at the door,
It looks like a . . . ghost.

*[Tired, Ato crumples on the terrace.]*

**1ST WOMAN**: I think it is the son.

**2ND WOMAN**: Ah, you are right.

**1ST WOMAN**: But what does he want at this hour?

**2ND WOMAN**: I do not know, my sister.
But it seems as if
Between him and the wife
All is not well.

**1ST WOMAN**: How do you know?

**2ND WOMAN**: Oh, I could tell you
The bird of the Wayside
Never tires of chirping.
But this is no secret.
My sons tell me this:
On their way home
From laying their snares
They saw the lady wife
Sitting on the grass in the school
With her head bowed.

**1ST WOMAN**: Oh . . . And when was this, my sister?

**2ND WOMAN**: Just this evening.
Darkness was approaching.

**1ST WOMAN**: Unlucky prophecies coming true,
I could excel one
Who has swallowed the dog's eye. . . .
But what was she doing there?

**2ND WOMAN**: I do not know.
And it is not part of my worries.
Besides, marriage is like *Oware*
Someone is bound to lose
And another gain.

**1ST WOMAN**: But if both players are good,
The game may end equally.

**2ND WOMAN**: And how do you know
The players in this set are not equal?

**1ST WOMAN**: One has backers
Another has not!

**2ND WOMAN**: People have been known to win
Who even continue on other people's losses.

**1ST WOMAN**: You are right.
And this is only the beginning.

**2ND WOMAN**: If we know this
Then, my sister,
Let us go back to mend our broken
Sleep.

[*They leave. Ato gets up and starts pounding on the door again and at the same time keeps calling his mother. Esi Kom opens the door and comes out. Ato stares at her as she starts speaking.*]

**ESI**: *Hei,* what has happened that you wake folks from their beds? Is it very serious? Shall I go and call your uncles? Why did you and your wife not attend the Thanksgiving this morning? Where did you go? All the food we reserved for you is cold. Is it the custom of educated people not to bid goodbye when they are leaving people?

**ATO**: It is not that. Eulalie is gone.

**ESI**: [*Moving towards the front of the courtyard followed by Ato*] Where is she gone to?

**ATO**: I do not know.

**ESI**: [*Sighing*] Or is she gone to your house in the city?

**ATO**: I am coming from there.

**ESI**: Then where can she be? We thought the two of you went away together.

**ATO**: No.

**ESI**: But why should she behave in such a strange way?

**ATO**: I slapped her.

**ESI**: You slapped her? What did she do?

**ATO**: She said that my people have no understanding, that they are uncivilised.

**ESI**: [*Exclaims coolly and nods her head*] Is that it?

[*She paces round then turns to Ato.*] My child, and why should your wife say this about us?

**ATO**: I do not know.

**ESI**: But do you never know anything? I thought those who go to school know everything . . . so your wife says we have no understanding and we are uncivilised . . . We thank her, we thank you too . . . But it would have been well if you knew why she said this.

**ATO**: [*Miserably*] I only asked her to come to the Thanksgiving with me. But she refused and . . .

**ESI**: And will she not refuse? I would have refused too if I were her. I would have known that I can always refuse to do things.

[*A pause*] Her womb has receded, has it not? But did you make her know how important it is for her to . . .

**ATO**: But her womb has not receded!

**ESI**: [*Unbelieving*] What are you telling me?

**ATO**: If we wanted children, she would have given birth to some.

**ESI**: *Ei,* everyone should come and listen to this.

[*She walks round in all attitudes indicating surprise.*] I have not heard anything like this before . . . Human beings deciding when they must have children?

[*To Ato*] Meanwhile, where is God?

[*Ato is confused since he does not know how to reply to this*] . . . yet only a woman who is barren will tell her neighbours such a tale.

**ATO**: But it can be done.

**ESI**: *Yoo,* if it can be done, do it. But I am sure any woman who does it will die by the anger of the ghosts of her fathers—or at least, she will never get the children when she wants them.

**ATO**: But, Maami, in these days of civilisation . . .

**ESI**: In these days of civilisation what? Now I know you have been teaching your wife to insult us . . .

**ATO**: Oh, Maami!

**ESI**: Is this not the truth. Why did you not tell us that you and your wife are gods and you can create your own children when you want them?

[*Ato is shamefaced and in spite of wide speculations and several attempts to speak, no words come out. There is a long pause.*] You do not even tell us about anything and we assemble our medicines together. While all the time your wife laughs at us because we do not understand such things . . . yes, and she laughs at us because we do not understand such things . . .

[*Here, mother and son face each other for a long time and it is Ato who is forced to look down at last.*] . . . and we are angry because we think you are both not doing what is good for yourselves.

[*She is almost addressing herself now.*] . . . and yet who can blame her? No stranger ever breaks the law . . .

[*Another long pause.*] Hmm . . . my son. You have not dealt with us well. And you have not dealt with your wife well in this.

[*Ato makes more futile attempts to speak.*] Tomorrow, I will tell your grandmother, and your uncles and your aunts about all this, and I know they will tell you that . . .

[*At this point Eulalie enters from the path on the right. She is weak and looks very unhappy. She nearly crumples in front of the courtyard while Ato stares dazedly at her. It is Esi Kom who, following Ato's gaze and seeing her, rushes forward to support her on. After a few paces into the courtyard, Eulalie turns as if to speak to Ato. But Esi Kom makes a sign to her not to say anything while she herself continues to address Ato . . .* ] Yes, and I know
They will tell you that
Before the stranger should dip his finger

Into the thick palm nut soup,
It is a townsman
Must have told him to.
And we must be careful with your wife
You tell us her mother is dead.
If she had any tenderness,
Her ghost must be keeping watch over
All which happen to her . . .

[*There is a short silence, then clearly to Eulalie.*] Come, my child.

[*And with that, Esi Kom supports Eulalie through the door that leads into the old house. Ato merely stares after them. When they finally disappear, he crosses to his own door, pauses for a second, then runs back towards the door leading to the family house, stands there for some time and finally moves to the middle of the courtyard. He looks bewildered and lost. Then suddenly, like an echo from his own mind the voices of the children break out.*] Shall I go to Cape Coast
Shall I go to Elmina?
I can't tell
[S]hall I?
I can't tell
I can't tell
I can't tell
I can't tell . . .

[*The voices fade gradually and the lights dim on him, gradually, too.*]

[ *Pause.* ]

# OVER MY DEAD BODY

*Violet Barungi*

Writing is my way of communicating with myself and my fellow human beings. When I am writing, I put my inhibitions aside and freely comment honestly about whatever concerns I have about life. Through writing I am able to make my contribution to society by highlighting issues I think need and deserve the attention of all of us.

**Violet Barungi, Uganda**

Violet Barungi, playwright, novelist, and short-story writer, was born in 1943 in Mbarara, Uganda. In 1967, she received her BA in history with honors from Kampala's Makerere University. In 1964, while still a student, Violet wrote her first short story, "Kefa Kazana." The story was published in *Origin East Africa,* a short-story anthology, and broadcast on British Broadcasting Company (BBC) World Service in 1964. Always literary, she worked as an editor for East African Literature Bureau shortly after graduation. After the breakup of the East African Community in 1977, she worked for the Uganda Literature Bureau.

In 1967, Violet married B. N. I. Barungi, a civil servant, and they have six children. While her husband held a variety of government positions, Violet concentrated on raising her family, allowing her little time to write.

It was only in the early 1990s, after her husband had retired and her children were grown, that Violet turned to writing professionally. Her first novel, *The Shadow and the Substance,* was published by Lake Publishers in 1998. In 1997, she joined Femrite, the only female publishing company in Uganda, as an assistant editor. Femrite published her second novel, *Cassandra,* in 1999. In 2001, Violet became the senior editor for Femrite. She has also published four short stories for children with Uganda Children Writers and Illustrators Association (UCWIA)—"Tit for Tat" (1998), "The Promise" (2002), "Our Cousins from Abroad" (2003), and "The Boy Who Became King" (2004)—and "Jogo Goes to School" (*Children Read Everywhere* anthology, 2004).

In 1996, Violet responded to an ad for the British Council International New Playwriting Award for Africa and the Middle East. She had never written a play but wanted to win the award. "I wrote the play *Over My Dead Body* in longhand, as I did not have access to a computer at the time. I saw the ad in July and wrote the play in August. No one proofed or read the play. I had no idea I would win." Her only other play, *Award Winner* (2000), commemorates women's literary achievements. Violet considers herself more a novelist than a playwright.

**Excerpts from Our Interviews**

***On the impact of Femrite and how it has elevated the interest of reading in the country:***

Femrite has played a significant role in nurturing and promoting creative women writers in Uganda by giving them a platform to air their views and by helping them to improve their writing skills through writers training workshops and seminars. I know in Zimbabwe they have an association of women writers, but I don't know if they have been as effective as our writers here because most of women's literary groups on the continent look to Femrite as a role model.

July 2006, Femrite celebrated her 10 Years Anniversary and women's literary achievements. When Femrite was formed in 1996, there were hardly any women writers in Uganda. Femrite's mission, therefore, was to build a sustainable platform for women to contribute to national development through creative writing. In ten years of existence, Femrite has trained and promoted women writers of formidable stature, many of whom have gained both national and international recognition by winning literary awards and other forms of acknowledgement. As one of the people who have been at the helm, I feel immensely proud and gratified at Femrite's achievements.

*On the reading culture in Uganda:*

You know something about reading culture here? It is nonexistent really. Other factors like poverty [stop] people from buying books—one would rather buy a pint of milk than a book. You find most people who buy books buy textbooks for their children because those are a must. Reading for leisure is considered a luxury many people cannot afford.

*On the audiences in Uganda:*

In our culture, drama is used as a source of entertainment. Most people go to the theatre to seek relaxation and be entertained, to laugh away their worries. What we usually have in theatres here is melodrama, which audiences find more appealing than serious or intellectual plays.

*On the situation of publishing plays in Uganda:*

Plays have no market in Uganda, so you can only write if you are commissioned to write.

# OVER MY DEAD BODY

Scene: Kampala-Uganda, 1997

**Characters**

Mbogo: Head of the family
Ngoma: His wife
Boona: First daughter
Sasha: Second daughter
Nunu: Third daughter
Bambi: Son
Tomusange: Boona's boyfriend

## ACT 1

*Scene 1*

[*A modestly furnished room with a cheap shabby sofa set and a thread-bare carpet covering only part of the room. In one corner there is a wooden dining table covered with a faded plastic cloth. Six rusty metal chairs are crowded under it.*

*There are three people in the room in the middle of a discussion. Mr. Mbogo, the father, a man in his early forties, is tall, broad and dark complexioned with serene intelligent eyes and regular features. His wife, Ngoma, is in her late thirties. She is pretty, but there is a perpetual hungry look in her eyes which mars her beauty.*

*The third person is their daughter, Boona, commonly known as Bo. She is about twenty with her mother's pretty features and her father's intelligent eyes. She is of medium height with lissom body whose main attraction is the full, well-rounded bust.*

*Mbogo is standing by the window, his back leaning against the metal frame, half-shutting out the rays of the mid-morning sun. Ngoma, who has just come from Church services, is still in her Sunday best. She is sitting in one of the armchairs, her restless hands beating a tattoo on the arm rests. Boona, who appears to be the subject of discussion, is sitting on the edge of the settee, her eyes downcast and her hands nervously plucking the frayed cloth of the chair.*]

**MBOGO**: [*Fixing Boona with a commanding gaze*]: I don't want to hear anymore talk of "I want to get married," is that clear?

[*Boona raises her eyes slowly and looks rebelliously at her father. She starts to say something, but falters under his gaze. Her lips trembling, she looks beseechingly at her mother who nods her encouragement before turning to her husband.*]

**NGOMA**: [*Anxiously*] Husband, I . . .

**MBOGO**: [*Impatiently silences her with his hand*] Quiet! Your turn will come when I have finished. So [*turning back to Boona*] I want you to go to your room and sit down and answer that letter from the University, accepting the course you've been offered. I myself will take it there first thing in the morning. In the meantime, I've arranged for you to go to your uncle in Jinja for the rest of the holiday to help in his shop. That should keep you out of harm's way in addition to giving you gainful employment. You'll be glad of a few extra shillings when the time to start college comes. Have I made myself clear?

**BOONA**: But, Papa . . .

**MBOGO**: [*Moving menacingly towards her. He stands towering over her, his eyes hard and uncompromising*] Yes, daughter?

**BOONA**: [*Sullenly*] Nothing.

**MBOGO**: [*Turning and striding back to his former position*] Good. We understand each other, I trust. You are an intelligent girl, Bo, so don't let anybody [*with a side-glance at his wife*] deceive you into thinking that there's a short cut to success. You've got to earn it all by yourself through sweat and endurance. And most importantly, you cannot depend on anybody else for happiness; you've got to make your own. No doubt you think that I'm a hard man and there are many who will concur with you. But I want you to know that I'm doing this for your own good. In years to come, you'll look back and thank me for it. You may go now and do me a favor, spare some time to reflect on what we've just discussed. [*Turns to look out of the window. Boona sits still for a minute, looking stunned. Then in slow motion, she gets up and starts to walk to the door.*

*Her mother ostentatiously runs to her side and puts her arms around her waist and walks her to the door. After she exists, Ngoma closes the door and stands against it, looking at her husband's back, waiting.*]

**MBOGO**: [*After a few minutes of silence, his back still turned to the room*] You have the floor now.

**NGOMA**: [*Carefully choosing her words*] Are you sure you're doing the right thing, husband? Bo's not a child and should have a say in a matter which primarily concerns her. I think her views should be taken into account.

**MBOGO**: [*Turning swiftly to face her, his eyes narrowed*] And if her views are wrong as they obviously are? Do we wash our hands of her and let her go her way? Bo is twenty years, yes, but she has not been exposed enough to the world and its evils to be able to tell good from bad. She is at crossroads and needs us to guide her in the right direction. I don't think, Ngoma, you realize fully what a bright girl Bo is and what a bright future lies ahead of her. With that in mind, do you still want her to throw it all over the fence for a few trinkets that swine has been dangling before her?

**NGOMA**: [*Her tone still mild*] You are quite behind times, husband. What matters these days is not how much education one has but how much money. I grant you in the past a good education was like a passport to success, but not anymore. How many young people, with their degrees and diplomas in their pockets roam the streets looking for non-existent jobs? Numberless. Jamil next door is a case in point. Armed with his degree in education, he wakes up early in the morning and comes back late at night with holes in his shoes but no job. This has been going on since he graduated three years ago, and his mother tells me he's getting quite desperate.

**MBOGO**: [*Unimpressed*] Jamil would have a job now if he were willing to work up-country. But all these young people want to hang around in the city. I've yet to see a doctor who was unemployed, though. In fact what they complain of is the reverse, overwork.

**NGOMA**: [*Nimbly*] And underpay.

**MBOGO**: [*Unruffled*] Yes, that too, but an enterprising young person can get around that by going into business or joining firms with better pay packages. A doctor is like a cook; there will always be need for one everywhere every time.

**NGOMA**: Teachers were like that at one time.

**MBOGO**: [*Sharply*] Why do you keep harping on teachers? You're surely a one track-minded person. Anyway, you were eager enough to marry one years ago, but with due respect, I don't consider the turn the discussion has taken relevant. If you have any more arguments you wish to raise as to why Bo should not pursue her education, speak now otherwise the subject is closed as far as I'm concerned.

**NGOMA**: You still refuse to consider Bo's feelings? Suppose she refuses to obey you and goes ahead and marries her young man?

**MBOGO**: Then that would be a tragedy.

**NGOMA**: Getting a son-in-law, who is kind, generous and rich would be a tragedy to you?

**MBOGO**: [*Cynically*] Shouldn't "rich" come before the rest of the embroidery to this superman? Hear me, woman and hear me well, my daughter is destined for better things than being a rich man's toy which he'll cast away the minute he tires of it.

**NGOMA**: There you go, looking at the dark side of the picture. If you had a more positive attitude to life, we would all be the better for it. So what if Bo's marriage to Tomusange doesn't last, so what? She's young and beautiful and cannot fail to secure another husband. But of more importance, she will have lived, really lived as some of us have never had a chance to do. She'll have something tangible to show for it. I'll make sure she realizes that from the beginning.

**MBOGO**: [*With a shocked expression*] What are you saying? Are you planning to swindle the man out of his wealth? Does your daughter know this? Somehow I knew this was about money and nothing else. Your greed and obsession to be better than your neighbor, to flaunt it around. Why use your daughter, why don't you marry the man yourself? You're certainly nearer his age than she is.

**NGOMA**: [*Jumping from her chair and going to face him with blazing eyes*] That's a filthy lie and very insulting to me. If I were a violent woman, I'd not take it quietly, I'd bring the roof of this house down, I'd . . . I'd make you eat your words. Bo wants to marry Tomusange because she loves him; not for any other reason. But I don't suppose you would understand things like that. You're the most insensitive person I've come across, and the coldest.

**MBOGO**: [*With contempt*] You certainly have a wide range of understudies from which to draw your conclusions.

**NGOMA**: [*Does not immediately react to his sally but turns away from him, her ample bust heaving with emotion*] Yes, I did have many opportunities of breaking away from the miserable hole you call a home, but unlike you, I always put the welfare of my children before my own happiness. For you, it's your pride which comes first although what you have to be proud about defeats me. I mean, look at this place, your castle, your heaven! [*She looks around the room with distaste, her finger dramatically pointing first at the rain-stained ceiling where the cardboard has been eaten away by mice in some places. The moving finger then pinpoints the dirty gray wall with peeling plaster before indicating the rest of the drab sights in the room.*] Is this place which makes for a happy family? Haven't you ever wondered why children never bring their friends visiting or do you think they have no friends? Do I need to spell it out to you? Yes, it irks me that we live in miserable surroundings and rub shoulders with the scum of the earth. It irks me that we eat cassava and ntura, and don't own even a bicycle when people of similar background like ours are out there, riding in cars and enjoying life to the full.

**MBOGO**: [*In a dangerously controlled voice*] Are you finished?

**NGOMA**: No. I was trying to show why Bo wants to break free from all this and help the rest of us to do the same. Be realistic, man, unless we grab this chance, we shall never do it under our own steam.

**MBOGO**: [*Visibly boiling with anger*] You're an incredible woman, you know. Quite incredible and thick too, in the head and very selfish. In the first place, it suits you to forget that if I had not left school prematurely to marry you and to take care of an unplanned family, I might have had a chance to realize my full potential instead of being trapped into teaching second rate primary schools. I want also to remind you that I do make efforts to provide for my family although I'm aware that these efforts fall short of your expectations. We've been over this argument over and over before. I wanted us to go to the village to farm our land, which we have in plenty. We would be much better off financially now, but no, you wouldn't go. You wanted your city life. Well, this is the only part of the city we can afford to live in. So whether you like it or not, this is where we stay. Bo will have to do as I say and join the university in September.

**NGOMA**: [*Warningly*] I shouldn't take that tone with Bo if I were you. She loves her man and will do anything, including disobeying you, to marry him if you persist in your arrogance. You remind me of my father before we were married. What do you think would have happened to us if my mother had not come to our aid?

**MBOGO**: [*With a malicious glint*] I know what would have happened to me. [*With emphasis*] I would not be married to you.

**NGOMA**: Obviously. You'd be married to that blousy fat Kirabo your father had earmarked for you—God, she looks so disgusting. I can't imagine what Ariyo ever saw in her!

**MBOGO**: But that doesn't stop you from envying her lifestyle. I'm sure if you had foreseen that Ariyo would turn out to be a rich man, you'd have dropped me for him.

**NGOMA**: Well, I'd certainly look better driving that Benz than Kirabo ever will. The woman has no class at all.

**MBOGO**: [*Maliciously*] Neither does Ariyo if it comes to that. You two would have suited each other up to the hilt. You'd probably be fat too since according to you, it's the worry and the inadequate diet which has turned you into a scarecrow.

**NGOMA**: I never said that.

**MBOGO**: But you've implied it often enough. [*Imitating her voice*] "Other people eat meat while we eat ntura; they eat bread at breakfast while we eat cassava!" I'd have to be really stupid not to read between lines. But we are diverging. Do you have anything more to say before I do my work [*indicating heaps of exercise books on the table waiting to be checked*].

**NGOMA**: [*Speaking slowly, her eyes suddenly becoming bleak, giving her an air of vulnerability*] Yes, before all this came up, I wanted to tell you that I went to see a doctor about the pain in my stomach.

**MBOGO**: [*Trying not to succumb to what he thinks are her tricks to get around him*] Yes?

**NGOMA**: Well . . . I don't know whether this is the right time to tell you. You seem in such a bad mood.

**MBOGO**: [*Impatiently*] Out with it, woman. I've wasted enough time as it is already.

**NGOMA**: [*Watching him anxiously*] The doctor said I have a tumor.

**MBOGO**: [*Quite alarmed, shouts*] The doctor said what?

**NGOMA**: Hey, take it easy, please. It's not as bad as that.

**MBOGO**: What do you mean it's not as bad as that? A tumor is a tumor, right?

**NGOMA**: Yes. But the doctor said it is still operable—yes that's the term he used. But he warned there should be no delay or it will turn malignant.

**MBOGO**: [*Greatly shaken*] When did you see the doctor? Why didn't you tell me immediately?

**NGOMA**: I wanted to but you've been so upset these last few days I did not want to worry you more.

**MBOGO**: Yes, this business of Bo has been preying on my mind. [*Stops and seems to be trying to puzzle out something. Eventually asks*] Is Bo aware of this?

**NGOMA**: [*Reluctantly*] Yes But I don't think that it has any bearing on her decision. She had already made her plans.

**MBOGO**: [*Unconvinced*] And this helped to clinch matters, right?

**NGOMA**: No, husband, truly.

**MBOGO**: Anyway, that's irrelevant now. We shall have to borrow the money needed for the operation.

**NGOMA**: For how long are we going to go on borrowing money we can't afford to pay back, until you're behind bars and we've been stripped of the little we possess? There is that outstanding loan from the bank, loans from your friends, relatives . . . Your friends now shun your company because every time you go near them, they think you want to borrow money. I'd rather die than plunge you into another debt.

**MBOGO**: And I'd rather go to prison than let you die for lack of funds. [*He looks desolately around the room as if trying to imagine it without her vibrant presence.*] No, I'll not let you die.

**NGOMA**: You won't have to bear the burden alone if Bo marries Tomusange . . .

**MBOGO**: [*Immediately alert and suspicious*] I thought all that was settled? Are you really in need of surgery or is this a ruse hatched between you and your daughter to mislead me into making the wrong decision?

**NGOMA**: [*Genuinely hurt*] What a contemptible thing to say! But don't worry, let me die and leave you in peace to order your children the way you think fit without interference from me. Anyway, why should I be afraid of death? It will be a relief from a world in which I'm not appreciated and will not be at all missed. Yes, a welcome release. [*She drops back in her chair, covers her face with her hands and starts to weep quietly.*]

**MBOGO**: [*Hurries to her and drops on his knee beside her chair. He clumsily tries to comfort her.*] Hush, dear, don't cry little one. I'll do whatever it takes to get the necessary funds, even if it means breaking into a bank. We shall get the money, little wife and you shall not die. Wait here for me; I'll be back soon. [*He walks to the door, throwing worried glances over his shoulder at her.*]

**NGOMA**: [*As soon as she hears the door closing, she takes her hands from her eyes which show no trace of weeping. She gets up and goes to peep out of the window.*] I wonder where he is going?

[*Turns and addresses the audience, talking confidentially*] That was a brilliant idea about the operation, disarmed him completely. Under that layer of impregnability there lies a soft heart, you know. Of course I do have this tumor and the doctor did suggest an operation would be advisable but he said nothing about it being malignant. So lucky Mbogo has never taken interest in my illnesses, thinks they are faked most of the time. So even if he became suspicious, he'll not know where to start making inquiries. This Tomusange is really a godsend and Bo says he is the most generous man she has ever seen—all those clothes, shoes and God knows what else. Dinners at Sheraton and Grand Imperial. But, I wish Bo would accept a little spending money he is always pressing her to take. She says it makes her feel cheap and will not accept his cash until they are married—strait-laced, that's what my Bo is, just like her father. I wonder if she'll have the courage to defy him.

I must get to her immediately before he does or all will be lost. I've been praying and dreaming about a thing like this for a long time—manna from heaven really and Mbogo wants us to turn our backs to all these blessings! Imagine if the Israelites had qualms about eating that mysterious food they found in the wilderness, would they have ever set eyes on the Promised Land? Never. Tomusange has been sent by God to rescue us from this misery and we would be mighty stupid if we did not welcome him with open arms. But first, let me find Bo and work on her. We say that when a hare grows old, it feeds on its offspring. It's now time for our children to start paying back a little of what we have invested in them. Fortunately, Bo is not like most children of her generation who think that the parents' role is to give, and go on giving. She has a sense of responsibility and understands that if she has to help us, she'll never have another chance like this one. [*Listening to approaching footsteps.*] Oh dear, there he comes. Now I can't get to Bo before he does, what shall I do? [*Runs back to her chair and sits down, assuming a melancholy aspect. The door opens and Mbogo comes in looking somber.*]

**NGOMA**: What's the matter?

**MBOGO**: [*Drops in a chair wearily and stares into space. After a long silence, he says to her*] When I left you, I went to see Mazima.

**NGOMA**: About what . . . [*breaks off and mutters*] as if I didn't know.

**MBOGO**: Just a little loan. A miserable fifty thousand for heaven's sake, not a fortune.

**NGOMA**: [*Gently*] And he was not in? I would have told you that, you know. After that, I suppose you went along to see Mukasa and got the same treatment, right?

**MBOGO**: [*Defensively*] What do you mean the same treatment? It just wasn't my lucky day. That's all.

**NGOMA**: I wish I had your faith in humanity! My belief is that people are basically bad, rotten through and through. It beats me how a man of your age and experience can fail to see that.

**MBOGO**: [*Irritated*] I don't need a lecture from you.

**NGOMA**: Someone has to tell you about your so-called friends who will never be at home to you until you've settled all the money you owe them. I suppose I'd do the same if I were in their shoes. That's why, dear husband, I suggest that we make the best of the luck that has come our way. It's not as if we were forcing Bo to do something against her will. She's head-over-heels in love with the man. I've never seen Bo so happy before. [*Getting up and going to her husband's chair. She puts a hand on his shoulder and continues.*] Don't worry about the money for the operation. Bo will see to it that we get it.

**MBOGO**: [*Almost shrugging off her hand*] I thought you said there was no time to lose, that it was urgent to operate on you immediately.

**NGOMA**: [*Puzzled*] It is.

**MBOGO**: Then how can you be planning to wait for Bo to get married, assuming of course she was indeed going to marry Tomusange, and get the money for you?

**NGOMA**: I wasn't actually reasoning that way.

**MBOGO**: [*Interrogatively*] Oh? So how were you reasoning?

**NGOMA**: [*Hesitatingly*] I thought that after the dowry is . . .

**MBOGO**: [*Throwing off her hand violently and jumping to his feet*] Dowry? What dowry? Absolutely not. [*Bending close to her and speaking slowly and emphatically*] Perhaps I did not make myself clear enough. There is going to be no marriage in this house in the foreseeable future. Once you have comprehended that, then we shall stop going round and round the issue like a dog chasing its tail. Neither illness, nor any other calamity will force me to change my mind on the subject of Bo and the need for her to continue with her education.

**NGOMA**: Well, of course you can afford to take a stand. It's not your life that is hanging in the balance, is it? You don't care whether I live or die. All you care about is your damned conscience. I'm tired of your "know it all" attitude, your self-righteousness. If you think I'm using Bo to get my hands on money that will save my life, so are you, trying to realize your unfulfilled dreams of becoming a scholar through her. I may not be intelligent in your opinion but I know you from A–Z.

**MBOGO**: Be quiet, woman! If this is about money for your operation, I have already told you that I'll find it. It's my duty as your husband to take care of you.

**NGOMA**: [*Caustically*] And in the inevitable event that you can't, what am I supposed to do? Watch my life ebbing away while you're engaged in the futile exercise of laying your hands on some money? Be realistic, Mbogo, nobody can lend you that kind of money.

**MBOGO**: [*Cautiously*] What do you mean? Do you know how much is needed?

**NGOMA**: Of course I know. I asked the doctor and he told me that his fee alone will come to shillings 150,000. To that, add the cost of drugs and hospitalization.

**MBOGO**: [*Profoundly shocked*] What? But that's preposterous!

**NGOMA**: No, it's called cost-sharing. His children need school fees, his wife needs new clothes, so you pay the bills.

**MBOGO**: [*Dangerously*] Are you trying to be funny?

**NGOMA**: [*Sighing patiently*] I'm trying to show you that none of our friends can lend you that kind of money. The only chance you have of saving me from a premature death, if you want to save me of course, is to come to terms with the idea of an early marriage for Bo.

**MBOGO**: [*Resumes his seat and bows his head in thought. After a few minutes he gives a gusty sigh and get up and walks to the window, avoiding his wife's keen eye. He stands there for a long time, gazing out of the window while his wife holds her breath, waiting for his verdict. Turning his face back to the room*] No, no, I can't do it. I know in my heart that I've made the right decision. We shall have to raise the money by a different method and not by sacrificing our daughter's future. I'll go home and appeal to the old man. I'm sure he'll sympathize and allow me to sell at least one cow.

**NGOMA**: [*Furiously getting up and walking rapidly towards him, she says*] I'm not interested in your dirty father or his dirty money. I'd rather die than allow you to use a penny of his money on me. One day, ask me to tell you why I hate him so much. [*Dejectedly*] That is if I live that long.

**MBOGO**: Why are you trying to load guilt on me?

**NGOMA**: [*Viciously*] Because you are responsible for whatever happens to this family.

**MBOGO**: [*Wearily*] If that's the case, let me figure things out by myself. But my decision about Bo still stands.

**NGOMA**: [*Walking around the room with long strides, her hands akimbo, she talks in a conversational tone*] You know, I pity you; you don't know how to live, how to enjoy life. You don't covet any of the good things of life; you don't seem to have any ambition at all to wish to improve your lot. Which other man would pass over a chance like this of living comfortably for the rest of his life? Wake up, man, you don't have forever to live. Look around you and see what other people are doing. They are driving cars, they are eating well and mansions, their own mansions are shooting up everyday. Do you think they do it by toiling and drudging day and night? No . . . o . . . oh. Shall I tell you how?

**MBOGO**: [*Sarcastically*] By selling their children?

**NGOMA**: [*Taking him seriously*] There was a time when having a couple of beautiful daughters could ensure that one's kraal would never be empty. But times have changed now. A wise man makes it by keeping his eyes open to grab whatever chance he can. This is our main chance, husband, let's seize it with both hands, before it's too late. [*She rushes to him and grabs him by the hands, looking at him imploringly*] Oh, Mbogo, you don't know how often I've prayed and dreamt of a chance like this, a chance to break free from the bonds of poverty and humiliation; of never having enough of anything, of longing for things that would never be all the time until your entire being is saturated with it. This must be God's answer to my prayers . . . please, don't say no, Mbogo, you can't do this to me! [*She falls down at his feet and begins to weep.*]

**MBOGO**: [*Having watched her performance with contempt, he pulls her up to her feet roughly saying*] You are mad, woman, stark raving mad. But nothing you can say or do will make me change my decision regarding Bo. So stop dramatizing yourself.

**NGOMA**: [*Speaking in her normal voice, without a trace of emotion*] You know, you're the most insensitive, cold-hearted man I've ever seen.

**MBOGO**: And you are the most selfish, unscrupulous woman I've ever had the misfortune to know, and a most unnatural mother too. Now that we've paid each other glowing compliments, may we close the subject?

**NGOMA**: The subject may be closed between us, but it does not mean that if Bo asks for my advice I'll not give it to her.

**MBOGO**: Don't try to turn Bo against me because if you do, you'll regret it.

**NGOMA**: I've already regretted having brought the matter to your attention at all. I should have advised her to go ahead and do whatever she wanted to do. She's of age and there is nothing under heaven you can do to stop her. [*She flounces out of the room, banging the door shut behind her. Feeling a murderous* *rage, Mbogo starts to run after her, but stops at the sound of the banging door. His shoulders hunched up, he walks back a defeated man and stands in the centre of the room brooding. He then walks towards a family picture on the wall and stands gazing at it.*]

**MBOGO**: [*Still gazing at the picture*] Bo, Bo, my pet, my little angel, why are you doing this? A little more patience and hard work and you would have it all, men and fame. Is it too late to talk some sense into you, to try and make you see reason? I'll give it a try, yes. I'll give it a try. It's all I can do. [*Hurries out of the room as curtain comes down.*]

*Scene 2 (Late Morning)*

[*A small kitchen-cum-store cluttered with cooking utensils and food stuff. There is a rectangular wooden table on which all kinds of paraphernalia pertaining to the preparation and serving of meals is to be found. Two girls in their late teens are sitting on metal chairs on either side of the table. Sasha, a dark, tall and moderately pretty girl with calm intelligent face, is crocheting a chair-back and listening to the incessant chatter of her younger sister, Nunu. Nunu bears a remarkable resemblance to their mother and makes no secret of being aware of her physical attributes. She is sullen most of the time, selfish, grasping and completely insensitive to the feelings or needs of others. She now sits fidgeting with an old radio, turning the knobs impatiently in search of a station with her kind of music.*]

**NUNU**: [*She gives the old machine a bang on top and pushes it away with disgust*] We need a new radio, a cassette player. In fact, we need a whole lot of new things around here. [*Putting her chin between her hands with her elbows on the table, she looks at Sasha*] What do you think is happening in there? [*Points with her chin and without waiting for an answer from her sister, provides it herself*] I'll tell you what is happening. I can see it all. Bo of course is wavering between pleasing Papa, who is being his usual block-head, and following the dictates of her heart. But you can bet Mama can fix Papa on that. Oh yes, she can.

**SASHA**: [*Stops crocheting and carefully puts the work on the table before raising her critical eyes to her sister*] Is that how you see it? A battle of wills between Papa and Mama?

**NUNU**: [*Carelessly*] What else would you call it? Ever since I can remember, it has always been that way with Mama wanting us to have the good things of life like other people and Papa subverting her every effort.

**SASHA**: [*Contemptuously*] You think he does that for the fun of it, do you? He works day and night so that he can earn enough money to support his family, and what do you do but criticize him and complain all the time. Don't you think that he too would like to have a good time, to rest from trying to imbue knowledge into those ruffians, and don't think I have not noticed how you flaunt yourself before them when they come here for coaching on weekends. Disgusting!

**NUNU**: You're jealous because they notice me and not you.

**SASHA**: [*Heatedly*] I'm not!

**NUNU**: Oh, yes, you are. You know you're not as pretty as I am, so you try to put down everything I do as bad or wicked. [*Bends across the table to scrutinize her face insolently*]: You know, sister dear, it's high time you did something about your looks. You could try some lightening cream and a bit of make-up. Then and only then might you succeed in catching somebody's eye.

**SASHA**: [*Upset but trying not to show it*] You know, for a seventeen-year old girl, you're completely evil. I don't care whether any man ever looks at me because I have a better vision for my future.

**NUNU**: That's what is generally known as sour grapes.

**SASHA**: [*Jumps down with anger from her chair and starts to chase Nunu around the room*] I'll kill you, minx, I swear I will.

**NUNU**: [*Cries out loudly*] Somebody save me. [*She runs towards the door, with Sasha in hot pursuit. The door opens suddenly as Nunu reaches it and she falls into Bo's arms and clings to her.*] Save me Bo, please, Sasha wants to kill me.

**BOONA**: And with good reason I'll bet. [*She closes the door and surveys the two younger sisters with amusement. Brawls between the two were a common feature in the Mbogo household.*] So what's the trouble?

**NUNU**: [*Looking at Sasha accusingly*] She wants my blood, I tell you. Though she's two years older and six inches taller, she still won't stop harassing me.

**BOONA**: [*Judiciously*] You must have provoked her. You know how insensitive you can be sometimes. But I want you now to shake hands and make up because I need both your advice on a matter of the utmost importance.

**NUNU**: [*Looking agog with excitement*] Would this matter be concerning a certain event uppermost in our minds?

**BOONA**: Could be. But sit down, both of you. [*Her sisters reclaim their former positions while she perches on the corner of the table.*]

**NUNU**: Well, tell us what happened. Did you manage to convince Papa? Hurry up, Bo, and tell us. Oh, I'm so excited I could die!

**BOONA**: [*Grimly*] No, I didn't, Nu. Papa's still adamant that I should go to university. As far as he's concerned, the subject is closed.

**NUNU**: But he's still closeted with Mama, isn't he? You can bet she's putting the pressure on him to agree. Mama can twist him round her little finger when she puts her mind to it. You wait and see.

**BOONA**: Not always. [*Turns to Sasha who is sitting quietly, taking no part in the conversation*] What do you think?

**SASHA**: [*Looking at her directly*] I think that you've changed a lot, Bo.

**BOONA**: How so? [*Defensively*] You think I'm about to mess up my life, don't you? You think that my decision to abandon my studies to marry Tomu is foolish?

**SASHA**: [*Brutally*] Foolish is too mild. I think it's suicidal. You're looking no further than the tip of your nose and putting your entire future at stake. And pray, for what? For promises of becoming rich quickly? What happens if these promises are not honored? Then you'll regret that you have nothing to fall back on.

**BOONA**: [*With asperity*] I trust Tomu implicitly. I don't think he can ever let me down.

**SASHA**: People change, Bo. Besides, I don't think you know enough about him to entrust him with your entire future. Even if he did not change, circumstances regarding his source of income could. Then what?

**BOONA**: [*In a passive voice*] You actually think I want to marry Tomu for his money?

**SASHA**: To be truthful, it did cross my mind.

**NUNU**: [*Appealing to Boona*] Don't listen to her, Bo. She is jealous, that's why she is saying those insulting things to you.

**BOONA**: Don't worry, Nu, I don't feel insulted by what Sasha thinks about me. On the other hand [*addresses Sasha*], your opinion means a lot to me because ever since we were young, we've shared our thoughts and secret dreams. Remember the vow we made on New Year's Eve of 1987? We said we would use our pens and brains to conquer the world and reach to the top. It seems so childish now, a mere fantasy. The real world is different, Sasha. Besides, when you fall in love, your whole outlook changes. Things you previously regarded as vital to your well-being suddenly lose meaning or pale into insignificance. You wait when your turn comes, you'll understand what I mean exactly.

**SASHA**: [*Incredulously*] You've actually managed to convince yourself that you're in love with Tomusange and not his bank balance?

**BOONA**: I'm sure you don't mean to be cruel, Sasha, but . . .

**NUNU**: [*Chipping in quickly*] She does, she does, I know. You don't . . .

**BOONA**: [*Cutting her vituperations short*] Please, Nu, let me handle this. What I was saying, Sasha, is that while it's true that I've always longed to escape from this wretched life, falling in love with Tomu was purely coincidental, I assure you. I genuinely like him and when he asked me to marry him I was elated. Of course I felt gratified when I passed my A levels and knew I would be granted the course of my first choice. But why should I spend five more arduous years at university when I can attain my goal now free of charge?

**SASHA**: Then you're proving my point. You're using the man as a stepping stone?

**BOONA**: [*Her face hardening*] So what if I'm, a little, anyway? They use us all the time for their selfish ends. [*She gets up and walks about the place thoughtfully, kicking at objects she finds in her way on the floor.*] All my life I've been poor; we all have. But the difference is that while you stayed in day schools, I was unfortunately sent to a boarding school. [*Pauses, her face reflecting the pain she is feeling.*] You've no idea how cruel and evil people can be until you've been to a boarding school—where snobbery, more than anything else, is bred. I was laughed at, ridiculed and ostracized because I was not rich, because I did not come from the right background. Every time those stupid girls passed near me, they would offensively hold their snobbish noses in the air because while their clothes had labels from famous couturiers, mine came from Owino market.

**NUNU**: Hey, don't knock them. They have some of the most famous labels "down town" too, I can assure you, like Nina Ricci and Louis Vertolli. What actually distinguishes them from the Wina Classic wear, apart from the staggering disparity in prices, is the pungent smell, which clings to them. Take this blouse for instance, bought six months ago, but [*bends to smell her sleeve*] ugh! It still stinks to high heaven. [*The other two regard her with despairing expressions.*]

**SASHA**: [*Addressing Boona*] Did it ever occur to you that those girls might have been jealous of you? Besides, the whole school couldn't have contained girls from rich families only. There must have been other poor ones like you, possibly even worse off than you were?

**BOONA**: You don't understand, Sasha. I wanted to be part of the real people, the magic circle. Not the poor wretches who had nothing to offer me.

**SASHA**: Except friendship.

**BOONA**: I didn't want their friendship. [*Pauses again recollecting*] It was horrible . . . Oh, you have no idea how horrible it was having nobody to talk to, to confide in. In the beginning, I used to cry myself to sleep every night. [*Pauses and gulps down a moan*] Eventually, I got used to my loneliness and misery and vowed that one day I'd have my revenge. I'd become so famous that those creeps would come groveling at my feet and I'd give them a taste of their own medicine. I directed all my energies to achieving academic excellence, which was not difficult for me. I was more than average and I had no distractions like other girls. I knew I could make it to the top . . . but reading for me still remained a means to an end, a weapon with which to beat my enemy rather than an intellectual pursuit.

**SASHA**: Whatever the reasons, you have now a chance of a lifetime to realize all those dreams without taking sidelines or clutching to the coattails of a man. How can men ever respect us if we keep giving the impression that we can never ever do without them?

**NUNU**: One man's meat . . .

**SASHA**: [*Interrupting*] Keep your inane sayings to yourself. Look, Bo, I have nothing against Tomusange or men in general. But I think the timing is wrong. Think this thing through before you commit yourself. I can imagine the temptation and the pressure you must be under to accept his offer of marriage, but don't act in a hurry. Give yourself time to reflect before you make your decision.

**NUNU**: Don't listen to her, Bo, she just wants to spoil things for you. Besides, you've already promised Mama you'd get us all out of this stinking place. You can't go back on your word now. Why should you listen to her anyway? She has never been in love and doesn't know what it feels like.

**SASHA**: [*Sarcastically*] And I suppose you do, numbskull.

**BOONA**: Please girls, stop it or you'll drive me crazy. Don't you see that you're trying to tear me apart? Anyway, there's nothing really to argue about. I love Tomu and he loves me. He has told me so countless times. He's totally committed to me and to prove it he's even [*with emphasis on each word*] bought me a car. A brand new Toyota Corolla, can you imagine that? [*She watches eagerly for her sister's reactions.*]

**NUNU**: Cripes, that's wonderful! [*She jumps up in the air in a state of ecstasy.*] Oh Bo, Bo, how exciting . . . aren't you excited?

**BOONA**: Of course I am, Nu, completely . . .

**NUNU**: [*Doesn't wait for her to finish*] What an incredible man! When can we see this car, Bo? Wait until my friends at school hear about it. They'll never believe it. Will you drive us to school at the beginning of term . . . Oh, happy, happy day!

**BOONA**: Keep your voice low, Nu, or they'll hear you in the next room. [*Turns to Sasha with an uncertain smile*] Aren't you thrilled for me too?

**SASHA**: [*Intentionally vague*] Buying you a car . . . that certainly tells a lot about the man, doesn't it?

**BOONA**: You bet it does. Tomu's a very generous man. I'm glad you can finally see my side. I wish you'd have a go at convincing Papa, if Mama fails. He'd listen to you, I know.

**SASHA**: [*Quickly*] No, don't drag me into that please. Besides, if you're convinced that you're doing the right thing, then you should be able to stand by your convictions. Papa's not a monster; he has only your best interests at heart.

**BOONA**: You sound like him.

[*Before anybody can say more, the door flies open and a boy of about fifteen, commonly known as Bambi, walks in. He has his mother's small bone structure and his father's loose-jointed frame, but otherwise resembles nobody in particular. He is now flapping his long arms, his eyes bulging with excitement.*]

**BAMBI**: You'll never guess what I've just seen down there.

**BOONA**: [*Glad of the diversion*] Then perhaps you'll tell us and save us all the agony of trying.

**BAMBI**: I say, Bo, is that super car really yours?

**BOONA**: What super car?

**BAMBI**: I have just told you. It's down there waiting for you—you don't look surprised? Then, it must be true. I thought the guy was pulling my leg, but apparently he wasn't.

**BOONA**: [*Ready to tear her hair off*] What in the name of God are you jabbering about, Bambi?

**NUNU**: [*Excitedly*] He's talking about the car, Bo . . . you're talking about the car, aren't you, Bambi? You mean it's down there with Tomu at the wheel?

**BAMBI**: Of course, how else would it have reached her?

**BOONA**: Is Tomu down there, Bambi? Why didn't you say so in the first place—Oh my goodness. [*She surveys her simple home dress and touches her plaited hair.*] I can't go to him looking like this. Oh what shall I do?

**BAMBI**: Let me go and keep him company while you get ready, Bo.

**NUNU**: Let me go, Bo. Bambi will bore him to death with his childish prattle.

**BAMBI**: You're a girl; you can't sit in a car alone with a strange man.

**NUNU**: He is not a strange man; he's Tomu.

**BOONA**: [*Flustered, walks up and down the room*] Oh, shut up you two and let me think. [*Bambi and Nunu watch her eagerly, waiting for her ruling.*] I wasn't expecting him so early, but I suppose he must be as eager as I am to know Papa's verdict. Oh, that reminds me, I can't see him before I've talked to Mama first.

**BAMBI**: Are you telling me that Papa's putting on screws. You cannot really let him do that, Bo. Isn't there a law or something about the rights of minors?

**SASHA**: [*With contempt for her brother*] Bo's not a minor.

**BAMBI**: Well, if she's an adult, then she can do as she pleases.

**NUNU**: Listen, I have a better idea. You and Tom can elope, Bo, can't you? It would be so romantic like those characters in Shakespeare—Romeo and Juliet, weren't they?

**BOONA**: Do stop blubbering you, two. I do really need to think . . . [*Stops pacing and turns to Bambi*] Go and tell him to go and come back at . . . let me see . . . no, tell him I'll give him a ring later in the day, okay?

**BAMBI**: [*Salutes smartly*] Okay, boss.

**NUNU**: Can I go with him and have a peep, Bo, please, please? I promise not to get too close. [*She runs out without waiting for an answer. Boona and Sasha are left in uncomfortable silence. The latter bends over her work, ignoring her sister's speculative glances at her. Boona shrugs.*]

**BOONA**: I'm going to the bedroom in case Mama or anybody else wants me. [*She walks towards the door. The door opens before she reaches it and her mother walks in.*]

**NGOMA**: Leave us, Sasha. [*Silently Sasha gathers her work and leaves the room. After the door has closed behind her, daughter and mother turn to look at each other.*] It's hopeless.

**BOONA**: What happened, Mama, what happened? What did Papa say?

**NGOMA**: He won't budge an inch.

**BOONA**: But I've got to, Mama. I've got to marry Tomu.

**NGOMA**: [*Anxiously*] What do you mean, child? Are you . . . you know?

**BOONA**: If you mean, I am pregnant. The answer is no. I'm not.

**NGOMA**: [*Excitedly*] But supposing you were . . .

**BOONA**: [*Impatiently*] But I'm not, Mama, I've just told you. Besides, is that the only reason why women get married?

**NGOMA**: You and I know you're not, but does your father? Supposing, for the sake of argument, we're to tell him you were, don't you see that it would be the perfect solution to our problem. He would have no choice but to agree to the marriage.

**BOONA**: [*Without enthusiasm*] Can't say I dig the idea much, Mama.

**NGOMA**: What other choice do you have? Don't be daft, girl. Once presented with evidence of this kind . . .

**BOONA**: [*Sharply*] There's no evidence, Mama.

**NGOMA**: You know what I mean. This kind of argument, if you prefer, once it's put before him, he'll have no choice but to escort you to the altar.

**BOONA**: [*Dryly*] He could try killing me.

**NGOMA**: Stop being flippant and pay attention, Bo. This idea of yours is quite a masterstroke really.

**BOONA**: Mine, Mama?

**NGOMA**: [*Irritably*] Don't be so tiresome, Bo. Whether it's your idea or mine's immaterial. The important thing's that it's an absolute cinch. There's no way your father can argue himself out of this.

**BOONA**: [*Looking unhappy*] I still don't like it, Mama. Supposing he were to find out that I was deceiving him? I'd never be able to look him in the face again.

**NGOMA**: [*Exasperated*] And how in the name of heaven, would he do that?

**BOONA**: [*Dubiously*] Well, Tomu could tell him, you know, could let slip that we've never been to bed together.

**NGOMA**: [*Disapprovingly*] For a modest girl, you do use some graphic expressions.

**BOONA**: Oh, Mama, I'm past the birds and bees stage. Besides, if I'm going to become a doctor, I . . . [*Her voice fades away and her mother watching keenly thinks there's a hint of sadness in her eyes. She shrugs and gives a high-pitched laugh.*] I guess I meant to say that to our generation, calling a spade a spade is quite normal, unlike yours where anything concerning sex was shrouded in mystery and hypocrisy.

**NGOMA**: Haven't we wandered away from the issue?

**BOONA**: Sorry, Mama. What were we talking about?

**NGOMA**: I was about to say that I can't see your father and your young man hob-nobbing. The two are totally different with nothing in common whatsoever.

**BOONA**: Except myself as the bone of contention between them. [*Rebelliously*] I still don't like your idea, Mama. There must be another way of convincing him. There has to be.

**NGOMA**: I don't understand you, Bo. I thought you wanted to marry Tomusange, were determined to? You certainly convinced me or I wouldn't have wasted my time trying to convince your father.

**BOONA**: Which you failed to do, Mama.

**NGOMA**: [*Indignant*] You think I didn't try? That man's as stubborn as a mule. Once he's made up his mind about something, nothing can change him. I tried reasoning with him, arguing, even threatening but all to no avail. I even told him about the money needed for my operation, but even that could not shake him enough to agree.

**BOONA**: [*Incredulous*] You mean he did not show any concern?

**NGOMA**: Well, he did, rushed off immediately to borrow the money from his friends, but of course nobody's willing to lend him more money. Besides, I'll not let him go to prison because of me and my useless life. [*Sniffing*] I don't even see the point of lingering behind in a world, in which I've become unnecessary [*sniff*]. You children are growing up fast and do not want or need me anymore . . .

**BOONA**: Of course we need you, Mama. You know we do.

**NGOMA**: No, you don't but I'm not complaining, mind you, because it's only natural. But I'd die a happier woman if I knew I was leaving you in the care of a good man to look after you. Then would my soul rest in eternal peace. [*She covers her face with her hands, overcome by the pathos of her own words and weeps earnestly.*]

**BOONA**: [*Distressed*] Please don't cry, Mama, please don't. I'll marry Tomu today if need be. You'll not die. Mama, I'll not let you.

**NGOMA**: [*Looking up pathetically, tears streaming down her face*] No, I don't want you to feel obliged to marry in order to get money for my operation. When you marry, I want you to marry for love because that's the right of every young person, boy or girl.

**BOONA**: But I love, Tomu, Mama, and I want to marry him. Only it'd be so much better if I had Papa's blessing. And he'll certainly not give it if he believed that I was pregnant. I'm sure you do see that, Mama. [*She goes and kneels down on one knee beside her mother, looking at her beseechingly.*]

**NGOMA**: [*Holding her middle and her face distorted with pain, she groans and tries to stand up*] Help me up, child.

**BOONA**: [*Alarmed*] What's the matter, Mama?

**NGOMA**: [*Standing up with Boona's help, gives heavy sighs*] Just a few aches to remind me that I'm not long for this world.

**BOONA**: Stop being pessimistic, Mama. I'm going to see to it that you get prompt treatment.

**NGOMA**: [*Signs of weakness forgotten*] What if your father puts his foot down? You know how he intimidates you.

**BOONA**: This is a matter of life and death; Mama, even Papa can see that. I've never disobeyed him before, but this time I'll have to do it if he refuses to be reasonable.

**NGOMA**: [*Listening to sounds of footstep, puts a finger to her mouth*] Shh, I think I hear him coming. [*She reclaims her chair and sits more squarely like someone preparing for battle.*]

**BOONA**: [*The look of determination disappears from her face and she casts a scared look at her mother*] Do you think he wants to talk to me?

**NGOMA**: [*Whispering*] There's nothing to be afraid of. Just stick to your resolution.

**MBOGO**: [*Opens the door slowly and looks suspiciously from one face to the other.*

*Sarcastically says to his wife*] It looks as if you've been preparing the ground for me and sowing a few seeds, no doubt.

**NGOMA**: [*Looking at him with defiance*] Bo and I have been sorting out our priorities.

**MBOGO**: I'll bet you have. [*He passes her chair and goes to stand in front of his daughter, his back to his wife cutting off her view completely. Softly to Boona*] Your mother told me that you've already made up your mind to marry the Tomusange fellow, is that correct?

**BOONA**: [*Nods feebly and whispers*] Yes, Papa.

**MBOGO**: [*Still speaking calmly*] Would it be of any use if I appealed to you as one adult to another to use your head rather than your feelings and reconsider your decision? All I'm asking you is that you give yourself enough time to examine all your options before committing yourself. Your entire future depends on it. Bo.

**BOONA**: I . . . [*About to answer, is attracted by her mother's frantic gestures. She's peeping around her husband's legs and is making signs of a swelling stomach with her hands. Without thinking, Boona seizes the opportunity to say*] But I have to, Papa, I have to marry Tomu. Otherwise I wouldn't be rushing into it.

**MBOGO**: [*Gently*] You mean because of your mother's condition?

**BOONA**: [*About to say yes, she notices her mother shaking her head vigorously while her hands wave a negative in the air*] Well, not exactly.

**MBOGO**: [*Beginning to lose patience*] Tell me exactly why you have to do it.

**BOONA**: It's not easy, Papa. You'll be angry with me.

**MBOGO**: Try me.

**BOONA**: [*Takes a deep breath and blurts out*] I'm pregnant

**MBOGO**: [*Exploding*] You're what? Pregnant? My daughter pregnant!

**BOONA**: [*Nods taking a step backwards*] I'm sorry.

**MBOGO**: [*Belligerently*] No, you're not. Not yet. But you will be soon, believe me. [*Turning to his wife furiously*] Did you know about this? Did you? Did you? I asked you a question, damn you! Did you or did you not know about this?

**NGOMA**: Well, naturally . . .

**MBOGO**: [*Barking*] Naturally? What's natural about this?

**NGOMA**: What I meant to say's that it doesn't matter now that she's getting married and . . .

**MBOGO**: Pregnant or not, she'll marry that man or any other man over my dead body, do you hear? Over my dead body! I've always had doubts about your competence as a mother, but I never thought you'd be so cold-blooded as to encourage your daughter to become a prostitute so that you can satisfy your avaricious nature. But don't think that I'm going to stand aside and let you get away with it. [*He moves menacingly towards her.*]

**NGOMA**: [*Shooting from her chair and confronting him angrily*] Who are you calling a prostitute, you evil man? How dare you?

**BOONA**: [*Reacting to the charge at the same time as her mother cries out*] How can you call me a prostitute, Papa? It's beastly unfair.

**MBOGO**: [*Brushing his wife aside and addressing himself to Boona*] When an unmarried girl shamelessly tells her father that she's pregnant, then prostitute's the only term that describes her.

**BOONA**: [*Shrilly*] But I'm not pregnant, I tell you, so stop harping on it for heaven's sake.

**MBOGO**: [*Puzzled*] You're not? But you said you were; you gave it as an excuse for . . .

**BOONA**: [*Cutting him short*] I know I did, Papa, but only to get you to be reasonable.

**MBOGO**: [*Not convinced*] Are you sure?

**BOONA**: Of course I'm sure.

**MBOGO**: Of all the damnable things to say! I'll bet your mother had a hand in this. [*Turning to his wife*] Did you? You would slander your daughter without a qualm in order to get your way? How ruthless can you be? Is Sasha to be the next, then Nunu? What kind of mother are you?

**NGOMA**: [*Unruffled*] A mother who cares what happens to her children when she's left this world. If I were married to a real man instead of an impotent, gutless effigy dressed up to look one, I . . .

**MBOGO**: [*Before she can finish, he swings into action and grabs her by the throat and starts squeezing, his eyes dilating further and further with the pressure of his hands*] I'll kill you. I swear by all that I hold dear.

**NGOMA**: [*Trying ineffectually to unclasp his hands from their grip, gurgles*] You're killing me, you're killing me.

**BOONA**: [*Stares, momentarily stunned. The next moment she is flying at her father, trying to pull him from her mother from behind. She shrieks*] Papa, Papa, please don't do it. Don't kill her, don't kill Mama, oh God!

**MBOGO**: [*Shrugs her off easily and she falls to the ground*] Today she dies or my name's not Mbogo-teitwa.

**NGOMA**: [*She's beginning to choke and weaken*] Mbo. .Mbo. .phuhpu. .h. .zi!

**BOONA**: [*Picks herself up immediately and scans the room for a weapon. Her eyes fall on a solid wooden pestle for pounding. She grabs it, raises it high and brings it down on her father's head resoundingly. Mbogo falls with a thud, dragging his wife down with him. Boona stares at them scared. She cannot believe what she's done. The pestle falls from her lifeless hands to the floor with a clang. She drops on her knees beside the still form of her father, crying*] Papa, Papa, please don't die! Oh what have I done, oh God, what have I done?

**NGOMA**: [*Recovering from the shock she pulls herself free and begins to rise up slowly rubbing her neck. She looks at Boona accusingly.*] Yes, what have you done? [*Hysterically*] You've killed him! You've killed your father!

**BOONA**: [*Defensively*] I didn't mean to: I was trying to stop him from killing you.

**NGOMA**: [*Panicky and flustered*] I know, child, I know. But you didn't have to hit him so hard. A tap would have brought him back to his senses. [*Wringing her hands*] What shall we do now, oh, what shall we do?

**BOONA**: [*Hopefully*] Perhaps he's not dead. Let me check—[*Puts her trembling hand inside his shirt and withdraws it quickly*] I can't feel it, Mama, I can't feel his heartbeat. [*Voice rising*] He's dead and I've killed him!

**NGOMA**: [*Sharply*] Don't talk so loudly. [*With her hand on her heart, goes to both doors, one leading to the backyard and the other to the sitting room and locks them.*] Let me think . . . where're the kids, by the way? I don't want them butting in now.

**BOONA**: [*Shaking all over says between chattering teeth*] Nunu and Bambi are down the road.

**NGOMA**: Let's hope they stay there long enough to enable us to do something.

**BOONA**: [*Stammering*] What're you plan-ning to-to-do? We can-not hide his-his body.

**NGOMA**: [*Thinking quickly*] I've got it. We can't hide his body but we can hide the cause of his death.

**BOONA**: [*Still kneeling down, touches the back of her father's head and her hand comes away with blood. She recoils and gets up quickly, runs to the sink, making retching sounds. She bends over the sink and is violently sick until she is completely drained. She drops down on the floor. Her mother runs to her quickly, wets a dish cloth and mops her face.*] I feel terrible, Mama!

**NGOMA**: [*Pulling her up to her feet gently and encouraging her*] Don't fail me now, Bo, you've been very brave so far. There, there, there's my girl. Put your arm around me . . . that's right. I'll take you to your room and then I'll find Sasha and send her up to you. Not a word to anyone about what has happened by the way, do you understand?

**BOONA**: Yes. [*As they pass the body on the floor, she steals a fearful look at it and whispers*] But what about . . . him?

**NGOMA**: Don't worry about the bo . . . your father. I'll think of something. [*They pass through the door and she locks it behind them and pockets the key.*]

[*End of act 1.*]

## ACT 2

*Scene 1 (Mid-afternoon)*

[*A medium-sized bedroom containing three single beds and hardly any other furniture except a study table near one of the two windows in the room. It is piled with schoolbooks. The walls are bare except for plastered cuttings from magazines of pop singers and fashion models. There is also a calendar, a face mirror and a scattering of nails on which the girls hang their clothes.*

*Boona is lying on her bed with her face towards the wall covered with kitenge cloth. She is pretending to be asleep. Sasha, wearing a worried expression, is sitting on her own bed, which is parallel to Boona's, her hands folded between her lap. The third bed, in a state of chaos, is at right angles with the other two. Quick footsteps coming towards the room are heard and the door opens and Nunu enters.*]

**NUNU**: [*Walks in quickly, goes to Boona's bed and stands looking at her puzzled. Without turning she asks*] What's wrong with her? Mama told me she's been taken bad.

**SASHA**: That's what I was told too. She hasn't said a word to me since I came in. I think she's asleep now, though.

**NUNU**: [*Still wearing a puzzled look*] She was fine a while ago.

**SASHA**: Keep your voice down or you'll wake her.

**NUNU**: What about lunch? I'm starving.

**SASHA**: You know what they say? The one who craves sleep makes the bed. So go and cook.

**NUNU**: How can I when the kitchen's locked and Mama told me to go near it at my own peril.

**SASHA**: Now you're being daft. Why would Mama lock the kitchen at this time or stop anybody going near it. You must have got it wrong.

**NUN**: I tell you it's . . . [*Stops as Boona's body's shaken by a violent spasm. Both girls look at her startled.*]

**SASHA**: [*Getting up and going to the sick girl the while whispering fiercely to Nunu*] I told you to keep your voice low. [*She touches Boona's face—and mutters to herself*] It feels clammy. [*Turning to Nunu*] Stay with her while I go and get something to sponge her.

**NUNU**: [*Looking at the strangely still form with trepidation, whispers*] You stay with her. I'll go for the water and towel. You saw what she did a minute ago: I wouldn't know what to do if she started kicking and raving.

**SASHA**: [*Looking at her with disgust*] She's not mad, for heaven's sake . . . [*The words are hardly out of her mouth when Boona, who has been suppressing her urge to weep, gives a tremendous hiccup, which sends both girls scampering to the door—with fear.*]

**SASHA**: [*Bravely taking a few steps back in the room*] Nonsense. You go and find Mama and ask her to come here pronto. [*She closes the door after Nunu and creeps stealthily past Boona's bed to her own. She's just lowering herself on it slowly when Boona suddenly rises to her knees, throwing away the kitenge and turns to face her. Sasha suddenly stretches up and stiffens as if to attention.*]

**BOONA**: [*Sits up on the bed, hugging her knees*] I want to talk, Sasha.

**SASHA**: [*Cautiously*] What do you want to talk about?

**BOONA**: Come here, Sasha, please, I won't eat you.

**SASHA**: [*Feeling foolish, starts to walk slowly towards the other bed. She is about to reach it when the sound of coming footsteps attract her attention. Changing course she goes to the door, and says with relief*] That must be Nunu. [*But it's Bambi who comes in prattling.*]

**BAMBI**: I say, what's going on? The kitchen's locked and there're no signs of anybody preparing lunch. [*Holding his thin waist, cries out*] I'm starving like Marvin—what are you two doing here, anyway, instead of being in the kitchen where you belong?

**SASHA**: [*Slowly*] Don't you ever think of anything else but food?

**BAMBI**: What else's there to think about? Food's my greatest joy in life.

**NUNU**: [*Walking right through the door Bambi has neglected to close*] I can't find Mama. [*She notices Boona sitting up quietly on the bed and points a trembling finger at her*] She's all right? She looks all right? [*To Sasha in a whisper*] I was about to tell Papa about her [*indicating Boona with her swiveling eyes*], but Papa's complaining about the delayed lunch. The strange thing is . . . [*But Boona, who has caught the gist of what she is saying, makes a choking sound, diverting their attention to herself.*]

**BOONA**: [*Urgently*] What did you say about Papa, Nu?

**NUNU**: [*Uncomprehending, looks at her and starts to answer hurriedly*] I said . . . nothing disrespectful, I swear. I only said . . .

**BOONA**: [*Hanging on her words*] Yes?

**NUNU**: Well, I said that he wanted his lunch.

**BOONA**: [*Whispering fiercely*] Where's he? Did you actually see him, touch him? They say ghosts don't appear during the day. So he can't be one, can he?

**NUNU**: [*Puzzled*] Why should I touch him and what do ghosts got to do with him? Although I'd sooner touch a ghost than disturb Papa at his desk.

**BOONA**: [*Her face suddenly radiant*] Papa's alive! You sure he's alive? [*She immediately springs to her knees, clasps her fingers together and in a fervent voice implores the three to join her in giving thanks to God. Tears running from her shining eyes down her cheeks.*] God is good and merciful. He's the mightiest ad deserves to be praised. He's . . .

**BAMBI**: [*Looking at her uneasily says in a loud voice*] She's gone cuckoo. [*Sasha and Nunu hug each other as they watch her with frightened eyes. With one accord they tiptoe quickly to the door and run out of the room with Bambi bringing up the rear.*]

*Scene 2*

[*The same room as in first scene. The time is approaching 2:00* P.M. *in the afternoon. Curtains are drawn against the glaring sun, but the glass door fac-*

*ing the street is wide open. Mbogo's sitting at his desk below the window, going through a pile of exercise books. Now and then he touches his temples with his fingertips, clenching his jaws at the same time as if he's in pain. He's just reaching for another exercise book on top of the pile when the three children burst in with worried expressions.*]

**BAMBI, SASHA, AND NUNU**: [*Chorusing*] You must come quickly, Papa, Bo's acting very strange. Please, Papa.

**MBOGO**: [*Turns slowly to look at them. He's feeling lassitude stealing upon him, slowing down his reactions. He removes his glasses and rubs the back of his neck. The children are watching him impatiently.*] Where's your mother? [*Before they answer, voices are heard outside. The three children run out the door and peep out.*]

**NUNU**: It's Mama.

**SASHA**: [*Surprised*] With the LC [*Local Council*] chairman? Why?

**BAMBI**: Proper hang-on is our gun-wielding old gizzer. Never passes up a free meal. Bet he's after the Sunday roast! What awaits him, though is a cold hearth and a locked room, ha-ha-ha!

**NUNU**: Shut up, you clown. Mama? [*She runs through the door outside.*]

**NGOMA**: [*Walking in with Nunu, takes a few steps inside the door, then stops. Her eyes open wide and her hands fly to her mouth as if to stifle a scream. She stares at her husband who's unconcernedly fidgeting with his books, stacking them in neat piles on the desk.*]

**MBOGO**: [*Gradually becomes aware of his wife and turning to her says brightly*] There you are, my dear. The children were looking for you.

**NGOMA**: [*Automatically walks towards him, hands outstretched as if to embrace a long-lost friend. A few paces away she stops and whispers wonderingly*] You're alive, Mbogo, you're alive! [*The three children stare at her in astonishment.*]

**SASHA**: [*Putting their feelings into words*] That's exactly what Bo said! What does it all mean?

**NGOMA**: [*Ignoring the interruption, shakes her head, still staring at her husband*] You're alive, Mbogo; I can hardly believe it.

**BAMBI**: [*Gives a high-pitched laugh and pointing at his mother says*] She's got it too, the jam-jams.

**NUNU**: Shhh! [*Whispers, nudging him in the side with her elbow.*]

**MBOGO**: [*Absently to his wife*] Believe what—ah, yes, I've remembered. I wanted to see Bo and talk some sense into her. [*Tries to get up holding onto the edge of the table but Ngoma quickly hurries to him and urges him back in the chair.*]

**NGOMA**: Don't strain yourself, Mbogo, you're not well.

**MBOGO**: Not well? Rubbish. I'm just worried about Bo. [*Puts his fingers to his temple and speaks slowly*] Bo must understand she's still too young to know what she's doing.

**NGOMA**: [*With her hands pressed gently on his shoulders soothingly says*] Don't worry; everything's all right.

**MBOGO**: [*Violently pushing her hands away*] No, it's not. I know your plan to encourage her to defy me but [*bangs the table, making everything on it jump and scatter in disarray*] she'll marry him only over my dead body.

**NGOMA**: Hush, husband dear, Bo's not going to marry Tomusange. She has changed her mind.

**MBOGO**: [*After a short puzzled silence, her words penetrate Mbogo's foggy brain, bringing some animation to his pallid face*] You're sure? You . . . [*He is beginning to quiz her when somewhere inside the house quick footsteps attract his attention and the attention of everybody in the room. They all cock their heads, listening as steps come nearer with varying expressions on their faces. The door flies open and Boona rushes in and falls directly at her father's feet, hugging his legs in a frisson of joy.*]

**BOONA**: [*Looking at his face with relief*] Oh Papa, Papa, I thought you were . . .

**NGOMA**: [*Interrupting her quickly*] Tell your father that you've decided not to marry Tomusange. That's all he wants to hear, dear, do you understand?

**BOONA**: [*Does not understand at first but after gazing at her mother and practicing her lip-reading skill, she nods, sobering up immediately. She takes her father's hands in hers.*] Listen, Papa, after thinking over what you told me, I decided to take your advice and not rush into marriage. I'll go to my room now and complete those forms. [*This revelation's followed by complete silence in the room until Mbogo's reaction, which is slow in coming.*]

**MBOGO**: That's my girl. I knew you'd make the right choice, told your mother so, didn't I, Ngoma?

**NGOMA**: [*Smiling broadly at him*] Indeed you did, Mbogo-teitwa. [*As she is speaking, a loud cough's heard from outside, which appears to discomfort her.*]

I'll tell you what, why don't you two go and complete those forms while the girls and I prepare a quick lunch.

**BOONA**: [*Gets to her feet and waits for her father to do the same*] Come on, Papa, I don't think I can fill those forms without your help.

**MBOGO**: [*Gets up rubbing his eyes and starts to walk vaguely away muttering to himself*] I feel as if I have not slept for days. [*Boona falls into step with him and takes his hand. The two exit from the room.*]

**NGOMA**: [*After watching the pair disappear, she turns to Sasha and Nunu*] Go and start lunch. [*Sheepishly*] Here's the key. I locked the door when I was going out; one cannot be too careful with all the pilfering going on in the neighborhood, can one? [*Like puppets, Sasha and Nunu speechlessly take the key and start walking to the kitchen door. Their mother hurries out of the front door, calling out apologies to somebody outside. Bambi is left alone and moves to the center of the room, shaking his head.*]

**BAMBI**: [*Imitating Boona's voice*] Papa, you're alive! [*Imitating Ngoma's*] Mbogo, husband, you're alive! [*In his normal voice*] Why shouldn't Papa—Mbogo—husband be alive? And all those goings-on in Bo's room. Are you thinking what I'm thinking? Yes, there's a mystery here and if anybody can crack it open, it's, I, [*with his hand on his chest, swaggering*] Bambi—Rutatiina. But first things first, and as always for me, food tops the agenda. Sherlocking can wait. [*Walking towards the kitchen, stops half-way to say over his shoulder*] Never work on an empty stomach or you'll end up with an ulcer. [*Winks and exists.*]

[*End of act 2.*]

## ACT 3

*Scene 1*

[*It is evening five years later, in the Mbogo living room of their new residence. The time is five in the evening. The room is large and airy with freshly white painted walls and unpretentious modern furniture. In one corner of the room, background music can be heard from a hi-fi and the other corner near the service hatch is a large dining table covered with a spotless white linen cloth. It is heaped with all sorts of eats and drinks but the center is conspicuously taken up by a large mouth-watering iced cake waiting to be cut.*

*There are seven people in the room all wearing a festive air. Everybody's attention is on Boona who is looking extremely beautiful. She is fashionably dressed in a long black skirt and a crimson organza blouse. Over this she is wearing a black academic gown and a sailor-like cap with strips of red ribbon at the back sits atop her head. She is sitting on a big sofa between her father and mother.*

*Her father, Mr. Mbogo, looks older with streaks of white in his black hair. He is dressed in a pin-striped black suit with a sky-blue shirt and a gray-blue-striped tie. His wife, Ngoma, looks unchanged except for a little plumpness around her cheeks. She is dressed in the traditional busuti and wears her hair short in shiny curls. The other members of the party include Sasha, Nunu and Bambi. Sasha looks almost as beautiful as her other two sisters but she has more poise and elegance. She and Nunu are suitably dressed for the occasion. Bambi, at six feet two inches looks too tall and awkward in his first ever evening suit. The seventh member is a man in his late thirties familiar to all present. His name is Tomusange. He is dressed in an expensive suit, has a crew cut and spots a small moustache which makes him look quite distinguished.*]

**MBOGO**: [*Gets to his feet, gestures to Nunu to lower the music and then clears his throat*] Ladies and gentlemen, may I have your attention please. [*The hubbub dies down and all eyes turn to him except Bambi who reaches for his camera and takes a snap of his father. After the flash, the speaker resumes.*] We have all had a long day, so I'll not make a speech. As you all know, we're here to celebrate Bo's graduation. It is one of the happiest days for me, all of which started twenty six years ago when my lovely wife here agreed to marry me. [*A burst of applause.*] A year later, a package of unforgettable joy in the form a squirming, squidgy little infant arrived. I give you one guess. Yes [*looking smilingly at Boona*], this lovely young lady was it. For the next five years, three more packages of the same arrived at regular intervals. Need I say more? What man would not be proud and grateful for such blessings! [*His eye roves the room, spotting each of these blessings. When they reach Bambi, they pause uncertainly. On being aware that he's under his father's scrutiny, Bambi's jaws work overtime chewing the ever present gum in his mouth.*] Yes, today's a memorable day in this family. Last year, Sasha did us all proud by graduating with a first class degree in Law. She set the course for all of you to follow. Bo has honorably acquitted herself. The onus now rests with Nunu and Bambi to keep the record untarnished. [*Everybody's eyes swivel to the two mentioned, dwelling longer on Bambi, whose increased tempo of gum-chewing threatens to dislocate his jaw.*] It is my custom [*the speaker resumes*] on such an occasion to ask the celebrant what she or he, so far only shes, would like for a present. My wife and I are ready and willing to grant any request within reason, and within our power to grant, of course.

But before that, Mr. Tomusange here [*in an aside*] he insists that I call him Tomu although as you all know he is my boss. [*Normal voice*] Anyway, Tomu asked to be allowed to say a few words. Tomu? [*More clapping of hands and flashing of bulbs from the camera.*]

**TOMUSANGE**: [*Gets to his feet*] Thank you, Mr. Mbogo. [*Pauses for the camera.*] Ladies and Gentlemen, I want, first of all to confess that I'm here under false pretences. It's true that Mr. Mbogo invited me here as the president of the company he works for, an honor which is not unappreciated. [*Bows to Mr. Mbogo.*] However, I want to tell you that I invited myself to this party five years ago when I made a pledge to Bo that I would be present at her graduation. [*Tender look at Bo during pause. Flash, flash from camera.*] That was after she turned down my marriage proposal to continue with her studies. I was shattered, of course and my ego suffered an almost irreparable damage. I mean here I was, offering Bo what most women would kill for and she said thank you, but no thank you? I could not understand it but later when I got to thinking about love, marriage, the lot, I discovered that while physical attraction might bring two people together, what actually sustains that togetherness, the marriage, is mutual respect and admiration. This may sound like a paradox but when Bo turned me down and her reasons for doing so became clear to me, my admiration for her grew by leaps and bounds. For the first time, Bo became more than a beautiful and desirable woman to me. She stood out as an individual in a crowd, a woman with an independent mind, a woman with a vision and a great deal of stamina. A woman—I could spend the whole day listing her qualities but I don't have the time. Having been rejected, I thought I could still stake my claim by giving her an engagement ring but again Bo would not have it. She advised me to keep my options open. What options? As far as I was concerned, she was the only one I wanted. That's when I made my pledge to her. I reckoned that since I had taken so long to find her, I could surely wait another five years for her. In the words of King Solomon: "A good woman is more precious than jewels . . . many women have done excellently but you surpass them all." [*Thunderous applause. Tomusange mops his glistening face before resuming.*] Forgive me, I got carried away there. The real reason for my standing here boldly before you is to ask your permission, Sir, Madam [*bows to Mr. And Mrs. Mbogo*], to be allowed to put this same ring [*dips his hand in his pocket and pulls out a small box. He snaps it open to reveal a small diamond ring of the most exquisite setting. Advancing towards Boona, he repeats*], this same ring on Bo's finger.

[*At a nod from her father, Bo gets up and extends her left hand. The two stand gazing at each other as Bambi's camera flashes. Loud clapping and Boona proudly flushes her ringed finger to all. She embraces her father and then her mother. The latter is smiling and crying at the same time. Mbogo gets up and slaps Tomusange jovially on the back.*]

**MBOGO**: I have now found a name for you . . . son-in-law-to-be. Welcome to the Mbogo family. [*The two shake hands.*]

**TOMUSANGE**: Thank you, sir, although I wish the last two words of the appellation could be dropped. [*Laughter and clapping. Tomu bows and resumes his seat.*]

**MBOGO**: I shall give it some thought. Before we proceed to the most important part of the ceremony, which Bambi will tell you is the cutting of the cake. [*Pause as general laughter ensues at Bambi's expense.*] I want to invite our guest of honor to make her request and perhaps say a few words. Bo?

**BOONA**: [*Stands up and moves to the center of the room. Bambi's camera goes into action again and again from different angles.*] With your permission, Papa, I want to reverse the order and start by saying a few words. First of all, I want to thank you all present for making this occasion possible. Without your support, I could not have made it on my own. Secondly, I wish to share a little secret I discovered five years ago. I discovered, that contrary to the belief that a person matures at a given age, growing up takes place suddenly in a flash and at any age. At twenty, I was a big baby; I had the mentality of a ten-year-old. I wanted to have the fruits on top of the tree without going through the struggle of climbing the tree to get them. But Papa made two significant observations at the time, which have more or less directed my step. He said, and I quote: "There's no shortcut to success. It's through one's sweat and endeavor that one achieves one's goal." He also said that each one of us make their own happiness, by which I understood to mean that you choose your own ingredients and make the kind of life you want to live. With these guiding principles, I was able to clear things in my mind and weigh my options. I did not love Tomu less then than I do now but I wanted to go to him without the slightest doubt. Forgive me: it was supposed to be a short speech but I'll get to the point.

**NUNU**: [*Chips in*] Don't stop please. We are all enthralled.

**BAMBI**: [*Hisses*] Speak for yourself. [*Looks at the buffet table longingly.*]

**BOONA**: [*Watching him with a smile puts up her hands pleadingly*] Don't shoot me please, Bambi but I promise to speak for only an hour or so more. [*In response, Bambi puts his hand in his pocket and gets more packets of chewing gum, which he opens and crams in his mouth as everybody watches amused.*] To continue, I want to emphasize that I've been lucky in having all your support and I'm very grateful. And who says that you cannot eat your cake and have it? I've trained for one of the most enviable professions, and I have for a friend and fiancée, a very dear person. [*She stops and gazes reflectively at the glittering ring on her finger. She then raises her eyes slowly and gazes at Tomu who is sitting directly opposite. Then turning she looks at her parents.*] Papa, Mama, I know this is supposed to be a graduation party, but as it has already assumed the aspect of an engagement party, may I put my request in the form of your permission to allow me to marry Tomu as soon as possible?

**MBOGO**: Not this minute I hope because I have ideas about what the wedding of my firstborn should be. [*He gets up and embraces her saying*] You have your request, daughter.

[*Suddenly everybody is on their feet embracing and laughing happily, Mrs. Mbogo alternating between tears and smiles. Bambi's camera flashes left and right and then with one accord, they move to the buffet table. Boona, assisted by her mother, cuts the cake to a thunderous clapping of hands and noisy rendering of:*]

She is a jolly good fellow × 3
And so say all of us × 3
She is a jolly good fellow × 3
And so say all of us!

[*Curtain.*]

### Glossary

**ntura:** vegetable, bitter tomato, symbolic of poverty.
**busuti:** traditional dress for women.

*Pause.*

# SHE NO LONGER WEEPS

*Tsitsi Dangarembga*

On campus, there were relationships happening all around us and many weren't working very well, and women were becoming pregnant. A friend of mine did fall into that circumstance. And I thought it was something that I could address in a drama.

**Tsitsi Dangarembga, Zimbabwe**

An award-winning novelist, filmmaker, and playwright, Tsitsi Dangarembga was born in Mutoko, Rhodesia, into a family of educators. Two years later, her family moved to England to take advantage of that country's educational opportunities. In 1965, her family returned to Rhodesia, where Tsitsi completed her secondary education at a mission school in Mutare. In 1977, she enrolled at England's Cambridge University, intending to study medicine. Homesick and isolated, Tsitsi returned to her native country in 1980. Shortly thereafter, Rhodesia was renamed Zimbabwe and came under black majority rule.

Now enrolled at the University of Zimbabwe, Tsitsi studied psychology after working as a copywriter for a marketing company. There she was soon writing and acting in many campus plays. In 1983, she wrote and directed *The Lost of the Soil. She No Longer Weeps* was performed in 1984 and was later published in 1987. She also joined Zambuko, the university's drama group. Headed by Robert McLaren, a noted scholar, Zambuko introduced Tsitsi to the craft of community theatre.

Tsitsi was not limited to writing plays. In 1985, she published a short story, "The Letter," in Sweden, but it was the publication of her first novel, *Nervous Condition,* written in 1985 but published in 1988, that catapulted Tsitsi to international recognition. *Nervous Condition,* the first novel published in English by a Zimbabwean woman, explores injustices against women and girls. The book won the Commonwealth Writers Prize in 1989.

In 1989, Tsitsi moved to Germany to study film direction at the Deutsche Film und Fernseh Akademie. For several years, until she left the country in 2000, she was involved in a variety of film projects. Her best-known film, *Neria* (1992), for which she wrote the story, supports women's right to own land in Zimbabwe. The film became the then highest grossing film in Zimbabwean history. In 1996, Tsitsi again made Zimbabwean film history as the first Zimbabwean woman to direct a feature film, *Everyone's Child,* an exploration of the devastating impact of AIDS on orphaned African children.

Her most recent film, *Kare Kare Zvako: Mother's Day* (2004), is based on a Zimbabwean folktale. Shown internationally, the movie was included in the 2005 Sundance Film Festival in the United States. In 2006, she released her second novel, *The Book of Not,* a sequel to *Nervous Condition.* Today Tsitsi resides in Harare.

### Excerpts from Our Interview

*On the drama group Zambuko:*

At that time—in the early eighties—the government was putting a lot of emphasis on culture as an institution. So there was a drama department that had just opened at University of Zimbabwe. They did a lot of outreach and I was able to benefit from that. . . . Its aim was to bring the university community together into a community theatre group. I think it succeeded very well because we had lecturers, students, staff, general workers . . . we all got together and produced some very good drama. . . . We would decide what stories we wanted to tell and we'd workshop [them] and produce . . . productions and they would tour in the country and in the region. . . . I think they had quite a great impact.

*On her status as a groundbreaking writer:*

Well, that's what people tend to say about a lot of my work, which I'm not conscious of at this time. Maybe as I grow older, I do become more conscious of that. At the time, generally, I was feeling that something needed to be said, so I would just go ahead and do it.

*On publishing in Zimbabwe:*

Zimbabwe does have a women's writers association, Zimbabwe Women's Writers. . . . That organization has been around for a long time, since the late 1980s . . . and we do have Irene Staunton, who founded and runs Weaver Press. She has been very encouraging to many women. She supported the late Yvonne Vera[1] in her work. . . . [P]ublishing may not be as bad as in other countries. I think the issue is whether women can write. I think if the writing is there, it can be published. I think it's becoming more and more difficult to write . . . Because of the time commitment, and also the Western alliance[2] has imposed sanctions on the country, everyone knows these sanctions exist, unofficial as they are in some cases and official in others . . . it has just made life that much more difficult.

*On the impact of economic sanctions on Zimbabwe:*

The sanction has impacted very negatively on women on a psychological level. I would say women are suffering levels of stress that are probably unprecedented. The economic situation is definitely exacerbated by the sanctions. . . . Practical things like, "How I am going to find the material I need to control my menstrual blood flow." That's just a major thing for every single woman from month to month. And, for example, if we don't have chemical for the water, then we don't have water to wash with. If you can't wash, you're not going to go to work when you are menstruating, are you? I do not believe that the people who impose these sanctions actually understand what they are doing. Or if they do, it is an evil of great order. . . . But this type of psychological terrorism has very insidious effects that I think are going to be far reaching.

***On her work with women filmmakers in Zimbabwe:***

We have an organization called Women's Filmmakers of Zimbabwe. It started as a workshop during the Southern African Film Festival, which used to be held biannually here. When the Film Festival closed, the women were tenacious enough to make sure Women Filmmakers of Zimbabwe survives. From the workshop it has grown into a fully fledged organization. We run a women's film festival where we screen women-centred films that feature a woman in a main role. We do training and production.

***How she views her work:***

I consider myself a producer of narratives.

*She No Longer Weeps* was first performed in 1984 at the University of Zimbabwe.
Telephone interview on August 8, 2006, from Harare, Zimbabwe.

# SHE NO LONGER WEEPS

*Tsitsi Dangarembga*

**Characters**

Martha
Freddy
Martha's Father
Martha's Mother
Joe
Lovemore
Gertrude
Chipo
Mrs Mutsika
Mrs Chiwara
Two Thugs
1st Maid
2nd Maid
Maid

## ACT 1

*Scene 1*

[*Martha's bedroom. She is sitting on the bed, propped up by a pillow. She is knitting an infant's garment. She is about five months pregnant. She has just arrived home and her suitcase lies open on the floor, clothes spilling out of it. A couple of drawers are open where she has attempted to unpack. She knits for a while and then throws her work down in disgust. She heaves herself to the edge of the bed. Momentarily she rests as though the effort were too much for her.*]

**MARTHA**: [*Muttering*] Ts! Knitting. Ha! I shall spend the rest of my life knitting at this rate . . . But it's bad—I've started too early. [*She gets up and goes to examine her profile in the full length mirror.*] [*Bitterly*] Yes, this slag heap proves it—I carry it everywhere; I shall knit for ever. I've been knitting for the past four months, I shall knit for the next four and the four after that . . . if I go back to Freddy. Oh God! Knitting and looking after Freddy! I hate knitting and I hate Freddy! I hate them both. I can't live with him . . . I should but when he looks at me I shiver. I get frightened because I see those little boy eyes of his looking at me from a man's face . . . and his body is definitely a man's all right. But his eyes are just like a little boy's. And he doesn't behave any better. I don't think his mother ever had to put up with as much nonsense from him as I did. [*Her face softens.*]

But, in a way, even after all that, I still do care about him. Perhaps it wouldn't be so bad if I went back—he's sometimes so sweet and gentle with me. It really surprised me that a man could be so warm and hold me so softly, and it's so nice, so nice to lie there cuddling and kissing in bed. I guess that's what it feels like to be a baby, all protected and warm and safe. I didn't know it could feel like that. Yah, when he's good to me, he's fine and his little boy eyes laugh at me and make me laugh at myself . . . and that's nice too because otherwise everything is so deathly serious. Heh! and things are really serious now [*indicating her pregnancy*]. So, I wonder, am I going to spend the rest of my life knitting, knitting like my mother and her mother and all the rest of them. I should . . . it's the right thing to do to go back there, but no, I can't. I don't have time to knit or look after Freddy. I haven't got time to look after Freddy's baby either. Oh Jesus, I don't really even have time to have babies. [*She is speaking more and more loudly.*] Lord in Heaven, I ask you, what do I want with a child? I won't know what to do with it. I'll be scared to even touch it in case it breaks. [*She pauses and makes a visible effort to be calm.*] Uh-uh, uh-uh. I must be sensible about this. Now let me look at it objectively. The child is mine. That is fact . . . or it will be soon enough. [*Enter maid.*]

**MAID**: Oh, it is you, Sisi Martha. I wondered who was talking in your room.

**MARTHA**: Yes, it's only me. Is my mother home yet?

**MAID**: Not yet.

**MARTHA**: Tell her I am here as soon as she arrives.

**MAID**: I will tell her. [*Exit.*]

**MARTHA**: I wonder whether Freddy is home yet. Is he thinking of me now? Or is it just the supper he's missing. I don't think he'll even notice I've left, I'm making such a habit of running in and out of his life. No, he was the one who was running. He never really stopped—I just started running with him, and, of course, I lost the race. But, Jesus, it was fun. Yah, being with Freddy was fun. Even the first time I met him was funny. I dropped in on him [*she chuckles*] just like that. There I was leaning against his bedroom door at college talking to someone—he opened the door and I dropped in! Hm! The fun beginning to everlasting love. Ts! The only thing that was everlasting about him was his erection. He used to boast about it, "Isn't it wonderful, darling, how long I can keep it up?" And, of course, I couldn't tell him that I didn't think it was wonderful at all. It was almost horrible, really—just one of the things that I did because I loved him. Hm. When did I love him? When did he love me—now, that's a better question. At first, it was O.K. But it didn't take long before I began to see the panic come into his eyes whenever I told him how much I loved him. At first it made me sad—I used to cry a lot in those days—but after a while it was really funny the way I could make him cringe just by telling him I loved him. Ha! The idiot. That's when he started beating me up, the son of a bitch. When did I love him? I swear I don't remember, but I must have done . . . otherwise I wouldn't have run to him and stayed all that time. He wasn't there when I arrived that day when I went to him, so I let myself in and waited in the sitting room.

[*Lights down. Scene changes to Freddy's partitioned bed-sitter. Martha, not noticeably pregnant, is sitting in an armchair reading. Her knitting is beside her. From time to time, she glances at her watch. Enter Freddy from work. He sees her immediately when he enters and stops in his tracks. Recovering himself he walks through to the bedroom section, carefully hangs away his velvet jacket, leaves his other clothes on the bed as he changes into jeans, T-shirt and takkies. Martha has stopped reading and has been watching. She follows him with her eyes as he fetches himself a beer and tumbler from the kitchen section. He sits down and begins to read a magazine.*]

**MARTHA**: Why are you ignoring me, Freddy?

[*Silence*] I am here, you know. I'm going to stay.

**FREDDY**: [*Shaking in spite of himself*] Get the hell out of here, you bitch.

**MARTHA**: If it weren't for your baby that I'm carrying, I wouldn't be here.

**FREDDY**: You don't look pregnant to me, girl. Even if you are, how do I know the child is mine, hey?

**MARTHA**: You know, Freddy, you know. I was a virgin when I met you . . . You used to call me your virgin because you were so pleased that you were the first.

**FREDDY**: That's what you say. So, even if it's true, how do I know what you've been doing since I gave you the green light? After me you had nothing to lose, so you could really enjoy, ha, with everybody. How many did you sleep with after that first time with me, hey? That child you are carrying could have a dozen fathers.

**MARTHA**: I never thought you would talk to me like this, not you . . . It's so . . . so dirty.

**FREDDY**: So now I'm dirty, hey? I was once clean enough for you. Ha. You forget. [*He finishes his beer and fetches another.*]

**MARTHA**: I'd like a beer too, Freddy.

**FREDDY**: [*Returning with one only*] Pregnant women should not drink. [*Martha rises to fetch herself a beer.*] You don't even care about that child, do you? What sort of woman would drink when pregnant, hey? Anyway, what sort of a woman would drink? [*Martha returns, sits down, stares at him steadily as she deliberately sips her drink. Freddy is getting angry.*] You want to know? You want to know? I'll tell you . . . a bitch. Only a bitch would do that. You are a bitch, Martha. Never forget that. No man will ever want you. Even if I hadn't spoilt you. You wear trousers like a man, you drink like a man, you argue and challenge men as though you were not a woman yourself. What you don't know is that that education of yours is good for only one thing . . . it lets you earn money. That's the only reason why men like women like you, otherwise you are useless. But even that education of yours is gone now . . . pregnant. You are finished. Women like you have no place in Zimbabwe. [*Silence. Freddy sits down.*] So now you have nothing to say. When it's too late, hey, that's when you got nothing to say. If you had always kept your mouth and your legs closed you wouldn't be in this shit now.

**MARTHA**: [*Stands to look out of the window*] They say you are my husband. [*Silence.*] They say a woman's place is with her husband. They won't let me stay at home.

**FREDDY**: So where have you been staying all this time?

**MARTHA**: With my sister. But my father found out and told her to send me away and her husband said she should obey my father so she sent me away . . . and here I am. [*She pleads with him.*] I've got nowhere to go, Freddy. They say I must be with my husband.

**FREDDY**: I'm not your husband. I haven't married you.

**MARTHA**: But you must, Freddy, please, you must. It will not be difficult or expensive—my parents are only worried about the rumours—you know how people are, they are talking already. All my parents want is for me to be married so that it's all right for me to have my baby. They won't charge much; they'll make everything easy for you. [*Getting hysterical.*] No one will refuse anything you say. They just want me to be Mrs Somebody . . . Mrs Anybody will do, just so I'm respectable and people can't talk. Jesus, Freddy, the way they go on you'd think they'd never done it themselves. "What I know," says my mother, "is that when a woman is old enough she gets married so that she can have her babies." And what about companionship and conversation, intellectual stimulation and basic human rights, I asked her? [*Freddy is getting uncomfortable but Martha is oblivious.*] She looked at me as though I was talking Greek. I don't understand Greek. How on earth could I speak it to her. Heh! It's bad. They don't want to hear, none of them. Not even my sister who's younger and ought to know better—she shouldn't be so set in her thinking. "There are some things" she told me . . . and I swear she looked just like my father. "There are some things," she said, "that simply aren't done. Decent girls don't sleep around or at the very least they don't get pregnant. You have done both. You will have to suffer the consequences. I wish I could help you," she said, "but I can't keep you here. Our father and my husband both say you must go." I cried and cried. I begged her, I begged her to let me stay, but even she believes that since I'm expecting I must have a husband somewhere. Somewhere there must be a man to go to.

[*She goes to Freddy, caresses his neck. Freddy stiffens.*] You know I love you, Freddy, and whatever else I am or whatever I do it's what I believe is right. That's why I'm carrying your baby. I thought it was right to love you. It was not only my body that was yours, I gave you my heart and my soul as well because I loved you and you said you loved me so I knew you wouldn't hurt me. How many times did we pledge our love to each other? So often. Every time we were together we . . .

**FREDDY**: [*Awkwardly patting her head*] I know, I know. I do love you, Martha, but I . . . I want to be . . . sure . . . that I'm doing the right thing.

**MARTHA**: Then let me stay. That is the right thing. I have nowhere to go and I'll only be here for a little while until University opens and I can go into residence. You've got a good job and if things work out, I'll have finished my degree by this time next year. Then we'll both be earning. The baby will be six months old this time next year. Just think, we'll be a family already. Oh, Freddy, it's not so bad. It'll be all right, everything will be just fine.

**FREDDY**: [*Moving out of Martha's embrace*] Hey, Martha, you think too fast and talk too much. It doesn't mean anything if I let you stay. It's just that you're in trouble and I feel responsible, that's all. You'd better understand you're just a friend staying here.

**MARTHA**: [*Mischievous*] Do you sleep with your friends? That's a lot of girls.

**FREDDY**: Don't talk like that, girl.

**MARTHA**: I'm sorry. I won't say it again. I won't say anything or do anything if I think it will make you angry. By the time I go back to University you'll see that we could have a good life together. I'll show you by being so quiet and obedient you'll fall in love with me all over again. [*Freddy looks at her with distaste. Enter Joe without knocking. Joe stops at the door. He speaks with a false American accent.*]

**JOE**: Say, am I interrupting something? [*Martha turns around, friendly, smiling, still holding Freddy who is only too pleased to be able to disengage himself. Freddy crosses over to shake Joe's hand.*]

**FREDDY**: Hey, man, you're late.

**JOE**: If I'd known you were in the arms of the beautiful Martha, I'd have been much later.

**FREDDY**: You said seven o'clock. It's quarter to eight now.

**MARTHA**: Actually it's only half past seven. [*To Joe*] You know how slowly the time moves for him when he's in my company.

**JOE**: Say, beautiful Martha, you're still spitting fire. It's nice Freddy's a tough dude so he don't get burnt.

**FREDDY**: Hey, I'm no fool. I don't want to get burnt. I'm afraid of getting burnt. So why should I go and play with fire if I'm afraid of getting burnt?

**JOE**: You've got a good man here, Martha—he's wise as well as tough. [*Freddy and Joe laugh and slap palms. Martha, annoyed, goes back to her original seat and begins to knit. Joe and Freddy both notice the knitting.*]

**FREDDY**: Her sister . . . the other one . . . Mercy . . . She's expecting. It's the . . . the . . . what is it Martha? . . . The third child. So, Joe, are you hungry? Martha, my love, aren't you going to cook? Joe and I are going to have a heavy night tonight. It's best to start with a full stomach. [*Martha crosses over to the kitchen without a word.*]

**JOE**: [*As she passes*] It's nice you've come back to him, Martha. Freddy was an unhappy man without you. In fact it was making him sick. You see how much weight he's lost? All because of you.

**MARTHA**: [*Laughing from the kitchen*] Sure he's lost weight. But I don't think it's because he was missing me. Was it Freddy?

**FREDDY**: Hey, darling. We know what's been bothering me.

**JOE**: That's right. The dude told me he was really cut up about you.

**MARTHA**: [*Coming out of the kitchen*] There's no food in there, only a little upfu, but nothing to eat with the sadza.

**FREDDY**: So go and buy boerewors or something. Come on, love. You're good at these things. You know what I need.

**MARTHA**: O.K. [*She goes and packs her knitting in her bag obviously dawdling.*]

**FREDDY**: Well? Aren't you going?

**MARTHA**: Will you come into the kitchen for a minute, please?

**FREDDY**: I don't want anything in the kitchen.

**MARTHA**: I just want a quick word with you.

**FREDDY**: You can have it here.

**MARTHA**: I don't have any money.

**FREDDY**: So you think I've got no money. You want to see if I've got money, hey? [*Extracting a $20.00 note from his back pocket and giving it to her.*] O.K. There you are. Now go and buy that food. I expect something good with all that money. [*Exit Martha.*] The woman is tight-fisted. I know she's got plenty of money. Her father's been working long enough, but she likes to come begging to me.

**JOE**: She's an interesting woman. But who wants an interesting woman—you just end up confused. [*Freddy goes to fetch more beer.*]

**FREDDY**: It's worse than that. They tell you things you don't want to hear. It's too bad most of it is true.

**JOE**: They expect you to do a lot of things ordinary women don't expect a man to do.

**FREDDY**: Yah. They say you can drink but you mustn't get drunk. Silly. So why drink?

**JOE**: They expect us to save money. They don't know anything. How can you save when brandy costs $10.00 for a bottle?

**FREDDY**: And they want us to keep them company even when we're not in bed.

**JOE**: That's bad. A man should be able to enjoy himself freely and know there's a woman at home waiting for him and keeping everything organised.

**FREDDY**: You know, she expects me to listen to her and take her seriously. [*Joe goes to get more beer.*]

**JOE**: That's difficult.

**FREDDY**: Why?

**JOE**: Because you can't take her seriously if you don't understand her.

**FREDDY**: You are a philosopher, my friend.

**JOE**: So you don't take her seriously?

**FREDDY**: I'm afraid of her.

**JOE**: So am I. [*They consider this for a while.*]

**FREDDY**: We are afraid of a woman.

**JOE**: We are afraid of women. Because they are no longer our mothers.

**FREDDY**: Instead of mothering us they expect us to become responsible citizens and marry them.

**JOE**: Does Martha expect you to marry her?

**FREDDY**: She wants me to marry her.

**JOE**: Congratulations, my friend. [*Joe shakes Freddy's hand.*] But what about Chipo? Mm! This is bad. Perhaps I should say commiserations. [*He shakes Freddy's hand again in condolence.*] Sorry, my friend.

**FREDDY**: I think I agreed to marry Chipo the last time she was here . . . that was two weeks ago.

**JOE**: Chipo is a lovely woman.

**FREDDY**: She is.

**JOE**: So is Martha.

**FREDDY**: I am lucky.

**JOE**: Why?

**FREDDY**: Because Gertrude likes me but she doesn't expect me to marry her. She doesn't even expect me to see her regularly. She doesn't expect me to take her seriously or talk to her or take her presents. She doesn't expect anything from me. All she wants is for me to make love to her when I feel like it. She's a nice woman.

**JOE**: She is. But she knows no man will ever do anything for her. She has to be a nice woman. She has no choice.

**FREDDY**: But really, that's why we won't do anything for her—she's too nice. Nice women are bitches.

**JOE**: Yes, it's true. You are also a philosopher tonight, my friend. Gertrude is a nice bitch.

**FREDDY**: I like bitches because they don't make demands on me. I thought Martha was a bitch because of the way she behaved. But I was wrong. So I'm trapped. Now what do I do?

**JOE**: Tell her the truth; tell her you only like bitches. She can't complain about that one.

**FREDDY**: She's pregnant.

**JOE**: Well then you certainly can't marry her.

**FREDDY**: It's my child.

**JOE**: [*Roaring with laughter*] You don't say! You actually managed it, you randy dude. I thought it was all talk but no spunk. Congratulations, my friend, and commiserations once again.

**FREDDY**: Perhaps you could marry her. And I could marry Chipo.

**JOE**: Say! I don't want to marry anybody.

**FREDDY**: [*Sighing*] Neither do I. But poor Martha. She needs someone to marry her. What shall we do?

**JOE**: [*Thinks*] I know. We must go and see Gertrude.

**FREDDY**: That's what we must do. And when Martha comes back and finds us not here she'll know we aren't going to marry her. That will make it easier for me.

**JOE**: Yes. She'll know because she's an intelligent woman. [*They sway to the door. Freddy stops Joe.*]

**FREDDY**: [*Very solemnly*] I think Martha will sleep here tonight, so I must not bring another woman back with me. Remind me, my friend, to be fastidious tonight.

**JOE**: I have a better idea. [*Joe goes to a drawer, pulls out a large piece of paper and red magic marker, writes in large letters "Martha is here. No women allowed," and holds it up for Freddy to see.*]

**FREDDY**: Very good, very good. [*Solemnly they stick the poster to the door.*]

**JOE**: [*Admiring his work*] Very nice. Even if you bring her, the whore won't dare come in.

**FREDDY**: It won't work.

**JOE**: Why not?

**FREDDY**: It will be too late. By the time she sees it she will already be inside.

**JOE**: That is true.

[*They remove the poster and go out with it. A little later, enter Martha holding poster and food. She looks around for Freddy and Joe, registers annoyance on seeing no one. She throws the notice on the table, goes to the kitchen and puts away the food. She tries to sit down to knit but is too restless. Eventually Martha gets up, fetches a broom and begins to sweep the room. She begins to cry as she works.*]

*Scene 2*

[*Freddy's flat two months later. The place has obviously benefited from Martha's presence in the way of ornaments, general cleanliness and tidiness. Martha enters from the bathroom now visibly pregnant. She is shabbily dressed in traditional print and doek. She has been doing the laundry and is perspiring. The smock is wet down the front. Martha carries a basin full of wet clothes. As she moves through the living room on the way to the kitchen, pegs fall off the pile of clothes. She tries to put the bucket down. As she does so she bends and jeans fall from the basin.*]

**MARTHA**: Shit. [*Martha walks to the kitchen, deposits basin and bucket, returns to the living area, picks up the jeans, shakes them out to demonstrate that they are Freddy's, throws them over a chair and begins to pick up the pegs. There is loud knocking at the door.*]

**MARTHA**: [*Stuffing the pegs into the jeans' pocket*] Coming. [*She moves towards the door, remembers the jeans and takes them hurriedly through to the kitchen. More knocking.*]

**GERTRUDE**: [*Off*] Hey! Is someone home? Hey, Mrs Mareya, come open the door.

**MARTHA**: [*Opening, speaking politely*] Sorry I kept you waiting. Come in. [*Gertrude enters just inside the door. Martha offers her hand.*] I'm Martha . . . Martha . . .

**GERTRUDE**: [*Ignoring the hand and swaggering over to a chair, throwing herself into the chair from where she examines Martha closely*] You are the one who calls herself Mrs Mareya?

**MARTHA**: [*Sitting at the table*] I am Martha, Martha Hatendi.

**GERTRUDE**: You are not Mrs Mareya?

**MARTHA**: I wish I was, but no, I'm just Freddy's fiancée. I'm staying here because . . . well, you can see for yourself. [*She laughs sadly.*]

**GERTRUDE**: [*Getting up to examine the room*] You are a fool if you laugh.

**MARTHA**: [*Becoming annoyed and therefore being particularly polite*] Would you like a drink . . . tea . . . a cold drink?

**GERTRUDE**: So this is how you are trying to catch him—with these [*raising a cushion by its corner between thumb and forefinger*], and these [*she tugs at a chair-back leaving it crooked*]. Hey, woman, our men don't care for this—just let them drink and let them fuck. Let them fuck anybody and everybody and they'll stay with you for ever.

**MARTHA**: [*Rising*] I'm busy, very busy. [*Martha goes to the door, opens it.*] You should leave now so I can get on with my work. [*Gertrude sits down again, takes out a packet of cigarettes, lights one, offers one to Martha who refuses.*] I would like you to leave.

**GERTRUDE**: Freddy doesn't like you to smoke. He doesn't want me . . . [*Gertrude pauses, disconcerted for a moment then carries on smoothly*] to smoke either. Even Joe. Especially Joe. Joe's my sweetheart and he doesn't like me to smoke so I smoke when he's not around. That way it's none of their business and if they listen to what people say and then come and ask me I tell them to go fuck.

**MARTHA**: [*Closing the door*] You are Joe's girlfriend! I didn't know.

**GERTRUDE**: Never mind, dear, just bring the cold drink.

**MARTHA**: Fanta, Ginger Ale, Coke?

**GERTRUDE**: Anything. Whatever you have.

[*Martha goes into the kitchen. Gertrude gets up and examines the posters on the wall.*] Ts! . . . Fuckin' bitch . . . I would like you to leave . . . O-o-h, I didn't know . . . O-o-h. Fanta . . . O-o-h, Ginger Ale . . . Coke! The bitch, but she's no problem. She's too soft to take it. She won't last. She'll leave him all by herself. I won't have to hit her. Fuckin' bitch! [*Enter Martha with a tray.*]

**GERTRUDE**: [*Turning to Martha with a smile*] I was admiring your pictures. Ey, they're nice. [*Gertrude pours herself a drink before Martha can serve her.*] Does Freddy like them? Is that why you bought them?

**MARTHA**: I bought them before I knew Freddy.

**GERTRUDE**: You must be very clever. You know what's nice.

**MARTHA**: Why did you come?

**GERTRUDE**: To see you.

**MARTHA**: To see me?

**GERTRUDE**: Freddy . . . Freddy and Joe . . . Joe and Freddy, they talk a lot about you. I wanted to meet you.

**MARTHA**: They refuse to bring you here?

**GERTRUDE**: Of course. They don't want you to know. They think I'll talk too much.

**MARTHA**: Talk. About what?

**GERTRUDE**: About the other women. There's hundreds of them. But you're no fool—I'm sure you know already so it doesn't matter if I tell you. Anyway, what's wrong with being the hundredth woman, it's like that for everyone—share and share alike. If you want a man you just have to settle for half or a quarter or even a tenth. That's not much when they are so little to begin with, but you don't joke with a woman. A desperate woman will take even a hundredth. Anyway I don't blame you. I would also be desperate if I was in your position.

**MARTHA**: Desperate? Me? [*She laughs genuinely.*] You don't understand. I love Freddy and he loves me, that's why we'll get married. We are very good friends, and the baby [*she pats her stomach contentedly*], the baby just makes things a bit more difficult. You see, I thought in a year or two Freddy would be able to settle down and cope with a family. Now the baby is making it happen a few years earlier, that's all.

**GERTRUDE**: [*Sympathetically*] That's what they all say.

**MARTHA**: Now what do you mean?

**GERTRUDE**: Ey, Martha, I don't like to say this because you'll just think I'm trying to break up your thing with Freddy. [*Enter Freddy unnoticed. He stops, backs out leaving the door slightly open so that he can listen.*] But it's true. Freddy is loose. If they called men whores, Freddy would be a whore with big capital letters. Ho! I know that one. He reckons you love him too much so you won't listen . . . but me, there's no reason for me to pretend anything and I know he's rotten. I can't count on one hand all the women he sleeps with [*Enter Freddy. Martha notices and stares not knowing what to do. Gertrude, still talking, turns to see what Martha is looking at.*] in a week. [*Seeing Freddy, Gertrude stands up.*] Freddy, I . . .

**FREDDY**: [*Grabbing Gertrude*] Get out of my house, you whore.

**GERTRUDE**: Please, Freddy, no trouble.

**FREDDY**: [*Dragging Gertrude to the door and throwing her out in spite of her struggling*] Out, bitch.

**GERTRUDE**: [*Forcing her way back in*] If I'm a bitch then you just love bitches. [*Freddy moves to strike her. They struggle. Gertrude yells as they fight.*] Yah, you love bitches. You leave this woman to come to me. Ehe. I'm a bitch, everybody knows it but you, you just love the way I open up for you.

**FREDDY**: [*At last managing to throw her out*] You stink. [*Freddy holds the door closed until Gertrude's screams stop after which he turns to Martha.*] She's mad. Don't listen to her. [*Martha opens her mouth to speak, closes it, shakes her head. She is grief stricken.*] You didn't believe her, did you?

**MARTHA**: I don't know.

**FREDDY**: Hey, my love. [*He moves behind her and holds her round the waist.*] Would I do a thing like that? Would I do any of those things? You can't believe what people say. Especially not a bitch like Gertrude. [*Martha disengages herself, walks stiffly to the bedroom entrance where she turns to face him apprehensively.*]

**MARTHA**: It doesn't matter. Even if it's true it doesn't matter. What does matter, what hurts me is that you don't care about me at all. You don't want me. Sure I'm convenient at the moment—I cook and clean and entertain your friends and hold you at night when you need me, but anyone else could do that—it doesn't have to be me. Find someone else, Freddy, you might as well because I expect something in return for what I do. I expect from you, your affection, respect and commitment to me and the baby . . . but I get nothing.

**FREDDY**: You get nothing? How can you say you get nothing when you live here for free. Tell me, my girl, who buys the food you eat? Who pays the rent for the flat where you sleep? I do. Even the soap that washes your body, I pay for that. Every day I go out to work to support you and you say you get nothing. I tell you, woman, you get an easy life from me. But it's not enough. You expect me to stay at home as if I'm the one who is having the baby. You want me to talk to you like a woman myself. You are mad, woman, crazy. Lazy. That's your problem. You don't want to do the work a woman is meant to do.

**MARTHA**: Let me tell you something, Freddy. I am not lazy. I'm not afraid to go out and work, so, if you want to sit and eat while I go out to work that will be fine with me. I don't like staying here. I hate the housework. I hate the cleaning and ironing, and now the sewing and knitting for the child. I hate waiting here for you every night and going to bed alone and getting up to put you to bed when you come home too drunk to know what you are doing. [*Her anger dies suddenly.*] I can't carry on like this, I can't. You are killing more of me than you bring to life, because you don't care about me, you don't care and I cared about you so much. I wanted to be cared for too. I wanted to be loved very much by you. I'd have done anything for you because I really did care. [*Martha begins to weep quietly.*] But I wanted you to love me too.

**FREDDY**: [*Sensing victory, takes her to the sofa to comfort her*] Don't cry. It's all right, darling. Feeling better now? Good girl. How about bringing me my lunch. I'm going to the football this afternoon—Dynamos and Saints—it's going to be a good game. [*Martha serves lunch. Freddy goes to sit at the table and eats. Martha sits in an armchair, watching.*] You're not eating? [*Martha does not answer.*] Well, you can't expect me to lose my appetite just because you're feeling bad.

*Scene 3*

[*About ten o'clock in the evening. The lunch has been cleared away; the room tidied. Martha is lying on the bed, awake but far away. Enter Chipo and Freddy, drunk, laughing and talking. Martha listens from the bedroom.*]

**CHIPO**: You're sure it's safe for me?

**FREDDY**: Yah, she's gone.

**CHIPO**: I'm so glad—I've been dying to be with you. [*Freddy laughs and sits down. Chipo follows to sit on his lap but he stops her with a hand on her bottom.*]

**FREDDY**: Go and fetch some beer, girl. The night is still young. [*He pats her bottom. She giggles and goes to the kitchen to fetch the beer and returns with two quarts.*]

**CHIPO**: She didn't take her things.

**FREDDY**: What things?

**CHIPO**: The cushions . . . the pictures . . . you know, the things for the house.

**FREDDY**: [*Nuzzling Chipo's neck*] Mm?

**CHIPO**: Maybe she's coming back.

**FREDDY**: [*Getting annoyed*] No—that's not possible. She's not the type. She said she couldn't carry on so she won't carry on. I know that one—she's tough. She does what she says. Now stop thinking about her.

**CHIPO**: Do you love me?

**FREDDY**: How many times do I have to tell you?

**CHIPO**: You've never said it.

**FREDDY**: I haven't?

**CHIPO**: No. You only ask how many times you have to say it. Just once would be enough.

**FREDDY**: All right. I love you, Chipo, my darling. [*Chipo takes a long sip from her bottle. Freddy draws back offended.*] So aren't you going to tell me anything? You won't even give me a kiss or tell me how much you love me?

**CHIPO**: I'm going to bed. Come on. [*Freddy sits back and sulkily drinks his beer. Chipo goes into the bedroom where she sees Martha. They look at each other for a minute in silence.*] He-e-e! Nhasi! [*Chipo goes back into the living room.*] You son of a bitch. Why do you bring me here when your wife is here?

**FREDDY**: How many times must I tell you, girl? I'm not married.

**CHIPO**: Then you must control your whores. There's one in your bed waiting for you.

**FREDDY**: Jesus Christ, she's still here! [*Freddy enters the bedroom. Chipo stands aside to let him enter. He pulls Martha to a sitting position.*] What are you doing here?

**MARTHA**: Freddy . . . I . . . [*Martha gives up because there is nothing to say.*]

**FREDDY**: You said you were going. What are you still doing here, hey? What are you doing? [*Freddy pulls Martha's suitcase out from under the bed and begins to throw her clothes into it.*]

**MARTHA**: Freddy, I can't leave now.

**FREDDY**: [*Pulling Martha off the bed*] Get out of my life. Just get out of my life and leave me alone. Get out of my life. [*Freddy pushes Martha out of the bedroom dragging the case with him.*]

**MARTHA**: I'll go if that's what you want, but I can't go now. Let me wait until morning.

**FREDDY**: [*Throwing the case down at Martha's feet*] Go now. Get out.

**MARTHA**: But I can't get home. There are no buses. Please, Freddy, just let me wait till tomorrow. I won't disturb you. I won't even say good morning. I'll just go.

**FREDDY**: You never listen to me, do you? I think today I must teach you a lesson. [*Freddy lifts his hand to strike Martha.*]

**CHIPO**: [*Who has been watching with great interest*] Leave her alone, Freddy. She's not worth it. You've said it yourself many times.

**FREDDY**: [*Pausing for a moment, relaxing*] O.K. [*Freddy throws Martha on to the sofa. She misses and falls on to the floor. Freddy begins to kick her, unable to resist her helplessness as she lies there.*] O.K. you can stay, but I'll teach you a lesson you'll never forget.

[*Chipo pulls Freddy away before he can really hurt Martha. Chipo takes Freddy to the bedroom. They begin to undress in silence.*]

**FREDDY**: What are you doing? What are you staying here for?

**CHIPO**: What's the matter now? I want to be with you.

**FREDDY**: What for? Why don't you go away? Why don't you go away and take Martha with you? I'm not worth anything. Just see what I've done, what I've done to Martha and what I'm doing to you. I'm not worth anything. [*Freddy lies on the bed with his back to Chipo.*]

**CHIPO**: [*Sitting on the bed and drawing Freddy's head on to her lap*] No, Freddy, don't worry. That's how things happen. Sleep now and forget all about it. [*Chipo begins to sing a nursery rhyme, rocking Freddy to sleep.*]

## ACT 2

*Scene 1*

[*Martha is sitting on the bed in her bedroom. Her mother is standing by the dressing table.*]

**MOTHER**: Have you heard my words, my child?

**MARTHA**: Yes, mother, I have heard.

**MOTHER**: So you will go back. [*It is a statement. Without waiting for an answer she goes to lay her head on Martha's shoulder. Martha remains motionless.*] I knew you would be sensible. You have always been sensible, and good too, except for your running around with this man. Come, [*she begins to pack, turning the clothes already in the suitcase out in order to fold everything neatly*] we must pack quickly. You must be gone before your father returns. Otherwise he will get angry. You know what he is like when he is angry. That is part of a woman's job, you know, protecting her man. You have to make sure he never loses control of himself.

**MARTHA**: Ha! So you must control him because he can't control himself. And who controls you?

**MOTHER**: You must just accept, my daughter, that by their nature they cannot take responsibility for themselves. Even when they are great men and achieve wonderful things they need to be controlled just like children. But it is only a wise woman who can do it.

**MARTHA**: Ts! And how does she do it?

**MOTHER**: By keeping quiet day and night and watching, watching what her man does, letting him enjoy himself like a child who does not know that soon it will be time to go home. Then, when the time is right, a wise woman knows that her hour has come.

**MARTHA**: She will be lucky if she lives to see it. [*Beginning to pack also.*]

**MOTHER**: Ts! You are right, my child, this is the difficulty, that that hour does not come early. But there is no other way. A woman must be patient and strong and bear her life bravely. If God is willing her time will come. And if he chooses not to bless you in this life you can be sure of your reward in the life to come.

**MARTHA**: So the hour does not come for all of us.

**MOTHER**: It comes in one way or another; a good wise woman always reaps what she sows. Even you will get your reward for bearing the burden of this man because this suffering will wipe away the sin of your fornication.

**MARTHA**: I haven't committed any sin.

**MOTHER**: You associated with this man without the Lord's blessing.

**MARTHA**: Mother, if I tell you I slept with Freddy because I loved him would you understand? I don't think so, because I don't want the things you wanted, I am not the same sort of person as you. You grew up in a world where women were made out of lace vests, or at least they pretended to be. But today we are not afraid to let it be known that we are flesh and blood too, so the problems of the flesh are our problems as well. We are not above them, so we must fight . . .

**MOTHER**: Fight what? Be careful how you talk, child. What do you know of flesh and blood? You don't even know enough to be afraid of eternal damnation. You are not even thankful that this man is free to make you his wife. Ts! Flesh and blood. Just see where it gets you. [*Martha sits down again, her fervour having disappeared.*]

**MARTHA**: It's no use, Mother. I love Freddy, but I can't go back.

**MOTHER**: You mean you will not go back.

**MARTHA**: I cannot go therefore I will not. Freddy may be my hell, but I will not endure it.

**MOTHER**: And what kind of love is this that cannot endure a little pain?

**MARTHA**: I can't go because I know Freddy is not a good man. Ts! He isn't a good boy. In fact he is a horrible, irresponsible, immature sort of person, but that's not why I fell in love with him. I fell in love with him because he made me laugh.

**MOTHER**: Eeh! Martha, you are still so young, if you can say things like this.

**MARTHA**: But it's true. What do we laugh at here? Either Father tells one of his stupid religious jokes—you know one of the ten we've all heard a hundred times each and we all laugh because we feel obliged to, or else I tell a joke that I think is really funny and all you do is tell me I'm going to burn for blasphemy. [*She absently begins to take things out of the suitcase, shaking them out and folding them very carefully before putting them back into the drawer.*] Freddy told me jokes that I could laugh at, and he even laughed with me. He told me I was beautiful, and I discovered I was, but the discovery didn't make me ashamed of my femininity . . . it made me feel good and fertile and clean to know that my body could make Freddy happy . . . and make me happy as well. You see, mother, I discovered that the object of life is not to get married like they taught you, but to celebrate our existence. I'm not saying you are wrong. I think that you've been really wonderful for the times and conditions that you are in, but the conditions are bad and have got to be changed. And that means everything has to change including us. That's why I can't go back to Freddy—he's not intelligent or brave enough to be able to change and I'm not strong enough yet to carry him. If I live with him he'll break my spirit—I'll have to give up everything I believe in and become a part of these bad conditions. So I think it's better for me to stay here until I'm strong enough and mature enough to be able to usefully contribute to the change. I don't feel ashamed of myself because my mind is free—it's the celebration rather than the marriage that becomes the important thing. I like to feel my life in every cell of my body—pleasure and pain, pleasure and pain, pleasure and pain. That's how it's always been and always will be. You tried to reduce your suffering by living a good life according to the rule of the Good book—but that also gets rid of pleasure. It's true you know—we never try in this family; Dad is a good stern principled man; you are a good principled woman—you aren't stern because good women aren't stern. You're both so perfect you can't tolerate imperfection. But you reckoned without me. I think your standards of perfection are false and I'm a bit too lusty to be good in the ways you want me to be. I like to shudder with pleasure, and sob with desire and know that tomorrow will come and we'll all be more beautiful because of what has been today. I like to feel myself actually living every minute of my life.

**MOTHER**: Now what madness is this? You sound like one of those we read about who are always being sent to jail, or getting themselves jailed, or something bad anyway.

**MARTHA**: Come on, Mum. I'm not so stupid. I have my priorities and I know my limitations. I know I must work hard. I must get my degree and live a productive life. But it will also be a satisfying life. I don't believe that just because I'm a woman I must sacrifice my potential to looking after some idiotic man and his off-spring; if he hasn't got the sense to know when the fun ends and the work, the real work, not just going to the office from 8–5, begins, then I haven't got time to teach him. I mean, if I thought he was a great man who would change the world for the better, well, I guess I could make the sacrifice, but what I loved in Freddy [*she shakes her head*] certainly wasn't his greatness. No, not that at all really, he's too little to satisfy the most undemanding woman. But, it's not his fault. He can't help being what his life has made him. But life must change so it doesn't produce people like him. If I become his good wife he'll have to accept it, but I can't because it's not right. Life must change, so it doesn't produce people like him. And besides, I want to remember the good things about him, so I can't go back. [*Martha is noticing that her mother is looking very upset.*] Don't worry, Mum. I'm only telling you the truth so you won't be disappointed. I know there's a lot of things that I'm wrong about, that I need to come to terms with. I need to do a whole lot of growing up. So does Freddy but he won't. I will, though. O.K. so the baby's a mistake, but I'll stay here and work hard, and you won't need to be ashamed of me.

**MOTHER**: Selfish child. How can you say that? Of course we shall be ashamed. Nothing is going to be all right. Once everybody knows that you refuse to live with your husband . . .

**MARTHA**: But he isn't my husband.

**MOTHER**: He is. You know it. Everybody knows it. And once they know that you aren't living with him, how, how is your father going to stand in the pulpit and preach a sermon on Sunday morning? You are a wicked girl. If I were your father I would whip you until the baby fell from your womb and then you would be punished and we would be saved. [*She moves to Martha.*] Even now I am tempted to do so myself.

**MARTHA**: Don't hit me, Mother. [*Enter Father as they confront each other.*]

**FATHER**: Now what is the problem? Martha, have you no respect for your mother challenging her like this. And what are you doing here anyway? I do not want to hear that you have left your husband because hearing such things will make me angry.

**MOTHER**: It is true. She has left him. But do not be angry, babawaMartha. She is headstrong and wicked, but she is our child. Do not beat her.

**FATHER**: I do not wish to beat her. I wish to find out what has happened. Martha, why are you not with your husband?

**MARTHA**: Father, you do not know what it is like to be with him. I cannot stay with him, and Mother was getting so unreasonable I . . .

**MOTHER**: She is tired and upset. Leave me with her now, I will talk to her.

**FATHER**: But I must know why this girl has left her husband. Did we not agree that she would stay with him and be the good wife the Lord has instructed a woman to be. Anyway, he has paid the damages and the roora is coming soon. She belongs to him. She should be with him.

**MARTHA**: Let me to tell you plainly now, both of you, I cannot go back. I swear, he'll kill me with his terrible ways. I'll die and then what will you say? You'll say "she was a good god-fearing woman who loved, honoured and obeyed her husband until death did them part." Whose death will that be? My death and nobody will ask whether he honoured and obeyed me. And even if you did, what use will it be to me? I'll be rotting in my grave.

**FATHER**: No, no, Martha. Stop this and be sensible. I don't understand why you are behaving like this—you were always a sensible girl. Tell me this, my child, what do you think that you a woman can do in life if not take care of a man?

**MARTHA**: A man should be able to take care of himself. And anyway I cannot take care of myself and Freddy at the same time. Freddy isn't a man like you, my father, one of the few men that I know and even you have faults that reduce you to no more than a suckling child.

**MOTHER**: Hush, my daughter, hush. You must not speak to your father like that.

**FATHER**: Do not speak to me like that, child.

**MARTHA**: Then how shall I speak to you? With smiles in my voice although my heart is breaking? No, today I will tell you, you had a daughter, but I am becoming a woman, and things are changing. To be a woman is no longer a crime punishable by a life-time of servitude to a man. I know that in your day there were so many pressures that prevented a woman from becoming independent. I know there were not even many women who could be independent because they couldn't work for a wage or a salary, but people saw to it that women would remain dependent because that was the only way of thinking that people knew then. Look at Mother, she wouldn't be a respectable teacher now if she hadn't got married. But the time has come for us to live differently; I don't have to be tied by those beliefs because I can support myself and I will not sacrifice myself to a man's eye just because society says I ought to. I'm as much a part of society as any one of you and where I see that change is needed, nothing will deter me from making that change in my own life or from working towards achieving that change.

**FATHER**: These are strong words, but you don't have the strength of will to do these things. This is only acquired through . . . [*Enter housemaid. She whispers to Mother and exits.*]

**MOTHER**: BabawaMartha, she says Freddy is here saying he has come to take his wife.

**MARTHA**: Don't let him near me. I'll kill him if he touches me!

**FREDDY**: [*Offstage*] Hey, Martha, where are you hiding, woman? [*He appears in the doorway.*]

**MARTHA**: [*Screaming at him and being restrained by her parents*] Bastard, whore, prostitute! Get away from here. Go wherever your penis points—go there and stick it in. That's all you are good for. Whore, bastard! Get out. [*She subsides onto the floor between her parents.*]

*Scene 2*

[*Her parents' bedroom. Very late. They are preparing for bed.*]

**FATHER**: Ma'a Mercy, do you think our daughter is mad? I think she is.

**MOTHER**: No, she is only unhappy.

**FATHER**: So unhappy that she must behave like a mad woman?

**MOTHER**: There are many things in this world that can make a woman unhappy.

**FATHER**: But surely not so unhappy that she cannot control herself?

**MOTHER**: She is not herself. These things that trouble us cannot be changed, so we hide from the world and from answers, doing only what must be done to give us a home and food for us and our children.

**FATHER**: But think of yourself. You are not unhappy, you are always calm and wise and content. I have always known that in my darkest struggles against temptation and sin I could depend on you for comfort and strength and guidance. I have praised the Lord that he saw fit to bless me with such a wife. But I also pray to him about my daughters. Mercy is not bad but Martha is like a wild animal.

**MOTHER**: It is true. But we are old and do not always know how to advise our children. For a girl it is particularly difficult—she feels very alone. Sometimes a woman sees that there is no one for her to turn to but God. She cannot even turn to other women because we are all so afraid of being alone and this fear poisons our thoughts against each other.

**FATHER**: But you know that you will never be alone unless God decides to take me first. And even then you will still have Him.

**MOTHER**: I know this, so I am not afraid. But few men and women are as content with each other and with God as we are. Usually a woman feels she must have a man to be something. Her man becomes her life and if she loses him she feels as though she is losing her life. I think this is what makes Martha angry. She thinks that a world in which such things can occur is not just and therefore it should be made just. I am afraid for her. I do not know whether she will learn in time that life is not just and that one must accept responsibility whether it is given fairly or not. Martha knows that no sensible man will put up with her talk of revolutions and women's rights. This is why she does it, because how can she tell others to let their husbands do the cooking if she is busy in her own kitchen?

**FATHER**: Then what will happen to her? I wish she would stop this because people are beginning to say bad things about this family. How can I preach when my daughter behaves like this? People will lose their respect for my word and I shall cease to be a sound instrument of God.

**MOTHER**: I told her this.

**FATHER**: And did she promise to improve?

**MOTHER**: No.

**FATHER**: She cares about nothing but herself and pleasure. She is truly mad.

**MOTHER**: She is not mad. I do not think that any of us can hope to understand the things she does, but if she is remembered by our grandchildren's children, I think they will remember her as someone who saw further than most of us are prepared to look. I think she has courage, but she will suffer for it. Most choose not to suffer, but some cannot avoid it because of the way they are made by that same God who created us all. Our daughter is like that and although I cannot tell her so because it would encourage her, I think there is some sense in some of the things she says.

**FATHER**: Mm! Ma'a Mercy. I do not like to hear you say such things. Next you will be saying that I should give to you my entire month's salary. Come, let us pray to drive away such evil thoughts. [*They kneel and murmur their prayers. They rise and get into bed.*] It came to me while we prayed, that we should send our daughter away. Then people will forget the scandal and I can continue to preach God's word with authority.

**MOTHER**: We cannot do such a thing. Send away my daughter when she needs me most. I cannot do it.

**FATHER**: We shall send her to relatives. She will stay with them during her vacations and soon she will be supporting herself so she can stay where she wants. We will tell her that she does not have to stay with this man, because today I have seen that there is the devil in him, but she cannot stay here. This is for the good of my name and also to teach her that she will have to bear the burdens that she makes.

**MOTHER**: We are in trouble because of Martha, but my heart tells me she must stay. She is young. She has not yet developed to an age of maturity where she can use her strong will and intelligence sensibly. Who will counsel her and guide her if we send her away? I think my child will die if we send her away.

**FATHER**: Are you questioning my judgement?

**MOTHER**: No, babaMercy, your judgement is sound; it is a mother's love that makes me beg you to let her stay.

**FATHER**: Let her go to your brother.

**MOTHER**: His wife will not look after her as I would.

**FATHER**: I have made my decision for the good of all of us. You will telephone him tomorrow. Martha must be gone by the end of the week. My conscience tells me I am doing the right thing. I know she does not want to go, but she is no longer a child. She must learn to face up to that truth. [*He turns to sleep.*]

*Scene 3*

[*A few weeks later. Mother is reading a letter from Martha.*]

**MOTHER**: "I still do not understand why father sent me away. Maybe he thought I needed to be taught a lesson and maybe he is right. Maybe he is trying to change me. I wish I could behave the way he wants me to, but I believe in the things I say and do. Maybe when I get older I'll see things the way you do, but not yet. I am quite comfortable here, but I miss you very much. Sometimes I feel very much alone and frightened. I am beginning to realise how big a person has to be in mind and spirit to do any of the things that are important and I know I am not ready yet. Please, Mother, ask Father if I can come home. Sometimes when I think about this I hate him very much. I feel myself growing to hate a lot of things—the baby, its father, my father and myself. I am realising that it is a dangerous thing, to hate so many things so much. So please ask Father if I can come home and learn how to love again." Ts! My child is suffering, but there is nothing I can do. Her father is a good man and just. It is up to her to find out how she can persuade him to change his mind. Hm! Let her begin her revolution by changing him. If only she would understand that things cannot be changed, only accepted.

## ACT 3

### *Scene 1*

[*Seven years later. The living room of Martha's large, stylish new house. One door, stage right, leads to the living room from outside. Another door, downstage right, leads to the kitchen, while another door, downstage left, leads to the bedroom. Martha is alone wrapping up children's clothes and toys in gift wrapping. Enter Lovemore from outside. He comes over to Martha and kisses her cheek. She briefly pats his hand, not wanting to interrupt her work.*]

**LOVEMORE**: Hi, darling.

**MARTHA**: Hi, love.

**LOVEMORE**: [*Making himself comfortable on the sofa in order to read the newspaper*] How was work? Any rape cases for you to get your teeth into?

**MARTHA**: I don't deal with rape cases. I'm only a junior partner. Anyway, we don't get many rape cases. Can you imagine anybody daring to stand up and admit they've been raped? Much too embarrassing.

**LOVEMORE**: How about wife beating then?

**MARTHA**: You're not being funny, Lovemore.

**LOVEMORE**: I was only joking, love.

**MARTHA**: I still don't find it funny.

**LOVEMORE**: [*Putting down his paper, sitting forward in his chair*] You don't find anything funny. All the time I've known you, I've never known you to laugh. Have you always been like this or is it something new. Sometimes I wonder whether you were ever able to laugh at anything.

**MARTHA**: [*Heatedly*] You have no right to judge me. You don't know what made me what I am so don't think you can walk into my life and tell me how I ought to be.

**LOVEMORE**: I never know anything about you because you never talk about yourself. You should. You don't talk but it shows how unhappy you are. You shouldn't let everybody see. You should talk to me.

**MARTHA**: It's none of your business. I'm not the talking type. If you don't like the way I am, just leave. I don't really care.

**LOVEMORE**: I love the way you are. So I won't leave.

**MARTHA**: [*Suddenly opening up*] Did I tell you it was Sarah's birthday tomorrow? I've bought her all these presents and ordered a huge chocolate cake. I told her she could bring all of her friends home after school.

**LOVEMORE**: Oh, so that's why there's so many presents, you're going to give them to her friends as well.

**MARTHA**: What do you mean? They're all for Sarah. I'll give her the little one tonight and the rest at the party tomorrow.

**LOVEMORE**: You can't be serious. How can you give one child so much for one birthday?

**MARTHA**: Easily. Sarah may not have a father, but I'm determined she won't feel any loss.

**LOVEMORE**: I don't want to interfere, darling, but I really think . . .

**MARTHA**: If you don't want to interfere, then don't.

**LOVEMORE**: I don't want to interfere but if I have to, I will! You're spoiling that child and you aren't doing yourself any good either. Just take it easy, honey, she'll grow up into a fine woman if you'll let her.

**MARTHA**: [*Abruptly*] Look at this dress. Isn't it sweet! She'll look so cute in it—she always looks so sweet in pink.

**LOVEMORE**: You're not listening.

**MARTHA**: I think she deserves lots of presents. All year I've been telling her that if she's a good girl and does what Mummy tells her, that is, if she gets good marks, sticks up for herself at all costs and doesn't cry even when she gets hurt, then I'll give her lots of presents.

**LOVEMORE**: That's blackmail.

**MARTHA**: But it works. She's turning into the sort of person I want her to be.

**LOVEMORE**: She is?

**MARTHA**: Yes, she is. Just the other day they had to write an essay about their favourite war hero. Do you know whom she wrote about? Teurai Ropa.

**LOVEMORE**: Well, that's all right, honey, but you're avoiding the issue.

**MARTHA**: If you mean that I don't want to fight—you're right.

**LOVEMORE**: You don't have to fight, but you do have to face the truth. You've got to stop hiding your head in this feminist fantasy of yours.

**MARTHA**: I don't have to do anything.

**LOVEMORE**: You do, you know. There are some things that have to be done. You've got to find out how you can live your life usefully now, not tomorrow when there's utopia on earth but now while it's violent and corrupt and sadistic.

**MARTHA**: I'm a woman, Lovemore. There's nothing you can tell me about violence and sadism. Now, do you want some tea? [*Martha gets up to make the tea. Lovemore grabs her arm.*] Let go of me. [*She tries to pull away but Lovemore holds her firmly.*] Beat me, then. If you want to prove how much of a man you are, go ahead and do it

**LOVEMORE**: [*Still holding her*] It wouldn't help, would it. A lot of people think it does. And I'd do it if I thought it would help. [*He lets go of her.*] Tell me, Martha, what is it you need?

**MARTHA**: I need nothing.

**LOVEMORE**: Then there's nothing I can do.

**MARTHA**: I'm glad you realise that. I don't want you thinking that just because I let you sleep in my bed you can come here and tell me how to live my life. Remember one thing, my love, my daughter is mine, mine, mine. She's all I have, the only thing I love.

**LOVEMORE**: The only thing you love?

**MARTHA**: Yes, the only thing.

**LOVEMORE**: The only person you love.

**MARTHA**: The only thing. Don't get ideas, Lovemore. You are something I need from time to time for purposes that you should understand well. After all, you are a man. Ha! We're all the same. In spite of having to say "no," we're all the same, I and you and all the men and women out there. So don't get ideas about owning me. Don't think you can tell me what I can or can't do. And never, never interfere with me or my daughter. As long as you understand that we'll get on together well enough. Otherwise we'll have to end everything right now. [*There is a knock. Martha's mood switches suddenly.*] See who it is, darling. [*Lovemore lets in Mrs Mutsika and Mrs Chiwara. They greet each other and then the women go and shake hands with Martha.*]

**MRS MUTSIKA**: Hello, Mrs . . . er . . . Miss . . . er . . . Martha.

**MARTHA**: [*Shaking hands, smiling*] Martha. Not Mrs Miss er Martha. How do you do?

**MRS MUTSIKA**: Sure, Martha. I'm very sorry. [*They all sit.*] Anyway, I'll get straight to the point. I'm Marceline Mutsika, Mrs Mutsika, and this is Susan Chiwara, Mrs Chiwara. We are representing the Women's Association for the Protection of the Illegitimate Mother. We call ourselves WAPIM. [*Lovemore and Martha exchange amused glances.*]

**MRS CHIWARA**: You are one yourself. Surely you have heard of us?

**MRS MUTSIKA**: Mrs Chiwara is trying to say that you have suffered this unfortunate experience yourself.

**MRS CHIWARA**: Yes, that is what I was trying to say.

**LOVEMORE**: [*Rising*] Excuse me, ladies. [*Kissing Martha's cheek.*] See you later. [*Martha kisses Lovemore on the cheek while Mrs Chiwara and Mrs Mutsika watch with distaste. Lovemore speaks to the ladies.*] Goodbye.

**MARTHA**: Don't worry, you haven't sent him away. He doesn't live here. [*Mrs Chiwara and Mrs Mutsika look at each other with more distaste.*] Can I give you some tea? [*Mrs Mutsika realises that Martha is speaking to them.*]

**MRS MUTSIKA**: What did you say? I mean, I beg your pardon?

**MARTHA**: Can I give you some tea?

**MRS MUTSIKA**: That would be nice. Thank you.

**MARTHA**: [*Rising*] I won't be a moment. [*Martha goes out to the kitchen.*]

**MRS CHIWARA**: We can't let her speak to our girls.

**MRS MUTSIKA**: We need her. She has achieved so much for a woman, especially the kind of woman who has had an illegitimate child. She must speak to the girls.

**MRS CHIWARA**: But she's so rude, so unfriendly. It isn't our fault if she couldn't find a man.

**MRS MUTSIKA**: She's trying to put us off, that's all. But we do need her. We must persuade her. [*Enter Martha.*] As I was telling you, my dear, we have a lot of unlucky young girls in our care. We would appreciate it very much if you would come and talk to them about how things are for us women and how these problems can be overcome. They must be inspired. You must tell them not to give up, that this is only the beginning of their struggle.

**MARTHA**: Their struggle?

**MRS MUTSIKA**: Yes, they will have to struggle for the rest of their lives, poor things. We need you to tell them that the way will grow rougher before it grows smoother, but that for their own sake and the sake of future generations of women like them they must be stronger than ever before. [*Maid enters with the tea.*] We would like you to come and tell our girls these things because coming from you they will understand that it is possible to fight and win. [*Martha begins to serve the tea.*]

**MARTHA**: What you say is true, but I can't help you. I'm sorry.

**MRS MUTSIKA**: Are you sure you cannot? A woman like you could do a lot to improve the condition of such unlucky women in this country.

**MARTHA**: How can I do that? I have no power.

**MRS MUTSIKA**: You can help by standing up and giving your witness. It's not many women without husbands, I mean unmarried mothers . . . I mean, I mean, I'm sorry, I don't mean . . . What I want to say is that it is only by taking power that we can ever have it.

**MRS CHIWARA**: You see, your story is . . . it's like something out of a novel . . . you were the quiet daughter of a respectable pastor . . .

**MARTHA**: Who told you these things?

**MRS MUTSIKA**: What Mrs Chiwara is trying to say is . . .

**MRS CHIWARA**: It was Rejoice. You remember her, don't you? She says you were at school together. She's now Mrs Gwanzura. Her husband's a doctor. Just last month he bought her a Golf and now she's off to England to do some shopping.

**MRS MUTSIKA**: But this is not what we came here to tell you. I'm sorry, Mrs . . . Miss . . . I mean Martha. You know how people like to talk.

**MARTHA**: Yes, and listen.

**MRS MUTSIKA**: Anyway, as we were saying, you were the daughter of a respectable pastor . . .

**MARTHA**: I still am his daughter. He still is a pastor.

**MRS MUTSIKA**: Of course, of course, but then . . .

**MRS CHIWARA**: But then you went . . . wild . . .

**MRS MUTSIKA**: [*Ignoring Mrs Chiwara*] But then you were led astray and fell pregnant at an early age. You were only twenty years old then. Nobody thought that seven years later you would be a partner in a successful law firm or that you would be living in this beautiful house or driving a brand new car.

**MARTHA**: I don't see that the fact that I "went wild" as you say . . .

**MRS CHIWARA**: As Rejoice said.

**MARTHA**: As Rejoice said. I don't see how the fact that I went wild can help anybody, not even your prostitutes. Let me tell you something. If I talked to your women I'd advise them to stay at home until the local teacher or doctor brought round the money for roora. I'd tell them that it's much easier to be a domestic slave to a man than it is to take responsibility for your own life, because when you are a domestic slave your problems aren't your own—they all come from your master, your man, and because the problems aren't your own, you don't have to solve them. All you have to do is go to your women's clubs and talk about how much you hate men on the whole and especially your husbands. Then when you've finished talking you can go back to the safe slavery of the home, feeling better and stronger and more defiant because you've talked. Meanwhile at home nothing has changed. Mrs Mutsika, do you really think your organisation, or I, or anybody can do anything for these women?

**MRS MUTSIKA**: You can't be serious when you say such things. You know very well these girls could not get married . . . You yourself know there are no men. That is why these women are so unlucky. So how can you say you would advise them to get married? I think you have learnt nothing from your experience with your child's father and the others that followed.

**MARTHA**: I knew it was coming. The others?

**MRS MUTSIKA**: Please understand me. I am not saying that you are loose, but there is the child, and naturally after that . . .

**MARTHA**: You should know one thing, Mrs Mutsika. I loved the man who fathered my child, but I couldn't live with him. I would have lived with him if it had been possible but it was not. Every day, every minute he was punishing me for loving him. That's how he killed the love. It was natural for him to treat me like that, it was natural. Our society expects men to remain children for too long and I, in the end, I rebelled. Now I have no desire to keep any child I have not produced. I refuse because it's bad, it's bad for women to live with men like that. All these household dramas make women feel so strong and virtuous and wise and maternal. We forget that there was a time when we had no alternative except to accept such domestic subservience, but now that part of the struggle has already been fought and won. We must continue it. We must not be afraid to go out of this man's home, your father, or that man's home, your husband. It is the only way, even for our children. Should a child grow up knowing only a drunken whoring middle-aged delinquent as his absolute authority? No. So we must be strong and give the men nothing. They should not even be allowed to see the children otherwise they will in their simple-mindedness be happy because they can have the pleasure without the responsibility. It is up to us women. We must take sole responsibility for everything we produce.

**MRS MUTSIKA**: Come and tell our unfortunate girls this. Because they have lost their self-esteem. They feel beaten, downtrodden and dirty. The hopelessness even drove some of them to prostitution. You must talk to them. You could make them feel like people again if you spoke to them like that.

**MARTHA**: I'm sorry, I can't help you. I don't want to become a public figure and I certainly don't want to speak for women who don't want to be spoken for. They'll only hate me for my success as they hate you for your families and husbands. I want to be left alone to live my life, that's all.

**MRS MUTSIKA**: But aren't you concerned for these poor, homeless, abandoned girls. If you, who have suffered in the way that they are suffering will also abandon them, then who is going to help them?

**MARTHA**: They will have to help themselves like we all do. I was abandoned once. I was forced to help myself. It has hardened me, Mrs Mutsika. Because of that I no longer feel pain or pity or sympathy, and that is good. To the extent that I am a woman and have my personal battles to fight with the taxman, my employers and lechers in the streets, I am fighting for all women. But I cannot help your prostitutes. I refuse to do it. [*Telephone rings.*] Excuse me. [*Martha exits to the bedroom.*]

**MRS MUTSIKA**: Heh! She's worse than they say.

**MRS CHIWARA**: She's like a stone. I wonder how any man could have found her warm enough to lie with.

[*Martha returns.*]

**MARTHA**: Have you finished your tea? Good. You see, that was the father of my child. He's coming to see me in a few minutes so I'm afraid I must ask you to leave. [*Martha shows the women to the door.*] Goodbye.

*Scene 2*

[*Martha's living room. Martha is standing anxiously by the door. She looks at her watch. Somebody tries the door handle from outside, finds it locked and so knocks. She flings the door open. Enter Freddy.*]

**MARTHA**: Bastard! What do you want?

**FREDDY**: [*Putting his arms round her and walking her backwards into the room. He kisses her.*] I've been missing you so much. Seven years is a long time.

**MARTHA**: Let me go.

**FREDDY**: That's not what you used to say.

**MARTHA**: We are not alone. [*Freddy abruptly drops his hands. Martha moves away.*] Fool! Do you think I'd let you come here without protecting myself? I'm not as trusting as I was, my friend.

**FREDDY**: There's no need to be so unfriendly.

**MARTHA**: I'm being unfriendly? Well, maybe you are right.

**FREDDY**: I came here to say I think we should be friends.

**MARTHA**: You do?

**FREDDY**: Yes, in fact I would be very happy if you would come and live with me again.

**MARTHA**: You would?

**FREDDY**: Yes, I would. Hey, you know that. I've been telling you that ever since you ran away, girl. I've been telling you how much I love you and asking you to give me another chance.

**MARTHA**: Lies, Freddy, lies as usual. Do you think I still don't know when you are lying to me? Or maybe it's just that my memory is better than yours. The truth is you started writing those letters after I graduated. In my third year when I was pregnant I got no help from anyone—as for you, I didn't see you that whole year, not even once. That was a bad time for me, you know. Even my parents wanted nothing to do with me. I was young and headstrong and naive. I desperately needed something to hold on to, but I had nothing except myself. Still, I survived. Now nothing can touch me or hurt me anymore—I have money and I have my child. You say you love me—even if it is true, I know you love my money and the comfortable life I could give you even more. I still remember the good things but I don't need you anymore. I have my child—what else could I need from any man?

**FREDDY**: If I remember you well you need company from men. Lots of it.

**MARTHA**: I get that without trying because all the hyenas are desperate for the scraps I throw to them. But my child and I are happy together, so I am content.

**FREDDY**: Actually, Sarah is the other reason why I came to see you.

**MARTHA**: What about her?

**FREDDY**: She belongs to me.

**MARTHA**: You're behind the times as usual, Freddy. No court in this country would grant you custody rights in a case like this.

**FREDDY**: Stupid woman. Do you think I don't know about the Age of Majority Act. It's all written down on paper, but it gets no further. All I have to say is that I can give her a stable home.

**MARTHA**: You! Stable! Ha!

**FREDDY**: And my wife would be a good mother to her.

**MARTHA**: You got married?

**FREDDY**: You were too proud to even think of me. Now look at you. This woman I married is not proud; she is grateful even to be allowed to call herself Mrs Mareya. She is a good woman, clean, smart, hard-working and she knows how to respect a man.

**MARTHA**: I don't understand you, Freddy. You've got a family, so why do you want to take my child from me. She's all I have.

**FREDDY**: I want everything from you, everything. I had your virginity and your love but you tried to prove that you could manage without me, so now I must teach you a lesson. You are not a good woman. You don't know your place in this world, which is underneath. You thought you should be on top.

**MARTHA**: No, what I wanted was side by side.

**FREDDY**: It is the same thing because a woman will never be as good as a man. Whatever the law says, society will remain on my side. Do you think any court in this country will give a child to a loose woman like you? Our moral standards in Zimbabwe are very high—we do not do such things.

**MARTHA**: I'll fight you, Freddy. I've done it before—I'll do it again. You haven't paid a cent for that child—she's mine.

**FREDDY**: That has nothing to do with it. It's not my fault you were too soft to make me pay maintenance. Ha! You call yourself a lawyer? You should have known better. Proud and soft, Martha, that is a dangerous combination. Anyway, even if the courts give you custody, I shall be allowed to see the child . . . I shall be able to come here to see her. That will be convenient for me. It will be good to see all your lovers trooping in and out of here, and know what sort of a woman I was lucky enough to escape.

**MARTHA**: You are evil.

**FREDDY**: No, I am only saying what everybody is saying. You have shut your eyes to what's really going on in this country, so much so that you haven't even heard what they say about you. They call you the cold bitch, the proud pussy. What good does that do me? If you were still my wife I would probably have to rent you out, like my car, to convince people that I knew what I was doing.

**MARTHA**: Get out of my house.

**FREDDY**: [*Going to the door*] Sure, but I'll be back to see my daughter.

**MARTHA**: You will never come back. Take your daughter, take your daughter and go. Go for ever. I never want to see you again. [*Shouting.*] Maria, Maria . . . come here . . . Maria. [*Enter Maria, a maid.*] Take this man, go and find Sarah, bring her back, pack her things and let her go with this man.

**FREDDY**: Hey, Martha, you can't be serious . . . hey, come on.

**MARTHA**: Go on. Go with her. If you don't take Sarah now I'll bring her to your house myself, and then what will your wife say? Go on, get out both of you. [*Maria and Freddy stand aghast. Martha picks up the bread knife and threatens them.*] Come on, get out! [*They go.*] Ha! The coward. The bloody coward—afraid of a little woman and her breadknife. [*She throws the knife down on seeing the presents, rips them open and starts tearing them up. Enter Lovemore.*]

**LOVEMORE**: Christ, Martha, what's wrong?

**MARTHA**: Don't talk to me, Lovemore.

**LOVEMORE**: But, darling, you're really upset. Why . . .

**MARTHA**: I'm warning you, man. Just get out if you don't want to get hurt. Get out. Get out. [*Lovemore steps towards her. Thinks better of it and quickly leaves. Martha goes back to destroying the presents.*] Cowards, every one of them. Who does he think he is, messing up my life? From the moment I met that man nothing has gone right, nothing. But at least I had my Sarah and he has to interfere with her too. Now he's taken everything from me. And he thinks he'll get away with it. The idiot. I'll show him. I swear to God he's going to regret the day he saw me and told me I had a cute ass.

*Scene 3*

[*Martha's living room. The room is empty. There is knocking at the door. It is three days later. Enter Martha. She opens the door. Enter Mother and Father. Martha embraces Mother, shakes Father's hand.*]

**MARTHA**: It's good to see you again, it's been a long time. [*They sit down.*]

**MOTHER**: Yes, it has been a long time—because you don't come home anymore.

**MARTHA**: I'm a busy woman these days, you know.

**FATHER**: Well, I can see you are working hard, otherwise you wouldn't be able to afford such a beautiful house.

**MARTHA**: I've been here for several months now and this is the first time you've been.

**MOTHER**: Better late than never. [*Martha gives Mother an odd look.*]

**MARTHA**: That's true. But how are you, Father? Mother, how are you? Is everyone well at home?

**MOTHER**: We are well; everybody is well.

**MARTHA**: I'm glad you are here. I've invited somebody else whom you haven't seen in a long time. [*There is a knock.*] This must be him now. [*Martha gets up to open the door.*] I hope it's a nice surprise for all of you. [*Martha opens the door. Enter Freddy. There are surprised greetings on both sides. During this time, the maid brings the tea including bread on a breadboard with a bread knife. Eventually everybody becomes settled.*]

**MOTHER**: Where is my grand-daughter? She is such a lovely child.

**MARTHA**: She must be playing outside. Freddy, my love, won't you go and find Sarah?

**FREDDY**: What are you saying? You know where she is.

**MARTHA**: No, I don't know where my daughter is. But I think she's playing somewhere. Let's go and find her together. [*Martha stands and offers Freddy her hand. Freddy hesitates looking at Martha apprehensively.*] Come, Freddy, we must find my daughter. [*Freddy gets up. They exit.*]

**FATHER**: I do not like this. Martha is having one of her moods.

**MOTHER**: I am also frightened. Martha has often worried me, but this time it is worse.

**FATHER**: Do you remember the time of Tete Enia's death? Martha stood there without a tear, only waiting to come back to Harare. That is when I noticed that she no longer weeps.

**MOTHER**: She has grown hard. Ts! It is not good. [*Enter Martha and Freddy.*]

**MARTHA**: We could not find Sarah. We could not find her, could we, Freddy?

**FREDDY**: [*Uncomfortable*] No . . . we could not find her.

**MARTHA**: Why couldn't we find her? Freddy, tell them why we couldn't find her.

**FREDDY**: I . . . I . . . Martha, this is enough. It's already too much.

**MARTHA**: Tell them. Tell them where my daughter has gone.

**FREDDY**: I . . . I . . . The child is at my home.

**MOTHER**: Is this good news? Are you together again?

**MARTHA**: We can never be together, not after what he has done. He came here and stole my baby. I shall have to teach him that that was a bad thing to do.

**MOTHER**: Be careful, my child. Do not be thoughtless. I know what you are like when you are angry.

**MARTHA**: I am not being thoughtless. I have thought about this for a long time. For eight years I have thought about how Freddy has ruined my life. Because of him I am an outcast. Because of him people say I am "that" kind of woman. Because of him I must live my life in loneliness and unhappiness. Before he came back into my life at least I had my child. I had something to fight for, something to live for. Now I have nothing. I have nothing. It doesn't matter what I do.

**MOTHER**: My child, you have us.

**MARTHA**: You sent me away a long time ago. Everybody did. I'm sorry, Mother. Perhaps I should have come back anyway, but I didn't because I was angry. Now it is too late.

**FATHER**: Martha, do not talk senselessly. Tell us plainly what you are trying to say.

**MARTHA**: You'll see. [*She goes to the bedroom exit and calls.*] Samson. Grey. [*Enter thugs. They manhandle Freddy from his chair and hold him facing the audience behind the chair. Father tries to rise but is pushed back by one of the thugs.*]

**MOTHER**: Yowe, yowe, yowe. Martha. Martha, my child, what is this?

**MARTHA**: Mother, be quiet. Father, don't interfere or else you'll get hurt. [*She picks up the bread knife.*]

**MOTHER**: No, Martha, pity your poor mother. Pity your poor father and mother.

**MARTHA**: Be quiet, both of you. This is a domestic affair. [*Father grapples with her and one of the thugs knocks him out. Freddy begins to struggle but is held firmly by the other thug.*]

**MARTHA**: [*Advancing towards Freddy*] How is my daughter, Freddy? Tell me, is she well? Is she missing me? Is she crying for her Mummy?

**FREDDY**: I . . . I . . . she . . . she is well.

**MARTHA**: But I am not well. I am missing my daughter and it is making me unhappy. I have been unhappy ever since you interfered with my life. The knife is sharp. I had it sharpened this morning especially for you. [*Freddy begins to moan. Martha speaks to the thug.*] Knock him out. I don't want to hear him scream. [*Thug obliges. Freddy slips to the floor behind the chair. Martha, visible to the audience, bends over him.*] I'm going to make you suffer for the suffering you caused me. [*She lunges with the knife.*] I shall take this for spoiling me. [*Mother begins to weep softly, nursing Father who is beginning to come round.*] And this because you took my daughter from me . . . and this I shall take for all the women you have betrayed. [*Freddy is now moaning subconsciously. Martha throws the bloody knife on to the table.*] Take him away. [*The thugs drag him to the bedroom. Martha turning to Father who is sitting up.*] It is done. Father, you were always strong enough to do the right thing. Phone the police. Tell them to come and take me.

**Notes**

1. One of Zimbabwe's most prominent writers.

2. The United States and the European Union (EU) imposed economic sanctions as early as 2003 in an effort to topple President Robert Mugabe. Zimbabwe currently has one of the highest inflation rates in the world with unemployment approaching 70 percent.

# BETTER DAYS COME IN BITTER WAYS

*Nathalie Etoké*

To me, the world is "gone mad." . . . When you look at what's happening in Africa . . . mothers are asking their daughters to become prostitutes or when you look at the way African rulers treat their own people. To me, madness is when the world is going mad. No values anymore. It's when you don't understand what's going on because there's something wrong at the core of society. The society is dysfunctional; the society is crazy.

**Nathalie Etoké, Cameroon**

Nathalie Etoké, a poet, novelist, and musician, was born in Paris in 1977. Her parents, both lawyers, returned to their native Cameroon in 1978 to raise Nathalie and her three younger sisters. In 1995, Nathalie attended France's University of Lille III, where she received a BA and MA in modern literature. She also earned a postgraduate diploma in modern literature from the University of Cergy-Pontoise (France) and a PhD in French literature from Northwestern University in the United States. Nathalie has been living and studying abroad since 1995 but returns to Cameroon for visits.

Nathalie's main interests are French African literature, diasporic studies (Africa, France, and Antilles), African American feminist theory, film, and cultural studies. In 1999, when she was only twenty-two, Cultures Croisées published her first novel, *Un Amour Sans Papiers* (*Love without Papers*), in Paris. Her other publications include the short stories "Bessombe Entre Terroir et Exile" (2002), "Bessombe: Between Homeland and Exile" (2004), and "Cameroun Mon Pays" (2004) and a poem "Song of Grace for African Women Writers" (2004). She is currently working on a second novel, *Le Reve de Weli* (*Weli's Dream*). Her monologue, "Better Days Come in Bitter Ways," is an excerpt from this novel.

Nathalie is a visiting assistant professor in the Department of French Studies at Brown University in the United States.

### Excerpts from Our Interview

***On writing her first novel,* Love without Papers:**

Something was happening in France. You had a lot of illegal immigrants. They had this movement called "Les Sans Papiers," "The Without papers." It was the mid-90s. They were on TV talking about the fact that the French government did not want to give them their papers. . . . They talked about the history between France and Africa; they mentioned the involvement of their ancestors in the Second World War. A war that did not concern them. How they were sent to the front lines and how they died in order to free France from the Nazis. They also argue that their presence in France is due to neocolonialism. And then there were protests in the streets. I attended some of the protests. But I'm not that kind of person to be on the streets yelling "give us papers; give us papers."

. . . That's kind of pointless. . . . I thought maybe I should write something about it. . . . I did not know I was going to write a novel, . . . but I needed to say something about the situation.

The objective was to talk about the immigrants in France, but somehow I ended up talking about myself without being the leading character because it is all fiction. But I talk about my social background; the fact that I come from a privileged family, was born in France, but grew up in Cameroon, went back to France for college. While going through college, I had to deal with white French people, and their ignorance about Africa. They always asked me about my origins. They saw me as a black woman, period, with all the stereotypes and clichés. It dawned on me that I was black. I am not talking about the skin color but all the stereotypical discourses associated with blackness in the West. Whereas, in Africa, it never occurred to me because I was surrounded by black people who do not see themselves as ignorant, poor, savages, barbaric, or oversexualized human beings. . . . Then I decided not to accept a racist definition of myself through the Western gaze. I decided to write stories that will address the predicament of postcolonial Africa without dehumanizing black people, stories in which being black means being human. Being black means dealing with the traumas of slavery and colonization, trying to survive in a postcolonial state that failed to provide for his citizens. Being black means experiencing a wide range of emotion: happiness, anger, sadness. Being black means being able to be good or be evil like any human being.

***On* Better Days Come in Bitter Ways:**

Nowadays you have many African women and young girls who are trying to find a white husband. . . . And people don't equate it to prostitution, but to me it is very close. . . . The last time I went . . . home . . . in 2002, I was very shocked to see all the women in Internet cafés. And I was like, wow, this is amazing. But you don't know why they are there. It's not like they are doing some intellectual research. They are looking for white men . . . and I thought this is very interesting; this is fascinating. . . . I'm going to use the idea of trying to leave Africa by being a prostitute, but, also, since writing stories and novels is about making up things, that prostitute, she's going to be a very special girl. She's not just going to be some prostitute. . . . I know some prostitutes who went to school and their parents couldn't send them to college, but they're smart girls. And they tried to find jobs, but it didn't work out because they only have high school diplomas. People with bachelor degrees and master's are unemployed. What are you going to do with your high school diploma? And also many young women are under a lot of pressure from their families. Your mother will not tell you go and be a prostitute, but she will be like . . . it can help, get some food. And you have all those women who leave as wives and mistresses and those who leave as prostitutes. These women live between Africa and Europe. They come on vacations to display their wealth. People see them as very successful. They build houses, they have cars, and their families are living large. . . . People end up admiring them because they got out of poverty and became rich according to their standards of living. So if you are in that kind of social environment, you feel like this is the path to follow. But I wanted my character to be a very special girl . . . and that's what I did.

***On African theatre:***

I was able to attend several African plays, not in Africa but in France, and that's very strange. . . . African books are published in France and read by the Western audience; African plays are performed in France. It's kind of amazing that I have to be in Paris to see African plays or to have access to African literature. I think there's a problem right there.

***On the reading culture in Cameroon:***

The literacy rate is high in Cameroon. . . . I don't know how high it is, but people read. They read newspapers and novels. In a country like Ivory Coast, you have this collection of love novels called *adoras*. They are very cheap and really popular. In Senegal, you have books that are published in French and Wolof. And if people were not so poor they will even spend more money on books.

Interviewed in Chicago, Illinois, October 8, 2005.

# BETTER DAYS COME IN BITTER WAYS

*Nathalie Etoké*

Life is rough. One must get by by all means possible. I still remember the night when I said stop. Stop to poverty. Stop to distress. I was trussed up in a stretch pant that showed off my curves. My tightly fitting low cut shirt displayed two shells targeting potential customers. Armed with my stiletto heels, I adopted a swaying and seductive gait. Dad was drunk. He stank of alcohol. With his husky voice he sang: "Amba amba amouchela amba." Mum looked at me askance without saying a word. She has been waiting so long for that day to come. Over and over again, she had said these words: "My daughter, you are twenty years old now. You are young and beautiful. You should be able to find somebody but you don't even try." Eventually I decided to be what she wanted me to be. A jobless drunkard husband. Eight children to take care of. She couldn't take it anymore. She needed my help.

After obtaining my high school diploma, I dreamed of leaving this neighborhood where disease and violence pace everyday life. I pictured myself going to college. Becoming a lawyer was my highest dream. But like many young people of my generation the hope of a promising future ended up in the trash. I wasn't the only one to choose the street. Was that a choice? My companions in misfortune were between fifteen and twenty-five years old. Most of them graduated from high school. The luckiest ones went to college. We were not some idle women looking for easy money. We belonged to this new trend of prostitutes, those maidens that the wheel of fortune had led to a sinuous path. At nineteen years, I was left on my own. What could I do? Sit down and wait for manna from heaven? At first, I tried to find a job that corresponded to my level of education. Naively, I thought my high school diploma would have opened many doors. I forgot all those street vendors who hold bachelor degrees and master's. They labored under the sun for salaries that are as devalued as our dear CFA franc. I stopped dreaming. It was absolutely necessary to find a way out. I was sick and tired of seeing my father sleeping off his hangover, my mother sitting all day long behind her vegetable baskets for zilch, my brothers and sisters wandering in the kitchen, looking for a nonexistent loaf of bread.

Before making my decision, I spent sleepless nights. Immersed in my teenage memories, I saw myself: a young high school pupil in my pretty blue uniform. The boys chased me. Fiercely, I resisted their assaults. I was a hardworking girl who didn't want to become infatuated with anybody. Finish my education, be economically independent, then marry a man that I would have chosen, this is the road my life was supposed to take. My girlfriends used to tell me: "Weli, you are so dumb. Get your head out of your books and have fun." I didn't understand them. Even the teachers tried to seduce me. Some of them offered me STDs. Those sexual transmitted degrees that were crowned with an unwanted pregnancy and a success at the HIV test.

So far away are the years when I could look at myself in the mirror without being ashamed. Without being afraid. I became somebody else. The one who brings money home. Money that I earned by the sweat of my body.

"Go looking for the WHITE MAN, more WHITE than WHITE. Don't even wink at BLACK MEN, they have no dough. North-South relations. Unequal distribution of wealth. Girlfriend, the money is on the other side. Get yourself a WHITE MAN, more than WHITE, the WHITEST, drop the hazelnuts, they're not worth a dime!" said Valerie, my best friend. "You'll get out of poverty. You'll leave your slum for the fashionable areas of Yagadoul before taking your flight for Paris. Put an ad in a specialized newspaper. Subscribe to one of those matrimonial agencies on the Internet. Obese, disabled, hunchbacked, bearded, dirty, decrepit, puny, hairy, young, sexagenarian, octogenarian, or septuagenarian with funny habits, I'll take him. I don't mind living with a senile bedridden invalid white jerk who dopes himself with Viagra or a Quasimodo who doesn't have anything between his legs. The money he has in his pockets is my only interest. Today, the most important thing is there and nowhere else. I want the dough. I got to get these papers. I need some cash. I'm not asking God for anything more. Anything less to the Devil. To push a man away because of his ugliness! What silly behavior! Come on now, even if he doesn't look like Richard Gere or Brad Pitt, his beauty lies in his pockets. Besides, you can't eat a pretty face, can you?" asked Valerie in a sarcastic tone that told me how motivated she was to leave Africa, the kingdom of poverty. She knew the six rules of success taken from a very special book: *How to Catch a White Man and Keep Him.*

*Rule 1:* Be obedient and malleable. Satisfy all his demands, even the craziest ones. *Rule 2:* Make the White Man believe that your encounter is God's graciousness. Blinded by his ego, he will think of himself as the savior. In his immense leniency, that Good Samaritan will help you. *Rule 3:* Forget how much money he has. The more you refuse his gifts, the more gifts you'll get. *Rule 4:* Put yourself on a starvation diet. The big soft black behind and rolls of fat that once upon a time were trendy are now out of fashion. Not recommended at all. *Rule 5:* Keep your dark skin and your kinky hair. Say goodbye to all those bleaching creams. Chlorinated black women are not popular. Black charcoal is in and beautiful. Alek Wek the stunning Sudanese model leads the show. Give up wigs and makeup. Be natural. Be yourself. *Rule 6:* To be or not to be pregnant? That is the question. . . . If your White Man is an old man, death is coming slowly but surely. The idea of leaving descendants will give him the illusion of eternity. And bingo: the wedding is on. Your financial security guaranteed forever. If he is a young one, take your birth control pills. If you get pregnant, he will lose his mind; run away and everything will be lost. You won't be able to take a slightly different tack.

That book wasn't available at any bookstore. It was saved on the hard drive of all the young women who were looking for the rare bird.

The evening of my first day on the street market, we met in front of the Benouri Hotel. Val held my hand: "Don't be scared, girlfriend," she said. "You'll see we will get through this together. We will drive expensive cars, wear fancy clothes, eat our fill, and go to Energy Fitness to lose the extra pounds." While listening to her, I remained silent and realized the new turn my life was taking. Val and I were the same age. But she started hunting the White Man when she was fifteen. She was very pragmatic. Her motto was: "I am from the bush. So why should I beat around the bush? If you have something to say, spit it out before you die. If you want something, get up off your ass and go get it."

From the beginning she told me: "Rule 1: Only two words: protection, condom. You won't have any trouble with white men, they are afraid of STDs, whereas your black brothers refuse to cover their scepter up. Their sacred seed guarantees eternity. It must not end its journey in a common sock. Rule 2: When it comes down to your wage, it is just a matter of how long you guys get busy. For an hour, charge $40. For more than two hours, there is a flat rate of $150. But be careful girl, sometimes you can come across athletes who will keep you up for hours and burn you out."

Val knows how and when to smile, cross and uncross her legs in a sexy and attractive way by rubbing them slowly the one against the other. She knows how to seduce a potential customer by giving him a glad eye to which he can't resist. She has a sweet bewitching voice. She teaches me how to fish. That evening, for my baptism of fire, she hopes I'll catch a big fish. I try hard to empty my mind. I don't want to think about what I am about to do. I am shaking like a leaf on a branch fighting against a hurricane. Seated by the pool, we are sipping Coke and whiskey. I have never drunk a drop of alcohol. That first glass feels like an erupting volcano in my throat. My saliva turns into lava and burns my stomach. Val looks at me mockingly, bursts into laughter, and welcomes me to the profession.

While she was trying to loosen me up, I noticed an old *white* man staring at me, his big eyes licking my body. Embarrassed, I switched chairs with Val. All of a sudden, he stood up. He was 6 feet 4, 195 pounds roughly, wearing a ragged shirt, and he was definitely bald. He came close to our table and offered to join us. Our conversation wasn't deep at all. In few minutes, we learned that his name was David Durand aka DD aka $D^2$, the king of wood. He was one of the famous lords of forestry who graze the green cathedrals of Africa while sipping champagne and smoking cigars. In Yagadoul for a short stay he "wanted to have a good time." We all drank some Moët Chandon and enjoyed an excellent free meal of boeuf bourguignon and gratin dauphinois.

Val was overjoyed. $D^2$ was a really good catch. Petrified and mortified, I dreaded the supreme moment. Time flew. Val pretended she had an appointment and disappeared in the dim light. I found myself in an uncomfortable tête-à-tête with $D^2$. He couldn't wait any more: "Come on sweetie, let's go! It's time to get busy!" he said. Because of the air conditioner, the room was cool, which made me forget how muggy Yagadoul was. $D^2$ vanished in the bathroom: "Make yourself comfortable. Give me a minute; I have to grab a condom. I'll be right back." I sat on the bed. Self-consciously, I started to take my clothes off. I was about to live my first time. To take a leap in the dark with a total stranger. I was racked by anxiety and fear. Stress. Sex. Latex.

After five minutes, $D^2$ was by my side. His penis was big. I wondered if it would hurt me. He slipped into the white sheets and rushed himself into my breast: "God, two calabashes filled with milk. Give me some milk honey, give me some milk," he said. His pudgy fingers massaged my behind while his rubber mouth swallowed my lips. His wet kisses made me want to puke. It was really unpleasant. My body went stiff. I was totally disconnected from what was going on. I closed my eyes. I couldn't step back. He wormed his way between my legs and came up against an impassible wall. "What's the matter with you? You want more money? It's OK. Come on now, give it up."

At that moment, I wanted to get up and leave, when suddenly, I heard my mum complaining about how hard life was, saw my two young brothers who died of malaria because my parents did not have enough money to afford the drugs, saw my sisters who left school, saw the scary face of our landlord threatening to eject us because the rent was overdue. Despair and sadness welled up inside me. But anger and survival instinct slapped me back into reality. I did not want this life of stricken poverty anymore. I did not want to live from day to day. I was determined to do what it takes to get out of this quagmire.

$D^2$ did not care about my coldness. He thought I was just being cranky. Resolved to break into my vagina, his strokes became more and more violent. At every new attempt, I bit my lips. So strongly that they started to bleed. $D^2$ was crushing my little body. His big flabby belly collapsed on my breast. As he penetrated me, I felt a throbbing burn. My muscle was tearing. I prayed he reached his goal as soon as possible. He yearned for my body. He wanted to eat the fruit that I secretly hid for years. The pain was unbearable. I tried not to show how afraid I was. But little by little, tears started to run down my cheeks and I swallowed them in silence. I was extremely tight. Eventually, he forced himself through me and it felt like a blade cut. Dead on the surface I was alive underneath. I was there but I wasn't there. I was out of my body. So far away from it. He was yelling: "Oh shit! It feels so good!" He came. He was happy and ready for another round when the sight of his bloody condom horrified him: "My God! What have I done?" Panicked, he threw it away on the bed. I stared at the sticky red liquid which had left stains on the sheets.

From that moment, $D^2$'s behavior changed. He held me in his arms and dried my tears with a lot of CFA bills. "You should have told me. Why didn't you? Why?" What was there to say? While he was harassing me with his questions, I felt his soft hands caressing my frightened face. The sweetness of compassion followed the violence of the act. A black skin and a white skin. A woman and a man. Our bodies intertwined in a halo of light. I closed my eyes and fell asleep in the protecting arms of my first customer, knowing that the money he gave me would help to ease the pain. Convinced that better days come in bitter ways.

[ *Pause.* ]

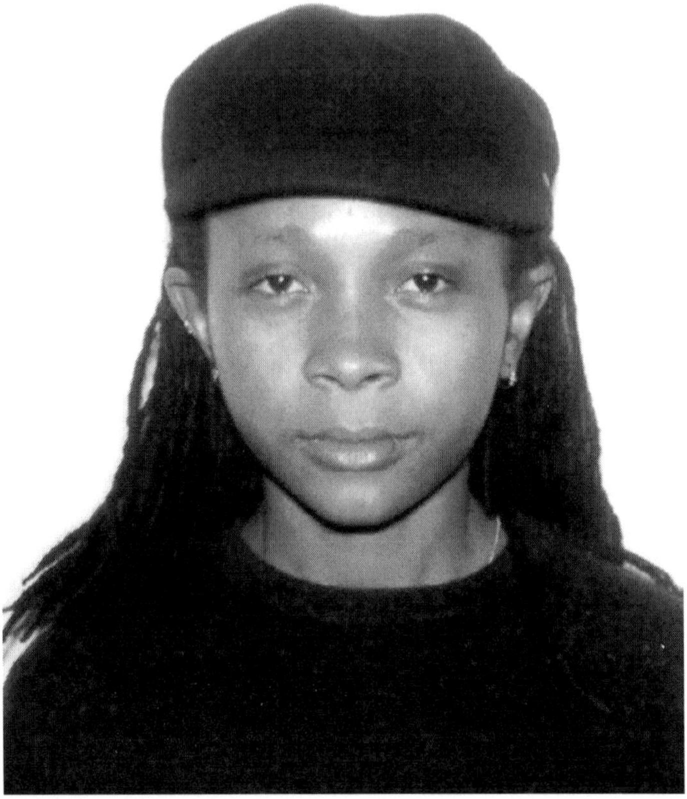

# HOMECOMING

*Andiah Kisia (Chika Okigbo)*

You meet people who are supposed to be responsible for some of the greatest atrocities and you find they are just regular human beings. . . . Someone who may have taken a lot of lives is probably someone's favourite son or someone's father or someone's brother. How do you treat a member of your family, whom you have loved, after they have done something you might consider inexcusable or unforgivable?

**Andiah Kisia (Chika Okigbo), Kenya, 2003**

A novelist, dramatist, and screenwriter, Andiah Kisia was born in Nairobi, Kenya. As a child, she frequently attended plays at Nairobi's Phoenix Repertory Theatre and discovered a lifelong love of literature and the theatre. She remembers writing her first piece of fiction when she was nine years old. In later years, her writings would be influenced by such playwrights as Samuel Beckett and Harold Pinter.

In 2001, Andiah published her first work, a short story, "A Likely Story," in *Kwani?* (So What?), a Kenyan literary magazine. She is also the author of two radio plays, *K Street* (2002) and *Homecoming* (2003), both of which won the British Broadcasting Corporation (BBC) African Performance Playwriting Competition and were later performed for BBC Radio. In addition, Andiah has written a stage play, *The Roosting* (2003), which premiered at the Phoenix Theatre in 2003. She has written a film, *The Aftermath* (produced by M-Net Nairobi in 2002), a dramatization of the plight of a child soldier returning from a civil war.

In 2004, Andiah was a playwriting resident at the Royal Court in London, where she began work on an as yet untitled play. That same year, she published a short story, "A Turn in the West," in the short story collection, *A Is for Ancestors: A Selection of Works from the Caine Prize for African Writing.*

Andiah's children's play *A Bronx Tale* is scheduled to premiere in 2009 at Riksteatern: The Swedish National Provincial Theatre. She is also writing her first novel.

**Excerpts from Our Interview**

*On her decision to set two of her plays (*K Street *and* The Roosting*) in prison, while at the same time the main character in* Homecoming *has returned from prison:*

It's just . . . a function of the place [and] the time that I was writing about or writing in. . . . In the late nineties . . . Kenya was still . . . a pretty repressive kind of place.

*On* Homecoming*'s protagonist, a convicted murderer and its basis in the Rwandan genocide:*

It was a moment of madness or something. . . . Some of them are perfectly nice guys in person. . . . Some of them feel bad about what they had done. But I thought: How could you do something like that? I am not sure that they completely understand what they were doing either.

*On using the radio drama format:*

It was easier. Not just . . . easier to write, but they were shorter and just in terms of a medium . . . that was available. It was easier . . . than writing a play in Kenya and trying to get it put up there.

*On why she has never written a play with a female protagonist:*

I have never really been able to write anything, prose or anything, from a woman's point of view. I don't know why that is. I need to try. Try it out. Get in touch with myself.

*On the role of theatre:*

I guess it's the same thing I think about the role of any writing in general . . . engagement with society, an engagement with the things going on around you. I'm not saying you're making pronouncements about it, but you're asking questions. I guess in some ways you are making statements, too.

*How she views herself as a writer:*

Actually, if I had to say what I consider myself, I think I am a novelist, even though I have not finished any yet.

*On her writing process:*

I'm not even sure what the process is. You have a thought, it's pretty tenacious, it sticks there and then it ferments, it does its thing.

*On the use of an alias name:*

When I was a little younger, I went through an Igbo phase wanting to be Nigerian. I was fascinated with Igbo writing, folklore, and Onitsha market literature. Christopher Okigbo, who died during the Biafran War,[1] was my favourite poet.[2]

Interview in Philadelphia, Pennsylvania, February 11, 2006.

# HOMECOMING

### Synopsis

One afternoon, Joseph, just released from prison for health reason, arrives at his daughter's house without warning. In spite of his release from prison, there are many people who would like to see him dead. He knows this, as does his daughter and her husband, Simon, who have spent the last few years trying to outrun his reputation. Neither wants anything to do with Joseph.

Joseph tries to convince his daughter to let him stay while Simon urges her to give him up to the mob who want him and end their predicament once and for all.

### Characters

Taxi Driver
Joseph: Marie's father
Marie
Simon: Her husband

## ACT 1

[*SFX: Sound of car engine and the crunch of gravel. Car engine goes off. A car door opens and shuts.*]

**DRIVER**: This is it I think. 19 Mwingi Road.

**JOSEPH**: 19 Mwingi Road. Good. Go on and see if there's anyone in. I'll stay here.

**DRIVER**: You want me to . . . Alone?

**JOSEPH**: I do.

**DRIVER**: They might not like that.

**JOSEPH**: I don't see why not. Unless I came with you that is.

[*SFX: Footsteps on gravel followed by knocking on a door.*]

**DRIVER**: [*shouting at man in car*] Nothing!

[*SFX: Knocks again and waits.*]

**DRIVER**: I don't think there's anyone in.

**JOSEPH**: Again. Try again.

[*SFX: Knocking on door, more insistent, followed by the turning of a key in the lock.*]

**MARIE**: Yes? What is it?

**DRIVER**: [*hesitantly*] I'm sorry to disturb you like this.

**MARIE**: What is it?

**DRIVER**: I have someone in the car for you.

**MARIE**: Some one? For me?

**DRIVER**: Yes. He asked for you. He wants to see you.

**MARIE**: He says he knows me?

**DRIVER**: Yes.

**MARIE**: Who is he?

**DRIVER**: I . . . I don't know exactly. He didn't tell me. But he knows you. I mean, he's here to see you.

**MARIE**: And who are you?

**DRIVER**: Oh, I just drove him here. Don't ask too many questions, as long as I get paid.

**MARIE**: And you're sure it's me he wants to see?

**DRIVER**: Yes. Quite sure.

[*SFX: Car door opens and shuts, crunch of slow footsteps on gravel.*]

**DRIVER**: Ah! There he is. Does he look like anyone you know?

**MARIE**: [*sotto voce*] Oh God.

**JOSEPH**: Marie?

**DRIVER**: He said you'd pay.

**MARIE**: What?

**DRIVER**: The fare. For the taxi. He said you'd pay.

**MARIE**: [*distracted*] Fine, fine. Let's get him into the house first.

**DRIVER**: Yes, but . . .

**MARIE**: Now. Quickly.

**JOSEPH**: Yes. That would be best. Get me into the house. Quickly. If you'd just get my bag out of the car. Thank you.

[*SFX (under): Car door slams, footsteps on gravel.*]

**JOSEPH**: Marie? Would you help me? Legs not what they used to be. Thank you. Sorry to drop in on you like this. I tried to find you, to call you first, but you'd moved. And changed your number. And God knows what else.

[*Pause.*]

Marie is a nice name. I've always liked it. Did you pick it yourself? Joseph, meet Marie. Joseph, meet Mary.

**MARIE**: [*distracted*] Yes, yes. Just leave it over there. Thank you.

**JOSEPH**: Yes. That's fine. Thank you very much. For everything. I'll be just fine here. Just fine.

[*Pause.*]

Janet? I'm sorry. Marie. Marie, would you pay the man?

[*SFX: House door slams shut. Moment of silence.*]

**JOSEPH**: This *is* a nice place. Very nice. Much better than the other place. I can see why you'd move. Much more room. Much more . . . private. Out of the way. Yes. Very nice.

[*Pause.*]

Very.

**MARIE**: You shouldn't have come.

**JOSEPH**: That's some welcome.

**MARIE**: You shouldn't have.

**JOSEPH**: Perhaps not. But here I am.

[*Pause.*]

No. Yes. You're absolutely right. I shouldn't have come.

**MARIE**: [*angry*] So why did you?

**JOSEPH**: Did you know? I mean, are you surprised? To see me I mean?

**MARIE**: It was in the paper yesterday. Everyone knows. They soon will anyway. And they'll know to come here.

**JOSEPH**: I doubt it. It's a hard place to find. It's why you picked it isn't it? To hide in?

**MARIE**: They'll find it. Why shouldn't they? You did.

**JOSEPH**: Yes. But then I so wanted to see you. To see your face.

**MARIE**: It's only a matter of time.

**JOSEPH**: Time. Yes. That's what I need. Time enough to think. Time enough to plan. Time enough to move. They won't find me here, when they find you.

**MARIE**: Who's seen you? Has anyone seen you?

**JOSEPH**: Of course they have.

**MARIE**: Of course. The taxi driver. Did he recognise you?

**JOSEPH**: He might have.

**MARIE**: Stupid.

**JOSEPH**: I didn't have a choice now did I? How else would I get here? You weren't waiting for daddy dear when he got out.

**MARIE**: It's the sixth house we've lived in in two years.

**JOSEPH**: I'm allowed to sit down am I?

[*SFX: Footsteps on wood floor.*]

Excellent. Tea would be nice by the way.

[*SFX: Rattle of teacups on tray.*]

**JOSEPH**: There's nothing like a few years in prison to awaken your appreciation of the finer things.

China tea. China. Porcelain I should say. If I ever see an enamel mug again, it'll be too soon for me. Wedgwood. Very nice. Did you know they still make their porcelain by hand?

**MARIE**: I don't care.

**JOSEPH**: No. In the larger scheme of things, I suppose tea is rather insignificant. No. Nor do I.

**MARIE**: What are you doing?

**JOSEPH**: Two spoons of sugar. And then we talk of greater things.

[*SFX: Tea being stirred.*]

**JOSEPH**: Where's Simon?

**MARIE**: Away.

**JOSEPH**: Good.

**MARIE**: Not for long.

**JOSEPH**: Pity.

[*Pause.*]

What happens when he gets back?

**MARIE**: What do you think?

**JOSEPH**: Let's see. *I* think, Simon says no dice. Simon says fuck off. Simon says, "I wash my hands of this man." Simon says, "crucify him." *I* think.

**MARIE**: You're not surprised, surely?

**JOSEPH**: Not at all. I know my Simon.

**MARIE**: What about you? What do you think we should do? With you? What do you think you deserve?

**JOSEPH**: What I'm going to get no doubt.

[*Pause.*]

**MARIE**: Where will you go?

**JOSEPH**: Would you?
You would!
You would, wouldn't you?
She would.

**MARIE**: Don't.

**JOSEPH**: You would let him throw me out. She would.

**MARIE**: Don't.

**JOSEPH**: Simon may be your husband, but don't forget what we are.

**MARIE**: Don't you forget what *you* are. And what you've made me.

**JOSEPH**: Which is what exactly?

**MARIE**: As if you didn't know.

**JOSEPH**: They're coming you know. We passed some of them in the taxi on the way here. Marching down the street, baying for blood.

[*Pause.*]

Don't let him. Don't let him give me up.

**MARIE**: You're not very convincing as a victim.

**JOSEPH**: Did it say in the paper, why they released me?

**MARIE**: Something about "humanitarian grounds."

**JOSEPH**: Nice word. Humanitarian. Concealing more than it reveals.

**MARIE**: I assumed you were ill.

**JOSEPH**: Mmm. I am. "Wounded unto death." Dying. More dead than alive. That's what it means. Pity. It means they felt so sorry for me, they let me go.

[*Pause.*]

And if they can, why can't you?

**MARIE**: If *you* cared about me, you wouldn't have come here.

**JOSEPH**: Did you never want to drop in by the jail to see your old father? Did you never think about me at all? Or did Simon help you change your mind?

**MARIE**: Why would I want to see you?

**JOSEPH**: You've been listening to Simon again. You shouldn't you know? He's every bit as stupid as he looks.

[*Pause.*]

No one is ever quite the monster they're made out to be.

**MARIE**: I've heard you're worse than that.

**JOSEPH**: Guileless. You *do* know that word? It's pretty. But really, it just means stupid.

**MARIE**: You're sure you're dying?

**JOSEPH**: You have my word.

[*Pause.*]

I take it you approve?

**MARIE**: What is it exactly?

**JOSEPH**: You don't have to be polite to me.

**MARIE**: I'm not. I want . . .

**JOSEPH**: It doesn't matter. It's a messy business though. *That* I would change. When you've made a point, there's no need to underline it. And this point is hard to miss.

**MARIE**: Are you taking anything for it?

[*SFX: Pill bottle is shaken.*]

**JOSEPH**: I have pills. Mostly for show. Whatever it is I'm paying for, it must have been very bad indeed. Maybe Simon's right after all.

[*Pause.)*]

The monster is getting his due.

**MARIE**: Daddy, don't.

**JOSEPH**: You just called me daddy.

**MARIE**: I've always done.

**JOSEPH**: [*urgently*] I need to rest. I need to lie down. Let me rest. Then I'll leave. Or you can throw me out.

**MARIE**: If they come while you're . . .

**JOSEPH**: They won't. We have a few hours at least. Please. Let me rest.

**MARIE**: One hour.

**JOSEPH**: We have more than that. Two hours. Maybe three.

**MARIE**: I don't know.

**JOSEPH**: Two hours, then I'm gone.

[*Pause.*]

**MARIE**: All right. Unless Simon comes back.

**JOSEPH**: We'll cross that bridge when it gets here.

**MARIE**: Come on then.

[*SFX: Footsteps.*]

The spare room's a bit of a mess I'm afraid.

**JOSEPH**: If it's any bigger than 4 by 6, it'll be heaven.

## ACT 2

[*SFX: Door slams. Footsteps on wooden floor.*]

**SIMON**: Marie?

[*SFX: Two or three more doors open and shut, footsteps on floor.*]

**SIMON**: Marie?

[*SFX: Footsteps stop.*]

**SIMON**: Marie. He's here isn't he?

[*Pause.*]

Well, he can't stay.

**MARIE**: That's what I told him.

**SIMON**: Good. Good. You did the right thing. Well, that's a relief. Where did he go?

**MARIE**: But you know how he can be.

**SIMON**: No! How? How is he? [*sighs in exasperation*] You mean he's still here? Where? Where is he?

**MARIE**: How did you know by the way?

**SIMON**: Yesterday's paper. Oh God. Oh God.

[*Pause.*]

Where is he?

[*Pause.*]

How did he find this place?

[*Pause.*]

You didn't . . .

**MARIE**: Me?

**SIMON**: I'm asking. Did you?

**MARIE**: You mean you haven't made up your mind?

**SIMON**: It *would* be just like you.

**MARIE**: Why ask me then?

**SIMON**: Because I'd like to believe you're not as stupid as all that.

**MARIE**: Generous to a fault as usual.

**SIMON**: Well?

**MARIE**: I didn't.

**SIMON**: But you took him in.

**MARIE**: He had no money. He was tired. I didn't know what to do.

**SIMON**: It's all right. I understand. Touching, yes. And stupid.

[*Pause.*]

Where is he?

**MARIE**: Sleeping.

**SIMON**: Good. Good. Let him sleep. It'll give us time.

[*Pause.*]

Now how are we going to do this?

**MARIE**: Do what?

**SIMON**: You know we have to give him up? You know that.

**MARIE**: No.

**SIMON**: Please. Don't start that now.

**MARIE**: I can't help it. I don't have your infinite capacity for cruelty. And he's my father.

**SIMON**: What's he been telling you?

**MARIE**: Nothing.

**SIMON**: We talked about this. For years. We planned it all. We agreed. We agreed what we would do if he ever came back. And now you're changing your mind? You can't believe anything he says. You should know that. You of all people.

**MARIE**: You know what happened before he went to bed? I found him in the bathroom. On the floor. He'd been there for a while. He couldn't get up. And he couldn't get his trousers back on. Do you think he made that up too?

**SIMON**: I wouldn't put it past him.

**MARIE**: He's an old man. Old and sick. Who shits in his pants and wets himself, and God knows what else. Leave him alone.

**SIMON**: No.

**MARIE**: He's no danger to anyone.

**SIMON**: That's not the point. You know that. It's about him and what he's done. About the real cost in lives and suffering that he's made us pay. Do you ever think about them? How they died? You'll be surprised what fear will do to a human bladder.

I'm sorry but I don't care what he's going through right now. And I know what I have to do. You?

**MARIE**: I can't.

**SIMON**: All right. You don't have to do anything. I'll call them. I'll tell them he's here. Then we'll leave. You and I will leave. We'll leave him here. That's all. That's all you have to do. When we come back, he'll be gone. It will be over.

**MARIE**: It sounds simple enough.

**SIMON**: But you won't.

[*Pause.*]

Do you know what would happen if they found out he was here? That we were hiding him here? They would drag him out and us with him.

**MARIE**: This has nothing to do with him does it? You're just afraid.

**SIMON**: I *am* afraid. But the thing is, he's going to die. We can't save him. But there's no reason we should die with him. No reason *I* should anyway. You can do what you want. If you insist on dying, there's nothing I can do about it.

**MARIE**: We could send him somewhere.

**SIMON**: We don't have the time. How long do you think before they get here? Besides, it would be wrong. I don't want to be on the wrong side of this.

**MARIE**: I *am* on the wrong side. This isn't some moral game for me.

[*Pause.*]

You realise what you're asking me to do?

**SIMON**: I'm asking you to do something that someone else in your position might not do, but should.

**MARIE**: Why would I want to be right?

**SIMON**: I've made my choice. I *will* call them. What's yours going to be?

**MARIE**: You call that a choice?

**SIMON**: He's going to die. And so will you if you stay.

[*Pause.*]

Well?

**MARIE**: If I warn him . . .

**SIMON**: He wouldn't get a hundred yards. Everyone's looking for him.

**MARIE**: I'm starting to wonder how that happened.

**SIMON**: What's that?

**MARIE**: Oh, I'm sure you didn't mean to do it. I'm sure you just let it slip. Inadvertently.

[*Pause.*]

You couldn't even just let things take their course, you had to chart it too.

**SIMON**: They would have found him.

**MARIE**: I'm quite sick and tired of your sense of duty.

**SIMON**: This isn't going anywhere. You can't justify your position and you can't vitiate mine. You have to agree with me.

**MARIE**: You've already told me what I have to do. Please don't tell me what to think.

**SIMON**: Fine. I'm going to call them.

[*SFX: Phone being dialed.*]

Hello? Hello? Yes. It's Simon. Excuse me.

[*SFX: Footsteps receding.*]

**MARIE**: [*sotto voce*] What am I doing?

**JOSEPH**: Simon says you're doing the right thing.

**MARIE**: What did you hear?

**JOSEPH**: I didn't think you had it in you. I told you not to listen to Simon. He's even stupider than he looks.

**MARIE**: I don't know. I don't know what I'm doing.

**JOSEPH**: Of course you do.

**MARIE**: He won't listen to me.

**JOSEPH**: I know. I know.

**MARIE**: If I stay . . .

**JOSEPH**: They'll kill you. He's right about that. First time in his life probably.

**MARIE**: You could still try to leave.

**JOSEPH**: You heard what he said. I wouldn't get very far.

[*Pause.*]

Twice in one day. What do you know.

[*Pause.*]

I suppose that's it then.

**MARIE**: [*whispering*] He's coming back. You'd better go.

[*SFX: Footsteps.*]

**SIMON**: Well that's done. They're on their way.

**MARIE**: Who are they? Who did you call?

**SIMON**: Jack.

**MARIE**: Who's Jack?

**SIMON**: It doesn't matter. Anyway, he's closest. It'll be easier. That's all.

**MARIE**: Easier.

**SIMON**: We should leave soon.

[*Pause.*]

If you want to see him, you should do it now.

## ACT 3

[*SFX: Key turning lock and door being cautiously opened. Creaking slowly and then stopping, then creaking again. Then slow deliberate footsteps, two or three followed by the crashing of furniture, a chair toppled over followed by swearing.*]

**JOSEPH**: You can turn on the light if you like.

[*Pause.*]

Ah! That's better. Simon. My very own Simon. Nice of you to come. I wasn't sure you would. Not absolutely.

[*Pause.*]

They're late aren't they? Yes, well. That's the trouble with mobs. What you gain in exuberance you lose in organisation.

[*Pause.*]

It's been a while hasn't it? You're looking well.

[*Pause.*]

But not at all happy. Aren't you glad to see me? You could pretend to be. It's the polite thing to do.

**SIMON**: Go on then. I haven't much time. And neither do you.

**JOSEPH**: Straight to the point. Good. Good. I have the same dislike for preliminaries. Fine. Well, it looks like you're finally going to be rid of me.

**SIMON**: It certainly looks that way.

**JOSEPH**: The last shreds of evidence, gone.

**SIMON**: Except the papers.

**JOSEPH**: The papers are safe. You can have them all when we're done. Lock, stock, and barrel.

**SIMON**: Just like that?

**JOSEPH**: Just like that.

**SIMON**: I don't believe you.

**JOSEPH**: But I need a favour first.

**SIMON**: That's more like it. Look, I can't let you go.

**JOSEPH**: Not that.

**SIMON**: What then?

**JOSEPH**: I need a lie. Well told, by you to Janet, aka Marie, née Janet.

**SIMON**: Well?

**JOSEPH**: She was never able to hate me as much as you do. She doesn't need to know the details of what happened here today.

**SIMON**: Paint her a pretty picture.

**JOSEPH**: Exactly. Tell her I got away. Tell her they came and found the bird flown. Tell her I disappeared without a trace. Tell her anything. Just make it good.

**SIMON**: That's it?

**JOSEPH**: Easy enough isn't it? And I know you're a good liar.

**SIMON**: And the papers?

**JOSEPH**: Oh, I got rid of those years ago. You don't have to worry about them.

**SIMON**: But I will worry. No. I want to see them. I'll get rid of them myself.

**JOSEPH**: I told you. I already did.

**SIMON**: Of course not.

**JOSEPH**: Of course not. But it's the truth. You'll have to believe me, as I have to trust you. Unpleasant yes. But what can we do?

**SIMON**: Why would you destroy them? It was the only thing tying me to you. Your safety net.

**JOSEPH**: My safety net was always full of holes. She loves you. I could never understand why, but there it is. Strange things happen.

[*Pause.*]

Well, that's it I suppose. You'd better be going.

**SIMON**: I wasn't joking you know. I did tell them you were here.

**JOSEPH**: I know.

[*Pause.*]

**SIMON**: All right. Look. I can call them and tell them you got away. They'll believe me. Buy some time. Then we can try to get you out of here.

**JOSEPH**: Don't bother. I'm quite resigned to my fate. I've been rather a bad man haven't I?

**SIMON**: Impressive. But I'm telling you there's no need for it.

**JOSEPH**: How about you Simon? Did you ever feel bad about what we've done?

**SIMON**: Me? What did I do?

**JOSEPH**: [*laughs*] Come, come.

**SIMON**: Can't you carry your own cross? I don't want any of it.

**JOSEPH**: That's exactly what I'm doing. It's you that refuses to.

**SIMON**: Everything I did, I did on your instructions.

**JOSEPH**: You could have said no. Just say no to corruption. The soul abhors its destruction. You could have said no.

**SIMON**: No one crosses Joseph. Everyone knew that.

**JOSEPH**: You were afraid to do the right thing.

**SIMON**: Until now.

**JOSEPH**: Is that what you think you're doing?

**SIMON**: I should have done it years ago.

**JOSEPH**: You should. And now it's too late. I'm too old and too sick to be dangerous now. But you. You were every bit as bad as I was. Now I think you're worse.

**SIMON**: I'm not the one they're coming for.

**JOSEPH**: Not now. But in a few years. . . . I would bet anything on it.

**SIMON**: Last chance. Will you come with me?

**JOSEPH**: Do you know what the worst thing is? I'm not even sorry. That's why I'm going to stay. And when they kill me, they won't get anything out of it. I'm not afraid. I'm in terrible pain already. And I'm still not sorry about any of it. Some justice.

[*SFX: Loud banging on door.*]

**SIMON**: They're here.

**JOSEPH**: Let them in.

**SIMON**: I could tell them . . .

[*SFX: Banging on door.*]

**JOSEPH**: Let them in.

[*SFX: Footsteps receding. Sound of door opening.*]

**SIMON**: Gentlemen. Thank you for coming. He's in the back room.

**Notes**

1. Nigerian civil war from 1967 to 1970.
2. BBC News, U.K. Edition, October 23, 2003.

[ *Pause.* ]

# VUKANI! (WAKE UP!)

*Sindiwe Magona*

There was this stupidity . . . people refusing to take responsibility for their actions; of being so bewildered and angry that they would go and want to believe—not even a myth—but something almost demonic, that, if I sleep with a virgin, I will be cured of this. There is no cure for AIDS. And this is what the play, among other issues, tries to address, that we must educate ourselves. We must accept what is happening and then deal with it in an honest and holistic manner. There should be no blame, there should be no finger pointing, people should not be stigmatized . . . behavior modification is the only way.

**Sindiwe Magona, South Africa**

Sindiwe Magona is one of South Africa's most exciting and prolific female writers. Born in 1943 in Gungululu, a village in the then Cape Province of the Union of South Africa, she is an award-winning novelist, poet, storyteller, children's book writer, inspirational speaker, and playwright. Her works have been published in South Africa, Great Britain, the Netherlands, Japan, and Sweden. She has written two autobiographical books: *To My Children's Children* (1990) and *Forced to Grow* (1995). The first volume is both a poignant evocation of the hardships of life under apartheid and a celebration of a young girl's endurance and eventual triumph; the second chronicles her struggles as a young teacher, activist, and single mother during the turbulent 1970s student revolt.

Sindiwe, who received a master's degree in social work from Columbia University, has worked tirelessly for various social causes. In August 1976 she was one of two South African delegates to the International Tribunal on Crimes against Women, held in Belgium. A few months later, she and five other women founded the Women's (Peace) Movement. From 1984 to 2004, she worked for the United Nations before returning to South Africa to write full time. She holds an honorary doctorate in letters from Hartwick College, Oneonta, New York. In 1999, she was awarded the New York Foundation for the Arts Award for nonfiction, and, in 2000, the BRIO (Bronx Recognizes Its Own) for fiction.

Sindiwe has published two collections of short stories, *Living, Loving, and Lying Awake at Night* (1991) and *Push-Push and Other Stories (1996)*, and a novel, *Mother to Mother* (1998), which details the 1994 murder of U.S. Fulbright Scholar Amy Biehl, who was fatally stabbed in a township in South Africa. Other publications include her AIDS anthology, *It's Up to Me!* (2004), and a children's book, *The Best Meal, Ever!* (2006). Sindiwe is also founder of the Guguletu Writers' Group, an amateur writers' workshop. She edited the group's first collection of short stories in the publication of *Guguletu Blues: Stories of Women of Township* (2007) in both Xhosa and Italian.

#### Excerpts from Our Interviews

*On why she became a writer:*

I was always good with words—if there was going to be one essay read at school, it would be mine. I used to win prizes a lot. At seventeen, my ambition was to . . . write a book. I didn't know anyone who wrote books, and the only books that we ever encountered were the ones at school. We never bought books except schoolbooks. So we didn't live with books, although I did more reading than the average child my age. Reading is not really part of our culture—storytelling is. Unfortunately, storytelling is dying out because of the breakup of the family.

*On why she left South Africa:*

When my husband left, I decided to make some changes. As a single mother, I knew I needed to do more. From 1976 through the early 1980s, I saw my kids' education going down the drain. . . . Now you find politicians, both black and white, talking about the "lost generation." I knew at that time that this was going to be a lost generation. I just saw young people who would never be able to recover. I had done a lot of work for various organizations working for change, but now I'd got fed up. At that time, I was at a white school teaching Xhosa, and it was difficult for me to educate these kids while my three were rotting at home. The situation was too much to deal with. When I left in 1984, there was no effective education for African children in South Africa. I had three kids and I believed in education!

*On the impact of AIDS in South Africa:*

Every family is losing children—not a child, but children. When I saw what was happening, it took me months before I could talk about it. [In New York] people would see me and ask, how was home? You just came back from vacation. Did you go home? Yes? How was it? And I'd burst into tears—to think, just to envision that the whole complexion, the demography of the country could change if this goes unchecked much longer. Black people in South Africa are a huge majority in the country. We talk about black majority rule. I don't know how long that will go on if we continue dying at the rate at which we are dying. And this is reality.

*On why she returned to South Africa:*

I had always intended to return, but, you know, life in the U.S. can be very seductive. Since I started writing there, I was scared that I would come back here and be ensnared in the same kind of situation where you start lacking in confidence and other things take the place of writing. . . . But I've sorted out things and realize that I could be of more use in South Africa than in the U.S. . . . And then there is the issue of my writing, which is rooted in South Africa. . . . There is only so much you can write from memory. I need to write about the current issues and I need to be back here. . . . There are other things I need to do. We're not going to get social transformation in Africa if we don't work at it. And that's another reason why I returned.

***On the writing program she has organized in South Africa:***

These are people who never thought they could write! I just made an announcement that I'm going to start a writer's group, and people came. The people who come are younger than I am—people in their thirties, forties, and a couple of high school students. We meet at a church in Guguletu. . . . This is something that I feel I need to do. I need to give birth to myself. I'm a writer. I really need, by the time I die, to have people say, "I write because Sindiwe wrote." I think this is the only true legacy we can leave: To inspire others to do the things that we hold sacred. Otherwise, what is there to show that you lived, if you leave no children who look like you, and by that I mean people who aspire to the same things that you hold dear in life?

*Author's Notes on the Play: Vukani!* deals with the issue of AIDS in the context of the other serious issues facing postapartheid South Africa. The play details the complex interaction between democracy and cultural values, mores, and rituals. This horrifying clash between culture, politics, and disease makes the AIDS crisis so difficult to address in a meaningful way.

*Production History:* First produced on September 26, 2003, at the Theatre of the Riverside Church in New York City, directed by Shirley Parkinson and starring Arthur French, Pawnee Sills, Joell Jackson, Sandra Mills Scott, Jonathan Anderson, Lincoln Brown, and Chantal Jean-Pierre. The play was also performed at New York's St. Bartholomew's Church in December 2003.

Interviews conducted on June 27, 1997, in New York City and in July 2005 in Cape Town, South Africa.

# VUKANI! (WAKE UP!)

*Sindiwe Magona*

### Characters

Nomandla Lonzi: Mid-40s. Domestic worker, with a half-day to be with her children, Zama and Jongi. She is Mfundo's wife.
Mfundo Lonzi: Late 40s. Educated, grade-school principal. Serious.
Jongilizwe Lonzi (Jongi): 17–year-old boy in high school. He is a loyal family member but a bit hotheaded and easily stung by injustice.
Zama Lonzi: 14 years old. Spirited, gifted, has talent for public speaking.
Themba Koyana (Koyana): 50s. He is a cleaner in the township's administration office. He is Mfundo's neighbor.
Nokwazi Koyana: Nomandla's friend and neighbor. Late 40s. Domestic worker. She is something of a gossip. Koyana's wife.
Vuyo Malunga (Vuyo): 17–year-old boy. Lives in the neighborhood. Known as a playboy. Son of Fina.
Fina Malunga: Late 30s. Vuyo's mother, also a domestic worker, but full-time. She is a devout Christian. Vuyo is the younger of her two sons.

### Setting

*Vukani!* takes place in NY200, a street in Guguletu, a few years after the end of apartheid. In the first act, we see the home of the Lonzi family, their side yard, the fence dividing their property from the Koyanas'. We see the kitchen, the living room and doors leading off to three bedrooms. The house is fairly well worn but well kept, a typical middle-class home in a township. Act 2, scene 3 is set on a different part of NY200, and the last part of act 2 takes place in the Community Center, a large drab building used for community events of all sorts.

### Prologue

**KOYANA**: Go to the nearest electronic-goods store and buy cameras by the score! Hurry! Go! Then go home; gather your families and take photographs.

Take photographs of them all! [*Pauses.*] Especially the children. Especially the young. Hurry! Hurry! Before it is too late—. Please, take photographs of them all. Take photographs of the children playing, crying, reading their books or doing their chores. Take photos of them laughing and dancing in the rain. Take photos of them fast asleep in their cozy beds. Take photos of them in their school uniforms, in their Sunday best or ragged day dress—But, please—Take photographs of the children and put them on the walls. Take photos of them and tell the children why. Before it is too late, before our tomorrow is no more. Before the promise that is their life—is snuffed, easy as candlelight. Please, hurry! Take photographs of the children who will not see thirty, the children who will never grow old.

[*Shouting.*]

Vukani! Vukani, Mawethu/My people! Wake up! Wake up!

[*Blackout.*]

## ACT 1

### *Scene 1*

**MFUNDO**: Mother of Zama, where are your children? The sun's long gone down. Even the streetlights are on.

**NOMANDLA**: Why are they mine today? Because they are out late? Strange how—when they do good they're yours and mine as soon as they mess up!

[*Laughs.*]

**MFUNDO**: [*Hands up*] Okay! Okay! *Our* children . . . where are they so late?

**NOMANDLA**: Youth Club.

**MFUNDO**: [*Looks at watch*] At this time?

[*Sound of Jongi and Zama laughing and talking.*]

**NOMANDLA**: A nurse to talk to them about . . .

[*Enter Jongi and Zama.*]

**MFUNDO**: Ah! Here are the prodigals home at last!

**NOMANDLA**: [*Whispers*] Condoms.

**MFUNDO**: [*It doesn't register*] And how was your meeting so late? [*It registers; to Nomandla*] Whaat? What? Did you say?

**NOMANDLA**: [*Trying to remain calm*] Condoms. The nurse was talking to them about protection . . . safer sex—You know—ABC . . . [*To Jongi and Zama. Trying to speak calmly.*] Isn't that right? Tell your father what did you learn from the nurse? [*Jongi and Zama jostle each other, mortified. Neither wants to speak. Zama tries to push Jongi in front of her.*]

**ZAMA**: You say!

**JONGI**: No, you go on. Tell her. She's the one who has to take you there!

**NOMANDLA**: Take her where?

**ZAMA**: [*Mumbles*] To the clinic.

**NOMANDLA**: What? Speak up! You are loud enough when you make your speeches for the youth club. Come on, out with it!

**ZAMA**: [*Takes a deep breath and blurts it out*] To the clinic. Jongi must wear condoms and I must go to the clinic. [*She covers her face with her hands.*]

**NOMANDLA**: To the clinic?

**JONGI**: To get an injection so that when she is raped, she doesn't get pregnant.

**MFUNDO**: [*Astounded*] When she is what? What did you say? Condoms! Injections! What has this world come to—for crying out loud! You're just babies [*Looks from one to the other. They hang their heads, not knowing how to respond, thoroughly embarrassed.*] I can't believe what I just heard from my own children. [*Pauses. Shakes his head.*] Let me remind you, I work hard for you, for this family. Being a school principal is a difficult and trying occupation. I support you and I expect you to respect me and not bring shame on our name. The only ABC I want you to know and concern yourself with is your alphabet . . . Do you hear me?

**JONGI**: [*Mumbles*] Sometimes these things may not be up to one.

**MFUNDO**: Abstain? Be loyal? Condomize? Oh, no!! You are not chaff, blown about by whatever winds happen to prevail on any given day. We are different from the riff raff all around us. We are different! Is that clear?

**JONGI**: If you only knew. This difference could bring more bad than good.

**MFUNDO**: Don't be absurd! You better watch yourself, Jongi! Now go! Get ready—dinner's spoiling.

**JONGI**: [*Aside, starting to leave with Zama*] And you've just spoiled *my* appetite, old man.

**MFUNDO**: What did you say?

**JONGI**: Nothing, Tata. Nothing!

**MFUNDO**: [*As he begins to speak, Zama and Jongi turn to listen*] Hey, hey, hey! Listen here! . . . No child of mine is using condoms when he's not married—when he's just a boy who can hardly wipe his backside. And no daughter of mine is going to get herself injected! [*To Nomandla, shaking his head. She wrings her hands, doesn't know how to respond.*] What is the world coming to that a grown woman, a wife and mother can talk such dirty things to our children?

Nurse, she calls herself! And every Thursday she wears the purple blouse of the Manyano, the Mother's Union—goes to church every Sunday—and this is what she tells our children?! ABC—indeed!

[*Dim lights.*]

*Scene 2*

[*Lights come up on Zama and Jongi alone in the kitchen.*]

**ZAMA**: You mustn't make Father angry.

**JONGI**: He needs to hear some truths. You know he lives in his own little world, his own country. Some of us have to walk the streets that everybody walks every day. He wants us to be so different; it's dangerous to be different. That's what I keep telling you.

**ZAMA**: Telling me what?

**JONGI**: You know that *way-way* I told you. Take care of business.

**ZAMA**: Mama would kill me. Both of them would kill me. You know . . .

**JONGI**: Yes I know . . .

**BOTH**: Save yourself for marriage.

**JONGI**: If you really must save yourself for marriage, fine with me, but people mustn't know. These days, it's dangerous to be a virgin; you know that. Old men, grown men, rape small children—all because they are virgins. Because the fools believe that if they have AIDS, sleeping with a virgin will cure them of the disease!

**ZAMA**: Oh, how stupid! We don't have such imbeciles in our township. It's the people in other townships and squatter camps who do those things.

**JONGI**: You are wrong little sister. Listen to me. I know boys my age in this very township who are sick! Who have gawulayo—the merciless, ruthless chopper!

**ZAMA**: But surely they don't believe that this raping virgins will cure them. They can't be that stupid. No one is that stupid.

**JONGI**: I know that. You know that, but who knows what a desperate man will force himself to believe to get back his hope? We can't take any chances. Oh sister, it would be so easy. I just have to drop a few words.

**ZAMA**: But you're not going to talk about me.

**JONGI**: Just a few words . . . just to give the impression.

**ZAMA**: But what if people believe it?

**JONGI**: I want them to believe it.

**ZAMA**: Oh no! Oh no!

**JONGI**: What's worse? A bad reputation or death? Let me help you in this! I want to protect you and this is the only sure way to do it.

**ZAMA**: All right, since you insist. But you have to talk to father . . . wait, no! Talk to mother and she will to talk to father. I don't want you killed trying to help me!

**JONGI**: I won't. And you'll be safe. All I want is that you be safe.

**ZAMA**: [*Laughs as the thought occurs to her*] Well, I guess I will have a little surprise for my husband when I get married. He won't know he's getting a good girl! That is, if mother and father agree to your crazy plan.

[*Exit.*]

[*Blackout.*]

*Scene 3*

[*Nokwazi stands in her yard watching intently offstage. After a moment Zama enters from that direction on her way home.*]

**ZAMA**: Oh Molo Mama. How are you?

**NOKWAZI**: Molo Zama. Was that Vuyo I saw you with?

**ZAMA**: Yes, Mama.

**NOKWAZI**: So now boys are walking you home from school?

**ZAMA**: Oh, no! I just saw him now. I just said hello.

**NOKWAZI**: Well you better watch out.

**ZAMA**: Don't worry, Mama. I'm not interested in boys.

**NOKWAZI**: Or men?

**ZAMA**: No, Mama, no. Not men either!

**NOKWAZI**: Well then, goodbye. Tell your mother I was looking for her.

**ZAMA**: Yes, Mama.

[*Exit Nokwazi. Zama enters the house and puts her books on the kitchen table. She is looking for a snack when Jongi enters, returning from school.*]

**ZAMA**: [*Cont.*] Hey, brother. Did you eat the last of the bread?

**JONGI**: No! And good afternoon to you, too! Why am I always accused of things when I enter this house? Six billion people in the world and I end up with this family! What did I do to God even before I was born for him to punish me like this? I am an absolute magnet for accusations!

**ZAMA**: Well, if the shoe fits!

**JONGI**: Ha. Well, sister, I've decided to talk with Mama tonight!

**ZAMA**: About what?

**JONGI**: You know, that *way-way* we talked about this morning.

**ZAMA**: Oh, no, I've changed my mind. Let's let sleeping parents lie.

**JONGI**: No! You said yes and I'm holding you to it. I'll talk to her as soon as she gets home.

**ZAMA**: Oh no! I'll die of embarrassment!

**JONGI**: Believe me, there are worse ways to die!

[*They don't see Nomandla enter.*]

**ZAMA**: Oh please don't talk to Mama!

**NOMANDLA**: Talk to me about what?

**ZAMA**: Oh no! [*She covers her face in her hands and runs into her room.*]

**NOMANDLA**: What? What? What's going on here?

**JONGI**: Oh, nothing Mama. I was just talking to Zama.

**NOMANDLA**: About?

**JONGI**: Something that happened at school.

**NOMANDLA**: What? What's this something that doesn't have a name?

**JONGI**: Ma'h! . . . It's nothing! I've just been telling Zama to let us do something for her.

**NOMANDLA**: I don't remember the last time I heard you *ask* for something to do!

**JONGI**: Mama, Zama is in danger . . . because of her reputation.

**NOMANDLA**: [*Misunderstanding*] After all I've said to her? All that her father has said? I can't believe it! What has she done?

**JONGI**: Nothing! Nothing. Calm down, Mama. Zama is a good girl. Everybody knows it. That's the trouble.

**NOMANDLA**: That's the trouble? What are you saying?

**JONGI**: I'm saying, let me say a few things to give the impression Zama is . . . experienced. Haven't you heard? Grown men are going around raping young girls thinking they can be cured of AIDS. We have to protect her.

**NOMANDLA**: What're you saying? Are you out of your mind?

**JONGI**: We'll know she is pure!

**NOMANDLA**: Oh, no! We can't soil her good name when I've raised her to be such a good girl. Why would I do that now?

**JONGI**: To be practical Mama!

**NOMANDLA**: *Practical?* What do you mean practical? Telling the world my daughter is a whore, what's practical about that?

**JONGI**: Mama, please, listen to me. Girls who are known to be virgins are being raped left, right, and center!

**NOMANDLA**: But Zama is safe. She's not one of these girls who go about, roaming the township all times of the day and night. Zama goes to school . . . comes straight home . . . I always know where she is . . .

**JONGI**: Mama, you think people get raped or killed because they were in a particularly stupid place? Remember, two days ago? The makhulu who was killed by her next-door neighbor's son here at this very NY200 of ours? Where was she killed? In her own house, on her bed. Mama, wake up! Danger comes to you wherever you are; there's no hiding from danger in this township . . . not anymore.

**NOMANDLA**: I can't believe this. I can't believe we're *standing here,* discussing spreading rumors about Zama's being immoral.

**JONGI**: Old men are raping four-year-old girls . . . *Two months old babies . . .* Haven't you heard? I'm only trying to save my sister . . .

**NOMANDLA**: Dear God, what has this country come to? How am I going to tell your father such a thing? How am I going to tell him this? Your father will never agree to something like this. He will think we're all mad.

**JONGI**: Then we must make him see reason, mustn't we?

**NOMANDLA**: He'll kill us.

**JONGI**: Does he want to lose his daughter? Does he want her to die?

**NOMANDLA**: Of course, not!

**JONGI**: Then we have to do this . . . *Must do this . . . Must*!

[*Cast sings Babephi N'abantu.*]

[*Blackout.*]

*Scene 4*

[*The following morning.*]

[*Lights come up on fence between the two houses. Nomandla is returning home from work with a bundle in her hands. Nokwazi is standing outside, waiting for her.*]

**NOKWAZI**: Mother of Jongi, I see you!

**NOMANDLA**: I see you, too, Nokwazi. How are you?

**NOKWAZI**: Fine, thank you. The cows' horns are already appearing on the horizon for your family.

**NOMANDLA**: What nonsense is that? Zama is the only daughter we have and she's still a child.

**NOKWAZI**: That's not what young men seem to think.

**NOMANDLA**: What do you mean? Zama does not fool around with boys; she's a good girl.

**NOKWAZI**: Hmm. By the way, did she tell you I was looking for you, yesterday?

**NOMANDLA**: No. Did you speak to her?

**NOKWAZI**: Well, my dear, I had to stand in line. This boy of Fina's, what do they call him, now . . . let me see . . . what's this boy's name . . . ?

**NOMANDLA**: Monde?

**NOKWAZI**: No, the younger boy.

**NOMANDLA**: Vuyo?

**NOKWAZI**: That's the one. The one they call Ladies' Man. Well, I think he has his eyes on your girl. You and Fina might end up abakhozi, mothers of a union, together!

**NOMANDLA**: Oh, leave me alone. Zama is a child, as I've just told you. It's years before she'll be thinking of marriage . . . never mind having children.

**NOKWAZI**: Oh, how like a mother! But, neighbor of mine, let me tell you something. As you know, I'm not one to meddle in the affairs of others, especially children . . .

**NOMANDLA**: [*Sarcastic*] I know.

**NOKWAZI**: But I'm bringing up what I saw only because I have heard that that boy, Vuyo, may be tainted . . . That he has this thing that's killing young people faster than the black plague. What do they call it now, heh, GAWULAYO, the chopper?

**NOMANDLA**: What are you talking about, Nokwazi? What are you telling me?

**NOKWAZI**: [*Nodding head up and down several times*] Yes, Yes, that's what's being said: Vuyo has this disease. So, I'd watch my daughter if I were you.

**NOMANDLA**: That's not true. I saw him only today. He looks just fine to me.

**NOKWAZI**: And do you think you're going to see a mark on his forehead? But I tell you—everyone says he's got it!

**NOMANDLA**: Oh, my God! Jongi was right.

**NOKWAZI**: What? What did you say?

**NOMANDLA**: Oh, nothing. Just thinking of a conversation we had, my son and I.

**NOKWAZI**: Okay, neighbor, I must leave you now, I see Koyana coming.

**NOMANDLA**: Goodnight neighbor of mine, goodnight! [*To herself*] I must talk to Jongi's father—*right now!*

[*They exit.*]

## *Scene 5*

. . . Evening . . .

[*Lights come up on Mfundo and Nomandla in the kitchen. Mfundo's papers are spread out on the table where he has been working. Now he is standing, making a show of cleaning his ears with a match.*]

**MFUNDO**: Now then, Mother of Jongilizwe, I've cleaned my ears, taken all the wax out so I can hear you *very, very clearly.* I've just cleaned out my ears because I am *most sure* I heard you wrong just now.

**NOMANDLA**: No, Father of Jongi, you heard me right.

**MFUNDO**: [*Continues as though she hasn't spoken*] I'm sure you cannot have said the words I thought I heard. [*Picks up tea cup from table and examines it*] Say, what did you put in this tea I've just had?

**NOMANDLA**: [*Sighs*] Nothing. Father of Jongi, please listen. Hear me out.

**MFUNDO**: [*Loud*] Listen to you? Listen to you? I listened. [*Sneers*] I listened to you speak and I must be *mad;* I know I'm not drunk. I must be out of my mind if—

**NOMANDLA**: If only you'd listen until I've explained everything. Jongi has made me see what we must do for Zama.

**MFUNDO**: And you listened to this?

**NOMANDLA**: Yes, Father of Jongi, I listened becau . . .

**MFUNDO**: [*Cutting her off*] Now you want me to listen to such an outlandish, stupid, sick, abominable proposition?

**NOMANDLA**: But Father of Jongi why . . .

**MFUNDO**: [*Cutting her off again*] Nomandla, Nomandla! Are you out of your mind? Have your brains left you where you stand? What is this? God! What is the matter with my family—with my wife? Listen to yourself, Nomandla! Just listen to yourself!

**NOMANDLA**: Do you love your daughter?

**MFUNDO**: What question is that? Of course I love Zama.

**NOMANDLA**: Then you will listen to me.

**MFUNDO**: Why should I listen to you when you come to me with madness from your mad, stupid son.

**NOMANDLA**: Our son.

**MFUNDO**: You know how this boy has been challenging me lately! Challenging my authority at every turn!

**NOMANDLA**: This is not about you. It is not about Jongi. It is about our daughter.

**MFUNDO**: Zama whose name you want to ruin, drag through the mud? And with it ours? She's only fourteen for crying out loud. She's supposed to be in the know at fourteen?

**NOMANDLA**: Of course not! She must save herself for her husband! But we must be the only ones who know that. We have to allow Jongi to let it be known she is not a virgin.

**MFUNDO**: Because of these rape rumors? Because of this disease thing? This gawulayo? But men who rape children are few and far between.

**NOMANDLA**: Few and far between? Didn't you say you've had a case like that in your own school? Last week, you told me about that little girl.

**MFUNDO**: Yes, but her mother's always drunk.

**NOMANDLA**: And the man who raped her? Was he also drunk?

**MFUNDO**: No, but . . .

**NOMANDLA**: You see! Sane, sober, grown men. Husbands of wives, fathers of children, sometimes grandfathers, molesting little girls. This is what is happening, this is what I'm talking about, Father of Jongi. So-called respectable men!

**MFUNDO**: But Zama stays home. She doesn't go out at night.

**NOMANDLA**: Let me remind you that Zama was created in broad daylight, Teacher. Sex doesn't happen only at night! And I hear boys are now getting interested in her.

**MFUNDO**: Boys! What boys? What on earth are you talking about?

**NOMANDLA**: Someone saw her with Fina's son. The lady's man.

**MFUNDO**: But this is insane! You're all insane!

**NOMANDLA**: Who is insane? Your son and your wife who want to do a simple thing to protect your daughter or the wicked men who would defile her?

**MFUNDO**: I'd kill a man who would . . .

**NOMANDLA**: That would not save Zama. That would be after the fact, I'm afraid.

**MFUNDO**: I'd kill him! On my mother's grave, I swear!

**NOMANDLA**: Fat help that would be to Zama. Don't you see? The damage would already be done.

**MFUNDO**: You have a better suggestion?

**NOMANDLA**: As I said from the very beginning, let's put out word that Zama is some boy's girlfriend.

**MFUNDO**: What kind of father am I who allows his daughter's name to be tarnished?

**NOMANDLA**: Her name? Her name? What about her body? Oh we'll be so proud standing before her coffin at her *funeral* proclaiming she died with no blemish to her character!

**MFUNDO**: But such humiliation! Dragging our name through the mud.

**NOMANDLA**: At least *we'll* be doing the dragging.

**MFUNDO**: And giving our enemies cause to gloat at our plight!

**NOMANDLA**: Giving Zama a chance to live a good, long life.

**MFUNDO**: I never heard such an outrageous idea.

**NOMANDLA**: The times we live in call for outrageous solutions.

**MFUNDO**: Oh God! God help us! What times we live in!

[*Collapses against Nomandla, conceding at last.*]

[*Nomandla holds him as lights fade down.*]

*Scene 6*

[*Inside the house. Nomandla and Zama are cleaning up before bed; Mfundo and Jongi are working, Mfundo with his papers at the kitchen table, Jongi reading in a chair in the living room.*]

**MFUNDO**: Zama, are you ready? Have you prepared your speech?

**ZAMA**: Yes, Tata. I've written it down and said it over and over.

**NOMANDLA**: Want us to hear it? We'll listen.

**MFUNDO**: We can tell you if it is any good!

[*Laughs.*]

**ZAMA**: I hope it is. Jongi says it is good.

**JONGI**: [*Looks up from his book*] I said it is *very* good.

**MFUNDO**: Well, come let's hear it!

**NOMANDLA**: If you don't mind.

**MFUNDO**: Why should she mind? We're only helping.

**NOMANDLA**: That's up to Zama, Father of Jongi! It's her speech, not ours!

**ZAMA**: I don't mind. I'd rather hear it from you if it needs improving.

[*Zama runs to her room and back with the speech.*]

**MFUNDO**: Now, I want you to remember to look up when you speak. Take your time. Look at the words, then look at the people as you say them.

**NOMANDLA**: You'll make her nervous!

**MFUNDO**: It's good advice!

**ZAMA**: Thank you, Tata. I will try.

[*Zama stands so that her parents can see her, facing the audience.*]

To the mothers here present: I greet you. To the fathers here with us: I greet you. To my sisters and brothers: I am with you. I stand here in the name of the young people of Elukhanyisweni Community Center, who have asked me to say what is in all our hearts on this sad day. Sad because we have lost a mother who worked so hard for us; sad because we lost her in the manner she was taken from us.

[*She pauses. To her parents*]

Then here is where I talk about all the things she did for us. How she believed in us and taught us to respect our hopes. So . . .

**MFUNDO**: So . . . Go on! Why did you stop?

**ZAMA**: How is it so far, Mama?

**NOMANDLA**: That's nice. Now do what your father says. Go on!

**ZAMA**: Okay, Mama. [*She pauses*] We, the youth of Elukh, have lost a great champion. We were lucky to have her. We will honor her memory by never forgetting her lessons, her example, by never forgetting who we are, by working hard to become who we are meant to be!

[*Pause.*]

To Mama Skonana's family: we thank you for sharing her with us. We express our deepest sadness on your loss. We hope you will take comfort in the riches of love and kindness she has built for herself in heaven by the love and caring she gave while on earth. Thank you.

**NOMANDLA**: Oh, Zama! That's great!

**MFUNDO**: [*Proudly*] Very good, Zama! Very good. I didn't know we had an orator in our midst.

**NOMANDLA**: Zama's always been good with words.

[*The lights fade as everyone exits to their rooms.*]

*Scene 7*

[*Enter Vuyo looking for Zama. He doesn't see her so he leans against a fence and waits. A moment later, Zama enters with her books, returning from school.*]

**VUYO**: Ja, Zama.

**ZAMA**: Hello.

**VUYO**: Hello, who?

**ZAMA**: Vuyo, please leave me alone.

**VUYO**: What did I do? I greet you and what do I get? Cheek! Who do you think you're talking to?

**ZAMA**: When have I been rude to you?

**VUYO**: Just now!

[*Imitating her voice.*]

Hello.

[*In his own voice.*]

No "Hello Bhuti?" No "Hello Vuyo?" . . . Why didn't you say "Hello dog?"

**ZAMA**: Vuyo, hello. Why aren't you at rugby practice with the other boys?

**VUYO**: Children play; a man's got important things on his mind.

**ZAMA**: So have I . . . [*Starts walking*] My chores are waiting for me.

**VUYO**: Hey! Listen here! I said come over, didn't you hear me? Woza la!

**ZAMA**: If there's something you want to say, then come to me and say it?

**VUYO**: Come here, you! Woza la! What's wrong with you?

**ZAMA**: Nothing! You're the one who wants to tell me whatever it is you want to say. You come to me.

**VUYO**: Come!

**ZAMA**: No!

**VUYO**: Stubborn girl! Awuva! [*He reluctantly crosses to her.*]

**ZAMA**: What is it? What d'you want?

**VUYO**: Eh—eh, Mmm—umm—eh . . . how was school today?

**ZAMA**: Why? You stopped me on my way to ask me about school? Who appointed you Schools' Inspector?

**VUYO**: You and your wisecracks!

**ZAMA**: Well, if you don't tell me why you stopped me—and it had better be good . . .

**VUYO**: Can I see you tonight?

**ZAMA**: Get away from me! What do you think I am?

**VUYO**: A beautiful girl. A princess. A vision who comes to me in my dreams in my sweet, sweet dreams.

**ZAMA**: Boy! They don't call you Sweet Mouth for nothing! You should be Mandela's Praise Singer. But me—leave me alone. There are lots of beautiful girls who have nothing better to do but listen to silly talk from silly boys! And besides, what's happened to your girlfriends? . . .

**VUYO**: Forget other girls. I'm talking to you. I need you. I love you!

**ZAMA**: Go away!

**VUYO**: I told you I'd get you someday, and I will.

**ZAMA**: Vuyo—No! I said no! Look at me carefully. I mean what I say. I said it yesterday, I say it today, and I'll say it tomorrow. I will never have anything to do with the likes of you!

**VUYO**: You think you're better than the other girls?

**ZAMA**: If they do what you want them to do, I *am better*.

**VUYO**: We'll see.

[*Zama walks toward the house and Vuyo falls into step with her. Zama stops.*]

**ZAMA**: Please leave me alone. Go to your girls, Vuyo; leave me alone!

**VUYO**: Jealous?

**ZAMA**: Don't make me laugh. You can only be jealous of a thing you want.

**VUYO**: I want you.

**ZAMA**: And I don't want you!

**VUYO**: Please!

**ZAMA**: I said leave me alone. I'll tell my father if you don't go away.

[*She walks away from Vuyo to the door.*]

**VUYO**: [*Calling after Zama*] You want me, too! You do. I know you do!

[*He watches as Zama goes through the door. A moment later he quietly walks to the door and tries it. It is unlocked. He enters. Meanwhile, Zama puts down her book and picks up a cracker for a snack and unbuttons her blouse as she goes into her room and half closes the door. She hears the door close behind Vuyo and calls out from her room.*]

**ZAMA**: Who's there? Jongi? Is that you?

[*Silence.*]

Stop playing the fool, Jongi! You're not scaring me! Do you think I'm a baby?

[*She pokes her head out the bedroom door and sees Vuyo.*]

You? What do you want, here? Get out!

**VUYO**: You are my baby! Come here!

**ZAMA**: No! Get out!

**VUYO**: Baby I want you. I told you . . . I need you!

[*Crosses to the bedroom door and pulls the knob out of her hand, revealing the unbuttoned blouse.*]

**ZAMA**: [*Pulls blouse together with one hand while she tries to pull the door closed with the other*] Get out of here! Get out! Can't you see I'm changing?

**VUYO**: That's why I'm here. Let me help you!

[*He pulls on her blouse.*]

**ZAMA**: Take your dirty hands off me!

[*He drops his hands.*]

Come on, Vuyo. Wait in the kitchen and I'll come out and we can talk.

**VUYO**: [*Grabbing Zama by the blouse and pulling her to him*] No!

**ZAMA**: Please!

[*He starts pulling her toward the couch, his free hand all over her.*]

**ZAMA**: [*Cont.*] No! No! No!

**VUYO**: You say that but you mean, Yes, Yes, Yes! You're going to like this. Come on relax!

**ZAMA**: Stop! Stop this!

[*Trying to get away from him.*]

No! Vuyo, No! I'll scream.

**VUYO**: [*Trying to pull her to the couch but not having much luck*] You stop fighting me. I don't want to hurt you. Give it up! Nikezela!

**ZAMA**: [*Terrified, whimpering*] Please, please leave me alone!

**VUYO**: [*Changing tactic and pushing her into her room*] I can't! I must have you!

**ZAMA**: [*In her room, she screams*] Stop! Help!

**VUYO**: Shut up! Just shut up!

[*He kicks her door shut from the inside. Another scream and then a muffled scream, then seconds later, Vuyo skulks away.*]

[*Lights fade.*]

*Scene 8*

[*Lights come up on the house, the door wide open, Zama crouched in a corner disheveled, catatonic, in shock. Sound of a clock ticking. Enter Nomandla carrying bags.*]

**NOMANDLA**: [*Calling from the kitchen*] Where's everybody? Zama? Zama!

[*To herself.*]

The door wide open! Are these children begging their father to chop off their heads or what!

[*Calling again.*]

Zama! Jongi! You'll get it from your father if thieves steal his TV because you leave the door wide open.

[*She enters the living room.*]

Maybe the lazy boy's finally raking the yard?

[*She hears Zama's sobbing and drops the bags and runs to her. Zama doesn't even flinch.*]

Zama!

[*Kneels and looks her over. Realizes what has happened to her.*]

Dear God!

**ZAMA**: [*Becoming aware of her surroundings. In a child's voice.*] Mama! Mama! Oh, help me!

**NOMANDLA**: Oh my God! Oh my God! Zama, my child! Zama! What's happened to you? I knew it! Oh no! Dear God no! My baby! My baby.

**ZAMA**: [*Wails*] Mama! Mama! You said I must keep myself clean. Well, look at me now! Look how clean and pure I am! For my husband? For my husband?

**NOMANDLA**: [*Reaching out to her*] Baby? Baby?

**ZAMA**: [*In fury*] Where's that husband now! Does he still want me? Does he care I love him so much I was saving myself for him? What is his name? Why did you teach me to care so much for the shadow of a man I do not know, who is powerless to say my name; who does not care that I breathe; who could not protect me from this this . . . this . . .

[*Screams out the last word.*]

evil?

[*She crumples and sobs uncontrollably. Nomandla holds her.*]

**NOMANDLA**: My poor baby! My poor, poor baby.

[*Lights fade.*]

*Scene 9*

[*A few minutes later. Zama is on the couch. Nomandla is kneeling, holding her hand while she drinks some tonic. Enter Jongi.*]

**JONGI**: What's going on?

**NOMANDLA**: [*To Zama*] Please, speak to me, my precious! Who did this to you?

**JONGI**: Did what? Did wha—t, heh?

**NOMANDLA**: [*To Jongi*] Nokwazi told me yesterday that Vuyo that son of Fina's they call the Ladies' Man, was bothering her. I'll . . .

[*Zama stiffens and then hides her face from her brother. Jongi realizes what has happened.*]

**JONGI**: Oh my God! Sisi? Was it Vuyo? Has he harmed you? That mad dog? No! NO! NO! I swear I'll kill him. If he has touched a hair of her head, I'll kill him!

[*Jongi looks about frantically*]

**NOMANDLA**: Jongi! Jongi! Come here!

**JONGI**: Mama, I have business with a dog. I'll be back.

[*Starts for the door.*]

**NOMANDLA**: [*Standing, loud, strong*] You will do no such thing! You sit down if you can't help your sister. You just sit down until your father comes home. Then we will decide what to do.

**JONGI**: [*Surprised by her commanding tone, sits*] Fine. We'll kill him together then. You know I tried to help my sister, but you wouldn't let me, just like you won't let me now.

**NOMANDLA**: You stop right there. I would give anything. *Anything* to take back this day and change what has happened. But it can't be done. So now we have to do what must be done. You have the rest of your life to remind me that you were right and I was wrong. So for this hour you can just keep still while I try to take care of your sister!

**JONGI**: [*Penitent*] I'm sorry, Mama.

**NOMANDLA**: [*To Jongi*] It's okay, son.

[*To Zama*] It's okay, baby, you're going to be okay.

**ZAMA**: No it's not, Mama. It's not okay. Nothing's okay. Nothing will ever be okay again.

**NOMANDLA**: My poor baby.

**ZAMA**: [*To Jongi*] You want to kill someone? Kill me! *Kill me!* I want to die!

**NOMANDLA**: No! No! No!

**MFUNDO**: [*Entering with briefcase*] What's this racket! Mother of Jongi, what's this? A man has no right to peace and quiet in his own home?!

**NOMANDLA**: Oh, there you are, Father of Zama!

[*She begins crying.*]

**MFUNDO**: Dear Heart, what's wrong? What's the matter?

**NOMANDLA**: Zama!

**MFUNDO**: Zama?

**NOMANDLA**: [*Blurts out*] Raped!

[*At this, Mfundo drops his briefcase and sinks to his knees, staring dumfounded at Nomandla. At the same time Zama struggles out of her embrace and jumps up. She runs to her room with her hands over her face and stops at the door. Nomandla sees her difficulty and speaks to her.*]

Zama, Sisi, go to my room, I'm coming!

[*Exit Zama.*]

[*To Mfundo*]

**NOMANDLA**: [*Cont.*] And you tie that son of yours down so he won't bring us all more trouble than we already have.

**MFUNDO**: [*Alarmed, standing*] What's *he* done?

**NOMANDLA**: He wants to kill Vuyo, Fina's son.

**MFUNDO**: [*In quiet fury*] The son of that drunk has done this?

**JONGI**: I warned you! Now we have to go and kill him, Tata. I know where he lives. Let's go.

**NOMANDLA**: Jongi! Stop!

[*To Mfundo*]

See what I'm talking about?

**MFUNDO**: My son, go get Koyana for me. Ask him to come at once!

**JONGI**: We don't need him, Father. I can do it myself!

**MFUNDO**: You do as I say!

**JONGI**: All right. All right!

[*Goes out the back door.*]

**MFUNDO**: The police will have to be called . . . How did this happen?

**NOMANDLA**: I got home late today because that woman I work for had me watch *her* children while she went to the place that washes her hair and paints her nails. When I got home I noticed the door was open. I came in and found Zama in that corner.

[*Points.*]

And the dog that had done this to her was gone.

[*Enter Jongi and Koyana. Exit Nomandla into her room.*]

**KOYANA**: Mmelwane, the boy says you sent for me.

**MFUNDO**: Son of Koyana, you saw me come to my home just now.

**KOYANA**: [*Nods*] Mh-huh, mh-huh. That's right.

**MFUNDO**: I walk in and find an abomination!—Isimanga! in my house.

**KOYANA**: What is it?

**MFUNDO**: Koyana, some dog has helped himself to my daughter!

**KOYANA**: My God!

**MFUNDO**: I thought I should call you in this, my hour of need; my hour of shame and defeat; you know, two heads are always better than one.

**KOYANA**: I thank you son of Lonzi, for thinking I'm a man who could help push the cart when the ground mounts and the cart is stuck. Let's see, how are we going to push this cart forward? What does the mother say?

**MFUNDO**: Let me call Nomandla—you'll hear for yourself.

[*Calling through the door.*]

Nomandla, Mother of Jongi, can you come in here?

[*Nomandla enters from her room, gently closes the door, and remains standing.*]

**NOMANDLA**: [*Speaking softly*] She's resting, but please be quiet. I don't want to upset her. She mustn't hear us talk about this.

**MFUNDO**: [*In a strong whisper*] All right, Mother of Zama, now! Tell Koyana here, in your own words—tell him what you know of this horrible thing that has happened to us.

**NOMANDLA**: As I told you, when I can home the door was open and I looked around . . .

[*She sniffs*] only to find Zama on the floor, in her room. And one look at her . . .

[*She chokes*] told me what had happened to her. She still won't say who did this to her. But yesterday Nokwazi told me she saw her with Vuyo.

**KOYANA**: You think the son of Fina has done this?

**NOMANDLA**: I'm not saying for sure. I wasn't here.

**KOYANA**: [*To Mfundo*] But you should ask him—at least ask the boy. Asking is not accusing.

**MFUNDO**: I'll break his scrawny neck for him! On my mother's grave, I'll kill him!

**NOMANDLA**: Father of Jongi! Father of Jongi!

**JONGI**: [*Jumping up*] Now you're making sense! Let's go!

**NOMANDLA**: Enough! Both of you! What would it help to kill a rapist? We should be focusing our energies on Zama and not the rapist.

[*Jongi is furious, pacing, seems ready to yell or bolt. To Jongi*]

You! I have one injured child tonight and that's enough. You cool yourself down!

**MFUNDO**: Oh are you saying we shouldn't ask this son of Fina if he did this thing?

**NOMANDLA**: No, I'm saying . . .

**JONGI**: [*Furious. As he speaks, Zama opens the door a bit. She stands back in the bedroom, listening.*] Don't you get it? Don't you understand? That dog Vuyo did this because he has AIDS! I told you!! He's killed her with HIV!

**ZAMA**: [*Shocked*] *O-o*-ooh!—Noooooo!

[*Blackout.*]

Intermission.

## ACT 2

*Scene 1*

[*Lights come up on the home as in Act 1. It is early. Nomandla is quietly getting coffee for Mfundo. She keeps looking out until she sees Nokwazi enter her yard. Then she goes out to greet her.*]

**NOKWAZI**: Good morning, Mother of Zama!

**NOMANDLA**: I see you, Nokwazi. The mornings have stopped being good, in my home.

**NOKWAZI**: I can imagine the pain . . . for our daughter . . .

**NOMANDLA**: Her eyes have not been dry, since this happened. She refuses to go to her room. Here is a girl, a young woman really, a child who's already seen her moontime . . . D'you know where she sleeps? In the same room as her parents! Is that natural?

**NOKWAZI**: The poor thing! How is she?

**NOMANDLA**: We've taken her to the doctor.

**NOKWAZI**: What did the doctors say?

**NOMANDLA**: She wasn't badly injured and, initial tests show she's not pregnant, thank God! But they can't know for a long time if he infected her. The disease can be in you for 10 years or more without showing itself. *Ten years!* And sometimes it even mutates . . .

**NOKWAZI**: Mutates?

**NOMANDLA**: Yes, it pretends to be something else, some other disease. So our Zama will have to go for tests for years and years.

**NOKWAZI**: You must be patient with her. Hurry slowly. Right now, she's fragile. Scared. And her room, the place of her violation, is defiled . . . it has become unholy.

**NOMANDLA**: You've given me an idea. Perhaps, they should exchange rooms, Zama and her brother.

**NOKWAZI**: Why not?

**NOMANDLA**: That would certainly be more help to her than what the mad boy and his father want to do. My teacher husband—mindful of his good name—didn't want her to go to the doctor!

**NOKWAZI**: Wha-aat? What?

**NOMANDLA**: I have my hands full, I tell you. And then, there is Jongi: all he wants to do is kill this boy!

**NOKWAZI**: Kill Fina's son? Jongi wants to kill Fina's son? Whoa, he's caught the Khayelitsha bug, where people have taken the law into their own hands.

**NOMANDLA**: And then, as though I don't have enough on my hands, doesn't this boy's mother send word she wants to talk to me? Talk to me? Talk to me?

**NOKWAZI**: Yho! Really, Fina has liver! *Unesibindi!* Where does she get such guts?

**NOMANDLA**: Truly, the trials God puts before me, sometimes.

**NOKWAZI**: Perhaps, she wants to say she's sorry.

**NOMANDLA**: Sorry won't mend my child's broken heart.

[*Blackout.*]

*Scene 2*

[*Evening on the street. Fina is in her church uniform. She catches sight of Vuyo.*]

**FINA**: There you are! I've been looking for you all over the shore. Why is it that on my day off, I must be going up and down the streets of Guguletu instead of resting in my house?

**VUYO**: Mama, I thought you were still in church.

**FINA**: You know the women's Manyano is over before the sun sets. Your older brother is home—why're you still out so late? You must be feeling better, then.

**VUYO**: I am, Mama. And I've missed my friends so I was visiting them.

**FINA**: Monde tells me something happened with the principal's daughter, at her home, and your name's come up in connection with that.

[*Vuyo is silent.*]

D'you know anything about that?

**VUYO**: No, Mama.

**FINA**: But why would anyone say you did this, if you did not?

**VUYO**: I don't know.

**FINA**: My child, you know you cannot lie because God sees what's in your heart. If this terrible thing is true . . .

**VUYO**: It's not true. Why does everybody want to believe I'm lying? She wanted me to . . . she . . . Like all the other girls, she's been showing me she wants me . . . making eyes at me, teasing me.

**FINA**: Did she ask you to her house?

**VUYO**: No.

**FINA**: No? Vuyo, then when did she ask you, show you she wanted you?

**VUYO**: Mama, first, she said yes and then she said no.

**FINA**: When was that, when she said yes? And when did she say no?

**VUYO**: When I asked her.

**FINA**: Were you already sleeping when she said no?

**VUYO**: No, Mama . . . but . . .

**FINA**: But, wha-at?

**VUYO**: Girls always say no when they actually mean yes.

**FINA**: Oh? Apparently this one said no and she meant no. Do you know the difference? Can you hear a no that is a yes and a no that is a no?

**VUYO**: No, Mama.

**FINA**: What does your mind tell you then? Don't you see that the only way you can be sure you are not making a mistake is to listen to what the girl is actually saying? What she's telling you? Take her no for a *no*—if she wants to say yes, let her say *yes.* Don't you see that, Vuyo?

**VUYO**: Yes, Mama, but she did want me . . . and showed me all the signs. I think she got scared, that's all . . . got scared her parents would know she'd done it.

**FINA**: When did she get scared?

**VUYO**: When I followed her into her house.

**FINA**: Followed her? Followed her? You mean you stood beside her as she opened the door and then you walked in after her?

**VUYO**: Yes, well, no. It was not exactly like that.

**FINA**: What was it like? Tell me. How did you *follow* her into her house?

**VUYO**: Well, I waited a little bit and then opened the door.

**FINA**: Did you knock and did she say, "Come in, Vuyo?"

**VUYO**: Well, I knocked and she thought it was her brother so I went in.

**FINA**: So you walked in and . . . ?

**VUYO**: She was in the bedroom.

**FINA**: And did she invite you into the bedroom?

[*Silence.*]

Did she Vuyo? Talk to me! Answer me! If you are having trouble answering me, what do you think will happen when the men of the principal's family fire questions at you? These men are not your mother. But worse still, how will you answer God when He asks you about this? You better not be lying to me . . . you know? You better not!

**VUYO**: I'm not lying, Mama. These girls . . . they say yes and then they get scared their parents will know. Then they want to say they never agreed to do it. She wants to get me in trouble and I can see you believe her although you are my own mother and I tell you it didn't happen that way.

**FINA**: My son, I just don't understand why she would lie. They say there were signs she put up a struggle. Why would she have done that? And why is she saying you raped her?

**VUYO**: How should I know? Maybe she liked it rough.

**FINA**: [*Slaps him*] Maybe? Maybe? But you were there! What do you mean maybe? Oh, the trouble you bring me! Why can't you be like Monde? Monde goes to school. He stays at home. Yes, he has friends, but he doesn't go vagabonding all over the place and he certainly doesn't get into half the trouble you do. He goes to church; you don't. Why, Vuyo?

**VUYO**: [*Hurt, angry*] I'm not Monde!

**FINA**: More's the pity. God help us! The disgrace! What will people say? Here I go to church every Sunday and, every Thursday, I wear the red blouse of the Methodist Women's Manyano. What will your poor father say, six long months away at sea so you can eat? [*Pause*] This thing you have done is something you have to answer for. These people are going to demand your blood. The police will put you in jail for a long time. The father of this girl is a school principal; he knows the law. He has money to hire lawyers. What have you got to say for yourself?

**VUYO**: I'm sorry, Mama.

**FINA**: [*Exhausted*] Sorry? Dear Lord, he's sorry. What is the matter with you?

[*Vuyo is silent.*]

What do we do now?

**VUYO**: Mama, can't you go and ask the principal to forgive me? Please—?

**FINA**: Forgive you? You didn't break the window in his house, Vuyo. D'you understand that? This is no small thing you've done.

[*Pause.*]

And forget about "you go, Mama." Mama didn't hurt anybody's daughter. *You* did and so, you go and apologize.

**VUYO**: [*Whimpering*] They'll kill me.

**FINA**: [*Shaking her head*] And so they should, Vuyo. I hope God can forgive you.

[*Sits down.*]

[*Blackout.*]

*Scene 3*

[*Same as in scene 1. Mfundo is in the living room, yelling through the door to Jongi's, now Zama's, room.*]

**MFUNDO**: The devil has come to rule my house. Well, Zama has to eat something, Mother of Jongi! Do you hear that, Zama! Eat what your mother brings you! The doctor said a good diet is important in keeping you healthy—Eat! And where is Jongi? He should be home now.

**NOMANDLA**: [*Through the door*] Out. The boy is out. She won't eat and he stays out.

**MFUNDO**: Wait! I hear someone coming. Maybe it's the prodigal son!

[*Enter Koyana and Fina, cautiously. They stand at the door.*]

**KOYANA**: We see you neighbor.

**MFUNDO**: [*Realizes who Fina is. Responds in barely controlled anger.*] Yes, Koyana, what can I do for you?

**KOYANA**: Our feet will take us no further.

**MFUNDO**: I don't remember calling a meeting.

**KOYANA**: No, Mmelwane, you did not call us.

**MFUNDO**: Oh! I thought I forgot because I see people come to my home *and* I know I have slaughtered no beast, I have brewed no beer.

**KOYANA**: [*Reacting a little to Mfundo's anger*] Okay! Okay! Okay! Mmelwane. I must beg your pardon! I myself, did not wake up thinking: Oh, I have nothing to do this Saturday and I'll go waste Mr. Lonzi's time because he also has nothing to do!

**MFUNDO**: What brings you here?

**KOYANA**: That is how a man welcomes visitors to his home? Thank you, son of Lonzi!

**MFUNDO**: No, thank you!

**KOYANA**: Before I got out of bed, this poor woman was already in my home. Mmelwane, Fina has asked me to come be her mouth.

**MFUNDO**: [*Giving in, motions for them to enter and points to chairs for them to sit. They remain standing.*] I'm listening.

**KOYANA**: It would not be a bad idea if you asked the mother of this home to join us.

**MFUNDO**: Mother of Jongi! Please come out here.

**NOMANDLA**: [*Enters, see that there are people in the living room*] Father of Jongi! Why didn't you say we have visitors . . .

[*Sees who it is, frowns.*]

Oh!

[*Turns as though to exit.*]

**MFUNDO**: [*Calmly, to all*] Sit down. Sit down.

[*They sit in the living room.*]

**NOMANDLA**: [*Aside*] The incredible nerve!

**KOYANA**: Neighbors of mine: the suffering brought by Fina's son is what brings me here today. As this boy's father is away at sea, she has asked me to accompany her here. May she speak?

[*There is a pause.*]

Mmelwane, and you, Mother of this home, may our neighbor speak?

**NOMANDLA**: [*Furious*] The time to speak is past. The deed is done.

**FINA**: A terrible deed, Mother of Jongi. A terrible deed. But that is why I am here . . . so we can talk.

**NOMANDLA**: Too late. The dog's already stolen into the coop and eaten my eggs.

**FINA**: It is never too late to do the right thing.

**NOMANDLA**: It is when the wrong thing's already done. Done! And can never be undone!

**KOYANA**: Let me break in, here, Mothers of children. Let me say, whatever we say at this time, we must not forget tomorrow and next week and next year—we will still be neighbors. None of us are moving away. I believe it is in that spirit, Fina has come.

**FINA**: My eyes cannot help but fix themselves on the door of this home! My eyes, filled with tears, remembering the pain my blood has caused the family of this home. Where shall I put my eyes? Where shall I look if looking here makes my heart leap to my throat with anguish?

**KOYANA**: Fina has come as a neighbor. Yes, a neighbor who has sinned against her neighbor. But, now she comes so that this terrible rift can be mended.

**MFUNDO**: And how is she proposing to do that?

**NOMANDLA**: How is that dog, her son, to restore what he has stolen from us?

**MFUNDO**: My child, my little girl, brutally assaulted!

**NOMANDLA**: [*Stands up shaking*] Do you know my daughter, my child, wants to kill herself! D'you know that? What's to be done? You tell me! What's to be done? When she has no way of knowing whether your son has given her this AIDS disease?

**FINA**: [*Surprised and a little offended*] I don't know what you are talking about. My son does not have that disease. He lost the weight because he had flu that became pneumonia. But he's fine now.

**NOMANDLA**: That's not what people say. And the doctors say, at any rate, we will have to worry for a long, long time.

**FINA**: [*On her knees*] Mother of Jongi, I have come to you about the bad thing my son has done. I have come to you mother to mother, so that we can see what can be done for the sake of our children.

**NOMANDLA**: [*Furious, raises her arm as if to strike Fina*] *Our* Children?!

[*Fina falls back, her arm bent to cover her face, frightened. Nomandla lets her hand drop.*]

You mean for the sake of *your* child.

**FINA**: [*Shaking*] No! For the sake of both of our children.

**NOMANDLA**: [*She sits back down, exhausted*] I don't know what you can do for *my* child. But I can see you want to save your son's skin.

**FINA**: [*Rises*] You mistake my intentions, Mother of Jongi, if you think my heart does not sorrow for your daughter.

**NOMANDLA**: [*Bitterly*] I can see that it sorrows more for your son.

**FINA**: I am a mother—with a mother's heart. That heart is grieving for what my child has done and what will happen to him as a result of his terrible deed—not just here on earth but the day he meets his Maker. However, that same heart bleeds for the pain brought upon your daughter—and she so young. So young! My heart is rent in two.

**KOYANA**: [*Moved by her sincerity*] Perhaps, Mfundo, we should leave the two women to talk to each other . . .

**MFUNDO**: Mother of Jongi?

**NOMANDLA**: [*Long pause, then resignedly*] Oh, all right!

[*Exit Mfundo and Koyana—Nomandla and Fina are silent—in their own thoughts . . .* ]

**NOMANDLA**: [*Sighs*] So, what do you want of me?

[*Lights fade on Nomandla and Fina as they continue talking and come up on Mfundo and Koyana standing in the space between their two houses. Mfundo is pacing.*]

**MFUNDO**: I should never have let that woman in my house. The dog, her son, should go straight to jail and die there!

**KOYANA**: But the boy's mother says something I think we should listen to. Think about it yourself, Titshala!—What will sending him to jail do except bring him back to us an even worse criminal? The jails teach nothing but how to be a better criminal. And there is no village out there for people who've been to jail . . . They come out—back here—to live among us.

**MFUNDO**: Balderdash! Stuff and nonsense! I don't want to hear about street councils!

**KOYANA**: You believe in jail? . . . the white man's jail?

**MFUNDO**: It is the only way. Lock him up in the darkest dungeon and throw away the key.

**KOYANA**: Why is it that we are such copy cats—So hasty in discarding what is truly ours, preferring what the white man brought with him.

**MFUNDO**: Are you saying evil people should be allowed to go scot-free?

**KOYANA**: *No!* but where were the jails in the times of our forebears?

**MFUNDO**: We had no jails . . . but [*Koyana cuts in.*]

**KOYANA**: But people broke the law even then. Even then, there were cruel people who sometimes did evil things. What happened then? *They* were dealt with by the community—by the village. They were *not* locked away anywhere. The village did not build special houses to put them away.

**MFUNDO**: You're right. We had no such places.

**KOYANA**: Even our language has no words for these monstrosities—places of banishment—where we lock up people; depriving them of all contact with others . . . That contact is vital; that's what keeps us human. We are human only because we daily drink from the fountain of our common humaneness.

**MFUNDO**: [*Dazed*] . . . drink from the fountain of our common humaneness . . .

**KOYANA**: And the village, in its wisdom, knew this.

**MFUNDO**: . . . the village knew . . .

**KOYANA**: The goal of punishment is not to destroy the transgressor, but to restore him to his basic humaneness. He was born human, let's help him die human and not a monstrosity, an animal, debased, stripped off all human dignity; completely and utterly bereft off all human affinity.

**MFUNDO**: Son of Koyana, you have taught me something, today. Yes, the boy must be punished . . . But . . . by *us!*

[*Lights fade on the two men as they continue talking and come up on the two women. Fina is in the middle of a speech.*]

**FINA**: . . . Let us cast our minds to our own truths, our own ways of doing things.

**NOMANDLA**: [*Pulling herself together, showing she has reached a decision*] I have often had words with my husband about bringing back the good from our past, the wisdom of our ancestors. My grandmother used to tell me, if you listen, you can hear the whisper of your ancestors, guiding you to the best path.

**FINA**: [*Her face fills with hope*] Oh Mother of Jongi, I came here chicken-hearted. I had little hope you would understand me! But I believe you do. You understand my desolation!

**NOMANDLA**: [*With some reserve*] I will talk with my husband. *If*, and I mean *if* I can convince him to call a meeting of the neighborhood, will your son abide by the decision?

**FINA**: I would be lying if I said I know my son's heart. But he seems to have remorse; and I should hope he expects, *must* expect reprisals for his wickedness.

**NOMANDLA**: Well, maybe some light can come out of this dark time after all.

**FINA**: [*Grimly*] May it please God! That boy has only begun to see the fury I am capable of. Let him try to resist my help!

[*Softening.*]

I can think of no way to repay your kindness.

[*They both stand and begin walking to the door—Fina Cont.*]

When I make my prayers, I will pray for God's blessings on your family first.

[*Nomandla nods; Fina exits, passing Jongi who is entering. Nomandla is standing near the kitchen door, thinking. Irate, Jongi charges into the kitchen.*]

**JONGI**: Is that who I think it is?

**NOMANDLA**: [*Surprised, then recovering herself*] Jongi! Where have you been?

**JONGI**: Out! Now tell me, was that the mother of the dog [*shouting, now*] *in our house?*

**NOMANDLA**: [*Forgetting how angry* she *had been when Fina arrived*] Yes, yes it was Fina. She came to apologize . . .

**JONGI**: Apologize! Who is she to apologize?

**NOMANDLA**: To apologize and ask us to consider leaving the police out of this.

**JONGI**: Oh, really! Leave the police out. Well, I agree with that plan!

[*Coldly*] I'll leave the police out of this all right! Did she say when that dog her son might be home alone?

**NOMANDLA**: No! She asked us to try him with a neighborhood council and decide his punishment among ourselves, to leave the white men's ways out of it.

**JONGI**: And you agreed? You agreed to this pale excuse for a remedy?

**NOMANDLA**: I said I will speak to your father.

**JONGI**: And he will bluster and blow and then do whatever you say. Like always. And what you will do will be too little too late. Like always. That bastard will get away with raping my sister.

**NOMANDLA**: No one wants him to go unpunished. Not even his mother.

**JONGI**: Is that what she told you? A clever witch; isn't she!

**NOMANDLA**: Jongi! Stop it. Listen to me.

**JONGI**: [*Pacing*] Too late. There is no justice to be had here. Zama's life is over before it began and mine has no meaning. Ugh. I wash my hands of you!

[*Heads for the door.*]

**NOMANDLA**: Where are you going?

**JONGI**: Out.

**NOMANDLA**: Why? Wait for your father.

**JONGI**: Are you kidding? I'm going to go to try to forget I have a father, a mother, to forget I have a family! At least I'll have some fun catching the disease!

[*Runs out, slams the door. Nomandla stands, aghast . . .* ]

*Scene 4*

[*Same as scene 3, a few minutes later. Nomandla is folding some clothes and she weeps and shakes her head, still upset by Jongi's outburst. Zama comes out of her room. She is disheveled, but wearing a nice night-gown. She quietly approaches her mother.*]

**ZAMA**: Mama? Was that Jongi I heard yelling? Has he left?

**NOMANDLA**: [*Pulling herself together for Zama*] Yes.

[*She leads Zama over to the couch and they sit together.*]

He's gone out with his friends. He's just upset over everything that's happened.

**ZAMA**: And that woman you were talking to?

**NOMANDLA**: That was the boy's mother.

**ZAMA**: You called him a dog before she came here.

**NOMANDLA**: Well, uh . . .

**ZAMA**: Now you want to let him go?

**NOMANDLA**: You misunderstand.

**ZAMA**: Do I? Do I, Mama? I heard what you said to her! You have no right to make father let him go! He didn't hurt you!

**NOMANDLA**: You don't know what you're talking about! *You* wait until you become a mother . . . until your body tears bringing new life into being. Then you'll know what a mother is . . . what she feels about her child. Let me tell you! I am angry enough to kill that child myself—But I know . . .

**ZAMA**: You want to let him go!

**NOMANDLA**: I don't want to let him go. I am saying, even if we send him to jail, eventually we have to forgive him.

**ZAMA**: Forgive? Mama? People will think what he did wasn't wrong.

**NOMANDLA**: His mother says he admits it was wrong. Your father and I and all the people of our street can sit and talk . . . and see what would be fitting punishment for a child who has done—and admits to—something like this.

**ZAMA**: But if it is true he has AIDS, then maybe he'll die in jail and we'd be finished with him!

**NOMANDLA**: My child—I pray that what has happened to you does not make you a bitter person. Bitterness only eats you up inside. Forgive and live a life that looks forward, not back.

**ZAMA**: Forgive? I'd rather see him cut to pieces and fed to the dogs.

**NOMANDLA**: Zama, my child, don't let the evil deed stick you, like glue, to the past. I'm not saying this is something you'll forget . . .

**ZAMA**: As long as I live, I'll remember. Mama, you can wash off dirt and cuts may scab over. But there are scars that will never heal. Do you want me to pretend this . . . this . . . this thing didn't happen?

**NOMANDLA**: No! But for you to heal, you have to understand—it was not your fault! You didn't bring this upon yourself! And you are not sullied, *your* reputation, your character, your soul, is intact!

[*Zama begins to cry. Nomandla gathers her up in her arms. Zama pushes her away.*]

Don't let this destroy you, darling! Remain this beautiful, young, trusting, brilliant, and outgoing woman you are! Go to school; stay in school. Do all the things you've said you want to do! Remember what the doctors say? Diet and exercise—even if you're infected—can slow the progression of the virus. Live—and live a full life—And be the woman you said you'd be when you grow up . . . be all these things you've dreamed of becoming since you were born.

**ZAMA**: My dreams are nightmares. That dog has stolen my future.

**NOMANDLA**: Oh, no, he didn't. Don't even think that.—Do not be a bitter woman—but forgive. Grudging vengeance eats you up. You don't want to be corroded by all that. You want to heal. Let go! Work on your healing, my Sweet!

**ZAMA**: I will never heal.

**NOMANDLA**: You will, my love—If you work at it, you will. Vuyo will live with the knowledge of this foul deed . . . *For the rest of his life,* he will know he once sunk this low. That is why it is good you speak out. *You* have nothing to hide. You have no shame; all the shame is his.

**ZAMA**: [*Starting to listen*] But, if we keep him out of jail, what's to stop him from doing it again?

**NOMANDLA**: No one wants to let him repeat his awful crime. Why don't we wait for the street court to decide his fate.

**ZAMA**: He *must* be punished! I want him to go to jail, Mama!

**NOMANDLA**: What will that achieve?

**ZAMA**: An ounce of recompense? It's my right as a victim!

**NOMANDLA**: Repentance rather than recompense is what we want. And to see you work on your healing. Don't be a victim, my love but work on your healing.

[*Zama begins to weep.*]

[*Nomandla reaches for her.*]

I'll support you all the way. I'll be with you always.

**ZAMA**: But Mama, I can't be strong like you!

**NOMANDLA**: You are my daughter, you are strong! Stronger than you know; you haven't begun to tap your strength. And together—we are formidable!

**ZAMA**: But Mama, I feel terrible. And I don't just feel terrible; I feel different . . . [*She falls into Nomandla's arms.*]

**NOMANDLA**: [*Gently*] You will always be my little girl! Life can be hard and God tests us in many ways. My heart is broken that I could not protect you when you needed me most.

**ZAMA**: I know . . .

**NOMANDLA**: Life can be hard, but you know what? This is not the end of your life! This may be the darkest hour but believe me, one day you'll look back even to this hour and, if you handle this the right way, you will see in today the seeds of an even better you, an even stronger you.

**ZAMA**: You think so, Mama? Do you really think so?

**NOMANDLA**: Yes, my heart, yes. *I know so.*

[*They embrace.*]

[*Lights fade.*]

*Scene 5*

[*The next day. Now tidy, Zama is alone in the house, lying on the couch, reading a book and munching on an apple. Jongi stumbles into the kitchen door, drunk and mumbling to himself. Zama hears the noise, bolts from the couch, flinging down book and apple and grasping a large knife from a sideboard drawer.*]

**ZAMA**: Oh! Not again!

[*Shouts*] Who's that?! Answer me or I swear I'll kill you this time!

[*Jongi comes into the living room*]

**JONGI**: Kill me, my little sister!

[*Zama sees it is Jongi and drops the knife.*]

My beautiful little sister! Come on, kill me! I deserve to die. I'm a useless dog. Couldn't even protect my poor, little sister. Kill me! Kill me! Kill me!

**ZAMA**: Jongi! What happened? Who did this to you?

[*Crosses to him and realizes that he is drunk.*]

Oh no! What have you gone and done Jongilizwe? Look at you! Just look at you!

**JONGI**: I am a worthless dog. Kill me!

**ZAMA**: Have you lost your mind? You, you . . .

[*Searching for an epithet; can't think of one. Growls*]

Urrgh! You went and got yourself drunk? Fool! Has this family not suffered enough?

[*Zama goes to the refrigerator and gets some milk. She pours Jongi a glass of milk, hands it to him and picks up her debris.*]

Here. Sit down and drink this.

**JONGI**: Drink milk? I'm not a baby.

**ZAMA**: Drink! It will help clear your mind. I'm making you black tea.

[*Jongi takes the cup and sloppily gulps down the milk. Zama goes to the stove and puts tea leaves into the kettle. As she starts to strain the tea into the cup, Jongi jumps up and runs to the bathroom. We can hear that he's sick. Zama frantically strains the tea, tastes it, finding it too hot. Adds a little cold water.*]

Please God, don't let Mama and Tata come back just now. Let them stay at Tata Koyana's till Jongi gets better.

[*Jongi reemerges holding his head and Zama turns on him.*]

You! Drink. Drink up! Drink up! D'you want to give our parents a stroke, eh?

**JONGI**: No . . . a heart attack!

**ZAMA**: You joke? This is a time for you to show the world you're a clown? Jongilizwe?

**JONGI**: [*Sobs*] I can't bear it! I can't bear to think of that stupid fool doing . . . doing . . . doing this to you.

[*Cries louder.*]

My poor little sister! My darling little sister! My beloved . . .

**ZAMA**: Is this how you show me sympathy? By getting drunk?

**JONGI**: I want to die.

**ZAMA**: Oh, you want to die. What exactly happened to you that you should be so sorrowful you want to die?

**JONGI**: I can't bear it! I can't bear it!

**ZAMA**: What can't you bear? Eh? Who asked you to bear anything?

**JONGI**: My poor little sister!

**ZAMA**: Stop it! Stop it! I am not poor. The dog who did this to me is poor—a poor excuse for a human being. And I stopped being little the minute he forced himself on me. And the last thing I need is people busy disintegrating around me. I need strong people.

**JONGI**: Need strong people.

**ZAMA**: Yes, strong people.

[*Pause.*]

Listen, my brother, this is time for action. Jongi, I had a strange dream, last night. Mama says it was Gogo, speaking to me. She says I have a path to follow; I have things to do . . . and I can't waste my time feeling sorry for myself any more.

[*Jongi pulls himself to an upright position. His eyes widen in an attempt to focus.*]

Brother of mine, son of my father, wake up! Be a man. Help me act . . . help me get even with that—.

**JONGI**: Now, you're talking! Look! [*He fumbles in his pocket and pulls out a gun.*]

I'll be a man, all right!—

**ZAMA**: A Gun! You've got a gu—

[*Enter Mfundo, unnoticed.*]

[*She sees father.*]

O, no . . . Tata! [*Runs out.*]

**MFUNDO**: Good God! Kwedini, what's that? Where did you get that thing?

**JONGI**: I'm going to shoot myself a mad dog . . .

**MFUNDO**: [*Yelling and then slowly approaching Jongi*] Look at me, son. This is not the answer. The boy has to pay for what he did—but this is not the way. Jongi . . . give me the gun.

**JONGI**: I did not protect my little sister.

**MFUNDO**: Give me the gun! Son, here, give me the gun . . .

[*Holds out hand, takes gun and embraces Jongi.*]

[*Slow fade to black.*]

*Scene 6*

[*Same place, an hour later. Zama is asleep on the couch, a book has fallen out of her hand and onto the floor. Enter Mfundo and Nomandla talking quietly. They smile a little sadly as they see her sleeping peacefully. Mfundo nods toward Jongi's room and shakes his head, a look of exasperation on his face. Nomandla beckons and leads him toward the kitchen where Mfundo sits at the table. Nomandla fixes him a bite to eat. They speak in subdued voices.*]

**MFUNDO**: [*Pushes plate away*] Food turns to sawdust in my mouth. Life has lost all meaning.

**NOMANDLA**: But Father of Zama, you've got to eat!

**MFUNDO**: What next? One child, defiled. Another, on the fast tract to the gallows! I don't deserve this! No, I don't! I work hard for this family. I give my tithe to the church . . . I—

**NOMANDLA**: It could have been worse. Thank God, you got here just in time.

**MFUNDO**: Worse? How could it possibly be any worse?

**NOMANDLA**: He could have hurt someone with that gun, you know . . .

**MFUNDO**: My natural inclination is to thrash that boy, but I don't think it would help matters . . .

**NOMANDLA**: No. It wouldn't. You handled a difficult situation very well. But we need to talk to him. He's hurting.

**MFUNDO**: I know how he feels. This situation has brought shame on our name.

**NOMANDLA**: Shame on us?! Father of Jongi! What are you talking about? How did I end up with two men in my life who are crazy? Both of you should be in Valkenberg! Your daughter has been raped by a boy who may be sick with AIDS and all you can think about is your good name?

**MFUNDO**: You don't understand what it is to be a man.

**NOMANDLA**: Oh no? Well, maybe I don't! But be a man and tell your son to be a man. It's not you or your name that's been assaulted—it's her body; her spirit; her soul. It's not you who is suffering, but that poor child you seem to have forgotten in your silly concern for your sorry good name.

**MFUNDO**: [*Trying to protest*] But . . .

**NOMANDLA**: I've never regretted I married you—don't make me regret it now! Shame on us? *Shame on us?* We have done nothing wrong!

**MFUNDO**: [*Holding up his hands in surrender*] I know! I know, Mother of Zama—and I am sorry. Bear with me—you have all these years. I don't know how you hold everyone's head above water all the time. [*Puts his arms around her*] I know you're a strong woman, but would it hurt to lean on me a little? Let me be the man?

**NOMANDLA**: [*She takes a breath as though to start another speech and then lets out the air and leans against him*] Of course, it wouldn't hurt. And, I will. So why don't we talk about what we'll be "having words" over next, Father of Jongi?

**MFUNDO**: [*With a wary smile*] So I can plan my argument?

**NOMANDLA**: Hmm. So you can encourage me to lean on you more and more. Anyway, my hero, next we have to talk about how to get these boys to be men. To get them to take responsibility for themselves and with their girlfriends . . . To A-B-C!

**MFUNDO**: Oh, A-B-C!

**NOMANDLA**: Yes, Father of my children . . . A! [*Mfundo responds: Abstain!*] B! [*Mfundo responds: Be loyal!*] C! [*Mfundo responds: Condomize!*]

**MFUNDO**: Mother of my children! Woman! Why do you think this will cause an argument between us? Believe me; I have seen the error of my thinking. This plague is no child's play. And unless we want to see a grim decimation of our race—young men and young women *must* practice safer sex . . . Indeed, we must all practice safer sex.

**NOMANDLA**: Now it is *my* turn to be amazed!

[*She reaches up to embrace him.*]

[*Blackout.*]

*Scene 7*

[*In the dining/living room. Lights come up on the family seated.*]

**MFUNDO**: Your mother and I have chewed each other's ears over this decision. We have decided it is not a bad idea to go to the Council. It shows a spirit of humaneness (ubuntu!). And despite everything, we must forge ahead . . . Think of the morrow. What happened isn't the woman's fault.

**NOMANDLA**: It is *not your* fault either, Jongi. And I want you to understand that, Son. It is not your fault . . .

**MFUNDO**: We all wish we could have prevented this. Protected your sister better. But . . .

[*Peters off.*]

**NOMANDLA**: In our sorrow, let us not lose sight of our ubuntu.

**ZAMA**: Then, Mama, may I address the Council? Promise me you will ask this for me.

**NOMANDLA**: Of course . . . That is only fair.

**MFUNDO**: Nomandla, do you think that is wise? Facing all those people? Zama has suffered enough!

**ZAMA**: Mama's right, I have nothing to hide. People must hear how I feel . . . what I think and what I believe!

**JONGI**: They'll certainly hear from Vuyo and his mother!

**NOMANDLA**: And they should! He has done evil—He's got to be man enough to admit his guilt, apologize to Zama, and accept what punishment comes his way.

**JONGI**: Vuyo must not only admit his crime but denounce this stupid belief that sleeping with a virgin cures AIDS! [*Sneers*] Cures AIDS . . . [*Shouts*] It only spreads AIDS!

**NOMANDLA**: That is why it will be good for Zama to speak—to bear witness to her suffering and demand redress! To help dispel that very myth.

**MFUNDO**: I gather this feeling, Zama must speak, is mutual, then . . . [*Heads nod*] . . . Well, I am right behind you. I support the decision of the majority.

**ZAMA**: You agree? Mama, Tata, you agree I should address the Street Council? [*Nods*] Thank you, thank you, so much!

[*Blackout.*]

*Scene 8*

[*The Community Center. Drab hall with rickety chairs and benches and peeling walls. There is a makeshift podium where Koyana stands. To his right sit Vuyo and Fina on a bench and to his left, on another bench, sit Zama, Nomandla, Mfundo, and Jongi. The Council is understood to be seated in the direction of the audience, slightly stage right. When not addressing specific individuals, speakers will address their remarks to this imaginary council.*]

**KOYANA**: This is a sad day, indeed. We are all gathered here because of two young people, children we know, children from our own street. One is accused of a heinous crime, the other, the victim of that crime.

[*Pause.*]

Vuyo!

[*Fina nudges Vuyo sharply and he stands.*]

You are here at your own request in lieu of bringing this case to the civil courts. And you have agreed to abide by our decision. Is that true?

**VUYO**: [*Under his breath*] Yes, Tatomkhulu.

**KOYANA**: Speak up, that all may hear the words of your mouth.

**VUYO**: Yes, Tatomkhulu.

**KOYANA**: Let me caution you. Many people run to the street court thinking the people of their street, because they know them, will be more lenient than the civil courts. Son, this is not always the case. The people you know may be harsher because: 1) they also know the victim; 2) they may fear you'll do the same to them; and 3) they do not particularly like you because of what you do not deny you have done; or 4) they may hold grudges against you from previous encounters. Do you understand all that?

**VUYO**: Yes, Tatomkhulu.

[*Koyana motions for Vuyo to sit. Vuyo sits.*]

**KOYANA**: Very well.

[*To the Council*]

Our daughter, Zama, has asked to address the Council.

[*To Zama. She rises as he speaks to her and walks to the podium. Nomandla grabs her hand and squeezes it.*]

Zama, please come forward.

[*Koyana steps back. Zama grasps the podium and gathers her strength. To the Council.*

**ZAMA**: Fathers and Mothers, this country has no death penalty, yet Vuyo . . .

[*She points in his direction but does not look at him. Vuyo, head down, looks off stage right.*]

has sentenced me to death. He has attempted my murder by defiling my body with his poisoned blood. Why should I die because of his actions? What is more, even before he did this to me, I lived in fear. Fear of being raped. I lived in terror no different to that of children in war-torn countries. Why? Why have our fathers and our brothers turned against us? What have we done that they hunt and harass us everywhere and every day?

[*Pause.*]

But our fathers and our brothers are protected by the law that says—even for such acts—they shall not die. What about us? What about the girl-children of this sad land? However, we are law abiding. We respect the law. Obey the law. So I come before this court, seeking redress. My case is in your hands.

**KOYANA**: Thank you, daughter—you may sit down.

[*He turns to the people assembled.*]

You have heard the words of this brave, young woman. Remember them as we go over this sad, terrible case—a case involving people who are neighbors. Now, it is only right, fair, and just that we hear from the accused; hear his side of the story; what he has to say for himself.

[*Turns to Vuyo.*]

**KOYANA**: Vuyo, do you deny these allegations of rape, made against you?

[*Vuyo nods.*]

**KOYANA**: Are you sick?

**VUYO**: Yes.

**KOYANA**: Tell this court what your illness is.

**VUYO**: Gawulayo.

[*Fina gasps audibly*—No!]

**KOYANA**: Is that what is also known as AIDS?

**VUYO**: Yes.

[*Outraged, Fina stifles a scream.*]

**KOYANA**: Is that why you did what you did? Raped this girl?

[*Vuyo nods.*]

**KOYANA**: Speak up! [*Shouts of: "Castrate him!" "Kill the dog!"*]

**VUYO**: I thought . . . I'd heard . . . they say if . . . [*Breaks down*]—They say if . . . [*shouts hysterically*] . . . you will be cured if . . .

**KOYANA**: Let me say it for you . . . "If you sleep with a virgin!" [*Pause*] Is that right? That's what you heard? What you believe is the cure for AIDS? Sleeping with a virgin?

**VUYO**: I wanted to heal myself.

**KOYANA**: You believed that you would be healed?

**VUYO**: Yes.

**KOYANA**: Well, are you?

**VUYO**: What?

**KOYANA**: Healed. Are you healed? You raped Zama Lonzi, a virgin, believing that would heal you. Are you healed now?

**VUYO**: I'm still sick. The terrible . . . what I did didn't help me, at all. I am still sick! Sleeping with a virgin didn't help me. It can never help any one! [*Sobs*] It doesn't help! It does not help!

**KOYANA**: Son, we hear your words. But, as you know, *must* know, those words mean little to the young woman you raped. Do you have any words to say to her?

**VUYO**: [*Slowly shakes his head. Silence—as the court waits for him to speak.*]

**KOYANA**: Vuyo! Have you anything to say to Zama? To her family? For the wrong you have done them? A wrong you admit?

**VUYO**: I am sorry! I am so-oo very, very sorry! [*Crumbles.*]

**KOYANA**: The Council will now continue its deliberations in a closed session. We will reconvene at 10:00 tomorrow morning—at which time, we hope to have come to a decision and have a verdict.

[*Cast begins to disperse. Vuyo pulls Fina aside. He is shaking.*]

**VUYO**: Mama! Mama! You can't let these people do these things to me!

**FINA**: You coward! Stand up and take your punishment like a man.

**VUYO**: But they're talking about killing me! You heard them! Mama, castration! You've got to stop them, Mama . . . please!

**FINA**: Vuyo, do not try God. You asked me to keep you out of jail and you got that. Now you want the Street to give you the sentence you want? You commit an outrage—an abomination—And then you want to be handled with kid gloves?

**VUYO**: Mama, you don't know what it's like. You think I'm a bad person but I only thought I could heal myself.

**FINA**: Heal yourself? Heal yourself? Vuyo, did you hear yourself in there [*points*]?

[*Pause.*]

Don't let these people make you believe you have AIDS. Yes, you were sick but look, you are better, now. We must get you tested so they can see they're wrong. Yes, that's what we'll do—get you tested and put a stop to all this nonsense. What you did is bad enough, the Lord knows. But no one must make it look even worse by adding AIDS to it. Dear God!

**VUYO**: I was tested.

**FINA**: What? You were tested . . . You were tested?—And . . . ?

**VUYO**: [*Surly*] Hell! What do they know?

**FINA**: *No,* it is not true. Tell me it is not true. You said you were feeling better; how could this happen, Vuyo?

[*He doesn't reply. She is appalled.*]

Oh! Holy Father of our Lord! It is true, then! You are dying . . . AIDS kills . . . You are dying and yet . . . yet you go on sinning. Have you no fear of hell? Do you not fear God's judgment? O, what've you done? That poor child!

[*Yelling and hitting him*]

Out of my sight. Out of my sight, you confounded sinner. You wretch, you are no son of mine! Get out of my sight you . . . you . . . you vermin!

[*Lights go down on Fina and Vuyo and up on Zama and Jongi on the other side of the Hall.*]

**ZAMA**: What if they just treat this as a joke and give him corporal punishment? Oh, God, I would die. Vuyo and everybody else will laugh at me, laugh to my face.

**JONGI**: Don't worry, little sister. I'm going to see that Vuyo gets what he has coming to him. And you're not the only one talking publicly about this. I have already started talking to the other boys. Everybody's appalled at what this lowdown coward has done. And I vow to start making sure we all see that the way we talk about girls, the way we like to rough them up even in play, the way we tell silly, stupid jokes about them *is not funny*. Such crude talk is what leads to bad attitudes.

**ZAMA**: And bad attitudes lead to atrocious actions—actions such as Vuyo's.

**JONGI**: That must stop. God knows, it has gone on long enough. I respect you as my sister. But I must respect all girls and women and behave towards them with civility and respect . . . at all times.

**ZAMA**: D'you think they'll listen to you, the other boys, I mean?

**JONGI**: Let me tell you something: you have no idea how my friends admire you for standing up for your rights—instead of hiding what has happened.

**ZAMA**: Do they? Do they, really?

**JONGI**: They do—all the ones with any brains. And they agree with me that real men do not abuse women. And that's what we're already working on—our own behavior and our own morals. We must do what needs to be done; including putting stigma where it belongs—to the witches who make the sick afraid to seek help.

**ZAMA**: Then, there's hope.

**JONGI**: Even Father's singing a different tune, these days. He now says we all *must* take a stand! Imagine that—I'm just sorry it has taken this to make me see what needs to be done . . . but, from now on, this Guguletu of ours is going to be much safer than it has been for some time . . . a long, long time.

**ZAMA**: Oh, Jongi, it is at times like this that one appreciates having a brother like you. I know how lucky I am to have you . . .

[*Lights fade.*]

*Scene 9*

[*Community Center the next day. Actors are councilors. All are gathered for the verdict. Fina has seated herself at the end of the Bench, away from Vuyo.*]

**KOYANA**: Vuyo! Stand, so you may hear what we have decided.

[*Vuyo stands. He is clearly frightened.*]

My son, we are glad you are repentant; that you have seen the folly of this misguided and cruel belief. However, your gruesome act deserves no less gruesome a reaction. Otherwise women will continue to be molested by wicked and cowardly men such as you; heartless men who see themselves as hunters in a field with no fences, who have declared open season on women, girls, and even infants. As a society, we must halt this barbarism. Many have demanded that you be castrated. Others say that putting you to death is the only way to ensure you will not be a repeat offender. Our council was evenly divided between these two punishments. But, remembering the words of Zama, that we are *and must be,* law abiding, and since, as of now, the laws of this country do not allow castration or capital punishment, it is the decision of this court that you will be shunned.

[*In turn, each councilor rises to deliver her/his part of the verdict.*]

**COUNCILLOR**: People will be informed of who you are and what you have done. Your photograph, name and address will be distributed throughout the community—glued to lamp posts and displayed at shop windows with an account of your crime and a clear notice of the sentence on your head and the duration of that sentence.

**COUNCILLOR**: For the next five years, you will not be welcome anywhere in NY200. You may go to work and to church and to the shop, but will be banned from any of the celebrations or social activities of this community.
**COUNCILLOR**: During that same period, one-half of your wages will be given to the Lonzi family as isihewula—reparation!

[*Vuyo's knees give way and he slumps forward onto his seat. Fina sits erect with tears streaming down her cheeks.*]

**COUNCILLOR**: Furthermore, to dispel this wicked myth once and for all—a myth that has given rise to terrible, vile deeds—[*Shouts:—2-months-old babies*—raped!]

—you will do community service—Go around to schools and churches and talk about your deed. Tell other men—young and old—that you are still sick—That after this act of savagery, you are not cured at all. Tell them rape is no cure for AIDS! As of now, there is no cure for AIDS! Virginity is not medicine for anything . . . And rape is a dastardly crime, a violation without parallel.

**COUNCILLOR**: You shall be the mouth of Zama's pain. You shall be the voice of her anguish—the voice of the anguish of the women of this sad land.

**COUNCILLOR**: You shall prize open the blind eyes of cruel men; clear stubborn wax out their ears till evil deafness leaves them forever.

**COUNCILLOR**: You shall be the key that turns their stone-hearts; the sure sun that thaws their frozen souls!

**COUNCILLOR**: Go and show the world your face. Open your mouth and confess to all the error of your ways . . . the evil of your deeds. You say you are sorry—now show us the weight of your remorse by your actions—by how you follow the instructions of this Council. And, if you do, one day, you may be reinstated to full membership of our community. It is up to you . . . Up to you and your conscience!

**KOYANA**: To all here present, you have heard the verdict, a verdict that is—yes—a compromise. But a verdict that conveys the deepest fears and the highest hopes of this community. Let this council and all the citizens join hands to demand legislation to make the punishment of castration or death a legal response to the crime of rape and mandatory when the rapist is HIV-positive or has AIDS—We will not rest until children like Zama are protected from the evil actions driven by the fear and stupidity of cowardly men, irresponsible men. We shall not rest till all children, all girls, and all women are safe.

[*Song: Raised fists. Sith' aba abantu!*]

Sith' aba abantu!
Sith' aba abantu—
Makulungiswe ukuhlala.
We must right what is wrong!

[*Sound: fades to a low hum as actors turn their backs on Vuyo.*]

**MFUNDO**: *Ma*-Afrika, *vukani!* This is war. We must all stand up and fight or we shall all perish. Vukani! Vukani! . . . [*Then the whole cast joins in*] *Wake up!*

[*Curtain.*]

## A COLOURED PLACE

*Malika Ndlovu (Lueen Conning)*

I consider myself African. But this is not a general Coloured perception. In fact, a lot of Coloured people deny their African heritage. There is an aspiration toward white beauty, although it's not overtly stated . . . they furiously straighten their hair so you can't see the African kink; they . . . consider a straighter nose, thinner lips, and lighter skin as beauty. And that's the aspiration. Apartheid still lives in our minds.

**Malika Ndlovu (Lueen Conning), South Africa**

Born in Durban, South Africa, in 1971, Malika Ndlovu is a poet, playwright, performer, arts administrator, wife, and mother of three. She attended state Coloured schools until the age of fifteen, when she successfully obtained a bursary to study drama at a private Catholic convent school during the apartheid era, one of first to begin admitting black pupils. After high school, she worked as an actress, touring South Africa with the highly acclaimed Theatre for Africa Company and later received her performing arts diploma from Natal Technikon. One year later, she completed her training as an arts administrator at the Durban Natal Playhouse.

In 1995, the SA Women's Arts Festival, after seeing the successful performance of her series of monologues called *U-Voice,* commissioned Malika to write her first full-scale professional play, *A Coloured Place.* Performed in 1996 at the Natal Playhouse, this multimedia show gives a woman's perspective on growing up Coloured in apartheid South Africa. The play has been performed frequently throughout the country, most recently in 2006 when the play celebrated its tenth anniversary at the tenth SA Women's Arts Festival.

Malika has also published four poetry anthologies, *Born in Africa But* (2000), *Womb to World: A Labour of Love* (2001), *Truth Is Both Spirit and Flesh* (2008), and *Exits and Entries* (2008). She was a featured poet at the 1998 and 2005 Poetry Africa International Festival, and her award-winning poetic radio documentary *Two Halves of the Whole* was aired on British Broadcast World Service Radio (2000). Malika is also a founder-member of the Cape Town–based women writers' collective, WEAVE, and coeditor of their multigenre anthology, *WEAVE's Ink @ Boiling Point: A Selection of 21st Century Black Women's Writing from the Southern Tip of Africa.* Today, Malika works with a variety of women's performing arts groups in Cape Town. She initiated the Word Was Woman Ensemble, which pairs established Cape Town writers with emerging talent, and she scripted the Mothertongue Project's multimedia production *Uhambo!: Pieces of a Dream,* which premiered at the 2004 Grahamstown Festival. In 2009, Malika will launch a national tour of her new play, *Sister Breyani,* which explores the complexity of family ties, in this case sisterhood, even beyond death.

**Excerpts from Our Interviews**

***On the lack of arts education in Coloured schools during the apartheid era:***

When I was young my creativity was seen as a hobby that you couldn't make a career of. There was no school subject that related to art. English was my only source of expression. I was highly frustrated because I realized that there were so-called white schools or private schools that offered drama as a subject and I wanted to study that badly. I knew from an early age that I wanted to perform and that I was an artist. There was also sense of animosity from friends because I wanted to achieve things they didn't believe people like us could achieve. . . . I started to go places that many Coloured people didn't go—like the theatre.

***On her initial inspiration for* A Coloured Place:**

It's something I've avoided—the issue of Coloured people . . . even relating myself to the term *Coloured* has always been a problem for me. Doing this play is a lot like a personal journey. The idea came from having so many . . . South African people asking me, "What are you?" . . . I would assume they would know the apartheid boxes we come from. But . . . there's not one particular face or type of hair or skin that you can say is Coloured or can really define us. Also, if you don't have a typically Coloured accent, it's hard to tell.

I decided to interview Coloured people from all walks of life in terms of age, class, levels of education, gender, etc. in the Durban area. I started with friends and moved on to strangers. . . . I also spoke to people of other racial groups to get their perception of Coloured people.

. . . The aim of the play is to feed and stimulate the questioning about identity and the significance of where we come from and why, as Coloured people, we've never acknowledged our roots. The play says . . . we can define our true identity and be at peace with that. A Coloured place means that there is a rightful place for Coloured people in South Africa; we do belong here, but many lack this sense of belonging. Coloured people were marginalized during apartheid and many believe that they are marginalized in the new South Africa because of policies like affirmative action. The most disadvantaged people and the majority, who are "pure" Africans, are being dealt with first in terms of reconstruction, development, and support, which is as it should be. Coloured people feel low on the waiting list, so there is a kind of bitterness that exists. . . . To acknowledge your Africanness is . . . part of the liberation process. . . . The whole perception that African is inferior, that there is nothing to aspire to, no beauty, no pride, nothing to revere, is an apartheid ideology, an apartheid illusion. These ideas are sadly still prevalent.

*Reflecting a decade after writing* **A Coloured Place:**

For me, the journey has really been about layers and layers of release, . . . of shedding of skin, and of rage and of fear, . . . [of] not fitting in and being accepted. It's really about self-acceptance and me getting more comfortable in my skin. More pride about the fact that I have so much mixed blood in me, and that that is a treasure that I was taught was something to be ashamed of. . . . It was a place of shame and rejection from both sides. . . . More and more, I come to understand that none of this is as simple as black and white—that's what the illusion of apartheid was about.

***The role of theatre in South Africa:***

Healing.

Interviews conducted in June 1995 (Durban), July 1997 (Durban), July 2003 (Cape Town), and July 2006 (Cape Town).

*A Coloured Place* premiered at the 1996 Southern Life Playhouse Company Women's Arts Festival in Durban, with Chantal Snyman and directed by Malika Ndlovu. The play has been performed throughout South Africa to enthusiastic audiences in such cities as Johannesburg and Cape Town.

A Southern Life Playhouse Company commissioned the work for the 1996 Women's Arts Festival.

# A COLOURED PLACE

*Malika Lueen Ndlovu*

I would like to think of this play as an instrument that strikes several chords at once. While it was borne of a very specific site, Kwa Zulu Natal–Durban and in response to a particular South African sociopolitical legacy, it also speaks of human experience at a level that is undoubtedly universal. *A Coloured Place* was written firstly to honour in some small way, those "mixed-therefore-historically-invisible" people who shared my birthplace and then on a national scale, for all those South Africans who inherited the racial classification "Coloured" in its many varied strains. Telling my story interwoven with that of many others through this play was a personal and collective healing process catalysed in 1996, but one that I pray will continue for all who recognize a part of themselves in it.

**Malika Lueen Ndlovu, 2001**

## Introduction

The performance begins with projected images depicting an intimate view of various locations, faces, and aspects of Coloured life in Durban, easily identifiable to the community for and about whom this play is written. Similar projections are interspersed throughout the play and are accompanied by a voice-over that incorporates extracts from interviews, quotes from source material, and improvised dialogue.

## Scenes

1. Born In-Between
2. Rehabilitation
3. Tips on Types
4. Celia in Me
5. When the Cycle Hurts
6. What's New?
7. A Coloured Place

**Cast**

A young Coloured woman

**Setting**

Time: Contemporary life in a Durban Coloured area.
Space: A symbolic set that can be used to represent various domestic interiors.

---

[*In darkness voice-over begins. The Real Ones: a capella rap song.*]

**CHORUS**: Bruinous, hey [×*2*]
The real ones

**VERSE**: We're kicking up the flow

Here we go [×*2*]
It's time to realise
That you're not a Negro
Listen up [×*2*]
Cos you're in for a blast
We're looking to the future
Free your mind from the past

**CHORUS**: Repeat

[*The following voice-over is accompanied by complementary or contrasting projected images.*]

[*Brothers squabbling.*]

**BROTHER 1**: Hey, what kind with you? Lemme alone, I'm not stealing it, how!

**BROTHER 2**: Ma lookit Mario, he's wearing my jacket. [*To Brother 1*] Take it off ha, its mine!

**MOTHER**: Your'll better shuddup before your father wakes up and fists the both of you. The man's working night shift and your'll got no consideration!

**NEWS REPORTER**: In 1972, a young Durban Coloured mother of five, Mrs. Patricia Justien, turned herself into a human torch and burnt herself to death over the Coloured housing shortage in Wentworth. On her deathbed Mrs Justien said she did it "to persuade the authorities to allocate a house for herself and her family in Wentworth."

**CHURCH CONGREGATION SINGING:**
Someone's crying Lord, Khumbaya
Someone's dying Lord, Khumbaya
Someone's praying Lord, Khumbaya
Oh Lord, Khumbaya

**PSYCHOLOGIST:** Lack of finance, power and social usefulness, heightened depression and limited milieu caused tension, frustration, estrangement and even fatalism.

**WEDDING GUESTS:** [*Singing*] For they are jolly good fellows
And so say all of us! Hip Hip . . . Hooray!

**H. F. VERWOERD:** One must distinguish between citizenship of a country and . . . what the components of a homogenous nation are. There is no doubt that the Coloureds are citizens of this country. There is just as little doubt that they are not part of this homogenous entity that can be described as the nation.

[*Young gangsters talking:*]

**GANGSTER 1:** Who, ou Gees? Whaa, dat ou got maaiberd 'cos he schemes he knows a span!

**GANGSTER 2:** Hey, you shoulda checked de ou kakking himself. Dey baamered him de by ou Solly's shop and the Y.T.F.'s were skopping and klapping him. But he kicked down. Dey jaared him into the bushes and ou Vince chooned him: You come back to dis district and we'll fucken steek you, your maader! [*All laugh.*]

**SOCIAL WORKER:** People in the ghetto follow the logic of survival, of doing from moment to moment, in apparently random fashion, whatever gives them the most intense sensation of being alive. This insight might help to explain the senseless gang warfare and vandalism that is so prevalent in the Coloured areas of Durban.

[*Young women talking:*]

**VOICE 1:** Who . . . Ha? He's been after em since school days, phoning my house, following me to the club, sending messages with my brother . . .

**VOICE 2:** Aah shame man, Babs. The poor man's got feelings for you.

**VOICE 1:** Hey, please. Just cos he's got that babyface, doesn't mean he's different. The only feelings men have, are when they're feeling with their fingers! [*Raucous laughter.*]

[*Men talking in bar:*]

**MAN 1**: Hey, my bra chooned me dat his divorce vied through in no time!

**MAN 2**: Ja, but how much did he have to pay and did he get his fair share, or did she vat everything?

**MAN 3**: With a vrou ladat bra, its better to take what you get and chuck. Did I choon your'll about the time ou Nobs vrou caught him in bed with her friend?

[*General responses of disbelief.*]

**MAN 1**: Whaa . . . you vatting me!

**MAN 3**: She fucken through them with boiling water, Ekse. Njannies! He was still tryna get his pants on when she got stuck into the other stekkie.

[*All roar with laughter.*]

**POLITICAL SPEAKER**: As a group the Coloureds have lacked the sentiments of unity, a territorial base and the numbers necessary for a politically effective movement of nationalism.

**OLD WOMAN**: Its like the wind that blew all these particles in different directions. A lot of things that originally united Coloured people have changed.

**TEACHER**: Now class, who can tell me how cross-pollination takes place?

**BOY**: Me Miss, Me!

**GIRL**: Ah but Miss, I had my hand up first.

**WHITE SOCIAL WORKER**: Those Coloureds who had European fathers formed a curious intermediate class between the Europeans and the mass of Coloured people. Very conscious of their kinship with whites they clung pathetically to such European standards as they knew, without having any hope of being admitted to that European society.

**YOUNG WOMAN**: My white auntie isn't proud of me, so why should I be proud of her?

**AFRICAN MAN**: Most of them are proud to be associated with white people, they live very white lives and they have inherited the white man's fears.

**WHITE SOCIAL WORKER**: With ambivalent and conflicting aspirations, the neglect by government of the provision of amenities and the constant reference to the uncertain origins, it is likely that Coloureds can be described as culturally deprived.

**AGGRESSIVE YOUTH**: What you mean? Of cause we got culture. Bruinous have their own style and there's a lot of talent in our communities, especially singing and dancing. Have you been to any of our variety shows ha, ha?!

**TEENAGER**: Who me? No Ha-a, I'm not a big mouth, I like to watch rather.

**PSYCHOLOGIST**: The imposed conviction of inferiority breeds apathy, low morale and a lack of self-confidence.

**ACTOR'S VOICE**: To the majority, Coloured people are just an invisible part of the masses.

*Scene 1*
*Born In-Between*

[*Tracey, a high school student, is seated, engrossed in her preparation of an assignment. She is interrupted by a shout from someone offstage.*]

**TRACEY**: Huh? [*Pause.*] What? . . . Who is it? [*Pause.*] Just take a message. But if it's Shaun tell him . . . tell him I never came home last night. [*Clicks her tongue in irritation*] Shit! I'm never gonna finish this. [*She reads*] Misege—what? [*Refers to dictionary, then reads aloud*] Miscegenation . . . They make it sound like contamination, a flippin' disease!

[*Thinking aloud*] What if God never made Coloured people?

I mean, were there "cocktails," mixed people like us in the beginning? Let's say there were these pure nations and they lived in separate corners of the globe and only after years of exploration, they discovered each other. [*Writing enthusiastically*] Only He [*referring to God*] knew that when these nations met they would start wars over territory, Earth's gold and even the colour of their skin.

[*Talking to herself*] Now that's where we would have come in, God's answer. People who would form the bridge and prove that unity is possible. [*Writing*] We are the overlappers, the people's people, yes, Man's creation! We are different but we are one. All over the world, but especially here and now, Coloured people represent a union . . . a blood-bond. [*Thinking aloud*] Instead we are rejected for not belonging to either clan and then what do we do? Reject ourselves. And our next move?

We start copying someone else's image. Some of us follow the wit ous, clutching any piece of evidence that we've got a great-great grandfather on that side. What about the rest our roots? [*Writing*] We must uncover them and take pride in the richness of our blood.

[*Voice-over continues with projected images.*]

**AFRIKAANS CLERK**: The Population Registration Act (no.30) of 1950 states: a White person is defined as meaning a person who in appearance obviously is or who is generally accepted as a White person, but does not include a person who, although in appearance obviously a White person, is generally accepted as a Coloured person.

**YOUNG GIRL**: Its the whiteness in us that black people can't accept and its the blackness in us that whites can't accept. My mother says in the past we weren't white enough and now we can't get jobs 'cos we not black enough!

**KUGEL**: I think that Coloureds are as much a part of the continent as the Zulu's, the Kenyans or for that matter, the White tribes who call themselves South Africans or Rhodesians.

*Scene 2*
*Rehabilitation*

[*Claudia sifts through a wooden kist full of family relics.*]

**CLAUDIA**: [*Stroking the dark, polished wood*] Recognise this? A kist, somewhere in your granny's house, usually at the foot of the bed with a special doily on top of it. When I was small, it was a box of untouchables. For some it was a young lady's "bottom drawer," where you kept your trousseau and any family treasures that were due to be passed down when you grew to a certain age or when your Gran died and it was time for the relatives to argue over what was rightfully theirs. It looks like a coffin doesn't it. It even opens like one. [*Lifts lid hesitantly*] At six years old my imagination told me that this was where granny kept grandpa's ashes. [*Mock shivers*] Whoo!

[*Imitating mother*] "Its made of solid Embuya wood. It'll be worth quite a fortune oneday, but you wouldn't think of selling it Claudie, would you?"

[*Reassuring*] No Ma, of course not.

[*To audience*] So here it is, just not at the foot of my bed with a doily on top of it!

[*She opens the chest and picks up a gaudy bib-tie.*]

[*Laughing*] Go dad! So he wasn't always such a stiff bastard. Its hard to imagine him stepping out dressed to the nines. He probably wore a polka dot shirt and purple bellbottoms to go with this. Thank God he met my mother. At least she's got some taste. She'd never have allowed him out of the house dressed like that. People used to call her a domineering wife, but she was always trying to put some life into him. His horizon stretched no further than work and home. Oh and soccer on the week-ends. So she stopped including him in her plans. Often she went to the dances, meetings or movies with friends and sometimes on her own.

**CLAUDIA**: [*Imitating grandmother*] That's no way for a married woman to behave! [*Pause.*] And my father? [*Imitating father*] You wanna make a spectacle of yourself, you carry on. Me, I know my place. Your bitch of a mother obviously never taught you that.

[*She rummages in the kist and picks out a pair of thick-heeled shoes and parades across stage.*]

**CLAUDIA**: Ooh, these must have been Aunty Selma's, some real kick-me-deads. They're back in fashion though. [*Imitating Aunty Selma*] These are the "real macoy" Aunty Selma would have said, "No-one will have a pair like these."

[*Her eye falls on a small cloth bundle in the kist. She slowly unwraps it, smelling the cloth tentatively.*]

**CLAUDIA**: I thought you'd almost still be able to smell it. That familiar whiff of burnt hair. [*Lifting an ironcomb from the cloth*] An instrument of torture, if you ask me. One strategic blow and that's it, your brains are on the floor. [*Pause.*]

Actually its an heirloom, carefully preserved and passed down from my great-granny . . . to me I suppose. The thing is I didn't need it. [*Mock Indian accent*] The Indian genes on my father's side blessed me with gladdes, almost stick straight hair. Combined with my dark skin it earned me nicknames like curryguts and chillipip. It also meant that my mother was asked:

[*Imitating inquisitive neighbour*] How come the coolie blood was so strong with her and not with her sister Charlene? Charlene inherited what most people refer to as croes hair, otherwise known as the bushie hair, frizzy hair, peppercorns, a korrelkop, a kroeskop. She had the fair skin and somehow missed out on the hair to match. That's were the ironcomb comes in. The saving grace for Coloured girls before they introduced:

[*Sings jingle*] *Wella . . . perfectly you* [×2]

A pioneer in the world of hair straighteners!

[*Imitating mother, she dramatises brusque combing and plaiting of a child's hair.*] Shame my child. Did God have to give you this unmanageable bush? Dammit! I just wish that you'd inherited your father's hair instead of mine. It would make your life and mine so much easier. At least if you were a boy, you could keep it short and still look decent. Ay, but nevermind. We'll try and see what we can do about these phutu-plaits; maybe even try a new style or something. You're still too young for us to start straightening it. Besides, your scalp is so sensitive. But don't worry, when you're a bit older we'll try some of that children's relaxer. OK?

That's about when the inferiority complex sets in. Charlene was six or seven when hers started to surface. Then there were the jokes about girls with hair that refused to respond to chemical taming.

[*Imitating jeering boys*] "Jarr ekse, even a galeforce wouldn't move that helmet. Real muntu's hair!"

By the end of class two she'd had enough. [*Imitating little Charlene*] "Ah please, Ma. I want my hair to be like Claudie's. It won't cost us anything if we do it at home, Ma. I'm not scared."

[*Demonstrating*] You'd heat the comb by placing it over the hot coals in the fireplace or on a hot plate or primer stove. When it was ready, you'd wipe off any ash or dust, before getting as close to the scalp as bearable for the victim. With each stroke the numerous unwanted kinks per inch where literally ironed out. I can still see her clutching her ears for dear life as my mother approached with the hot comb. Still, she was sick of her middle path and two thick plaits, weighted down at the ends by a pair of blue or white baubles to match her uniform. Her little set of anchors to prevent those plaits from sticking up in the air. More of a ball 'n chain than ball and elastic!

**CLAUDIA**: Without those anchors, Charlene's hair had a mind of its own. Plaits would come undone, or resisting wind and rain, would point to the sky like aerials, mini-antennae from her head. As her hair grew more accustomed to curl-evicting heat and chemicals, its will-to-frizz was conquered. The result? Charlene with a head of hair she could be proud of. With the aid of rollers, blow drying and swirling she was transformed. She conformed. Of course there were endless compliments to reinforce her new self-image.

[*Imitating Aunty Selma*] Oh, your hair came out so nice, you can't even see that it's been done. Who did it for you, Lovie?

[*Imitating mother*] Now you look a bit more like your sister. Just watch, even the boys will start taking more notice of you, you'll see sweetheart.

Now for the rest of her life she'll have to maintain that picture, I thought. No matter how much it costs. As long as she avoids wet and windy weather, she'll never have to fear that her hair's gonna "go home." What a joke! Going home means going back to your roots, your natural state.

The hair can dry out, fall out, break, split, thin out and die. You may even have a don a wig to hide the damage, but as long as it's not croes and you're not completely bald, you'll survive. [*Packing items into kist*] Almost twenty years later, Charlene is beginning the process of rehabilitation. Not only of her hair, but of her being. No more efforts to please family, boyfriends, neighbours who may reject you for not being absorbed into the Coloured crowd. We often speak about it. It's that fear of rejection that cripples you. You get swallowed by what everyone thinks and soon *they* determine what you do, what you wear, where you go and hell, even who you go out with!

I love Charlene's attitude 'cos it's not the typical defensive "So what?"

But rather: "Shame. I understand, you're so afraid of who you are."

And if she's in a good mood she might smile and say: "You should try it sometime. There's nothing wrong with being yourself. It's what makes you unique!"

[*Voice-over continues with projected images.*]

**ENGLISH HISTORIAN**: Cape Coloureds originated from Khoi San, White and Oriental. Natal Coloureds are different in many respects from the bulk of Coloureds in the rest of the country. Their origins can be traced to three groups, Mauritians, St. Helenans and Euro-Africans.

**CAPE COLOURED PERSON**: The term Coloured is not of our own thinking, and if we look at the circumstances of the South African situation then you must ask why. We have no peculiar colour, we have no peculiar language and if other people see these peculiarities, they see them not because they see them . . . but because they want other people to see them . . . I don't want to be labelled Coloured . . . all I want to be known as is South African.

## *Scene 3*
## *Tips on Types*

[*Jennifer enters. She is a drunk Cape Coloured "bergie," a middle-aged woman clutching her shabby jersey to keep out the cold. She is looking for Fransie. Her eyes eventually settle on an audience member; she pounces.*]

**JENNIFER**: Ag Fransie, what am I gonna do with you. Sitting kaalgat opie witman se stoep. Wag jy vir iets? Daa's niemand binne daai huis, so you might as well forget it. Margie's looking out for my things there by the bridge and you know I don't trust her. [*Pause.*] I saved 'n eintjie for you. Hoor jy, Fransie? Daa's nog iets in my borrel, 'n laaste mondvol plesier. Kom jy saam? Kom moegoe, dis laat!

[*Jennifer abruptly changes character, speaking directly to the audience as Samantha, a vibey, smooth-talking teenager.*]

**SAMANTHA**: [*Stripping off "bergie" clothes*] No, I do not stem from a long line of toothless fishermen and grinning flower sellers. I'm no tourist attraction spicing up the beach front. Neither have I or any of my immediate family been to Cape Town for anything other than a holiday and to see the mountain, like everyone else. Afrikaans is not my mother tongue, yet you will be amused as I'm to note that many of us were registered at birth as Cape Coloured, Cape Malay, or swept under the distinguished umbrella . . . Other Coloured.

I am also not the knife-weilding-slang-chooning-dagga-rooking-club-crazy-adolescent-alcoholic-type. I am not the taxi-addict-hanging-out-of-windows-in-peak-traffic-to-let-everyone-being-deafened-by-my-amps-know-and-see-that-I-am-here-and-I-am-loud-and there's-F-all-you-can-do-about-it-type.

Play-white? I couldn't even if I tried. Besides it's far more fashionable these days to be pro-black. And please, I don't mean African as it is, but psuedo-homey-nigger-lingo-baggy-jeans-and-jiving-hands-gangsta-black-into-rap-hardcore-rap-at-that-type.

The female equivalent being the tough-and-sexy-beer-and-cigarettes-who-says-girls-can't-rap-so-dress-me-skimpy-'cos-a-woman's-not-a-woman-with-out-a man-type.

It's obvious that I'm not the nice-and-decent-get-me-to-church-so-I-can-strut-my-fashion-down-the-aisle-to-get communion-oh-so-innocent-marry-the-boy-next-door-with-a-veil-over-my-face-'cos-believe-me-daddy-I'm-still-a-virgin-at twenty-five-type.

My mother is not the babalaas-rollers-in-the-street-swera-my-father-for-her-Friday-nite-blue-eye-and-fat-lip-type. My brothers and sisters and I have never been the sit-on-your-ass-blame-and-complain-it's-our-parents-it's-apartheid-this new government-affirmative-action-welfare-mentality-type.

I fought not to be the abandoned-and-pregnant-at-sixteen-give-up-my-dreams-'cos-your-life's-over-and-education-doesn't-pay-so-I-better-just-get-a-saleslady-job-like-my-aunty-so-me-and-my-child-can-wear-nice-clothes-type.

All types! A frame created specially for you, by someone else . . . an outsider who's opinion matters more than yours or mine. But its not what they see that robs us our identity. We betray ourselves. We play the part. We stick to what we know, malicious when one of us chooses a life beyond those confines. It takes courage to change your point of view and unashamedly do what your gut tells you to do.

[*Voice-over continues with projected images.*]

**WOMAN IN STREET**: Coloured people are only a community in that they generally cling to the same ideas.

**INDIAN MAN**: We must each follow the path we want to, but bruin ous just seem to follow everyone else.

*Scene 4*
*Celia in Me*

[*Zoe pages through her photo album, reminiscing.*]

**ZOE**: I was born where most of Durban's Coloured population was born, Addington hospital. My family shifted about fourteen times before I was ten, but somehow we inevitably settled in a historically Coloured area, even after it was legal to live somewhere else. There were never any public signs saying Coloureds only, but like an unspoken law, you went to a Coloured school, a Coloured church, had mostly Coloured friends, listened to popular Coloured music and followed Coloured fashion . . . or else!

[*Imitating teenage peers.*]

**GIRL 1**: Whehe, that one thinks she shits ice cream. One-two klaps and she'll come right.

**GIRL 2**: Ja, she better watch it, 'cos me I got nancy time for people who think they too clever.

**ZOE**: I grew more determined to make my own choices, be myself and eventually I got used to not fitting in. My Dad built a kind of pedestal for me and through me, my mother saw a dream for herself realised. Being, as my Gran would say, "a Coloured girl with her head screwed on right," was a safe place to be. So I thought. But I was now at that age when losing that "precious gift for your husband oneday" was the warning on my mother's lips and the gossip on the tongues of the neighbours.

[*Imitating neighbours.*]

**WOMAN 1**: I mean, are our schools not good enough for them that they must send their daughter to a white school. Just watch. Just know she'll start "twanging" like a witou and listening to opera music, as if she's got a clue of what's going on! They need to come out down a peg or two, the lot of them.

**WOMAN 2**: You know what it is? It's that mother of hers a real jitterbug, always flitting around. I see her from my kitchen window every Tuesday, dashing off to play tennis in that mini-skirt of hers. Please, at *her* age!

**ZOE**: And then it happened. Yet another Coloured teenager pregnant, straight out of school. The neighbours were delighted.

[*Imitating neighbours.*]

**WOMAN 1**: What I did tell you? Private school and all. At least my daughter's looked after herself. She will be going to Varsity next year. [*Pause.*] Oh. I don't know, but she'll have a degree behind her name when she's finished.

**ZOE**: Everything changed. My gran's praises fizzled. [*Imitating grandmother*] Oh well, my son. She isn't the first and she won't be the last.

While the other granny on hearing the dreaded news, left my mother speechless as she burst into sobs. [*Imitating grandmother*] Hai no, child. Not her too. Such an intelligent girl wasted like that. Ag no, man. What are these children getting up to these days. What did her poor father have to say?

**ZOE**: Not much actually. I thought he'd be the one to blow a fuse, but he didn't. Even before I said it, I sensed that he knew. He curled up on my bed with his head at my feet and said: What is it, my baby? The speech I had spent almost two weeks agonising over, fell out of my mouth in monotone.

"Dad, the worst thing that could ever have happened, has happened. I don't know how else to say it . . . I'm going to have a baby." I had repeated my mother's pattern to the T, pregnant at the same age from a man I never intended to marry. She was furious that all her attempts to keep me from making her mistakes, had failed. I wanted to scream at her too. [*Shouting*] I'm going away, so you won't face the sniggering neighbours and sorrowful relatives! I intentionally had my baby in another city, a distant hospital and as far from a Coloured environment as possible. *I* saw the arrival of my son as a sign for me to change direction. Together we made a new beginning. I went ahead with my career plans, baby at my side.

[*Imitating peer.*]

**GIRL 2**: You going back to study? For what? Whe-ma-me, you've got time.

[*Imitating neighbour.*]

**WOMAN 1**: Ooh, she's definitely missed the boat. Can't wear white at her twenty-first, that's for sure. [*Laughs.*]

**ZOE**: They began to ridicule again and I could feel my old self coming back. I graduated with distinction and my Dad resurrected his pedestal.

My parents broke tradition too, by not forcing me to marry the boy.
Not that I'd wouldn't let them. Oh and about that prize package "for our

husbands oneday," I just remind myself that they're talking about a part of *my* body as if it doesn't belong to me. I guess to let go of an old way of life you have to dare to step outside, choose your own angle. Why the hell not? Nowadays almost everything I do is the breaking of the mould and each time I realise a new part of myself. Coloured is not always what it seems and I'm not what *you* think I am, but what *I* think I am.

[*Zoe speaks as Samantha.*]

You could call me the never-surrender-'cos-it's-not-over-till-the-coloured-girl-spreads-her-wings-type!

[*Voice-over continues with projected images.*]

**PSYCHOLOGIST**: There is a tradition of retraction and at the same time violence has become a symbol of manhood.

**COLOURED SOCIAL WORKER**: Coloured women are survivors. If they can withstand all the verbal, physical and psychological abuse that they do and still wake up in the morning and find something to laugh about, just imagine how much more powerful they would be in the absence of that abuse.

*Scene 5*
*When the Cycle Hurts*

[*Brenda enters in semi-darkness, humming a popular tune. She stumbles and curses, then realises that there is someone in the room. Her mother is not physically present on stage, but Brenda speaks to her as though she is. Her "mother" is seated in a large armchair.*]

**BRENDA**: Mummy? Is that you? What you doing sitting in the dark, Ma why don't you switch the light on? [*She does so and steps back in shock*] Oh fuck, Ma!

[*Long pause. She stares at the couch her mother is seated in.*]

Where is he? [*Pause.*] Gone where? Flippin' coward. Are you OK, Ma? Can I get you something? [*Pause.*]

[*Angry*] I stay out one night and he has to make the most of it! I'm not that stupid child who can't fight back anymore and he knows it. Why didn't you phone me, Ma. You knew where I was. Or even call the bladdy cops for once in your life. Jesus, I'm sick of this.

[*Pause. She sits.*] You know Ma, I could have got that flat with Clarissa and Ashley, but I thought of you alone in this house with him and I said nevermind, I can wait a bit longer till you pull yourself together. I wouldn't have been able to go to bed in peace anyway, wondering what he's doing to you at night. But Ma you can't go on like this forever. I can't. I'm spending my life being your bodyguard and he hasn't stopped hitting you in all these years. What makes you think he'll ever change? He doesn't even need an excuse these days. You just have to look at him sideways and he say's asking for it.

I mean, tell me Ma. What was it this time, the food? Did he go off 'cos of something you said? [*Pause.*] Me? 'Cos you let me go out last night? No, it can't be me. I'm in his good books. I'm not "living in sin" with Ashley and he wanted a teacher or a doctor or a lawyer, so now I'm doing the fuckin' LLB, so he can "broam" about it. I mean, even Bradley's out of his way. Always throwing it in his face that he wasn't his real son, so now he doesn't have one. The dog should be smiling. [*Breaking*] Look at you man, Ma, what are you holding on for? So one day he can hit you so bad that the stitches and ice-blocks won't even help. Is that what you want, Ma? And for what? So he can live? [*Long pause.*] You remember that blue floral dress you had, Ma? You made it, hey. The one with the two pockets in front that you used to dig in for your hanky or some tissues. [*Silence*] Well, I remember it, it used to be your favourite. But you stopped wearing it that day after Aunty Sandra's wedding, remember Ma? The day your blue dress turned red. You know, that's one thing about my father. He never leaves a job till it's finished. Standing there breathing like an ox, with his shoe in your face. He knew we were watching. It was like he was trying to show us a point, but he just made us hate him more. [*Pause.*] Ma, listen to me. We could find a flat together, you and me. I could work some nights in the week instead of only on the weekends and you could start working from home like you're always joking about. You've already got the sewing machine and all those stylish patterns in your head. I mean, look at the outfit you made for my matric ball. No-one could believe that you copied it from a magazine and in no time. Ma, are you listening? Imagine Ma, "Gloria's Garments" or better " G. Designs." You could take orders. Half the neighbourhood already knows how good you are. [*Pleading*] Ma! [*Frustrated*] Ma, don't sit there like a bladdy statue. You could do it Ma, start looking after yourself, instead of slaving in this fucked up house, just waiting for your next hiding. Ma . . . ?

[*Her eyes follow her "mother" crossing the room and exiting the stage.*]

[*Raging*] Ma . . . Ma! For fuck sakes, at least tell me what's wrong with what I'm saying. Please Ma, don't just walk away, I'm serious. I'm prepared to take the chance if you are, he can't touch you!

[*Sound effect of dishes being cleared and washed up offstage.*]

[*Defeated*] What do you think you teaching me, Ma? How to stay faithful to a man, even if it kills me? How to make a dead marriage work, so I won't be a "divorcee" or cause a scandal. "The wife packed up and left her husband, just like that!" At least you stuck it out till the children were old enough and when is "old enough" Ma? You're not going anywhere and Bradley's already following his stepfather's example. Am I supposed to follow yours?!

[*To herself*] Well you are one outstanding example, Ma. A fuckin' classic!

Just like your mother.

[*Voice-over continues with projected images.*]

[*Middle-aged Coloured women talking:*]

**WOMAN 1**: Its always some old white lady or a bladdy Indian winning the jackpot and what about us?

**WOMAN 2**: Ja, hey, people like us don't win lotteries.

**COLOURED HOUSEWIFE**: In the twenty years that I lived in that block of flats, I watched the mother, the children then the grand-children sitting and drinking on that same staircase.

*Scene 6*
*What's New?*

[*Evette is doing a "langarm" dance by herself. As the song ends, she relaxes, pours herself another drink and collapses into a couch. She is a witty and outspoken woman in her mid-forties, who becomes progressively drunk and abrasive through the scene. At times she speaks directly to the audience and then sometimes she seems to be talking to herself.*]

**EVETTE**: You must be wondering what I'm doing here all by myself, like some old cow in a nursing home on New Year's Eve, mind you. He's gone to that stupid party alone this time, 'cos me, I'm not a false person and I'm sick of pulling a mask for those in-laws. His family never took to me in the first place, so it's no skin off my face. Besides, I'm in no mood for the same boring conversations about how big the children have grown and comparing husbands who can cook to husbands who won't. They're a bunch of liars anyway. Everyone knows that Shirley's man is forever getting some young fool pregnant and Pasty acts so shocked, like André's any better. As for poor Merna, she'll get a allergy one of these days, with all that cheap make-up she plasters on to hide her bruises. Oh and let's not forget madam Cookie herself. The party's at her house this year, and I'm sick of hearing her stories about how Jerry bought her this gold ring last year and that gold chain for her birthday and for the tenth time, how he sent her this huge bouquet of flowers when she went into hospital to have her [*gesturing*] "wardrobe" taken out. Dripping in jewellery like a bladdy coolie! Looks like a damn Christmas tree, if you ask me. I doubt she ever asks where that money comes from or thinks how it would feel if it was *her* son buying those drugs from Jerry. Poor Tyrone, that's their son. Imagine what it's like for him, knowing what his father does on the side. Watching his father buy anyone and anything he wants. No bladdy principles, like money's the answer to all your problems. Me? I may be poor, black and ugly but at least when I sit in church, my conscience is clear.

[*Makes the sign of the cross.*] My child knows the difference between right and wrong. He knows that if I catch him hanging around with those button-head cornerboys, I'll klap him, pull his ears in front of them, no matter how big he thinks he is. [*Suddenly overcome with pride*] My boy . . . He just started this nice job my friend's husband organised for him. Every Friday he comes straight home with his pay packet, not even opened yet. After he's paid his board and given me some money towards a carton of cigarettes, a box of wine or something nice for myself, only *then* does he think of himself. I just hope he doesn't let me down now that he's out of school. You know how they get . . . full of big ideas like buying a car and shacking up with that girlfriend of his. Ay, but what can a parent do to stop them. He keeps saying that they're in no hurry to get married, so why must they live together is what I can't understand. [*Panicking*] Maybe she's pregnant and he's too skrik to tell me. Ooh and she's from one of those snotty uppercut families too. They're not exactly rich, but they live in a white area and it'll be a big disgrace, you know what I mean. They'll say it's all his fault and then what'll do?

[*Calming herself*] Anyway I told him not to bring shame to this house, just because his father's not here to put him in his place. You see Barney's not his real father and they never really hit it off, so it's only me listens to.

[*She sighs and takes a long sip of her drink.*] Ooh, it's almost half-past eleven, they must be really making a noise by now. With those people, once they've had a few shots, all that stiffness is out the window. The woman are screeching with laughter, the kids are running amok and the men are babbling about engines and what have you or else they're showing off with their guns. Hmph! No thank you. I'm quite happy having my own private celebration for a change. Anyway Cookie probably wasn't expecting me to show my face at her house after the fight we had. We haven't spoken to each other for . . . must be five months now. I told her off about minding other people's business and you know what she had the nerve to tell me? That I'm forever living in other people's houses and that I don't know when to go home. That's the problem with her type of person. You can't put a mirror in front of them, 'cos they won't like what they see.

I hope Barney remembers to bring my share of the food home, especially my favourite potato salad and Granny Williams must have made her usual delicious trifle. Mmm. The old lady can bake, man! Sponge cake, chocolate cake, koeksisters, biscuits, Christmas pudding, you name it. She makes everything the old way, using the recipes her mother gave her. She refuses to give away her baking secrets. Ja, I suppose she just loves being told that her cakes come out the best and she's bang that one of us will outshine her.

Bladdy old cow! [*She pours herself another drink.*] Now Cookie on the other hand, loves to tell everyone how to cook and it got to the stage where I used to hear her starting to preach and I'd just get up and walk out. I'm not gonna sit there acting polite, while madam tells me how to do better in the kitchen, as if that's the way to improve my marriage! [*Whispering*] Of course *she* knows men inside out and she's not shy to tell you. [*Aside*] That's because she slept with so many of them before she became the faithful housewife that she can't even remember their names! [*Chuckles to herself*] Oh, I better phone Barney to remind him about the food before they start the countdown, 'cos that's all he's gonna have for lunch tomorrow. I refuse to stand and sweat over those pots, when there's only two of us eat it. I don't know what's so special about New Years anyway.

[*She lights a cigarette, dials and waits for someone to answer.*]

Hullo . . . who's that? Oh Tyrone sweetheart, you sound so big over phone. It's Aunty Evette here. Please can you call Uncle Barney for me, lovey. He's wearing a green-and-white stripe T-shirt and denim bermudas. Thank you, boy. I'll hold on. [*To audience*] Just like I said, a bladdy madhouse. Oh and Merna's smoking too much, sounds like a dog barking. They probably had a good scandal about me already. No-one will stand up for me too, except Pasty maybe. She's the only one I can tolerate from that whole Williams clan.

[*She is interrupted.*] Barney, is that you? Here! You sound like you drank a whole case by yourself. But listen, I'm phoning about the breyani, don't forget to bring me some. [*Pause.*] You can put it in my Tupperware that I sent the beans salad in. And bring some meat and potato salad too . . . What you mean you can't hear me? Since when do your ears get blocked just 'cos your tongue is thick? [*Raising her voice*] I said don't for . . . Oh, so now you heard me. Just bring back my bladdy bowls; I know how those sisters of yours are forever snatching other people's Tupperware by mistake. OK? [*Pause.*] I'm watching

TV, so if I fall asleep in the lounge don't disturb me when you come in. Ja, and let someone sober drive you home, alright? OK. Bye. [*Abruptly replaces receiver and pours herself another drink.*]

[*To audience*] . . . As was saying . . . this thing about New Year. What exactly are we celebrating? I'm not getting any younger and this place hasn't gotten any better. The bladdy kids are growing up too fast. It's all that American trash they listen to, blasting a person's eardrums in the taxis. If the girls are not pregnant, then it's the boys stabbing each other or trying to drink themselves to death. It was exactly the same when I was young. Only that time you were forced to marry the boy who spoiled you and the gangsters were much more sophisticated and organised. Not like these goofballs we have today. Lucky for me, my parents were a bit strict. If it wasn't for my mother forcing me to go to church and my father checking up on my friends, I might have ended up a whoring alcohol like Tessa down the road. Tessa the "town mattress."

"There's a screw just waiting for you."

[*She notices the countdown on TV, quickly turns the volume up and tops up her drink.*]

Oh, just listen to me selling my mouth for-a-win-and-a-place.

I nearly missed it. [*She raises her glass motioning for the audience to join in.*]

Five . . . four . . . three . . . two . . . one? What the hell, Happy New Year!

[*Fade to black as she dances alone.*]

### *Scene 7*
### *A Coloured Place*

[*An older Tracey randomly covers areas of the set with white sheets, to signify the closing of each character's story.*]

**TRACEY**: Even before my granny died, our family used to joke about how we'd have to hire a stadium and the whole Mayville bus service, to cart all the people who'd insist on being at her funeral. Each with their own story of why they came from hell-and-gone to pay their respects, to this one unforgettable woman. [*Pause.*] Yesterday the rain didn't stop them. Those who couldn't fit into the church stood outside with umbrellas. Others sat closeby in parked cars, behind streaming windows, waiting for the procession to Stellawood cemetery. I don't know if it was all the crying last night or just the presence of all these people, but as my eyes glazed over the large bouquets, the front pews packed with relatives and close family friends, it all seemed unreal. The faces and flowers blending, my tears and the numbing rhythm of the rain gainst the church building. How long will it take them to forget her? Will her story be kept alive, after the sensation of this massive turnout and the drama of my grieving relatives becomes stale news? So many like my grandmother have their place in our history but there is no local museum or library that tells these stories. How can someone whose life meant so much, someone so big, be so invisible? This place she called home, the history of it that only she remembered, will die too. When our children look back, searching for where their stories began, will they turn and find this same emptiness? If our stories are left untold, our triumphs unheard of, our faces and voices unrecognised, there will be a hollow place where our pride should be. Our histories form the map that can lead these children to a coloured place, not rotting with division or inertia, but a coloured place of power and diversity that they will not be ashamed to call . . . home.

[*Voice-over continues with projected images.*]

**INDIAN MAN**: I think of Coloureds as outspoken people, down-to-earth.

**COLOURED MAN**: A Coloured person does not believe that he can invent anything. He can only watch, take, copy and buy, because he cannot see himself as a creator. With me, with everything I touch I ask myself—hey, why can't I do that?

**ELDERLY COLOURED WOMAN**: Our Coloured youth are far too Americanised, but what we see on TV is not reality. Americans are selling us their garbage and we're buying it!

**ACTOR'S VOICE**: The future of Coloured people lies in the hands of each Coloured individual. It's the universal question of choice.

**TEENAGER**: The term Coloured is something for other people to identify me by.

**YOUNG WHITE WOMAN**: I think Coloured people are beautiful and as soon as they can realise it, the sooner they can make the world around them beautiful. You know, spread that beauty.

**COLOURED WOMAN**: I've always thought that having mixed blood in my veins makes me an interesting person.

**TEENAGER**: Coloured is a piece of art, the meeting of extremes.

**INDIAN MAN**: To me, Coloured women are the most beautiful women in South Africa.

**YOUNG COLOURED GIRL**: If you can be at peace with yourself then you can promote peace in your community.

**ACTOR'S VOICE:** May the new year bring into our minds and souls an awareness that we are our own bondsmen and by our endeavours free ourselves. And in this awareness we will find the beginning of the thread of oppression and subjugation, which permeates the entire fabric of our being. And finding it is not enough. We must eradicate and destroy it, first in our souls and then, wherever else it may manifest itself.

[*Projection fades to black as voice-over ends.*]

## Glossary

**Bruinous:** (Afrikaans slang) literally meaning "brown guys," referring to Coloured people. Term most frequently used by people in Durban or KwaZulu-Natal province, in contrast with terms like *kleurling* or *chlora* in the Western Cape region where the largest Coloured population exists.
**Chooned:** (slang) scolded.
**Coolie:** derogative term for Indian person.
**Dagga-rooking:** marijuana smoking.
**Gladded:** (Afrikaans derivative of *glad,* meaning "smooth") straight or sleek hair.
**Jennifer:** Ag Fransie, what am I gonna do with you. Sitting kaalgat opie witman se stoep. Wag jy vir iets? Daa's niemand binne daai huis, so you might as well forget it. Margie's looking out for my things there by the bridge and you know I don't trust her. [Pause.] I saved 'n eintjie for you. Hoor jy, Fransie? Daa's nog iets in my borrel, 'n laaste mondvol plesier. Kom jy saam? Kom moegoe, dis laat!
**Jennifer:** (rough translation) Oh Fransie, what am I going to with you. Sitting naked on the step of the white man's door. Are you waiting for something? There's no one inside that house, so you might as well forget it. . . . [Pause.] I saved a cigarette butt for you. Do you hear, Fransie? There's still something in my bottle, a last mouthful of pleasure. Are you coming with me? Come on idiot, its late!"
**Kakking:** (Afrikaans derivative of the word *kak*) shitting.
**Lang arm:** (Afrikaans, literally meaning "long arm") a style of ballroom dancing, particularly popular among older generations of Coloured people; Coloured people also nationally recognised by others as having natural talent in this dance.
**Maader:** (corruption of Tamil swearword) insult equivalent to "you mother's . . ."
**Maaibered:** (lang) beaten up.

**Njannies!:** (slang derivative of Isizulu expression *Inyaniso Ngempela!*) "For real!"
**Steek:** (Afrikaans) stab or poke.
**Stekkie:** (slang derivative of Afrikaans word *stukkie,* meaning "a piece") derogative yet popular term for a girl/friend.
**Vatting:** (Afrikaans derivative of the word *vat*) kidding, to take for a fool.
**Vrou ladat bra:** (colloquial speech) "With a wife like that . . ."

*Pause.*

# EDEWEDE (THE DAWN OF A NEW DAY)

*Julie Okoh*

Edewede means: "The Dawn of a New Day." I am telling those who firmly believe that circumcision is a part of their culture that must be adhered to, that no culture is static. Every culture changes according to time.

**Julie Okoh, Nigeria**

A member of southern Nigeria's Edo tribe, Juliana Okoh was born in 1947 into a family of fiction writers. As a young girl, she wrote poems and short stories but later turned exclusively to drama, studying with Ola Rotimi, the renowned Nigerian playwright. She received her BA in French and English from Chicago's Loyola University, her MA in French literature from the University of Alberta, and her PhD in African and Caribbean theatre from the University of Bordeaux III in France.

Juliana is the author of more than a dozen plays. Her published works include *Mask* (1988), *The Mannequins* (1996), *Edewede* (2000), *In the Fullness of Time* (2000), *Who Can Fight the Gods?* (2002), and *Aisha* (2005). Unpublished plays include *Austerity* (1984), *Mary, Model for All Women* (1996), *In Search for Jesus* (1998), and *The Nativity* (1999). She has also written numerous articles and critical essays on various artistic and sociopolitical issues. Juliana teaches theatre history and playwriting at Nigeria's University of Port Harcourt. She also directs.

### Excerpts from Our Interview

*Why she chose to write plays:*

The majority of Nigerians are illiterates. Even many of those who are literate do not . . . read. Thus theatre performance . . . is the more appropriate and more effective medium for reaching my target audience.

*On her choice of subject matter:*

As an educator and social activist . . . I want to be a part of the ongoing global struggle against . . . gender discrimination. . . . My artistic work serves . . . as a platform to express my response to oppression, injustice, and violence against women . . . in my sociocultural environment. By naming, describing, analyzing, clarifying, and contesting issues relating to women's subjugation and oppression, my work assumes the role of conscientization [*sic*]. By proposing solutions to [these] issues . . . my theatre work aims to encourage . . . my audience and reader to take positive action that will eventually bring about attitudinal transformation in society. For this reason, vivacious, courageous, intelligent, and progressive women—intended to serve as role models—generally populate my plays.

*On female circumcision:*

It is in line with the above mission that I wrote the play *Edewede,* which deals with the problem of female circumcision. . . . Contesting the validity of the practice in contemporary African societies, the sociocultural myths surrounding the practice are analyzed and debunked on one hand, and, on the other, some of the adverse effects of the operation on women's physical health and psyche are explained.

The idea . . . came to me one day in 1991 in . . . France as I was watching a televised debate between the French West African immigrants living around Paris and the French institution, made up of lawyers, psychologists, medical doctors, etc. A woman named Soko Aramata Keita was accused of having circumcised some girls from Mali and Senegal who were now living around Paris. One of them hemorrhaged to death. When interrogated, the woman and some of the African immigrants pleaded not guilty [to] any crime, claiming that they were acting according to the dictates of their indigenous culture. So after listening to the debate, I started to ask myself questions about culture.

. . . Where I come from, the practice of circumcision has long faded away. So I decided to write *In the Fullness of Time,* which deals with culture and change. Female circumcision is one of the issues discussed in that play. But it is built on metaphors, allusions, associations, etc. Halfway into writing it, I felt it would be very difficult for the native people to understand. So I left it for a while to write *Edewede,* which is situated in a village environment and simple enough for everyone to understand.

*While writing* Edewede, *Juliana interviewed several African women who still practiced circumcision:*

Some of them saw it as a mark of cultural identity, a rite of passage, or . . . to receive favor from the goddess of fertility. For others it was for hygienic purposes; for example, to prevent body odor. However, the main reason given by the majority of the people is that female genital mutilation (FGM) prevents women from having sexual desires.

*On the problems West African playwrights face:*

There are many female playwrights in West Africa, including Nigeria, but they are hardly known outside their immediate environment because their plays are neither published nor publicized. It is very difficult to publish plays in Nigeria due to lack of funds. Novels have a better chance and also have a larger market. For example, . . . when my play *Mask* was performed, many people advised me to have it published for schools and colleges [to perform]. I showed it to some publishers. . . . Their response was always the same. They would like to publish the play but I would have to foot the bill. . . . All my published plays so far are self-sponsored.

The same thing applies to the production of the plays. The building of sets, props, the hiring of lighting equipment, the making or hiring of costumes are self-sponsored. But I usually use students, so there is no pay involved except to provide them snacks during rehearsals and . . . their transport. . . . At the end of the show, we are entitled to just 30 percent of the gate fees irrespective of the production cost. It is a complicated issue.

I love theatre. I love to see my creations gain full life on stage. That is my reward. If I neither produce nor publish my plays, how would the public hear my voice?

Interview at Smith College in Northampton, Massachusetts, June 30, 2001.

**Production History**

Codirected by Julie Okoh and Friday Nwafor, *Edewede* premiered at the University of Port Harcourt Arts Theatre in August 1998. In 1999, it received a command performance at the university's convocation ceremony. Since then, the play has been performed in several universities across Nigeria.

## EDEWEDE (THE DAWN OF A NEW DAY)

*Julie Okoh*

*Dedicated to all the EDEWEDES in Africa.*
*Cultural practices are resistant to change.*
*But culture is never static but dynamic.*
*May you ever remain dauntless.*
*In your pursuit of freedom*
*From nefarious cultural*
*practices and traditions*
*For the African woman!*

**Characters**

Edewede (Wede): A housewife
Mother: Her mother
Ordia (Ordy): Wede's husband
Izenebu (Ize): 11 years, their first daughter appears in the flashback scene
Oseme: 12 years, their second daughter
Ejimien: Her friend, also appears as young Wede in the flashback scene
Ebikere: Ordia's mother
Adawan: His paternal uncle
Eriala (Mama-Nurse): A midwife, owns a maternity home
Ebungbe (Ebun): Wede's friend
Iriata: Ebungbe husband
The Seer
The King
The Village Matron
Her Assistant
First, Second, Third, and Fourth Market Women
First, Second, Third, and Fourth Elders
Some Young Girls (to dance the choral parts)
Some Old Women (to perform the ritual parts)
The Town Crier

A Masquerade
Its Attendant
The Crowd
A Band of Drummers

The play *Edewede* was first performed on August 25, 1998, in the University of Port-Harcourt Arts Theatre

**Theme Song**

| | |
|---|---|
| Aie ze n'oria | No one chooses for another |
| *Oria to bo'ze* | *One chooses for oneself* |
| *Aie ze no oria* | *No one chooses for another* |
| *Oria to bole ze* | *One chooses for oneself* |
| *Enó khole mhen tale* | *My personal convictions* |
| *Ole iyiarekhan* | *Shall dictate my course of action* |
| *Aie ze no oria* | *No one chooses for another* |
| *Oria to bole ze* | *One chooses for oneself.* |

## DRAMA I: CRISIS

[*The action takes place in a remote village, in a hilly area of Otoedo land, that old Mid-Western part of Nigeria comprising the Edos, Urhobos, Ikas, Kwale, and the Ijaws.*

*One early morning, the cock crows, followed by the singing of the birds, all suggesting light chasing away darkness. Next comes the sound of chickens, goats, and dogs denoting a village setting. Some wooden chairs and stools are strategically placed in front of Mr. Ighalo's house, which is, at first, barely visible under the milky morning dew.*

*Humming the Theme Song, Oseme sweeps the floor from inside the house to outside. Suddenly, she starts up, looks right and left, sees nothing, resumes sweeping. Ebikere's voice is heard from afar.*]

**EBIKERE**: Get out of my way, you stubborn goat. You almost made me fall down this early morning.

**OSEME**: [*Stretches her neck to see who is coming along the path*] That sounds like my grandmother's voice. [*She falls on her two knees as soon as Ebikere appears.*] Good morning, Nene.

**EBIKERE**: My beloved grandchild!
She who knows to warm the heart of an old widow!
She who knows when my drinking pot needs fresh water!
She who knows when my fireplace needs fresh wood!

She who knows when my hut needs scrubbing and fresh coating!
May you be blessed abundantly!
May you live long enough to harvest
All the joys of womanhood!

**OSEME**: Ise! Nene, Ise!

**EBIKERE**: Are your parents within the compound?

**OSEME**: My father left yesterday for the cocoa market. He is not expected back till two days. My mother was not feeling well last night. She left very early this morning for town.

**EBIKERE**: To see that her "dokita" friend, I guess?

**OSEME**: Yes, she has gone to see Mama-Nurse. I am sure she is already on her way back, by now.

**EBIKERE**: And here you are all alone. We pray that the gods bless this house, one day, very soon, with the cry of a newly born baby boy!

**OSEME**: Ise! Amen!

**EBIKERE**: How is my favourite grandchild doing today?

**OSEME**: [*Showing off herself*] See for yourself.

**EBIKERE**: I can see you are growing every day into a very beautiful young woman. Ehenh! Come, I have something to discuss with you.

**OSEME**: Something like what?

**EBIKERE**: Don't be too curious. First of all, let us have a seat. [*Oseme sits on her laps.*] My daughter, as you can see I am getting very old. Do you know what will really make me happy?

**OSEME**: What is it, Nene?

**EBIKERE**: Your marriage. Although your father hasn't discussed it with me yet, I know that many eyes are already on you. Very soon, you will be the happiest woman in this village. Ehenh! That reminds me. The initiation ceremonies are about to begin. You must not miss them this time.

**OSEME**: [*Moving away from her, reproachfully*] Grandmother!

**EBIKERE**: Why did you call me like that? Have I said anything bad?

**OSEME**: Have you forgotten Ize so soon?

**EBIKERE**: How can I forget my own granddaughter? May she rest peacefully at the bosom of our ancestors!

**OSEME**: She was very sick before she died a few years ago.

**EBIKERE**: I remember that very well.

**OSEME**: I don't want to die like her, Nene.

**EBIKERE**: May our ancestors protect you!

**OSEME**: May you too protect me from circumcision!

**EBIKERE**: I can not do that, my child.

**OSEME**: Why can you not, Nene?

**EBIKERE**: Circumcision is part of our culture. My mother was circumcised. So also were her grandmothers, great grandmothers and great, great, great grandmothers. It is a rite that every woman in this land goes through.

**OSEME**: Why?

**EBIKERE**: Well. Well . . . , well . . . , em . . . em . . . Oh yes! It's part of the initiation rituals. Yes, yes. The initiation ceremony is an occasion that every young girl looks forward to in this land of ours. Oh! I can still remember how it went in my days. On the night of departure, we hardly slept. Anxiously, we waited for dawn to show its face. Then the clarion call was heard at the first crow of the cock. Young maidens assembled at the market place for the onward journey to the camp. On the way we sang:

**Departure Song**

| | |
|---|---|
| *Imhan rie egbo* | *We are going into the forest* |
| *Imhan rie* egbo | *We are going into the forest* |
| *Imhan khia do so odoni-Oh* | *We are going to touch over there* |
| *Imhan rie egbo* | *We are going into the forest* |

We spent seven days in the camp. Each day had its special activities. We ate, sang and danced. Then the day of circumcision came to spoil it all. [*Simultaneous miming of the events described. Alternatively, the director may choose the narrative technique.*] The matron and her assistant arrived. We filed in one by one to lie down on a carpet of leaves and palm fronds, before them. The assistant helped to hold our legs apart and the operation was performed. Rising from the ground each girl intoned a song of valour. The others responded hailing her courage [songs]. You will be brave my grandchild. Yes, you will be brave. Your bravery in the camp of circumcision will be the pride of your family and lineage. You are from a family of a brave warrior. Ah! The descendant of Edokparu, the Ogbomhagbesin, revered far and wide in Otoedo land for his military prowess. Oh yes, you will be brave.

**OSEME**: But Nene, I am afraid. Any time I think about circumcision my heart beats Pomp! Pomp! Pomp!

**EBIKERE**: There is nothing to be afraid of. Circumcision is a thing of joy. Ah! Look! The homecoming day is the most interesting of all. [*Simultaneous miming resumes.*] As soon as the girls approach the village, drumbeats rend the air. The whole village is agog with excitement. Friends and relatives rush forward to welcome the girls at the entrance of the village. Drumming and singing increase. Then, beautiful girls gorgeously dressed in intricately worked necklace, their body adorned with multicoloured designs of clay, come into the village singing:

**Home Coming Song**

| | |
|---|---|
| *Esin gono gono* | *The meandering horse* |
| *Dughere, Eh dughere* | *Has come to the arena* |
| *Obhiye mhen nusunnobu* | *Brethren far and near* |
| *Noi tua khian-oh* | *Come and see who* |
| *Eh dughere* | *Has come to the arena* |

[*The villagers respond singing and dancing:*]

| Leader | Chorus |
|---|---|
| *Bhokhi* | *Onyiomhen non* |
| *Bhokhi* | *Onyiomhen non* |
| *Onyiomhen egbedan* | *Onyiomhen non* |
| *Onyiomhen odo* | *Onyiomhen non* |
| *Onyiomhen omo* | *Onyiomhen non* |
| *Onyiomhen igho* | *Onyiomhen non* |
| *Onyiomhen afe* | *Onyiomhen non* |
| *Bhokhi* | *Onyiomhen non* |
| *Bhokhi* | *Onyiomhen non* |
| *What is it?* | *It is joy* |
| *What is it?* | *It is joy* |
| *Joy of good health?* | *It is joy* |
| *Joy of marriage?* | *It is joy* |
| *Joy of children?* | *It is joy* |
| *Joy of money?* | *It is joy* |
| *Joy of wealth?* | *It is joy* |
| *What is it?* | *It is joy* |
| *What is it?* | *It is joy* |

The procession is led from there to the Market Place by the old women of the village, followed by the crowd, then the girls. The village matron and her assistants come last. The former holds a white fowl. At the Market Place, after making some incantations, with a sharp knife, the matron severs the head from the fowl, throws it up into the air, the blood spurting to every direction. Avoiding the blood, the crowd disperses. The matron picks up the head of the fowl to bury at the Market Shrine. Thus all the evil spirits are interred with the chicken head. [*Mime stops.*] My daughter, you will see what I will do for you on that day. I have been keeping my best jewellery for the occasion. I will sing and dance as I have never danced before. Dance for the daughter of my only son, that has always been my dream. Yes, even though my legs are no longer as strong as they used to be, still, I will dance for you, my dear. I will dance and dance.

**OSEME**: Nene!

**EBIKERE**: Yes.

**OSEME**: Isn't it possible to sing, dance and feast during the initiation ceremonies without the circumcision?

**EBIKERE**: Oh no! My child, happiness and sorrow go hand in hand like day and night. That is the pattern of life itself.

**OSEME**: I know, but I still can't see how circumcision and initiation are connected.

**EBIKERE**: Both of them are landmarks in the life of a woman. The initiation ceremonies are the period of transition from girlhood to womanhood. My child, listen very carefully. The peanut is very delicate. It is the source of confusion, impurity and imperfection. [*Edewede arrives, listens unnoticed.*] So during the initiation ceremony, it is carved out of its pod. And the girls are taught about the taboos of our land. They are fortified for their future roles of wives and mothers.

**EDEWEDE**: What about those girls who do not return to the village and are never even mourned, after bleeding to death? Regarded as sacrifice, they are left behind for the vultures to feed on. Tell her also about those girls who do not live long enough to see the days of their marriage and motherhood because of the infection contacted during the operation. Go on; tell her about all of them.

**EBIKERE**: [*To Oseme*] My child, go inside the house. Your mother is about to let loose her evil tongue again.

**EDEWEDE**: Stay there! This is for your benefit as well. Mother-in-law, please sit down. Let us discuss woman to woman, the three of us.

**EBIKERE**: Me discuss with you?

**EDEWEDE**: Yes, Mother-in-law. Let us discuss circumcision. To be frank, I too want to know everything about it. Kindly educate us on the subject.

**EBIKERE**: This is early morning. No one starts the day by raving, not even a mad person. So, subject closed.

**EDEWEDE**: This is your granddaughter. She needs to know about these things from you.

**EBIKERE**: She has already known all she needs to know from me. The others she will discover by herself later.

**EDEWEDE**: You are dodging the issue.

**EBIKERE**: You are misleading her with your blab-blab talk. No wonder she is afraid of circumcision! My grandchild, do not listen to her vile tongue. Circumcision is a thing of joy, prestige and cultural identity.

**EDEWEDE**: When those who know no disaster hear weeping, they think it is a song. Circumcision has brought tears to my eyes many times. So I know exactly what I am telling her about it.

**EBIKERE**: A young person can have fine clothes like an elder, but she can never have rags like an elder. So, what do you know about circumcision that I do not know?

**EDEWEDE**: I know that it is a destroyer. It killed my daughter, Ize.

**EBIKERE**: I have been watching you because of her. Oseme should have been circumcised by now. The nuts are already out on her chest.

**EDEWEDE**: Oseme will never be circumcised, even when she is on a third foot. [*To Oseme*] Go inside the house.

**EBIKERE**: I see! Each year, you give one excuse or another to prevent her from going to the camp with the other girls. Now I understand your plan. All right, we shall see. Oseme must be circumcised this year unfailingly.

**EDEWEDE**: Please, go to your home. Go and take care of your other grandchildren. That child is mine, "Osemera."

**EBIKERE**: Listen to her. [*Mimicking her*] "That child is mine, Osemera." Since when have women started to claim children as theirs in this village? If you want to become a man, why don't you first of all grow a tail between your thighs? Go on and do it. Let's see.

**EDEWEDE**: I have said what I have to say on the issue.

**EBIKERE**: Who are you to say anything on any issue in this house? You are going too far! You can not throw sand on our traditions like that. I warn you. She, who gathers a bundle of troubles, carries it on her head.

**EDEWEDE**: You can not put fear into me.

**EBIKERE**: Continue to wag your foul tongue. One day, one day, the child who boasts she can recognize in the market place the faces of her mother's goat shall be made to identify the ancestral spirit behind the masquerade.

**EDEWEDE**: Let that day come.

**EBIKERE**: Spoilt child, your mother should be very proud of her handiwork.

**EDEWEDE**: Leave my mother out of it. This problem is between you and me and not between you and my roots.

**EBIKERE**: You have always been headstrong. Too stubborn! Humility means nothing to you. A well brought up woman should know her place and respect her limits. But you, oh no! You want to be in every place, have a word on every issue. You don't even know that you are only a wife in this house. And as such, your place is in the kitchen.

**EDEWEDE**: I have played that role for many years. Then, I was too afraid to say or do anything. Afraid of what people would say. Afraid of what people would do. Afraid, so much so that I found myself always doing what others wanted and never what I wanted. One day, I realized that I was merely an object, used by others. Then I said to myself "Edewede! You are a human being. You must kill that fear in you. Kill it!" Mother-in-law, I have killed that fear implanted in me from childhood. Now, I take my destiny in my hands. I speak on issues that concern me. And I follow my own advice. Nobody, I repeat, nobody can intimidate me again, not even you. Understand?

**EBIKERE**: [*With self-pity*] "Oyia-oh!" Oh, Ebikere of the luckless soul! See how life is treating you. Your son's wife talking to you anyhow. [*To Wede*] Do I blame you? It is my son that gave you the mouth to address me like that. You tell a child that vulture is not edible, he insists on eating it. I showed him many other girls, he insisted on marrying you. This is what I get.

**EDEWEDE**: A rat in the bush is more venerated than the one inside the house. What qualities do those girls have that I don't have?

**EBIKERE**: No doubt, you have very many qualities. See what they have done to my son. The child that I raised to be a man is now a woman.

**EDEWEDE**: He is a man. A man who understands that a woman is not just an object to carry out commands, but a human being with feelings and emotions.

**EBIKERE**: How many men in this village treat their wives like he does? Others in his place would have since married another woman. His homestead is empty, yet he calls you: "My wife!" "My wife!" Go away! Barren woman!

**EDEWEDE**: Barren! Haven't I confirmed my fertility? [*Pointing a finger at Oseme*] That child is the fruit of my womb. What other proof do you need?

**EBIKERE**: Having only one issue is like having none at all. And a girl too. [*Hissing*] Chiew! Nonsense!

**EDEWEDE**: I have had male issues. My first son, Itoya was bitten to death by a snake in your rubber plantation. Six years ago, I had another baby boy. He cried. Mama, I heard him cry. But nobody came to his rescue. They said he was an evil child, for he wore the cord around his neck like a necklace. I would have died too, while waiting for the medicine man to come and separate him from me. But God saved me.

**EBIKERE**: It is your stubbornness that was undoing you. "Evil begets evil," said the oracle.

**EDEWEDE**: Away with superstitions! The priests merely make you believe whatever they want you to believe. My son would have survived if only that cord was removed from his neck in time.

**EBIKERE**: What? Touch an evil child! "*Awah!*" Forbidden!

**EDEWEDE**: Ignorance is worse than any disease. My child was normal like any other child. Mama-Nurse explained it all to me.

**EBIKERE**: That is the woman who has been misleading you. Every day, Mama-Nurse said this. Mama-Nurse said that. One two, you run to consult her like an oracle.

**EDEWEDE**: She is my light, my oracle!

**EBIKERE**: She is your doom. One day, you will end up like her, a woman without a husband, a whore!

**EDEWEDE**: She has a husband.

**EBIKERE**: Why is she living out there, all alone by herself?

**EDEWEDE**: Her husband is from a tribe far, far away. He was the District Officer in charge of this region so many years ago. One day, he was touring the rural area under his care when he saw her. He paid bride price on her and married her according to customs. He sent her to school in the city. He has seven children by her: four boys and three girls. When he got his pension, they returned to his village. Then, her troubles began: her co-wives wouldn't let her know any peace. So, she decided to return home. He comes to visit her from time to time.

**EBIKERE**: You call that marriage? Part-time marriage!

**EDEWEDE**: In this village, there are many women living in the same compound with their husbands, yet for months and months, they do not see their husbands' loin cloth. Mama-Nurse has her husband's full attention whenever he visits.

**EBIKERE**: And when he is not visiting?

**EDEWEDE**: She devotes herself to her work. Many women have gained from that, Ebungbe for example. In fact, infant mortality is now rare in this land because of her.

**EBIKERE**: If her medicine was that reliable, why couldn't she save your daughter, Ize?

**EDEWEDE**: I got to her too late. At first, I was afraid of you. But none of the medicine men you were bringing could help my daughter. That evening, I saw how you and the medicine man from across the river were speaking in low voices. He shook his head and I knew my daughter's case was beyond his power. So, I took the risk. But it was too late.

**EBIKERE**: It was her destiny. That is what the oracle said.

**EDEWEDE**: Enough of your oracle! Any time anybody is sick, we kill fowls, we pour libation, we spray white chalk powder everywhere to chase away evil spirits, because that is what the oracle says. Yet every day, our children die in great number. Each time, the oracle pushes the cause on human maliciousness. But, Mama-Nurse can explain the cause of the deaths in this village. And she can cure many diseases.

**EBIKERE**: Why hasn't she cured the disease in your belly? For seven years now, my son's blood only fattens your buttock and not your belly.

**EDEWEDE**: Babies are not mushrooms that one goes to pick and drop into a pot of soup. Tell your son to cut down on his travels. Today to this market, tomorrow to that market, buying cocoa and rubber sheets from villagers to sell to exporters. How can a baby come like that? There is nothing wrong with my womb. Mama-Nurse said so and I am hopeful.

**EBIKERE**: Okay oh? Stay here and be hopeful: "Mama-Nurse said this, Mama-Nurse said that." I have heard enough about that woman. Let me go and listen to what my fellow village women have to say. They too have their own knowledge and wisdom.

**EDEWEDE**: Please, go to them, quickly.

**EBIKERE**: Are you driving me out of my son's house?

**EDEWEDE**: You said you were leaving. So, go at once.

**EBIKERE**: Stubborn goat! If you don't learn to control that foul tongue of yours, your legs will be swept out of this house, one day. Bet me. [*Walks out of the compound furiously.*]

**EDEWEDE**: Goodbye mother-in-law!

[*Fade out*]

## DRAMA II: IN SEARCH FOR A SOLUTION

[*Same place, few days later. Ordia is at dinner. Edewede serves him with tenderness.*]

**EDEWEDE**: [*Bringing a bowl of soup*] Here it is. Have some more. It is your favourite soup.

**ORDIA**: I like it very much. That is why I ate so much. Look at my stomach. It is bulging out like that of a pregnant woman.

**EDEWEDE**: Don't exaggerate. You have not eaten very much.

**ORDIA**: Where did you find the vegetable at this time of the year?

**EDEWEDE**: Far, far away in the mountains. I spotted them growing here and there around a brook some time ago. This morning, I said to myself, "When you are away, I do not know what you feed on. Now that you are here, I must make sure you feed well." Have some more, my husband.

**ORDIA**: Thanks for caring. That is one of the reasons I married you. You always care about other people's well-being.

**EDEWEDE**: What are the other reasons?

**ORDIA**: Ehenh! You don't praise a woman; or else her head begins to swell up with pride.

**EDEWEDE**: Please, tell me. I want to hear about my other qualities.

**ORDIA**: You don't give up, stubborn goat.

**EDEWEDE**: [*Sulkily*] Ah! That is unfair. I am not a goat.

**ORDIA**: But you are stubborn. [*Pause.*] Come on, cheer up. I have really had enough. You can keep the remaining soup for another time.

**EDEWEDE**: [*Genuflecting*] "*Alemhengbe*" May the food nourish your body!

**ORDIA**: "*Agboleakhor*" May tomorrow bring some more. [*She carries up for him a bowl of water to wash his hands, after which he rubs them on his legs to dry, saying*:] Whatever one eats must be seen on the body. [*Wede gathers the remaining dish, goes to the kitchen. Ordia picks his teeth. Calls*:] Wede!

**EDEWEDE**: I'll be right there. [*After a moment, she appears.*] At your service my husband.

**ORDIA**: Have a seat. [*She sits. He clears his throat.*] What is this I heard about you, Wede?

**EDEWEDE**: [*A bit aghast*] What did you hear about me, Ordy?

**ORDIA**: I stopped by my mother's house this morning.

**EDEWEDE**: Oh, you did!

**ORDIA**: Yes, I did.

**EDEWEDE**: What did she say this time?

**ORDIA**: That you are causing trouble in the village.

**EDEWEDE**: She actually told you that?

**ORDIA**: Something like that. Is it true?

**EDEWEDE**: My husband, I respect you greatly. But please, permit me to say that your mother is a louse, a jigger, a bedbug, and a flea that likes to live on other people's life.

**ORDIA**: You speak about my mother in such raw terms?

**EDEWEDE**: I wished she didn't put me in such a raw mood. I have always wanted to respect her as I do you. She gave you life. But her attitude forces vile words from my mouth, in spite of myself. She is a liar, a slanderer, and a traitor. What is she up to this time? Turn the whole village against me? That is very mean! People should learn to respect themselves so that others will respect them.

**ORDIA**: I am very patient. Yes, I am. Both of us can not be mad at the same time or else this house will be on fire. So, go on! Let me know when you have let off the steam from your ribs.

**EDEWEDE**: [*Kneeling*] I am sorry, my husband. I am very sorry. [*No response.*]

Please pardon me. [*Silence.*] Ordy-y-y! I am sorry. [*Pause.*] Answer me please. I said, I'm sorry.

**ORDIA**: Are you sure?

**EDEWEDE**: Yes, I am.

**ORDIA**: Rise up, sit down and explain to me calmly what happened in my absence between both of you.

**EDEWEDE**: Nothing new.

**ORDIA**: Look, I know you have been having problems with her. But this is the first time she is accusing you of causing trouble in the village. What have you done?

**EDEWEDE**: Nothing that I know of.

**ORDIA**: Unbelievable.

**EDEWEDE**: My husband, don't you believe me any more?

**ORDIA**: I don't know whom to believe again. Trouble, trouble every time . . . ! But why would she accuse you of something you haven't done? That's unlike my mother. You must have said or done something. Think well, Edewede.

**EDEWEDE**: Well, the other time she visited, I went to town. I met her preparing Oseme for the initiation ceremonies. I told her not to waste her time for Oseme will not participate in them. Angrily, she stormed out of here fuming. We have not met since then.

**ORDIA**: Hmm! The initiation ceremonies, I see. [*Pause.*] Why don't you want Oseme to take part in them?

**EDEWEDE**: I don't want to lose her.

**ORDIA**: Lose her! Why do you think so?

**EDEWEDE**: My husband, can't you see? These things are under the control of blind furies. No one can predict who the next victim will be. All of a sudden it happens, then we wrestle helplessly to save those that cannot be saved. Ordia, my daughter will never be circumcised.

**ORDIA**: She needs to have it done like every other woman.

**EDEWEDE**: There are so many women out there who are uncircumcised.

**ORDIA**: Really! How many of them do you know?

**EDEWEDE**: Quite a number.

**ORDIA**: Name them.

**EDEWEDE**: Mama-Nurse's daughters and grand daughters. They don't practise it in her husband's village. And that doesn't prevent the women from fulfilling their roles as wives and mothers. My husband, you have travelled far and wide. You know the customs in these other places. Is it true that people in some towns and villages far away no longer circumcise their daughters?

**ORDIA**: Yes. It is true.

**EDEWEDE**: If so, why do we still practise it in this village?

**ORDIA**: Well, it is part of our culture.

**EDEWEDE**: Listen, I am tired of your mother wanting to draw us back to the past. She lives her life according to the needs of her generation. Let her leave us to live according to the demands of our time. Is that difficult for her to do?

**ORDIA**: It is difficult to give up an age-long tradition.

**EDEWEDE**: Nothing remains the same forever. Like the vicissitude of the sea, like night and day, season succeeds season giving way to new. Today, we must choose our values and live by them. Tomorrow comes another season, another choice. Man is what he does in his time. Circumcision has lost its old value.

**ORDIA**: That may be right. But right now, our people have in their hands problems more serious than female circumcision.

**EDEWEDE**: What problems could be more serious than the loss of human lives. Or is the death of innocent young girls of no serious concern to this village?

**ORDIA**: I'm sure, it is of great concern.

**EDEWEDE**: Why don't they do something about it, then?

**ORDIA**: With time, they will learn to do something about it.

**EDEWEDE**: We can't afford to lose lives anymore. It must be stopped at once.

**ORDIA**: How?

**EDEWEDE**: By explaining to everyone the harm caused by the evil blade. Education will make them see things differently.

**ORDIA**: Who will educate them?

**EDEWEDE**: They who suffer know how to describe the pain. So, our women should open their mouths to talk about their suffering because of circumcision.

**ORDIA**: Men do suffer too.

**EDEWEDE**: What do men know about that kind of suffering and pain? You stay far away while women suffer. At best, you come to console us, and then you take off. You were not even there when Ize was sick. Oh that night, that fateful night she passed away. What a night!

[*Fade out.*]

[*Flashback: A Traumatic Experience*]

[*On a bush path leading from the village to a town at the bottom of the hills. In the middle of the night, the atmosphere is calm but dreary. Carrying Izenebu, Edewede and Oseme stagger in.*]

**OSEME**: Mother, those footsteps again. I can hear them as if someone is following us.

**EDEWEDE**: I can't see anything. It must be your imagination.

**OSEME**: Is the place still far?

**EDEWEDE**: We are almost there.

**OSEME**: I am tired.

**EDEWEDE**: Please, be strong for her sake. She needs our help.

**OSEME**: She is getting heavier and heavier.

**EDEWEDE**: Be brave. The Maternity Home is right there after that corner.

**OSEME**: She is now too heavy. I am crushed. I'm shaking. I'm going to fall. She is going to fall too.

**EDEWEDE**: All right, let's put her down to rest for a while. This will be our last stop. [*They put Ize down, exercise their limbs and neck to ease off the fatigue. Ize groans with pain. They rush to her.*] That pain again. Let's go quickly to Mama-Nurse.

**OSEME**: My legs are still tired.

**EDEWEDE**: I know. Groping through these bush paths at night is not an easy task for a child.

**OSEME**: I wish father were here with us.

**EDEWEDE**: I sent for him. I wonder why he hasn't returned. Not that he would have agreed to our plan, anyway.

**OSEME**: Why not? He cares about Ize.

**EDEWEDE**: No doubt he does and very much too. But you know how he adores his mother. He will not want to offend her in any way. Well let's go. I will carry her by myself. The distance is not much again. [*She tries to carry Ize; the latter groans with pain.*] It is no use. The pain is too much.

**OSEME**: What do we do now? The weather is very cold. I am completely tired. I'm shivering. I can not go any further.

**EDEWEDE**: You stay here with her then. I'll go and call Mama-Nurse. [*The owls hoot.*]

**OSEME**: [*Coiling unto her mother*] Mother! The owls! They are hooting again.

**EDEWEDE**: They have been hooting all night as if they were having a meeting.

**OSEME**: And those footsteps too. Can you hear them now? They are closing in on us every minute by minute. I am afraid!

**EDEWEDE**: Be courageous. We have come this far. We must make it to the end.

**OSEME**: Is she really going to be all right?

**EDEWEDE**: She will be as soon as she receives good treatment.

**OSEME**: Go and call Mama-Nurse. Go well mother.

[*Edewede runs off. Izenebu moans with pain.*]

**OSEME**: Has it started to hurt again? "Rielamhen ley!" Be brave! Grandmother said it is normal for it to hurt. We just have to bear it. "Rielamhen ley!" But you have been sick for too long now. Other girls have started going about their normal business. They plan to learn "Agbega" dance for this year's new yam festival. You must get well quickly to join them.

You will beat all of them as you did last year. You were born a star. [*Ize groans with pain.*] Ah! Your body is hot! What can I do now? I'll sing for you to ease off the pain. [*Sings.*]

| | |
|---|---|
| *Rielamhen ley* | *Be brave* |
| *Rielamhen ley* | *Be brave* |
| *Rielamhen ley-oh* [2×] | *Be brave* |
| *Rielamhen ley* | *Be brave* |
| *Akhi mi u' u guina* | *You unappeasable death* |
| *N'omi asagbonhi* | *Violator of earthly wishes* |
| *Tohan mhan rebhe-oh* | *Have mercy on us* |
| *Imhan bhi-e* | *We pray thee* |
| *Toham mhan rebhe* | *Have mercy on us* |
| *Toham mhan rebhe* | *Have mercy on us* |

| | |
|---|---|
| *Tohan mhan rebhe-oh* [3×] | *Have mercy on us* |
| *Imhan bhi-e* | *We pray thee* |

My sister, be brave. Rielamhen ley! [*Starts up with fright.*] Who's there? [*Looks around.*] I hear some sound but I see nothing. I'm afraid. No, I must be brave.

Fear go! Fear go!
Fear go, go, far away!
Fear go! Fear go!
Fear go, go, go, far away!
Fear go! Fear go!
Fear go, go, go, go far away!

Well, I'll just lie down, close my eyes and ears and wait for my doom. [*Lies down beside Ize, and sleeps off. The cock crows, Edewede and Mama-Nurse enter.*]

**EDEWEDE**: They are over there. [*Edewede moves Oseme aside. Mama-Nurse examines Izenebu.*]

**ERIALA**: [*Shaking her head*] It is too late.

**EDEWEDE**: Meaning what?

**ERIALA**: She is dead.

**EDEWEDE**: Dead! Just like that?

**ERIALA**: Unfortunately.

**EDEWEDE**: Impossible!

**ERIALA**: Accept my sympathy.

**EDEWEDE**: I am doomed! [*Cries while singing:*]

| | |
|---|---|
| *Iye! Irie emhin ye-eoh* | *Mother! Is this how thing are?* |
| *Domhan ni gha tona man,* | *To whom shall I narrate this,* |
| *Iyemhen!* | *Mother?* |
| *Oya non vumhen eko na* | *I am overwhelmed with pain.* |
| *Domhan in gha tona man,* | *To whom shall I narrate this,* |
| *Ebaba-oh* | *Father?* |
| *Osa non nya agbon* | *God! Creator of the universe!* |
| *Uwe okpa ni gha tona man,* | *To you alone shall I narrate* |
| *Eramhen!* | *This, Almighty.* |
| *Yeh yeh yeh yeh.* | *Yeh yeh yeh yeh* |
| *Yeh yeh yeh yeh-oh.* | *Yeh yeh yeh yeh-oh* |
| *Domhan nigha tona man* | *To whom shall I narrate this?* |
| *Ehi mhen-o-o-oh!* | *Oh my destiny!* |

[*Collapses.*]

**ERIALA**: What a waste! The same thing keeps on happening every time, since I came to this land. You advise them, they will not listen. They only run to me when it is too late. Well, rise up. Let's go. [*Hallucinatory atmosphere. Several corpses wrapped in shrouds appear everywhere. Slowly, Wede rises to a sitting position, stares fixedly at a spot.*] What are you staring at?

**EDEWEDE**: Corpses.

**ERIALA**: Corpses!

**EDEWEDE**: Yes, corpses.

**ERIALA**: Where are they?

**EDEWEDE**: Over there.

**ERIALA**: I can't see any thing.

**EDEWEDE**: Look over there. [*Rises and moves forward.*]
In this corner, there are corpses
In that corner, there are corpses
Of innocent children, plucked from earth
Season after season.
Corpses of beloved ones
Yearning for life, pleading for help.
But helplessly, we watched them struggle
Hopelessly through their premature journey
To the land of no return.

> *Yeh yeh yeh yeh*
> Yeh yeh yeh yeh-Oh
> Donhan ni gha tona man
> Ehi mhen-o-o-oh

[*The corpses open out like hyacinth flower. As counterpoint to Wede's narration, they sing:*]

> Oh why
> Do they do that to us?
> Oh why
> Do they do that to us?
> Why, why
> Oh why, why
> Oh why, why
> Oh why?

[*They close up again.*]

**EDEWEDE**: How many corpses have I seen so far?
How many sorrows have I known so far?
How many tears have I shared so far?
Since my childhood because of circumcision?
Oh! My senior sister, Azelu.
That day, after spraying white chalk powder everywhere
The medicine man went away with his loot, smiling.
A minute later, I peeped into her room,
Stuffed with the fetid odour from her infection
She groaned and writhed with pain.
To mother, I ran as fast as I could. But,
Before she could call back the medicine man,
Azelu was no more.

Yeh yeh yeh yeh
Yeh yeh yeh yeh-oh
Domhan ni gha tona man
Ehimhen-o-o-oh!

[*Ghosts sing and close up.*]

**EDEWEDE**: I was seized with fear.
And my fear increased as I matured in age.
Then came our turn to face the evil blade.
We all walked to the initiation camp
But some never walked back from there.
Akalo bled to death. Denowe died few weeks later.
As seasons rolled by, many more maidens
Passed away for the same cause.
Others remain destroyed for life

Yěh yeh yeh yeh
Yeh yěh ye hyéh
Domhan ni gha tona man
Ehimhen-o-o-oh

[*Ghosts sing and close up. Exeunt.*]

Look at Ize, my daughter
She was so full of life
Always smiling like the rising sun.
Soft, and gentle in every way

Like the morning dew.
Never said any hurting word to anyone.
But like the hummingbird
Keeps the whole house alive
From morning till night,
With her songs and mirth
But, now, she lives no more.
*Yeh yeh yeh yeh*
*Yeh yeh yeh yeh-oh*
*Domhan ni gha tona man*
Ehimhen-o-o-oh

**ERIALA**: Why didn't you protect her from the evil blade?

**EDEWEDE**: I tried for many years, but my mother-in-law will not leave us alone. This year, she wrenched her from my arms. And she has been sick since then. [*Sings:*]

Yeh yeh yeh yeh
Yeh yeh yeh yeh-oh
Dormhan nigha lona man
Ehimhen-oh

**ERIALA**: No amount of tears will bring her back. So stop crying.

**EDEWEDE**: What else can I do but cry?

**ERIALA**: You can do much more.

**EDEWEDE**: I can do absolutely nothing. I am a helpless woman.

**ERIALA**: Do you know what your problem is? Inferiority complex! Do you know what that means? [*Wede shakes head negatively.*] That means you under-value yourself. You see yourself as a cripple, incapable of doing anything for yourself. So, you wait for others to think for you, show you what to do and how to live. Are you really a cripple? Answer!

**EDEWEDE**: Much worse than that.

**ERIALA**: I can't believe my ears.

**EDEWEDE**: What do you expect? We live in a land where men are born to dish out commands and women to carry them out and suffer in silence.

**ERIALA**: You are a human being, capable of doing many things men can do, if only you'd try. But you wouldn't try because your mind is weak, weakened by fear. That is why you lack confidence in yourself.

**EDEWEDE**: You may be right.

**ERIALA**: Listen to my strong advice to you. When death comes, sickness goes. This is the time for you to act and not to cry "*Yeh yeh yeh yeh!*" Away with fear and resignation! Think of yourself as superior in some way. Summon up courage! Call forth hope! Use your anger and grief wisely to reverse the order of things. But do you have the will and determination to start a new beginning? That is the big question. If not, look out! That daughter of yours over there will be a victim one day, very soon. And once again you will cry: "*Yeh yeh yeh yeh!*"

**EDEWEDE**: No! She is my only child.

**ERIALA**: Then you must do something to protect her from the evil blade.

**EDEWEDE**: How can I do that? Circumcision is part of our tradition.

**ERIALA**: A tradition that is of no value to anybody.

**EDEWEDE**: Why do we practise it then?

**ERIALA**: It's because of ignorance.

**EDEWEDE**: Ignorance!

**ERIALA**: Yes, ignorance.

**EDEWEDE**: Ignorance alone?

**ERIALA**: Ignorance and superstition still weigh down heavily on your village behind the cloak of customs and traditions.

**EDEWEDE**: Do you really mean that our women suffer from circumcision season after season just because of ignorance and superstition?

**ERIALA**: Yes, just like the tortoise who dips its finger into the cricket's hole only to be bitten by the snake. So, go home and talk to your fellow women. Make them know the grave harm they do to themselves by adhering to those useless traditions.

**EDEWEDE**: What harm?

**ERIALA**: I will explain it to you at the right time. Meanwhile come with me to the Maternity Home.

**EDEWEDE**: It is getting to dawn.

**ERIALA**: Yes, the darkness is fading away.

**EDEWEDE**: I must return to the village, immediately.

**ERIALA**: Not until full light appears. You were coming to me for help. Isn't it?

**EDEWEDE**: The reason for that is gone. My daughter is dead.

**ERIALA**: Is the cause of her death gone?

**EDEWEDE**: No.

**ERIALA**: You have come this far. You must pursue your goal till the end.

**EDEWEDE**: I must inform my people about her death at once.

**ERIALA**: You are in no position to do that right now. Feel your strength. You are very weak. How do you climb those hills? You might not even make it to your village. Come and have some rest. By the time you recover, you will be fortified enough to face your people. Besides, what are you doing about your daughter? You know very well that your people will deny her burial rites. Are you too going to abandon her here for vultures to feed on? Once you turn your back, they will descend on her.

**EDEWEDE**: Oh no! She must be buried, at once.

**ERIALA**: The doors of the Maternity Home are opened. Walk right in. I'm going to arrange for the funeral service. [*Exit.*]

**EDEWEDE**: [*Waking her up*] Oseme! Wake up. Let's go.

**OSEME**: [*Goes to Ize*] Ize! Wake up. Let's go.

**EDEWEDE**: She is dead.

**OSEME**: No!

[*While they both wail over Izenebu, the sound of a church bell is heard. Light fades out slowly to total darkness. A solemn dirge swirls the air.*]

> Help, Lord, the souls that thou host made,
> The souls to thee so dear,
> In prison for the debt unpaid
> Of sin committed here!
> These holy souls, they suffer on,
> Resigned in heart and will,
> Until thy high behest is done,
> And justice has its fill.

[*End of flashback. Lights fade on gently onstage, the action goes back to Ighalo's residence.*]

**EDEWEDE**: I was sick after that awful experience. So also was Oseme. Can you remember?

**ORDIA**: Yes, I can still remember very well.

**EDEWEDE**: You see, I know exactly what I am talking about. Enough of suffering! Away with out-dated traditions! Everything has its time.

**ORDIA**: Agreed, things have to change. They are bound to change, not suddenly but gradually. If not, our people will lose grip of their bearing. With time, they will learn to appreciate new values.

**EDEWEDE**: And our daughters? What will happen to them meanwhile? No, needless to waste time. They must be protected from this day.

**ORDIA**: There are too many obstacles.

**EDEWEDE**: One needs not fear obstacles when one is fighting a noble cause.

**ORDIA**: Wede! I am your husband. It is my duty to protect you too. So, listen to my advice. Do not allow that painful experience to becloud your reason. Give up this suicidal idea of yours.

**EDEWEDE**: I can't. Any time I see people suffering, I am overwhelmed by the urge to act to alleviate their pain. It is my nature. I can not help it.

**ORDIA**: I know you've always been like that. I can still remember the first day I saw you. It was in the market place. Two children were fighting. The crowd gathered around them watching hilariously. But you rushed forward to separate them.

**EDEWEDE**: If I hadn't intervened, both could have injured each other.

**ORDIA**: But you went home with swollen black eyes. All the blows they had intended for each other ended up on your body.

**EDEWEDE**: One of those things that cannot be avoided.

**ORDIA**: Wede, severing a people from their culture is just like separating those children wrapped up in scuffle.

**EDEWEDE**: Really!

**ORDIA**: You might be destroyed in the process.

**EDEWEDE**: What a noble death to die.

**ORDIA**: What about us, our marriage, our dreams and plans? All these mean nothing to you? What do you want that I haven't given to you? Is it affection, happiness or liberty?

**EDEWEDE**: You have tried for me, my husband. I recognize the sacrifice you've made for me in the past. And I appreciate the way you carry me high in the present. I consider myself very lucky to have a husband like you. But when life is good for oneself, one should not forget others.

**ORDIA**: So, you'd rather destroy our marriage because of others?

**EDEWEDE**: On the contrary, I am fighting to make it stronger. Remember it is our daughter's life that is at stake. How can we be happy if she dies?

**ORDIA**: I understand your fear. But be patient. He who has patience has everything.

**EDEWEDE**: Be patient till when?

**ORDIA**: Until I am able to find a place for us, somewhere in town.

**EDEWEDE**: Will your mother leave us alone? Of course, not. Like a shadow trailing a body, she will come after us. So there is no need to run. I will stay right here to protect my daughter's life.

**ORDIA**: Well, on my part, I have tried to protect you.

**EDEWEDE**: You have, my husband. Kindly understand that I am fulfilling my motherly duty.

**ORDIA**: Don't forget that I too have my filial duty to fulfil; She who has a bad child is the enemy of the community.

**EDEWEDE**: Yes; I do understand. [*Pause.*] Ordy!

**ORDIA**: Yes, Wede.

**EDEWEDE**: I have a request to make.

**ORDIA**: I am listening.

**EDEWEDE**: Please, note that this is not a personal war between you and me.

**ORDIA**: I know that.

**EDEWEDE**: So, promise that no matter what happens, you will not let hatred replace your affection for me.

**ORDIA**: What differences will that make?

**EDEWEDE**: It will make the burden lighter for me to carry. You mean a lot to me. So far, our marriage has been fulfilling because we value each order highly. I'll want to still sit high in your mind, no matter what happens.

**ORDIA**: You can not be hurting me and at the same time you ask me not to feel anger and hatred towards you. Your stubbornness pierces through me like an arrow.

**EDEWEDE**: The stubbornness is for a purpose. The purpose is good.

**ORDIA**: But I feel pain. And pain kills affection.

**EDEWEDE**: Just for a while. Soon, the trial will be over. Kindly endure.

**ORDIA**: There is limit to human endurance.

**EDEWEDE**: I know. Well, be it as it may; at least tell me you do understand why I am doing it. [*Sings.*]

| | |
|---|---|
| *Eeh Obhiye-o och* | *Oh my kinsman oh* |
| *Eeh odor mhen-o eeh* | *Oh my husband oh* |
| *Lumele nimen hnvele* | *Because of vengeance* |
| *Olukholorkhi fo bhagbon-o eh.* | *Evil doing will never end in This world.* |

**ORDIA**: You place me in an awkward position.

**EDEWEDE**: Please, do not talk like that. Or else, you make things difficult for me. At least tell me you do understand. [*No response.*] Ordy, speak to me, please. [*Ordia merely looks at her defiantly, storms out of the room furiously.*] Poor man!

It is not going to be easy for you either. [*Enters an inner room.*]

[*Fade out.*]

## DRAMA III: DILEMMA

[*Same place. Same day. Edewede emerges from an inner room speaking.*]

**EDEWEDE**: To do or not to do, that is the question.
Whichever I choose, I'm bound to lose
One of the two dearest people in my life.
One is urging me to act; the other restraining me.
Husband, daughter; marital love, maternal love:
Both equally important; both deserving equal commitment.
But which is stronger? Which should I protect?
If I protect him, I'll earn her contempt and hatred.
If I protect her, I'll provoke his anger and vengeance.

I owe much to my husband as to my daughter.
I think it is better to kill myself.
In that way, I'll offend neither of them. But—eeh
Kill myself? What right do I have to do that?
It is only He who creates life that can destroy it.
Besides, I could never bring myself to do such a thing.
Even mere thought of it is appalling.
If only I could make them understand.
But how do I make them understand?
Nobody wants to understand.
Mother! Why did you bring me into this world
Where people refuse to see things as they really are?
What should I do now? I am confused.
Oh my mother! [*Pauses. Reflects.*]

[*From the fore stage, far right, Mother enters, unnoticed.*]

Mother -er-er-er-er! [*Whirls around, slowly.*] Where are you?

**MOTHER'S VOICE**: Right here -ere-ere-ere.

[*Cross fade. Her paternal home. Edewede to be played by a younger girl, runs in from outside to meet Mother.*]

**EDEWEDE**: Mother, I need your help.

**MOTHER**: What kind of help?

**EDEWEDE**: Kindly speak to father. If not, I'll kill myself.

**MOTHER**: Why would you do such a thing?

**EDEWEDE**: He's been talking to me too much about the son of Itua. I don't want to hear any thing about that man again.

**MOTHER**: Why not? Don't you want to get married?

**EDEWEDE**: But I have already told you about Ordia.

**MOTHER**: Ah! You want to choose a spouse for yourself? You are a woman. Don't you forget that!

**EDEWEDE**: I haven't forgotten, Mother. But I was hoping that . . .

**MOTHER**: [*Cutting her short*] You hardly know that man.

**EDEWEDE**: Even if so. He is the right man for me.

**MOTHER**: How do you know that? Just from seeing him in the market? Who are his parents? From which village is he? What does he do for a living? You don't even know if he is one of those procurers or even a ghost prowling the markets.

**EDEWEDE**: It doesn't matter. He is going to be my husband some day. That, I do know for sure.

**MOTHER**: What gave you that assurance?

**EDEWEDE**: My feelings tell me so.

**MOTHER**: You are day-dreaming.

**EDEWEDE**: I am not. Mother, I have made up my mind. It is either I marry him or I remain at home forever.

**MOTHER**: "Shut it up!" In whose home? May God forbid bad thing!

**EDEWEDE**: My wish is to make him happy all his life. Will you talk to my father about him?

**MOTHER**: Oh no! Do not drag me into your scheme. You should be ashamed of yourself: A girl rejecting the spouse chosen for her by her father. Unheard of!

**EDEWEDE**: I know. But, I really like Ordia a lot. And I was relying on you to help me out. Mother, please, I am on my knees. Kindly help me.

**MOTHER**: Hmm! Well, I'll think about it.

**EDEWEDE**: Oh! I shall always be grateful to you.

**MOTHER**: Calm down. I haven't promised you anything.

**EDEWEDE**: All the same, thank you.

**MOTHER**: Right now, it is time to prepare supper. I am going to the kitchen. You come with me right away. [*Exit.*]

**EDEWEDE**: I must be brave if I am to win. Defeat is the reward for cowardice.

[*A knock on the door cross fade. Ordia's residence.*]

**EDEWEDE**: If I am to win, I must be brave. I must be . . .

**EBUN**: [*Knocking*] Anybody in this house?

**EDEWEDE**: Who is there?

**EBUN**: It's me, Ebungbe.

**EDEWEDE**: Come in.

**EBUN**: Are you all right? I have never seen you like this before. Except perhaps when Ize passed away.

**EDEWEDE**: The whole world around me is crumbling. I am afraid.

**EBUN**: Afraid of what?

**EDEWEDE**: Of destroying my marriage. You need to see his eyes when he left here a while ago. They were as red as the ember. I don't want to lose him.

**EBUN**: What happened?

**EDEWEDE**: His mother is coming between us.

**EBUN**: Is that why you're looking like this? I thought it was something more serious.

**EDEWEDE**: It is very serious. I need your help.

**EBUN**: You have it already. One good turn deserves another. Wede, come and feel my stomach.

**EDEWEDE**: [*Touching her stomach*] You mean another baby is on the way already?

**EBUN**: Before long, I may smile again.

**EDEWEDE**: Wonderful! You see what I mean? People thought that your womb was locked up because of a curse on your family.

**EBUN**: For ten years, I went from one native doctor to another. We killed fowls. We killed goats. We made sacrifice upon sacrifice, yet my womb had no fruit. Then you came and took me to your friend, Mama-Nurse. She only treated me for three months and my womb was blessed. And now, another baby is on the way. Wede, what can I do to help you save your marriage?

**EDEWEDE**: The help is also for every female child in this village today and for those yet to be born.

**EBUN**: You are alarming me. What is wrong? Say it!

**EDEWEDE**: My mother-in-law wants Oseme to be circumcised.

**EBUN**: What is wrong with that?

**EDEWEDE**: Remember, Ize died few years ago because of circumcision.

**EBUN**: Now I understand your fear.

**EDEWEDE**: Circumcision has destroyed many women in this village. They suffer from different types of infections and complications after the operation.

**EBUN**: On that point, you are right. Some even carry from it that disease they call AIDS [*Acquired Immunity Deficiency Syndrome*]. They say it kills human beings like fowl. There is no cure for it.

**EDEWEDE**: Do you remember Akalo?

**EBUN**: Yes I do.

**EDEWEDE**: She died of V.V. F.

**EBUN**: V.V.F.? Tell me, what does that really mean?

**EDEWEDE**: Vesico-Vaginal Fistula. According to Mama-Nurse during circumcision, when the clitoris is being removed, the labia and the surrounding tissues are damaged. The girl suffers from stenosis that is healing with the narrowing of the birth canal. This process makes the muscles surrounding the vagina and the urethra to become very tight. Later in life, during labour the narrowed birth canal makes it difficult for the baby to come out easily. The baby's head is forced to create an opening between the walls of the bladder, urethra and the vagina. If the woman survives, she begins to leak urine because the damaged bladder, urethra or vaginal outlet can no longer control the urine.

**EBUN**: So, is that why some women are always wet and smell of urine.

**EDEWEDE**: Yes oh.

**EBUN**: Is that so?

**EDEWEDE**: Do you know that the delayed childbirth can cause death or brain damage to the baby?

**EBUN**: Ewoh! I am afraid. So, all these are side effects of circumcision!

**EDEWEDE**: Yes; moreover, the narrowing of the vagina also makes sexual intercourse painful.

**EBUN**: But how many of our women know about these things?

**EDEWEDE**: Very few.

**EBUN**: Hmm! Ignorance is very dangerous.

**EDEWEDE**: It is worse than any disease. May God forbid bad thing! My only daughter will not be the victim of circumcision.

**EBUN**: Wait a minute! Does it mean that some day, I too will have to send my daughter to that initiation camp? The child I spent ten good years looking for?

**EDEWEDE**: So it appears.

**EBUN**: And if she dies? Ah! The native doctors! What will they say? That their juju has caught up with me? Oh no! That must not happen. But what can we do?

**EDEWEDE**: I think the only way out is to make everyone know why female circumcision is bad.

**EBUN**: The idea is not bad at all.

**EDEWEDE**: How do we spread the information without offending our husbands and mothers? That is my problem right now.

**EBUN**: I see! In that case, we do it step by step. First of all, we talk to the young mothers one by one. Then, we move on to discuss it in our weekly meetings. Finally, we launch a public campaign.

**EDEWEDE**: You know our women. They may think that we are fighting against female circumcision because we find it difficult to have babies.

**EBUN**: Some may think so at first but when they know about the dangers of circumcision, they too will support our action. Without knowledge, self-determination simply can not exist.

**EDEWEDE**: You know, until I met Mama-Nurse, I never knew that my partial barrenness is due to the infections I suffered from after the circumcision.

**EBUN**: I am also a living evidence of the same problem. Our women need to know about all these things. They need to be educated on the subject.

**EDEWEDE**: But how do you educate a people that see every new idea as threat to traditions?

**EBUN**: It is very difficult. Well, can you get Mama-Nurse to come and talk to our women about those things she usually tells us at the Maternity Home?

**EDEWEDE**: How well thought!

**EBUN**: Leave our women to me. I know how to handle them.

**EDEWEDE**: What about our mothers? They constitute a force to reckon with.

**EBUN**: Yes, they are the custodians of our customs and traditions. But we are the controllers of life in this village. We feed them. We breed and raise the children. We keep the village itself alive by providing for every event in it. Since we are the ones who suffer the pain of all these labour, shouldn't we have the right to express our opinion on the issues in this village? As for female circumcision, don't worry. Whether they like it or not, we will fight against it with every breath and strength in us until the end comes. The sun is on our side.

**EDEWEDE**: That has always been my wish. But wishes like the ivory, are rare to come by.

**EBUN**: Be hopeful. I hold the key to the success or failure of any event in this village. Yes, I can see it coming. One day very soon, we shall celebrate in this village the dawn of a new day.

**EDEWEDE**: "The dawn of a new day!" That's my name: "*Edewede.*" Surely, I must be hopeful.

**EBUN**: It is not going to be easy, though. It may even take many years, just as it took me to have my first issue. But in the end, victory will be ours. Go and bring Mama-Nurse. Our women will be at the market place in great number and in their best to listen to her.

**EDEWEDE**: You have lifted up my sagging spirit.

**EBUN**: May the plan succeed.

**EDEWEDE**: May it succeed.

**EBUN**: Wede!

**EDEWEDE**: Yes.

**EBUN**: Have hope, Ordia will come back. If I could keep my husband on my side during those years of my infertility, you too can do the same. You know, many people advised him to marry another woman. But I used my natural gifts to keep him on my side. Go and prepare a nice supper for him. Then talk things over with him calmly tonight. I wish you happiness.

**EDEWEDE**: Thank you.

**EBUN**: Good night.

**EDEWEDE**: Same to you.

[*Fade out.*]

## DRAMA IV: A GLIMPSE OF HOPE.

[*Market place. Midday. The atmosphere is filled with music and hilarity. A table and three chairs are set up for Wede, Ebun and Eriaja. Others sit on stools or wooden chairs. Ebun rises, and goes to the middle of the arena to address the ladies.*]

**EBUN**: Daughters of our ancestors, I greet you all.

**MARKET WOMEN**: Same to you.

**EBUN**: Market women, I greet you all.

**MARKET WOMEN**: Same to you.

**EBUN**: The market is the heartbeat of the village. You are the central nerve of the market. The market dances according to your drumbeat. Agile women of this land, beat me some sound, to shake off the rust on my legs. [*Drumbeats. She dances a little while they sing:*]

| | |
|---|---|
| *Edelena eghongh on nor.* | *Today is a day of joy* |
| *Edelena eghonghon nor-oh.* | *Today is a day of joy* |
| *Eghonghon.* | *A day of joy* |

My fellow women, once again, I greet you all! We all agreed to gather here today to meditate upon issues touching all of us. As you may have noticed, this is an age-group meeting. Our president and her age-group were not invited because the matter at hand is for young mothers and mothers to be. We shall inform our elders later about our activities here today. Two women shall lead the discussion. Two women you know very well. After their talk, others who may so wish can make their own contributions. Meanwhile be patient. Listen carefully to them. Fellow women, I greet you all.

**MARKET WOMEN**: Same to you.

**EBUN**: Esan khide!

**MARKET WOMEN**: Imban khide.

**EBUN**: Esan khide!

**MARKET WOMEN**: Imhan khide.

[*Drumbeats, Ebun dances to Wede inviting her to address the audience.*]

**EDEWEDE**: Noble women of this land, my greetings!

**MARKET WOMEN**: Same to you.

**EDEWEDE**: Able women of this land, my homage!

**MARKET WOMEN**: Same to you.

**EDEWEDE**: Today, you have set a record. For the first time in history, you left your homes, your business, everything to come together, not just to eat, dance and celebrate, but to listen to words about womanhood. You are gre-ea-eat!

**MARKET WOMEN**: Great!

**EDEWEDE**: You are grea-ea-ea-eat!

**MARKET WOMEN**: Great!

**EDEWEDE**: You are gre-ea-ea-ea-ea-eat!

**MARKET WOMEN**: Grea-ea-ea-eat!

**EDEWEDE**: May your desires be fulfilled.

**MARKET WOMEN**: Iseh!

**EDEWEDE**: May this occasion be blessed abundantly.

**MARKET WOMEN**: Iseh!

**EDEWEDE**: My fellow women, once again, I salute you all.

**MARKET WOMEN**: Same to you.

**EDEWEDE**: I bring you nothing but words.
Words to help you know yourselves better
So as to be able to choose for yourselves
Between light and darkness.
If by so doing I've offended any one
Let that person raise up her hand
For to her, I do owe an apology.

**MARKET WOMEN**: You've offended no one. Go on!

**EDEWEDE**: Recently, I have been accused of many things:
Of disturbing the peace in this village,
Of planting bad seed in the minds of women,
Of talking about things that are better buried in silence.
But I ask, "Is there any woman here, right now,
Who has not passed through sleepless night,
Watching over a dying child or relation,
Victim of that dreadful evil blade?"
If so, let that person raise up her hand.
For to her, I do owe an apology. [*Pause.*]

**MARKET WOMEN**: None, please go on.

**EDEWEDE**: Our mothers practised circumcision
Because they knew nothing about anything
Except for laws and taboos imposed on them

To stop them from thinking for themselves
So that from childhood, they learn
To be shy, silent and docile
Until they see themselves
As objects for men's pleasure.
They got so accustomed to this condition
That they see any deviation from it as a crime.
But today, light has chased away darkness
And women must change with time.
Wake up! Wake up fellow women!
Gird up your loins.
Rise up! Rise up fellow women
From your impotence to dazzling height.
Step out boldly! Step out proudly!
Proclaim your right!
If one never risks anything
One can never gain anything.
Is that true or false?

**MARKET WOMEN**: It is true.

**EDEWEDE**: What is good is worth keeping.
What is bad is worth throwing away.
Is circumcision good or bad?
For whom is it good or bad?
Since women are the ones who carry
All the burdens of circumcision
Isn't it right for them to decide
Whether to keep it or throw it away
These are the questions before us today.

**MARKET WOMEN**: We should have the right
To express our opinion on the subject.

**EDEWEDE**: To help us make a valid decision
Let us first of all know more about the issue
From someone, some of you have already known.
Someone, most of you are yet to know.
Someone, who has been in this land:
The strength of the weak
The rock of the broken-hearted
The fortress of the homeless
The mother of the motherless

The nurse of the sick
The light of the blind
The hope of the hopeless
The future of the destitute
Everybody, please rise up and welcome
Our mother, fondly called Mama-Nurse.

[*Drumbeats and standing ovation.*]

**ERIALA**: I thank you all.
Today, I am the happiest woman on earth
To see women gather like this
To discuss their own problems
Freedom to womanhood!

**MARKET WOMAN**: Freedom to womanhood!

**ERIALA**: My speech will be brief.
You all already know what circumcision is.
You have all gone through it.
In this society, many young girls have lost
Their lives because of circumcision.
Many women are suffering from different
Types of diseases because of circumcision:
Tetanus, urinary infections, V.V.F.,
HIV/AIDS are all dangerous
Afflictions contacted through circumcision.
Yet they see nothing wrong with it!
Of course they do.
Women! Do you know the exact reason
They make you go through it?
Do you know what harm you do
To yourselves by agreeing to do it?
Do you know the answers to these questions?
Go on tell me. Do you know?

**MARKET WOMEN**: No, we don't know.

**ERIALA**: Don't you think you ought to know?

**SOME MARKET WOMEN**: We think so.

**OTHER MARKET WOMEN**: We have the right to know.

**ERIALA**: Fairly well then.
First of all you must know that
God created man and woman in his own image.
If the image of God is one
then man and woman were created equals.
But society made one master and the other slave.
Circumcision is a form of slavery
imposed on woman to dominate her.

**FIRST MARKET WOMAN**: Is that so?

**EBUN**: Women! Open your ears and listen properly.

**SECOND MARKET WOMAN**: Our elders said that circumcision is good for us. Do you want us now to believe that they have been telling us lies all these years?

**ERIALA**: I am aware that the custodians
of our customs and traditions claim that
your peanut is the source of confusion and impurity.
So, they carve it out of its pod
to prevent you from having impure thoughts.
But women! For once in your life, stop and think.
Think for yourselves. Think about yourselves
Think! Think! Think!
Do you think with your brain or bottom?
Do you see with your eyes or bottom?
Do you desire with your heart or bottom?
Go on! Open your mouth! Speak out!

**MARKET WOMEN**: No one thinks with one's bottom.

**ERIALA**: If so, tell them to leave your bottom alone.
Evil thoughts dwell not in the bottom but in the mind.
Circumcision neither encourages nor discourages lust.
Women! Use your brain.
Reflect on what I have just said.
Come on! Think about it.

**THIRD MARKET WOMAN**: I think there is sense in what she is saying.

**FIRST MARKET WOMAN**: Truly speaking, circumcision neither prevents a woman from admiring a man, nor from nursing secret desires for that man.

**SECOND MARKET WOMAN**: That is not completely true.

**FIRST MARKET WOMAN**: Really! Come on; remember Aimufia. She was circumcised. But how many times was she caught sneaking behind her husband to sleep with other men?

**MARKET WOMEN**: Uncountable!

**THIRD MARKET WOMAN**: If circumcision does not prevent promiscuity, why then do they make us go through it?

**SECOND MARKET WOMAN**: Ehen! Go on; explain.

**FOURTH MARKET WOMAN**: I don't know. But listen, she is speaking again.

**ERIALA**: My children! Listen carefully to the truth.
Your peanut is an organ for sexual enjoyment.
It is only active when a man and a woman are together.
If it is cut off, the woman is unable to enjoy sex.
She becomes a mere vessel for man's pleasure.
Women! Are you bowls, pots, or mortals to be used
And thrown to the corner, until the next time around?

**MARKET WOMEN**: No! We are not.

**ERIALA**: Do you forbid enjoyment?

**MARKET WOMEN**: No, we don't.

**ERIALA**: If you want to savour
The greatest joy of life
You must rise up and fight.
Fight against female circumcision.
Fight against female oppression.
Fight for your rights.
Fight for womanhood.
A word is enough for the wise.
Thank you all for your attention. [*Standing ovation.*]

**EBUN**: Women! You have heard it all. From now, what do you say to circumcision?

**MARKET WOMAN**: We say no to circumcision.

**EBUN**: Again!

**MARKET WOMEN**: We say no to circumcision!

**THIRD MARKET WOMAN**: Down with circumcision!

**MARKETWOMEN**: Down with circumcision!

**THIRD MARKET WOMAN**: Up, up, freedom!

**MARKET WOMEN**: Up, up. Freedom!

**THIRD MARKET WOMAN**: Freedom! Freedom! We want Freedom.

**MARKET WOMEN**: Freedom! Freedom! We want freedom.

**EDEWEDE**: [*To herself*] At last! The silence is broken. I wished my mother were here to listen to you all. [*Mother appears from behind the crowd. Alternatively, their prerecorded voices could be relayed while Edewede looks at a spot lost in thought.*]

**MOTHER**: Edewede!

**EDEWEDE**: Ah! Mother, what brought you here, today?

**MOTHER**: Just to find out how you are doing.

**EDEWEDE**: See for yourself.

**MOTHER**: How is your husband?

**EDEWEDE**: He is fine.

**MOTHER**: I hope you are taking good care of him.

**EDEWEDE**: I'm trying my best. But it's not easy.

**MOTHER**: Who told you it would be easy? However, remember your great dream. You wanted to make him happy all his life. And you made me help you to become his wife to your father's greatest chagrin. Wasn't it so?

**EDEWEDE**: So it was, mother. I love him very much and I hope it will ever remain like that.

**MOTHER**: If so, you must look for a way to create happiness between both of you.

**EDEWEDE**: Happiness in marriage is difficult to maintain. No matter how hard one tries, there are always obstacles. At times, ordinary question or innocent answer takes on values that are out of proportion to their intent. Mother but . . .

**EBUN**: [*Moving closer to her*] Wede! Whom are you speaking with?

**EDEWEDE**: With my mother, of course.

**EBUN**: [*With surprise*] Your mother! How can?

**EDEWEDE**: What do you mean? Look at her over there.

**EBUN**: Impossible! She died years ago. Wede, are you all right?

**EDEWEDE**: Pardon! I was carried away.

**EBUN**: You must be missing her a lot.

**EDEWEDE**: Life is difficult.

**EBUN**: Yes. But one mustn't lose hope. After rain comes sunshine.

**EDEWEDE**: Certainly. But I wished she were here to listen to the women. Ebun! Listen. They have broken their silence. They are clamouring for freedom. Can you hear them?

**EBUN**: Yes I can, Wede. This is the dawn of a new beginning. Things can never be the same again.

**EDEWEDE**: Never!

**EBUN**: Come, let's join them to celebrate the dawn of a new day. [*Sings:*]

"Freedom! Freedom! We want freedom!"

**MARKET WOMEN**: Freedom! Freedom! We want freedom!

[*Drumbeats. This is repeated several limes, as the Women sing and dance around the arena proclaiming freedom.*]

## DRAMA V: SHATTERED DREAM

[*Same day: Same place. At the entrance of the market, the Town Crier beats his gong. Every woman is aghast. Holding a short broom, a ritual Masquerade enters. A rope tied around his waist is being pulled by a man. He also serves as an interpreter for the Masquerade who only makes unintelligible guttural sound. After walking around the arena he stands in front of Wede. A feather across his lips, Ordia enters flanked by some old women holding short brooms. The Masquerade directs Edewede to step out into the arena facing Ordia. Ebikere gives seven cowries or coins to the Village Matron who in turn hands them over to Ordia. He looks at the cowries then at Edewede sternly.*]

**EDEWEDE**: [*Gently to Ordia*] I am sorry to put you through all this, Ordy. Please don't hate me. I need you. We need each other. But, I do understand. Go on, play your role.

[*She stretches out her hand. Ordia counts into her palm the seven cowries, then walks out briskly from the arena without uttering a word.*]

**MASQUERADE**: [*To Wede*] Bru brughu ghughu.

**HIS ASSISTANT**: [*To Wede*] Body of a woman! Do you know me?

**EDEWEDE**: Spirit of our ancestors! Your identity is beyond common knowledge.

**MASQUERADE**: Khio khior khioeu.

**HIS ASSISTANT**: They say you claim to know things even beyond common knowledge.

**EDEWEDE**: Those who say so do me great wrong.

**MASQUERADE**: Yhou yhou yhing yhwing.

**HIS ASSISTANT**: But you claim to know more than your mothers do about womanhood.

**EDEWEDE**: Ah! On that subject, that may be true to some extent.

**MASQUERADE**: Hue, hoe hum foe fou.

**HIS ASSISTANT**: How far can this knowledge of yours carry you?

**EDEWEDE**: For the moment I know not. All I know is that knowledge is valuable. Through knowledge one learns to conduct oneself wisely in a world that is always in the process of becoming.

**MASQUERADE**: Ghri ghru ghan. Ghni ghri ghrin ghrim.

**HIS ASSISTANT**: Of what use is a knowledge that is alien and obscure? The community is the source of knowledge for the living.

**EDEWEDE**: Some knowledge may seem useless for the present but may not be so for the future. Before you came the women over there spoke out their mind boldly. Today is the dawn of a new day. The things of the past belong to the past. Henceforth we look forward to a brighter future. Edewede!

**MASQUERADE**: Yegulu gulu gho ghoo.

**HIS ASSISTANT**: You have spat on the traditions of this land. Temper is high. Go before it becomes tempestuous.

**EDEWEDE**: No matter how violent a storm may be, it will surely calm down afterwards.

**MASQUERADE**: Ahiana! Aikhelu! Ufidon! Ughogholo!

**HIS ASSISTANT**: Forbidden! Abomination! Cursed! Crushed! Go away quickly.

[*As she walks out slowly from the market place with Eriala and escorted by the Masquerade, Edewede intones very emotionally the Theme Song. The women repeat it after her in chorus. This is repeated until she finally leaves the stage. The Old Women perform the Broom Dance to the sound of drumbeats. Exeunt.*]

## DRAMA VI: SOLIDARITY

**EBUN**: Market Women! Are you all here?

**MARKET WOMEN**: Yes, we are here.

**EBUN**: Market Women! Are you all awake?

**MARKET WOMEN**: Yes, our eyes are open.

**EBUN**: Did you see what I saw, few minutes ago in this very market, our market?

**MARKET WOMEN**: Yes, we saw everything.

**EBUN**: Anger! Fury! Vengeance! Calling forth justice. Market Women! Do you feel what I feel?

**MARKET WOMEN**: Yes, we feel anger inside us.

**EBUN**: Anger swells up in my chest like a mountain. Anger makes my body hot like iron on the hearth. Anger rumbles in my bowel like a volcano ready to erupt. Aie! Repudiate a woman publicly like this! It has never happened before in this village.

**MARKET WOMEN**: Not even in the history of this land.

**THIRD MARKET WOMAN**: Khai! Public humiliation! Awooh!

**FIRST MARKET WOMAN**: By the way, why did they come here to wash their family dirty linen?

**SECOND MARKET WOMAN**: Why couldn't they wait till she returns home?

**THIRD MARKET WOMAN**: And those old women looked on, as if they were no longer women.

**FOURTH MARKET WOMAN**: He who curses the whole market does not exclude his mother.

**MARKET WOMEN**: Not at all.

**FIRST MARKET WOMAN**: Did you notice how they danced with great satisfaction as they swept out her footsteps?

**THIRD MARKET WOMAN:** Yes. I wonder why?

**FOURTH MARKET WOMAN:** Can't you see? It is very obvious.
They are fighting all of us. Wede is only a scapegoat.

**EBUN:** That's right! It was well planned. Our mothers conniving with men to declare war on us. They have slapped us, What do we do now?

**SECOND MARKET WOMAN:** What can we do? Nothing.

**THIRD MARKET WOMAN:** Nothing! What do you mean by that? We should go home and lick our wounds?

**FOURTH MARKET WOMAN:** No one goes to lie down to sleep when there is a snake on the roof.

**FIRST MARKET WOMAN:** She means we should go on our knees before them saying, "Master please pardon me, your slave, for daring to discuss issues that are better buried in silence."

**SECOND MARKET WOMAN:** Not exactly.

**THIRD MARKET WOMAN:** Exactly what do you mean then? That woman has been exiled because of all of us.

**FIRST MARKET WOMAN:** She means we should let her suffer on our behalf like the carrier of the village filth.

**FOURTH MARKET WOMAN:** Well that is what they say men do these days in the cities. Once their leaders are locked up in cell, they forget all about them. It is a question of cash! Slip money into their pocket, seal up their lips.

**FIRST MARKET WOMAN:** We are not men but women. Besides, this is the first time we are fighting for a cause. We either fight to win now or remain slaves forever.

**THIRD MARKET WOMAN:** If we do not fight now, we could never open our mouths in this village again.

**SECOND MARKET WOMAN:** Fight whom? How does one fight against one's superior? They have shrine, masquerades and occult power. What weapon do we have?

**EBUN:** Women have weapon!
A very powerful weapon for that matter!
It brings the kings from their high throne,
Down on their knees before their slave,
Creeping and peeping.

It makes even the Chief High Priest of the oracle
Shiver like a leaf before his helpless client,
Fluttering and flapping.
It disarms even the most powerful man on earth,
Jinglelet Yekpete.
Yes, women have a very powerful weapon.

**SECOND MARKET WOMAN**: What weapon is that? Name it.

**EBUN**: Our bottom. Yes, our bottom is our power. As from this day lock it up until they crawl to us for reconciliation. Is that clear?

**MARKET WOMEN**: Yes, it's very clear.

**EBUN**: Good. If death does not kill the sacrificial hen, some day it will bear some chicks.

**FIRST MARKET WOMAN**: Women!

**MARKET WOMEN**: Bottom power!

**FIRST MARKET WOMAN**: Women!

**MARKET WOMEN**: Bottom power!

**FIRST MARKET WOMAN**: Together!

**MARKET WOMEN**: We stand!

**FIRST MARKET WOMAN**: Divided!

**MARKET WOMEN**: We fall!

**FIRST MARKET WOMAN**: Women!

**MARKET WOMEN**: Bottom power!

**FIRST MARKET WOMAN**: Let us take an oath of solidarity to prevent the weaker ones from falling by the wayside.

**MARKET WOMEN**: Yes, the oath! Let us take the oath.

**EBUN**: Very good, we will take the oath. Who knows the right procedure?

**FIRST MARKET WOMAN**: Well. I can't remember exactly, but I think it goes like this. First of all, we remove all our clothes, Next, we . . .

**THIRD MARKET WOMAN**: What? Remove all our clothes!

**FIRST MARKET WOMAN**: Yes. That is what I said.

**THIRD MARKET WOMAN:** You mean I should get naked! Oh no, not me!

**SECOND MARKET WOMAN:** You must remove all clothes. That's how it was done in those days.

**EBUN:** Yes, indeed, that is how it was done in the past. But time changes everything. With time, we learn to winnow grain from chaff. So also must we learn to sift from every tradition only the useful parts, others left to be blown away by the wind. Therefore, we will take the oath without the nakedness.

**WOMEN:** Right! Away with nakedness!

**FIRST MARKET WOMAN:** Just a minute. I think we can still do that symbolically.

**MARKET WOMEN:** How?

**FIRST MARKET WOMAN:** By removing only the top of our wrappers.

**MARKET WOMEN:** Not bad at all. That is done. Go on.

**FIRST MARKET WOMAN:** Pile them up in a heap.

**MARKET WOMEN:** That is done. Go on.

**FIRST MARKET WOMAN:** Next, we form a circle around it.

**MARKET WOMEN:** That is done. Go on.

**FIRST MARKET WOMAN:** Then you repeat after me: "Idigun gbee-e-e! ldigun gbe!" Repeat!

**MARKET WOMAN:** Idigun gbee-e-e! Idigun gbe!

**FIRST MARKET WOMAN:** God of wisdom and justice! We present our grief before you. Idigun gbee-e! Idugun gbe!

**MARKET WOMEN:** Idigun ghee-e-e! Idigun gbe!

**FIRST MARKET WOMAN:** Whosoever will betray our plans

**MARKET WOMEN:** Idigun gbee-e-e! Idigun gbe!

**FIRST MARKET WOMAN:** Whosoever will plan evil against us

**MARKETWOMEN:** Idigun gbee-e-e! Idigun gbe!

**FIRST MARKET WOMAN:** Whosoever will break our rank

**MARKET WOMEN:** Idigun gbee-e-e! Idigun gbe!

**FIRST MARKET WOMAN:** Whosoever will slander us

**MARKET WOMEN**: Idigun gbee-e-e! Idigun gbe!

**FIRSTMARKET WOMAN**: Idigun gbee-e-e! Idigun gbe!

**MARKET WOMEN**: Idigun gbee-e-e! Idigun gbe!

**EBUN**: By this oath, we swear to stay together as one till our goal is achieved.

**MARKET WOMEN**: We swear!

**SECOND MARKET WOMAN**: Wait a minute. One thing bothers me though.

**THIRD MARKET WOMAN**: Ehenh! She has come again with her fear.

**EBUN**: What's bothering you?

**SECOND MARKET WOMAN**: Suppose my husband comes to me today and touches me gently, I push him away. If he comes tomorrow, I push him away. The next day, will I be able to push him away again? You know it is hard to say no all the time. The body is not wood but flesh.

**EBUN**: You are under oath. So, lock up your bottom. Lock it up tight.

**SECOND MARKET WOMAN**: Under the heat of desire, who will remember the oath?

**THIRD MARKET WOMAN**: Hear her! A traitor!

**SECOND MARKET WOMAN**: I am not a traitor. It could happen. You all know that for sure. So I suggest we move far away from their reach for some time.

**THIRD MARKET WOMAN**: You mean, we should abandon our homes and children?

**SECOND MARKET WOMAN**: Our husband will take care of them. That will make them realize our importance.

**FOURTH MARKET WOMAN**: Good idea! For once, you are talking sense. But where can we all go together at the same time. We must stay together. That is very important.

**SECOND MARKET WOMAN**: How about the Maternity Home! I'm sure Mama-Nurse will not mind.

**FIRST MARKET WOMAN**: Agreed! Let's go to the Maternity Home.

**EBUN**: If so, everybody fall in, let's go quickly before darkness comes.

[*Before proceeding to the Maternity Home, they perform some choreography to the Theme Song:*]

| | |
|---|---|
| Aie ze n'bria | No one chooses for another |
| Oria to bo'ze | One chooses for oneself |
| Ale ze n'oria | No one chooses for another |
| Oria to bo'ze | One chooses for oneself |
| Eno khole mhen tale | My personal convictions |
| Ole iya re khan | Shall dictate my course of action |
| Ale ze n'ria | No one chooses for another |
| Oria to bo'ze | One chooses for oneself |

### DRAMA VII: DRAMATIC TURN OF EVENTS

[*One early morning in a bush path leading to the stream, holding their water gourd, Oseme and her friend Ejimien enter.*]

**EJIMIEN**: Have you heard the latest?

**OSEME**: No, tell me about it.

**EJIMIEN**: They said that some men went to town to see our mothers.

**OSEME**: Really! What message did they bring back?

**EJIMIEN**: Nobody knows for sure. They only speak in low voices.

**OSEME**: When the rope is tight on the goat's neck, it will cry out "Me-e-e-eeh!" Meanwhile, no matter what they say or do, we must not yield.

**EJIMIEN**: Never!

**OSEME**: Remember, no initiation ceremonies this year until they call back our mothers.

**EJIMIEN**: Agreed.

**OSEME**: You must advise the other girls to hold on till the end.

**EJIMIEN**: Don't worry. Most of them are fully with us. And they are asking questions about circumcision.

**OSEME**: Good. Let them continue to ask until the elders do something about it. Come, let us go quickly to the stream.

### DRAMA VIII: NO CONDITION IS PERMANENT

[*Seven weeks later. One early morning in a village street, the Town Crier enters and beats his gong. People gather around him.*]

**TOWN CRIER**: [*Beats his gong*] Gboi! Gboi! Gboi!
Edion! Egbama! Egbonughele! Egbonefa! Ibha ka eho!
The different age groups of male adults! Listen-oh!

Through this medium, you are all summoned immediately
To the king's palace!
Gboi! Gboi! Gboi!

[*Exit. Feeling very dispirited the Crowd also disperses.*]

[*At the King's Palace, simply represented by his throne. As the villagers arrive, they gather in small groups to discuss the events of the previous days. Fear and anxiety are prominently visible on their faces. Some of them sit among the audience, thus integrating the latter as part of the village crowd.*]

**THIRD ELDER**: I could hardly sleep last night.

**FIRST ELDER**: How could anybody have slept under the circumstance.

**FOURTH ELDER**: It is getting unbearable.

**IRIATA**: Yes, it is. But what do we do now?

**SECOND ELDER**: We need to offer sacrifice.

**IRIATA**: Haven't we offered enough? All our goats and chickens are gone.

**SECOND ELDER**: Have our problems been solved? No. So, we must offer more sacrifice.

**IRIATA**: My people let us be realistic. Look, since the gods have failed us, let us look for other ways to solve our problems.

**SECOND ELDER**: Keep quiet! Which other ways?

[*The King emerges from an inner room. Everybody rises saying "Za-a-a-iki!" He sits on his throne.*]

**KING**: My people, I greet you all.

**CROWD**: Za-a-aiki!

**KING**: Perhaps, some of you are wondering why I called for this meeting.

**CROWD**: Well, may be.

**KING**: Is there any one present here who is unaware of the mysterious things that have been happening recently in this village?

**CROWD**: We are aware of them.

**KING**: By the way, have you all heard about Adawan's torchlight?

**THIRD ELDER**: Yes.

**FOURTH ELDER**: No.

**ORDIA**: Which Adawan?

**IRIATA**: Your uncle.

**ORDIA**: What is it about his torchlight?

**IRIATA**: They said that it flashes on and off by itself. But when the old man tries to switch it on, it wouldn't work. The batteries have been dead for years.

**ORDIA**: A white man gave that torchlight to him long time ago. He used to work for him then in the city as a night watchman.

**FOURTH ELDER**: In those good old days, whenever we saw a light flashing on and off at night, we knew Adawan was in the village visiting.

**FIRST ELDER**: Ezomo, please leave the past alone. Let us discuss the present. Zaiki! You were about to tell us something.

**KING**: Yes, yesterday, three children ran back to the village from the river, leaving behind their calabash.

**CROWD**: Why?

**FIRST ELDER**: According to them, as they approached the river, they heard people singing. When they got there, they saw no one. But as they bent down to fetch water, suddenly they were surrounded by music. So, they ran home shaking like leaves.

**SECOND ELDER**: One of them even said she saw maidens dancing inside the water.

**FIRST ELDER**: Their fathers went to see for themselves. They too came back with the same story. The elders were informed. After a long deliberation, we consulted our chief priest. He referred us to the blind seer of Emado.

**KING**: Let the messengers tell the crowd about their journey.

**FIRST ELDER**: Osuma, go on, narrate your story to the crowd.

**THIRD ELDER**: When we got there, we met a young girl outside the door.

**KING**: A young girl? That's strange!

**FOURTH ELDER**: It was a boy we saw.

**THIRD ELDER**: To me he looked like a girl. Anyway before we could say anything the person said: "Elders of Otoedo! The seer said, 'You have walked well. However, you cannot see him today for this is the last of his seven days retreat. Tell your people that they shall see him tomorrow morning at the king's palace'"

**FOURTH ELDER**: We were surprised. How did the seer know that we were there?

**THIRD ELDER**: How did he know about our mission?

**FIRST ELDER**: They said that although blind, he sees visions by feeling the air.

**SECOND ELDER**: Some even said that he could communicate with the dead.

**THIRD ELDER**: On our way back, as we were talking about the old man, suddenly we heard people singing. We looked around, saw no one. But we heard the song, very loud and clear. So, my people, we took to our heels.

**FIRST ELDER**: Can you recall the song?

[*Adawan arrives, goes to sit quietly.*]

**IRIATA**: [*To Ordia*] Your uncle has just arrived.

**ORDIA**: I've seen him.

[*The Third and Fourth Elders try to sing the song, but they can't. Ordia hums the tune of the sung: "Why Do You Do That to Us?"*]

**THIRD ELDER**: [*With surprise*] The song! That's it.

**FOURTH ELDER**: No doubt! That's the song. But you didn't go with us.

**ORDIA**: That's true.

**THIRD ELDER**: How did you come about that song, then? Zaiki!

This is amazing.

**KING**: Ordia, we need an explanation.

**ORDIA**: Zaiki, it's a very long story.

**KING**: Narrate it. Perhaps, it will help us to understand some of these omens.

**ORDIA**: Strange things have been happening to me lately, things that I am not too sure about. Could they be the fruits of my imagination, I sometimes wonder. Hence I couldn't mention them to anybody. It all started one day, while waiting for my mother to send down my supper. Suddenly, the door clicked, opened, remained ajar, but nobody came in. I thought it was opened by the wind, so I closed it back. Few minutes later, the door reopened, remained ajar. Again nobody came it. From then on, I started bolting the door. One afternoon, I heard three taps on the door. I opened it but saw nobody. I went outside, looked everywhere; nobody was visible. As I was about going in, I heard distinct footsteps crunching behind me. I turned around, there was no one around. But I noticed that our oldest goat was wagging her tail as if seeing someone familiar. These things continued to happen on and off before I travelled. I returned yesterday from my trip feeling very tired. I laid on my bed in a troubled doze, my mind tormented by bitter memories. I didn't know when sleep finally silenced my mind. I dreamt that I was in an arena. Drumbeats ushered in some maidens, singing that song. Ize, my daughter was one of them. She danced and danced, just like she did last year.

**FIRST ELDER**: Oh! The girl with feather-legs, she used to dance as if there were no bones in her. She would have been my daughter-in-law by now.

**ORDIA**: As she danced, everybody hailed her. I went into the arena to "spray" her according to tradition. She stepped backward asking: "What are you doing here all alone? Where is my mother?" I looked around, my wife was not there. I searched for her among the crowd. She was nowhere to be found. For the first time, I noticed that the crowd was made up of men alone.

**IRIATA**: Just as we are right now?

**ORDIA**: Yes, I started to shout, "Wede! Where are you? Wede!" When I woke up, I touched my face; it was wet. Have I been crying in my sleep? Me! A man? Doubt, fear and pride wrestled against one another inside me. Life is unpredictable.

**KING**: It would seem that your dream and the various omens occurring in this village are connected.

**FIRST ELDER**: Zaiki! I agree with you completely.

**THIRD ELDER**: What could be the meaning of all these?

**FIRST ELDER**: Let us hope that when the blind seer arrives, he will unravel the mysteries.

**THE SEER'S VOICE**: He is already here.

**CROWD**: [*Some rising, some bending to search under their seat*] Where?

**SEER**: Right here. [*Walks into the arena with an aura of dignity and reverence.*] Sit down, everybody. Here I am before you. Why do you stir an old man from his recluse?

**KING**: Pardon our temerity. The palm kernel does not shed tears except it is under pressure. This village has been under confusion and fear for so long.

**SEER**: For exactly how long?

**KING**: For about seven weeks now.

**SEER**: Seven weeks you said?

**KING**: Yes old one, seven weeks.

**SEER**: Hmm! That's about the time one of your wives was repudiated in the market place.

**FIRST ELDER**: Come to think of it, that's right.

**KING**: Since then, this village has not been at peace. We have consulted oracles and we have offered sacrifice. We no longer know what to do, hence we seek your help.

**SEER**: [*Sniffs the air*] Hmm! The air! [*Sniffs again.*]
Yes, that's right. The air is heavy.
Some obscure forces are pulling the strings
The future is shaping itself.
It may assume any form.
But the events of the future
Are already present.
Just as the events
Of the past are present.
Today, the self is no longer
What it was yesterday
But another self:
And tomorrow, another.
They who tamper with nature
Can never be at peace.

[*Pause, sniffs the air.*]

Yes. The air is heavy.
The place is crowded.
Ah! What a crowd!
But where are those
Who ought to be here,
But are not here?
Where are they?
Hmm! A huge sacrifice,
Too heavy for the vulture!

Behold it staggers beneath
The weight of its victim!

[*Pause, sniffs the air.*]

Hmm! You think the worm is dancing,
But that's the way it walks.
You think the thunder is angry,
But that's just the way he is.
Calm down! Calm down!
Calm down your fear.
The leopard may look ferocious,
But a cat is a cat.
A cat can be tamed.

**SECOND ELDER**: Who wants to do anything with a wild cat?

**ELDERS**: Will you shut it up!

**SEER**: [*Does as if hypnotizing them*] Sh-sh-sh-sh!
Silence! Complete silence!
I hear some sound.
Cripples are weeping.
Orphans are wailing.
And widowers are snivelling.
Listen! Listen carefully to the noise.
Come on! Step down!
Step down, down and down
To the deep sea of your mind.
Hark! I hear some sound.
The leopards are beginning to rouse.
They open their eyes.
They stretch their body.
Here comes the chance for peace
To enthrone herself over this land.
Humility is the enemy of pride
As peace is of war.
Look! The leopards are prowling
Stealthily, they mount up to the palace gate.
With their snout, they push open the doors.
Yes, look at them assuming former forms.
Music is the food for the spirit.

Beat them some sound to inebriate them.
For here they come. Here they are.
Asking questions.

[*Like puppets, the Elders move away from the arena to beat the drums. Music, snorts, eerie sound. The Maiden Ghosts appear, perform synchronized choreography to the following song:*]

*I*
*Why did you do that to us?*
*Why did you do that to us?*
*We were so healthy and strong*
*Before you sent us away*
*Far, to the sacred grove*
*That's where they cut us*
*With the evil blade*
*And sent us to Hades*
*With speed*

*II*
*Why did you do that to us?*
*Why did you do that to us?*
*After you sent us to Hades with speed*
*We cannot rest in any peace*
*For, we've been denied the chance*
*To life full life*
*Hence now we roam in space*
*Longing and sighing*
*Through time*
*Chorus*
*Oh why?*
*Why did you do that to us?*
*Oh why?*
*Why did you do that to us?*
*Why? Why?*
*Oh why? Why?*
*Oh why? Why?*
*Oh why?*

[*Drumbeats switch to that of "Agbega Dance." The Maidens dance until the Seer waves his hand into the air. The Ghosts disappear. The Elders return to their former seats.*

*Simultaneously, Ordia screams: "Ize-e-e!" The Elders are dehypnotized. They look at each other with bewilderment.*]

**THIRD ELDER**: [*Touching him*] Iriata! Is this you?

**IRIATA**: Yes. It is I.

**THIRD ELDER**: Edogun! Is this you, yourself?

**SECOND ELDER**: It is my very self, Osuma.

**THIRD ELDER**: What is happening? It . . . It . . . It seems I saw just now, my twin sister. She was here dancing. But she died long time ago; we were about ten or eleven years old then. She got sick after circumcision.

**FOURTH ELDER**: And I saw my betrothed, my ebony, and my rising sun. I went to see her the eve before they went to the initiation camp. She never came back to the village. Life is unpredictable. Aye-e-e!

**SEER**: Sh-sh-sh-sh- silence!
The air is bubbling
The place is crowded
But where are those
Who ought to be here,
But are not here?
Where are the pearls of the sea?
Are they cast before the swine?
Where are the bright eyes of the forest?
Are the twigs holding back
The tigress by the tail?
Wisdom is the chief path to happiness
But rashness pays a price
Of great magnitude
And teaches wisdom in old age.

**KING**: The price has been paid.
But happiness is not yet in sight.
We need your help.

**SEER**: The solution you seek is within you.
Prudence shall be your guide.
Sh-sh-sh-sh-! I hear some sound. [*Listens.*] Umhum!
Speak! I am listening.
Yes. [*Pauses, listens.*] Edokparu,
He who glared at the lion and the lion recoiled.
What's about him? [*Pauses, listens.*]
"His heir should not forget in the dark
What he learnt in the light.

He should hold out the light
That all may see through the woods. [*Pauses, listens.*]
War may last with foreign foes
But love will always band those
That it once had bound.
If the market steams,
It is people that gather there.
Each village chooses its own market day."
All right. I believe so.
They have heard everything.
[*To the Elders*] You've heard it all.
So spoke the oracle.
I am only a messenger.

[*The Seer disappears.*]

**FOURTH ELDER**: Where is he?

**THIRD ELDER**: He's gone!

**IRIATA**: Gone?

**KING**: Yes, he is gone. However, you all heard what he said. It is now left for us to search within us for the solution to our problem. Is Adawan here?

**FIRST ELDER**: Yes. He is over there.

**KING**: Old one! My homage! Wisdom comes with age. So says our sage. You are the oldest living descendant of Edokparu.

So, show us the way out of the woods.

**ADAWAN**: [*Clears his throat*] Hm-mh. Do we all know those who ought to be here but are not here?

**SECOND ELDER**: Of course, we do. They are our wives roaming about in town like wild animals.

**THIRD ELDER**: How did you know that?

**SECOND ELDER**: If they were not, why are they not where they ought to be, among us?

**FOURTH ELDER**: You speak as if you don't know why they went away.

**SECOND ELDER**: Listen to that! Women took off abandoning their husband and children, yet we have done nothing. What are men becoming? Have we lost our authority? Have our medicines lost their potency? If not, those women should have run back to us, naked and crawling. But here we are paralyzed as if under hypnosis. We are unable to do anything except to listen to an old blind man recommending an old dying man to be our leader. My friends! Wake up from your stupor! Let us act as men.

**FIRST ELDER**: Edogun! Shut up your mouth! Sit down! Enough of your foolish talk! See where your rashness has led us. Some of us objected to the repudiation rite. We thought it was too severe. We wanted the family to settle the problem quietly. But you, in particular, insisted on the ritual to teach the other women a lesson. You never thought for one minute that the situation would turn out to be like this. You never imagined that women could stick together to fight for a cause. This is the seventh week they went away. Who in this village can boast that all has been well in his home since then?

**IRIATA**: My life has been disorganized since then: No rest during the day, no sleep at night. My twelve months old baby is always crying. I have never been so terrified in my life as I was the other day she was sick. No. Enough is enough!

**THIRD ELDER**: I have seven children. I can't get them to do anything. The whole house is turned upside down. I can't stand it any more.

**FOURTH ELDER**: [*Pointing to his phallus*] Look! This thing is lifeless. For seven weeks now, it has not seen the loin of any woman. We must look for a way to bring back our women immediately.

**KING**: Ezomo! That is what we are doing right now. It is not as if we have not tried to do so. Ihama! Tell them about our previous attempts.

**FIRST ELDER**: First of all, we sent people to carry our message to the women. We asked them to either return home immediately or face banishment. What did they do? They defied our order. Then we sent some other people to explain to them the situation at home since they left. If need be, they should appeal to them to return.

**SECOND ELDER**: Beg them! *Chei!* The world is spoilt!

**IRIATA**: Let it be.

**FIRST ELDER**: Iriata! You are the husband of their leader. We thought you could reason with your wife that was why we asked you to lead our men. Please narrate to the crowd the message you brought back.

**IRIATA**: Yes. I can still remember their words vividly: "We are women. We love being women, wives and mothers. But each woman wants to be herself, think for herself, and express herself in her own way as a unique being. Circumcision takes these rights from us, makes us objects. Today, we reject that status. We can no longer live by simply following the ideas handed over to us. So, ban circumcision, repeal Edewede's repudiation or forget about us." My people! That was their message.

**ORDIA**: How can I forget my Wede?

**ADAWAN**: It is difficult to forget those that one has had certain ties with. Memories only bury themselves deep down in our mind. Mere sound, taste, sight, odour or even a flash of thought suffices to stir them up from their recluse to open up a vast universe where the past and the present fuse into one.

**ORDIA**: Just like the other day I dreamt about Wede. Oh, I miss her a lot. She means so much to me.

**THIRD ELDER**: Who knows how they are doing over there?

**IRIATA**: The day we went there, they looked very happy. In very high spirits, they explained to us how they fill their day with different activities. They built an orphanage for the maternity home. Can you believe that?

**SECOND ELDER**: We know that you miss your wife. But don't exaggerate.

**IRIATA**: If a blind man can not see, does it mean that the leaves on the trees are not green?

**SECOND ELDER**: Who is the blind man? You insult me, an elder!

**FIRST ELDER**: Behave like an elder, then. Sit down! Let us discuss the issue before us like elders. Zaiki! To you, we are all listening.

**KING**: This matter concerns all of us. We have to take a collective decision on it. You have all heard about their demands. So do we ban circumcision or banish the women?

**SECOND ELDER**: Banish the women.

**ORDIA**: What! Are you out of your mind?

**SECOND ELDER**: Not at all.

**THIRD ELDER**: Do we also banish our young daughters?

**SECOND ELDER**: Who is talking about children right now?

**THIRD ELDER**: Are they not in the middle of all this? Besides, they have refused to go in for the initiation ceremonies. No matter what their grandmothers say, they remain silent. Do I speak for everybody or is it just my children that are behaving like that?

**FIRST ELDER**: According to report reaching us, it is so with all the young girls in this village.

**FOURTH ELDER**: Are we surprised? They witnessed the repudiation rites. And they know the reason behind it.

**SECOND ELDER**: [*To Ordia*] That's your daughter's handiwork.

Like mother like child! May they be banished forever!

**FOURTH ELDER**: Iseh! Amen!

**THIRD ELDER**: Ezomoh! Are you on his side?

**FOURTH ELDER**: Who said so?

**THIRD ELDER**: You said Iseh to his malicious prayer.

**FOURTH ELDER**: Mere routine. Each day we say things without really meaning them.

**THIRD ELDER**: Ah! I was going to inform you that he has been quarrelling with his wife, lsemua, over the young girl he is intending at Ugbegun. So, Isemua might as well stay in town forever.

**ORDIA**: Let us ignore that man. My people come to think about it. Of what use is circumcision to us today? Does it in anyway, threaten our manhood? Those in town have done away with it. Why can't we do the same here?

**SECOND ELDER**: You mean we should destroy our tradition?

**FOURTH ELDER**: Indeed an ancient tradition. But its validity today is worth looking into.

**SECOND ELDER**: It served our forefathers some purpose and we are their offspring. So the same goes for us.

**FIRST ELDER**: We are not talking about what was, but what is. Right now, we have found ourselves in a difficult situation. We must choose a line of action, for the sake of progress.

**IRIATA**: What progress can we make when fear and anxiety weigh heavy on our mind?

**ADAWAN**: My children listen to me. I have seen more days on earth than any of you. I have been to places more than any of you have. In all these places, I have seen changes upon changes. Values are not eternal, but constantly changing. We all know this fact. And it isn't as if we don't know that circumcision has lost its value. But our real problem right now is fear. We are all prisoners of fear.

**SECOND ELDER**: Hear that! I told you all before. Listen to him.

He said we are prisoners. [*Laughs.*]

**ADAWAN**: Yes. I repeat, we are all prisoners of fear. Why are we afraid of change? Can anyone evade what is?

**FOURTH ELDER**: No, we can only make attempt.

**ADAWAN**: Mere illusion.

**FOURTH ELDER**: Mere futility.

**ADAWAN**: Borne out of ignorance.

**FOURTH ELDER**: Native to man from pristine time.

**ADAWAN**: My children enough! Put away your fear. Fight for your liberty. True liberty is the ability to act freely in full knowledge of what one is doing and why one is doing it. True liberty gives more sense to one's life. So my people fight for your freedom. [*To the King*] Zaiki! This is my old torchlight. I entrust it into your care. When they shall have overcome their fear, it will see them to town through the woods.

**KING**: We appreciate your precious gift.

**ADAWAN**: Zaiki!

**KING**: My people, the old one has spoken deeply about knowledge, freewill and human action. So, on this issue before us, what have you all to say? Please speak out your mind freely.

**FOURTH ELDER**: Tendency to resist change is a common trait in man. But sooner or later, change will come despite all resistance.

**KING**: Ah! See oh! Light! It came on just like that.

**ELDERS**: Are you sure?

**KING**: Yes. I can't believe it.

**FIRST ELDER**: Your Highness let me see.

[*They pass the torchlight from hand to hand interjecting some expressions of surprise as the torchlight switches on and off automatically from hand to hand.*]

**SECOND ELDER**: Put away that torchlight! My people remember Ikeken. Few years ago the people suffered from some strange disease and they were almost wiped out. Our gods are supreme. They are the authors of everything. Let us not call upon our heads the anger of the gods. We must protect our customs and traditions.

**IRIATA**: That is for you. As far as I know, we were too severe on our wives. That is why they abandoned us? If I remember correctly, we all took a collective decision to repudiate Ordia's wife. There were no gods among us then. Or were there? [*Some murmuring among the Elders.*] Therefore our suffering is of our own making.

**SECOND ELDER**: Sit down! You don't know what you are saying.

**IRIATA**: Hear this fool! Do you know anything at all about life? To you, human relationship means nothing? All you know is to talk about gods and sacrifice.

**FIRST ELDER**: Enough, you two!

**ORDIA**: My people, I greet you all.

**CROWD**: Same to you.

**ORDIA**: Our elders, I greet you all.

**ELDERS**: Same to you.

**ORDIA**: Esan khide!

**ELDERS**: Imhan khide.

**ORDIA**: Esan khide!

**ELDER**: Imhan khide.

**ORDIA**: The Zaiki has enjoined us to speak out our mind freely. So, I beg you all to grant me that favour. You all know that at the beginning of all this, I gave you all my full support. I carried out faithfully the repudiation rites, not that my wife offended me in anyway, but as my mother would say, the village is bigger than one man. So, I gave up my happiness for the village. But since then, the village has not been at peace nor have I. Right now, we are all lost in an ocean of confusion. However, my mind is made up. I am ready to pick up my life and move on. If you all still decide to hold tightly to worn out tradition, then I will say goodbye to this village. A man does not make up a home. A home is where a man lives with his wife and children. So I am going to look for my wife. Wherever she is, there, will I be. [*Sings the Theme Song.*]

**IRIATA**: [*Rising*] Ordia! Wait for me. [*To the King*] Zaiki! My baby needs her mother. I need my wife. With humility, I say goodbye.

[*Except for the First and Second Elders, others join in saying: "Me also, I need my wife. Goodbye."*]

**KING**: Wait! Everybody wait! if you all go away, who will live in this village?

**SOME ELDERS**: [*Pointing to the Second Elder*] Him.

**KING**: Himself alone?

**SOME ELDERS**: Yes, himself and people like him.

**KING**: Ihama! What do you say to that?

**FIRST ELDER**: Your Highness, it would seem that they are asking you to ban circumcision.

**KING**: Is that the wish of everybody?

**SOME ELDERS**: Yes.

**SECOND ELDER**: No! Zaiki, let's put it to vote.

**SOME ELDERS**: Yes, yes. Let's vote on it.

**KING**: All right then. Everybody sit down. Ihama!

**FIRST ELDER**: Yes, Your Highness.

**KING**: You've heard them. Go on, conduct the vote.

**FIRST ELDER**: All those in support of female circumcision lift up your right hands. [*They do so and he counts and records.*] All those against female circumcision lift up your right hands. [*He repeats formalities.*]

**KING**: [*To a spectator*] You! You didn't lift up your hand at all. What's your opinion on the subject?

[*Some spectators are interviewed here. Thus integrating the audience in the debate.*]

**FIRST ELDER**: Everybody! Listen to the result of our vote. [*He reads it out accordingly. Those against circumcision outnumber those for it.*]

**KING**: You have all expressed your opinion on the subject. Majority carries the vote. Ihama!

**FIRST ELDER**: Za-a-a-iki!

**KING**: Send for our wives without delay.

**FIRST ELDER**: Your Highness, what shall we tell them?

**KING**: Tell them that I, Edeikholor, The Ojiso of Otoedo land, descendant of Oba Ewuare, the wicked but magnanimous enough to grant his fugitive lords chiefdom, want to see them immediately. Arrange for their homecoming. We shall welcome them with festivity.

**FIRST ELDER**: The king's order must be obeyed. We are your subjects. Za-a-a-aiki!

[*The Theme Song filters in softly during the changing of the scene. Fade out.*]

## IX: RECONCILIATION

[*Seven days later. Early in the morning, on a village street. The Town Crier enters, beats his gong. People gather around him.*]

**TOWN CRIER**: Gboi! Gboi! Gboi!
Men! Women! Listen-oh!
Through this medium
You are all reminded
To assemble today in Eguale
At the Royal Palace
To welcome our women
Back home from abroad.
Gboi! Gboi! Gboi! [Exit.]

[*Later that same day. It is a bright sunny day. Soft, cheerful drumbeats warm the atmosphere. The Palace is already fully crowded with men dressed in colourful Esan traditional attire known as "Igbulu-ododo." Joy and doubt alternate with each other on their faces as they await the arrival of the women. The old women of the village come in one by one carrying their stools. They are casually dressed in locally loom-woven material. All of a sudden, coming from the direction of the town, the sound of singing is heard:*]

| | |
|---|---|
| *Ebholo do ghe-e-e-e* | *People come out and see* |
| *Ebholo do ghe-e-e-e* | *People come out and see* |
| *Imhan nikhwo Otoedo* | *We, the women of Otoedo* |
| *Imhan tu bha hia* | *Greet you all* |
| *Imhan ne erumhun* | *We pray that God* |
| *Nosa deba mhan hia* | *Be with us all* |
| *Iseh! Iseh! Iseh!* | *Amen! Amen! Amen!* |

**FOURTH ELDER**: [*Jubilating*] They've lived. That must be them singing.

**SECOND ELDER**: Calm down, my friend!

**FOURTH ELDER**: Shut up! Who's your friend?

[*At the palace gate, the Town Crier blows his horn. The King, in full regalia, emerges from an inner room, mounts his throne.*]

**CROWD**: Za-a-a-aiki!

**KING**: Have they arrived?

**FIRST ELDER**: Not yet, Your Highness. But, we heard some women singing. They can't be far away from here.

**IRATA**: [*Looking down the pathway*] No doubt, they will be here any moment from now. Ah look! Someone is coming.

**THIRD ELDER**: [*Joining him*] That's the Town Crier.

**TOWN CRIER**: [*Runs in to prostrate before the King*] Za-a-iki! The women greet you all. They say they thank God that their legs have touched the soil of Otoedo once again. They asked if they could advance forward?

**KING**: Tell them we are waiting for them. But first of all get the mother of the village to wash their feet.

[*Drumbeats. The Village Matron and her Assistant dance in to perform the rites of restitution on the women at the entrance of the palace. The latter are wearing "Iro" and "buba" in the latest lace material design. After the cleansing rites, the women dance to the king singing.*]

| Ebun | Chorus |
|---|---|
| *Awe no gigan nu ghe mhan yore Awe* | *Awe* |
| *Awe no gigan nu ghe mhan yore Awe* | *Awe* |
| *Eboka rogo, boghede rogo Awe* | *Awe* |
| *Ebi toito ehe no bhie-e Awe* | *Awe* |
| *Aie rebe okhwenkhwen ghale ebhiyin* | *Awe* |
| *Awe o-oh nu ghe imhan yore* | *Awe* |
| *Awe o-oh-oh ghe imhan yore* | *Awe* |
| *Oh-oh ghe imhan yore Awe* | *Awe* |
| *Awe the great see we have gone and come back* | *Awe* |
| *Awe the great see we have gone and come back* | *Awe* |
| *The leaves of maize and of banana are in the farm* | *Awe* |
| *The leaves of itoito are very broad* | *Awe* |
| *The leaves of okhwenkhwen are not used for wrapping things* | *Awe* |
| *Awe o-oh! See we are back* | *Awe* |
| *Awe o-oh! See we are back* | *Awe* |
| *Oh-oh! See we are back* | *Awe* |

[*To be repeated all over until they get to the King.*]

**EBUN**: Za-a-aiki! We learnt that you sent for us.

**KING**: Yes. You are welcome. [*Clears his voice.*] Yes. About circumcision, while you were away, we have all thought about it. Everybody has expressed his opinion on it. Now, I make my declaration public. As from this day, whereas, the initiation ceremonies shall still be performed, female circumcision is banned in this village. Whosoever is found practising it in any form, will not step out of this village alive. Let those who have heard tell those who have not heard.

[*Signs of joy from the young women, but sighs of disapproval from the old women. Edewede who has been standing alone at the gate intones the following song:*]

| | |
|---|---|
| *Uluese baba-oh* | *Father you have done well* |
| *Uluese Abhulimhen* | *Fair verdict you have done well* |
| *Uluese Uluese* | *You have done well, done well* |
| *Uluese baba-a* | *You have done well father.* |

[*The women go to bring in Edewede. As they dance to their husbands, they sing:*]

| | |
|---|---|
| *Osa lumhen nose Oluese* | *God has done me well, has done well* |
| *Oluwe nose Oluese* | *God has done you well, has done well* |
| *Olumhan nose Oluese* | *God has done us well, has done well* |
| *Oluese noigbokan* | *He does good without ever berating one* |

[*Drumbeats increase, followed by general jubilation. Husbands embrace wives; they dance out of the arena. As if rooted to a spot, Ebikere stares at a distance. Edewede and Ordia dance towards her. She picks up her stool, walks out of the arena calmly. Followed by Ordia and Edewede. Fade out.*]

### Glossary

**Ale mhen egbe:** May the food nourish your body.
**Agbo le akho:** May tomorrow bring some more.
**Chieu!:** A hissing sound of disapproval.
**Dokita:** Local way of pronouncing "doctor."
**Ehenh!:** Yes.
**Esan khide:** Esan will never fall.
**Imhan khide:** We will never fall.
**Idigun gbe:** May this fetish kill.
**Iseh:** Amen.
**Nene:** Granny.
**Oyia-oh!:** Expression of self-pity.
**Jingletet yepkete:** Colloquial descriptive expression of helplessness.
**Zaiki:** Your Royal Highness.

# IN THE CONTINUUM

*Danai Gurira and Nikkole Salter*

*In the Continuum* was born out of our profound concern for . . . black women fighting against HIV/AIDS. Black women currently represent the highest rate of new infections—both in the U.S. and Africa—and this . . . story is told from that perspective. Developed during our third year at New York University's graduate acting program—with an invaluable artistic community of students and teachers—it is a representation of the humanity behind the statistics and an invitation for more unheard stories to be brought "In(to) the Continuum."

**Danai Gurira, Zimbabwe, and Nikkole Salter, United States**

*In the Continuum* concerns two black women—living on opposite sides of the Atlantic Ocean—who are diagnosed with AIDS. Danai Gurira and Nikkole Salter, the play's coauthors, portray multiple roles in this ninety-minute exploration of the devastating effect AIDS has had on black women. Begun as a graduate acting Freeplay project at New York University (NYU) in early 2004, *In the Continuum* quickly caught the attention of the New York theatre community. Chosen by both *The New York Times* and *New York Magazine* as one of the top four plays of 2005 and the winner of an Obie Award and the Outer Critics John Gassner Award, the play will soon be published in Jeffrey Jenkins's *The Ten Best Plays Yearbook 2005–2006*. In addition, *In the Continuum* received the 2004 Global Tolerance Award from the Friends of the United Nations, was featured at the 2006 Edinburgh Festival (Scotland), and has toured both South Africa and Zimbabwe. For the 2006–2007 theatre season, the play toured throughout the United States. Dania and Nikkole completed their tour in July 2007 at the renowned Grahamstown Festival in South Africa.

## DANAI GURIRA

> When I was growing up in Zimbabwe during the eighties and nineties, it [HIV/AIDS] was around me all the time. And I think that's what really made me . . . create pieces about HIV and African women. I felt like their stories were so unheard and they were just statistics, and that was truly upsetting me.

Danai Gurira was born in the United States, to Zimbabwean parents, where her father was a professor at Iowa's Grinnell College. In 1983, when she was five, the family returned to Zimbabwe. Danai attended local primary and secondary schools and was also a member of the Children's Performing Arts Workshop (CHIMPAWO), founded by renowned playwrights Robert McLaren and Stephen Chifunyise.

She returned to the United States to attend Macalester College in Minnesota, where she majored in psychology and also took several theatre courses. In 1999, during her junior year abroad, Danai traveled to South Africa to participate in an arts and social change program. Transformed by the experience and frustrated by the scarcity of literary works written by and for contemporary African women, she created her own pieces upon returning to the United States. After graduation, Danai entered New York University's graduate acting program, where she received an MFA in acting.

A talented actress, Danai has appeared in several plays in New York City, including *Forbidden City*, a Lincoln Center Workshop production, and *God Botherers*, part of the Public Theater/New York Shakespeare Festival New Works Now series. Other theatrical credits include *The Story* (Philadelphia Theatre Company) and *King Baabu* (at Scotland's prestigious Edinburgh Fringe Festival). She is a recipient of a 2007 Helen Hayes Award for Outstanding Lead Actress. Danai has also appeared in the television series *Law and Order: Criminal Intent* and the films *Patience* (for the United Nations Educational, Scientific, and Cultural Organization), *Trial of Charumathi*, and is featured in Tom McCarthy's *The Visitor*, the story of illegal immigrants living in New York City. Danai has also recorded *The Stone Virgins*, by late Zimbabwean writer Yvonne Vera, as a book on tape. Danai is a 2007 recipient of a Theatre Communications Group New Generations Award to travel to Liberia to conduct research on her new play *Eclipsed*, scheduled to open at the McCarter Theatre in 2009.

**Excerpts from Our Interview**

*On her 1999 trip to South Africa and her decision to pursue theatre:*

During that time . . . we went to see plays in Johannesburg, and we met artists from all genres, from photography to sculpture . . . painters . . . poets . . . actors . . . and they really transformed me in terms of realizing that I needed to do what they've done and have the courage to step into this art form as my career or as my life's work. I knew this was what I wanted. . . . In a way I felt like I didn't want to be an entertainer. I wanted to explore hard-hitting issues . . . social-changing issues that I felt passionate about.

I think there was a part of me that didn't feel that this art form [theatre] could do that as much as I would like. I think this was something holding me back. When I realized that this was where my passion and love was . . . and meeting these amazing South African artists who were in a far less beneficial situation than me—and yet they were making that choice to work in their craft—that really . . . gave me a very clear realization that I needed to dedicate myself to what I love.

*On the character of "Abigail":*

The world thinks that . . . African women are so deficient and problematic and that's why we have this issue [HIV]. In reality, there are so many amazing, highly intelligent, complex, highly functioning . . . people in society who get struck down by this disease. . . . I grew up in a middle-class Zimbabwe environment and people right there. . . . I have many relatives and family friends who have died of AIDS. . . . When I left home and I saw how . . . riskier it was to be a married woman in Africa than single . . . that's why I chose the character I did for the play.

***On her intended audience:***

Everybody! I had the West in mind for the simple reason that I feel they need to see . . . subjective, humanized portraits of . . . African people. That was something that really fueled me, the fact that we are so underrepresented. Also, for my own people, I wanted to address an issue which we never speak of in our culture: women tolerating promiscuous men who expose them to HIV. It just goes so unspoken. We don't talk about this issue, even though we know that HIV is a big killer. We have all the advertisements, we have all this awareness, but we never go into the real nitty-gritty of what in our culture is perpetuating this problem. For me, that was very frustrating . . . how many women are . . . blamed . . . and punished for contracting HIV, even though they receive it from their husbands.

***Where she would like to be in ten years:***

I'd love to have written a couple of plays and books. I'm interested in making and being in films. I want to continue telling the stories of African people. There are so many to tell. . . . I also want to help create acting conservatories in Zimbabwe. That's my optimal life: to spend a certain number of months here in the U.S. and a certain number . . . in Zimbabwe. Gradually, however, my time will be more spent on the continent than here.

Danai Gurira, telephone interview, October 5, 2006.

## NIKKOLE SALTER

> I believe in the power of storytelling. I know that it can move people, not merely down the path of diversion, but to the heights of . . . enlightenment, education, advancement, growth, healing, understanding, inquiry, and reflection. I have, therefore, made it my mission to produce—through glaringly honest, thought-provoking, and memorable performance and literature—stories that reveal the gamut of the human experience. The stories I tell will entertain and, most importantly, spiritually and emotionally move people to act in ways that promote self, societal, and cosmic understanding, the value of human existence, and the affirmative evolution of life.

Born in 1979, Nikkole Salter is a native Californian. Her interest in theatre began when her mother enrolled the young girl in a summer theatre program hosted by television actress Danielle Spencer (*What's Happening!!*) at Southwest Community College. Nikkole played the lead role in an adaptation of *Cinderella*.

Determined to pursue acting, Nikkole, on the advice of her mentor, television actress Wendy Raquel Robinson (The Steve Harvey Show), enrolled in Howard

University's Theatre Arts department, where she received her bachelor of fine arts. Nikkole also studied at the British American Drama Academy (BADA) at Oxford University and later received her master of fine arts in acting from New York University.

She has played a wide range of roles on stage and in film and television. Her stage work consists of *King Hedley, We Won't Play, Gum, Three Sisters* (NYU), and *Jitney* (the Studio Theatre in Washington, DC). Other credits include the televisions shows *Moesha* and *L.A. Kids*, the 2003 Sundance Film Festival Official Selection short film *Whispers* (2003), and the feature films *The Architect* (2006) and *Pride and Glory* (2007).

**Excerpts from Our Interview**

*On her inspiration for the play:*

There was something about the statistics [on AIDS] . . . that hit me in ways that statistics don't usually hit me. . . . I heard them on a special that MTV did about the celebrities who had been infected, such as Arthur Ashe and Eazy E., and what the surrounding celebrity community thought about their diagnosis and their ultimate deaths. The show actually wasn't about the larger community, but they mentioned statistics about African American women. . . . This was late 2003 when I determined that I would write about AIDS and black women.

*On the play's title:*

The title was my idea. I lived in Bedford Stuyvesant, in Brooklyn, and I would walk down the street and . . . see a group of guys on one side of the street, loitering—a group of young guys. They would always be there . . . day in and day out. . . . And across the street from them was . . . a group of older guys, well over fifty, who also loitered . . . day in and day out. One day, I wondered if the young men could look across the street and see the older men and see where they were headed. And then I wondered if the older men looked across the street and saw the younger men and saw where they came from.

And then I began to think about my own life and my own family and about what they do in terms of employment. . . . I thought about what an anomaly I am. I was trying to it figure out: How did I break that cycle, that continuum? There is nothing about what I do, or what I've done, that necessarily coincides with the hand that was dealt to me or what the world expects of me. . . . I'm one of the few members in my immediate family who has a college degree and the only one to pursue and complete college right after high school. I'm the only one with a graduate degree. There are no actors, no writers in my family;

none of them have moved out of LA in pursuit of their dreams. Maybe it's the weather. . . . I must admit, I miss it!

***On whether she was targeting a specific audience:***
Not so directly, but, yes, I definitely wanted to perform this for African Americans. I definitely wanted to perform this in LA, definitely for young people, or at least people who remembered what it was like to be young.

***On any difficulty co-writing* In the Continuum:**
No, actually it was very helpful. It was good to have another perspective to make sure I was being clear with what I wanted to say. It also helped me to refine and define my intention and make sure my execution was clear.

***On her desire for* In the Continuum's *future:***
I . . . hope that it will take the country by storm and people will perform it everywhere. And it will begin to be deconstructed and taken apart. It can be played by ten different women instead of two. . . . I want the message and the work to live and the spirit in which it was created to be preserved and multiplied. I believe in collaboration: The artistic input and creativity of others have the potential to make this piece something greater than either Danai or myself could have ever envisioned. That is my hope: That the play continues to grow and positively influence all it touches. That is my vision for this piece.

Nikkole Salter, telephone interview, September 20, 2006.

*In the Continuum* received a workshop production at Robert Egan's Ojai Playwright's Conference in August 2004 and its first professional production at the Mud Bone Collective in September of that same year. Under the direction of Robert O'Hara, the play had its New York debut at Primary Stages, an Off-Broadway theatre, in September 2005. A month later, it moved to the Perry Street Theatre, where it ran for four additional months. The play, produced by Primary Stages in association with Martin Platt, David Elliot, Patrick Blake, Cheryl Wiesenfeld, and Richard Jordan, then enjoyed a yearlong international tour, traveling to the Harare International Festival of the Arts (Harare, Zimbabwe), the Baxter Theatre (Cape Town, South Africa), the Market Theatre (Johannesburg, South Africa), the Traverse Theatre (Edinburgh, Scotland), the Woolly Mammoth Theatre (Washington, DC), Cincinnati Playhouse in the Park (Cincinnati, Ohio), the Kirk Douglas Theatre (Los Angeles), the Yale Reparatory Theatre (New Haven, Connecticut), the Philadelphia Theatre Company (Philadelphia), and the Goodman Theatre (Chicago), where it ended its tour in June 2007.

### How This Piece Is Performed

This piece was born of two actors deeply concerned about the experience of black women in the present fight against HIV/AIDS. Presently, with black women being the population with the highest rate of new infections both in the United States and Africa, the co-creators of this piece (one African and one African American) felt the need to have a story told from the black woman's perspective; for her to be more than a statistic on a news report. This piece is designed for two actors to incorporate separate, yet parallel, stories of an African and African American woman and for both worlds to parallel and sometimes collide. Each character is real and is performed as such, not a commentary on a stereotype but an illustration of three-dimensional human experiences in these societies. The piece as presently designed allows each actor to create her own environment, both with sound and movement and minimal props. It is a minimalist piece, performed with no set and only two chairs onstage. Lighting and sound elements can enhance the creation of each world but are used supportively and only when necessary—the actors create the environment with their bodies and voices. Though the piece is performed primarily with only one character onstage at a time, there are moments in which the worlds are shuffled in such a way that both the performers and worlds flow, overlap, juxtapose, and cohabitate the stage throughout the performance. The stage directions are meant to clarify the way the piece is presently performed but are by no means meant to restrict future incarnations of this piece.

# IN THE CONTINUUM

*Danai Gurira and Nikkole Salter*

Prologue: Back in the Day

[*Children playing together—Child #1 in South Central, Los Angeles, California; Child #2 in Harare, Zimbabwe.*]

**CHILD #1**: Come on! Com' on! I wanna play . . . I wanna play hopscotch! C'mon! Hopscotch! Just get some chalk! No, get a brick! Just bang it out. Then draw a circle. Yeah! [*Draws circle on the ground with a "brick."*] All the way around. I'ma show you how to play like this! Alright, I but I'ma go first cuz I drew the circle. Huh? Okay, okay . . . One! Two! Three! [*She throws her marker into the circle.*]

**CHILD #2**: Okay saka, totamba chi? Totamba nodo? Here. Ya! Saka une chalk here? Saka hauna? Oh, ndaiwona pano, mirai,—ngatigadzire circle, rakadai, rakadai. [*Draws circle on ground with chalk.*] Okay, ini ndotanga, one, two, three . . . [*Throws stone in the air, tries to catch it and it flies behind her.*]

**CHILD #2**: Oh, shiiit.

**CHILD #1**: What?

**CHILD #2**: Aiwa, richiri jana rangu, aiwa, no man, iwe waka pusa! Ahh, saka hapana achatamba, hapana achatamba! [*She rubs out the chalk with her feet.*]

**CHILD #1**: No! It's got to land in the middle of the circle. That's not the way you play the game. You stupid! Fine! [*She rubs out the chalk with her feet.*] Then nobody's playin' this game then! Ain't nobody playin'!

**BOTH CHILDREN**:

[*Singing and dancing together.*]

Tomato sauce, sauce,
Sauce, sauce, sauce, sauce [*2×*]
Elizabeth, abeth,
Abe, be, be, beth [*2×*]

Chipikinringo, go
Go, go, go, go [2×]
Cousin's on the corner in the welfare line
Brother's in the slammer, he committed a crime
Preacher's in the club on the down low creep
And yo' mama's in the gutter screamin' HIV.

[*The children separate into their distinct worlds, no longer playing together.*]

**CHILD #1**: What you say about my mama?

**CHILD #2**: Saka wati amai vangu vari HIV?

**CHILD #1**: *Yo'* mama got HIV.

**CHILD #2**: Amai vako ndivo vari HIV.

**CHILD #1**: Yo' mama, yo' daddy, yo' whole generation got HIV!

**CHILD #2**: Amai vako, nababa vako, nevese vemumhuri menyu, vari HIV!

**CHILD #1**: You stupid! And *you* got HIV! And yo' mama got a cauliflower growin' out of her pussy!

**CHILD #2**: Iwe waka pusa, newewo uri HIV; futi Amai vako vane maronda panapa!

**BOTH CHILDREN**: Uuuggh!

## ONE: IN THE BEGINNING

[*The two actresses continue in their separate worlds as Abigail and Nia. Abigail walks in looking over a news report at Zimbabwe Broadcasting Corporation Studios. She takes a seat. Nia is in a stall of a bathroom in a hip-hop nightclub, hovering over the toilet.*]

**ABIGAIL**: Good evening and welcome to the 8 o'clock main news bulletin.

I am Abigail Murambe.
Harare: The minister of agriculture comrade Nixton Chibanda warned against any reports by the biased and slandering Western Media which assert that Zimbabwe is facing a famine. He further commented that these irresponsible journalists and their evil cohorts have been the source of Zimbabwe's expulsion from the Commonwealth as well as the crippling sanctions imposed by the United Nations. He asserted that contrary to such reports, Zimbabwe will in fact produce a surplus of agricultural crops in the coming harvest. He admonished against nastyers who . . .

Ahh, ahh, what is nastyers? Naysayers? Whooa, ah, but it says nastyers ka. And what is naysayers, someone who says nay? Ah, hey, are we in Shakespeare or what. Okay, why can't they just say liars or something?

Ahh, ahh, look at all these typos man!! And since when was the vice president's name Janet Mujuru? Its Joyce Mujuru man, you want to get me fired?

**NIA**: [*She vomits.*] It feel like I'm dying.

No, I'll be okay. Just give me a second.

I haven't had nothin' to eat—I keep throwin' everything up. Nasty cafeteria food. All I had was a Long Island Iced tea. I know I should eat something.

Just give me a second. I'll get it myself.

I don't know, Trina. It mighta been in the weed—I ain't the weed expert. They was passin' it, it was free, I took just some. [*Abigail sits at mirror—touches up makeup with tissue.*] I think it's somethin' else. Cuz nothin' taste the same, don't nothin' smell the same—I ain't old!

Just cuz you popped outta yo' mama coochie yesterday don't make me [*starts to throw up*]—.

Trina, just pass me some tissue!

**ABIGAIL**: Ewe, wait, is there any shine here? Okay. [*Dabs side of face, drops tissue to the floor, Nia picks it up.*] Thanks. And, can I have the rest of the report please?!

[*Perusing report.*] Hey, it's getting harder and harder to even say this crap man. I can't believe—

Huh? No I wasn't saying anything. But, Evermore, have you gotten your pay check? Ah, NO I haven't, its been six weeks now, how am I supposed to pay school fees with air? Right now I am near penniless. This is what we get for working for the government, ini I want to move into the private sector, South Africa man! SABC! Real money, shamwari! Ah, I am just as good as them, probably better! Then from there CNN!!! Why not, I bet I am just as good as them, probably better. [*Nia flushes the toilet and exits the stall.*] Where is my tea by the way, Evermore, can you please, please bring me my tea *before* we start, I need to calm my nerves. Four sugars. [*Abigail sits—jots notes on her tasks for the day on news report.*]

**NIA**: My breath smell like raw fish and old tacos.

No, I don't wanna go. [*Looking into an imagined full-length mirror.*] I got all dressed up so I could celebrate with Darnell, so that's what I'ma do. Cuz, I don't see him everyday no more, so when he get here I wanna look good.

[*Fixing her hair.*] No, he just be out, doin' his *college* thang, but in two more days, all this scholarship stuff will be done. We been together ten months and three weeks, I can wait two more days.

Huh? Yep, it's almost been a year. He practically my husband. [*Fishing out lipgloss.*] Cuz we been through so much! Like last summer, when he got jumped by them Piru niggas; girl, I was so scared! But I was the first one to visit when he got home. And when everything went down with my mom's I would run away from the foster homes and Darnell would let me sneak and stay with him till I got my spot at Good Shepard. And if that ain't love,—He even came to see me when I won that poetry contest. [*Applying lipgloss.*]

Girl, yes!

They gave us a big banquet; I got $500—and a plaque. And the judges said I was—what they call it?—"full of potential." I know, I didn't have no potential before, but now that I can talk they poetry language, I'm "full of potential." [*Closing lipgloss.*] It ain't hard, all they have you do is follow a pattern and write it out—

A pattern!—

Okay, like: [*Using the lipgloss to count the syllables on her hands.*]

*Bright ass sun-ny day*—5 syllables

*Burn-in' the shit out-ta me*—7

*I wish it was cold*—5

See. No, I think about them all the time. It just come to me. It's just like flowin'. Try one. Just try one. Alright, I'ma start you, okay? Okay.

*Dir-ty ass, skank . . . humm?*—[*Waiting for Trina to fill in the blank.*] Hoe! Good!

*Wit yo' crun-chy hair*—[*to Trina*] wit yo' fake weave?—no, no, wait I got it- *wit yo' crun-chy ba-by hair*—7

*Leave Dar-nell a-lone*—5

[*Begins fishing mascara out of her purse.*]

**ABIGAIL**: By the way, before I forget, next time I want to be dressed by Truworths—because Edgars keeps bringing these clothes that make me look like I have grandchildren or something. Thank you for that Evermore, I know I am a married woman, that doesn't mean I have to look like I am selling vegetables paroadside. Next time they bring such things I am just going to say no, they must know I am their model, saka they're supposed to make me look good.

**NIA**: [*Applying mascara.*]

Shut up, Trina! I always look good.

Please! I look better than those groupies! Did you see that girl that had on the—

So. [*Putting mascara away.*] So what! So, Darnell looks at them, so what! Girls walking around with they titties hangin' out tryin'ta get looked at. [*Fixing her clothes.*] He might look at them but he goin' home with me. Don't worry, tonight, I'ma just let him celebrate. But Saturday night, after his scholarship ceremony, [*imitating "video hoes" in hip-hop music videos*] I'ma give him somethin' to look at. [*She laughs.*]

Huh?

What, my new purse?

Yeah, it was a gift—courtesy of Nordstrom. [*Fishing for and applying perfume purse.*]

Girl, please. A playa like me don't pay fo' nothin'. [*Pretending to steal the purse.*] Everything I got on was a five finger discount.

Wait! No! Cuz the way I see it, it only cost fifty cents for these companies to make; they only pay Javier and them ten cent to put it together; they pay me five wack ass dollars an hour, then they go sell it for a hundred and fifty? Do I look like a dummy? Please, me takin' this purse is part of my community service. I wish I would pay a hundred and fifty!

**ABIGAIL**: Mmm, mmm, Evermore, forget about that tea. I am not feeling well. Ahh, we better do this thing quickly guys. Where's the cameraman? Oh oh oh, is Gibson not here yet? Finish. But shame—he told me he has no transport, hanzi he has to wake up at 3 A.M. to reach here by 7! [*Nia returns to the bathroom stall.*] Ahh, times are hard suwa. MunomuZimbabwe sha. Oh is he still feeling sick? He wasn't looking very well. Shame . . . But Evermore, you are looking plumper these days, where are you finding sadza munomuZimbabwe? Please can you direct us all there? No, no tea please, I'm not feeling well . . .

**NIA**: I never get sick.

No, never! When have you seen me—?

I don't be sick for real at school.

No! I be fakin'! Yeah.

I guess I'ma good actress—

—liar, actress, whatever. Like you ain't never lied about havin' cramps to get outta sex ed. Shoot, when I realized that worked, I would be havin' my period like two, three times a month. I mean, it's not like they gon' check! What they gonna do, look?—

Oooh! Hay! Shh! Be quiet.

You hear that?

**ABIGAIL**: Ahh, I think I hear Gibson out there.

**NIA**: That's my jam. Me and Darnell always dance to that. They would play our song when I'm on the toilet.

**ABIGAIL**: [*Gets up*] Yes Gibson, muri right? / Are you feeling better—good good. / Evermore checkai for lint! / Lets go. [*Looking in the mirror.*] / Yes I am ready! / Wait where is my special ballpoint?! / [*Finds it in her hand.*] Oh, its right here. / Totanga ka! / Lets go!

**NIA**: Trina . . . ? / Trina, why you so quiet? / You takin' a dump? / You don't take a dump in a public bathroom! / You nasty! / [*Looking in the mirror.*] Yeah, I guess I feel a little better. / Do me a favor: go get me a breath mint or somethin. / Hurry up!

[*Gunshots. Nia runs out.*]

[*Blackout in both worlds.*]

**ABIGAIL**: Oh, no tell me your joking, another powercut!! This is the third one today! We won't be finished till night time! Twenty minutes? Okay please, ndapota. *And* can we get some sort of lights here please! [*Sits back down.*]

Better be twenty minutes, last time it was three hours. Ha, its bad enough we had to work so late all last week, you know ma in-laws they start to say marara—"hey hey that is why she only has one child"—imagine! "We want more children here, Simbi is getting lonely! You mustn't work so much!" This coming from inlaws who have never given me a bubble gum or a fork at my wedding. But, [*looks around*] they can shut up now Evermore, baby number 2 is on the way!! Ya! Pururudza! Tofara tese! Hmmm? I just found out on Monday! Stamford doesn't even know yet, I am going to tell him and that family of his at Simbi's birthday party on Sunday. Ya, he's turning seven, he's a big boy now—time for another, one that looks like the mother. Simbi? He looks just like his father man, with that big nose—shame. Stamford? He's fine . . . he just keeps doing too much of those late nights I told you about—I don't like it man! These men, they want to play away and have us at home at the same time—he's got to stop that. But, you know, I think another baby will make him act better; Auntie always said showing the husband you are a good and fertile wife will keep him indoors. Oh, by the way Evermore—you chased your man out when you caught him with the other woman? Ah no that's not the answer man—no it's not, because then that other woman, hure that she is, will get everything you have been working for! Ah no me, I realized the solution: men are like bulls searching for pastureland, you show them greener grass and they stay put, and this baby is greener grass. He's going to stay put now. Hey, Stamford, he wants to forget how hard he had to work for me! *Me?* I was known as the Ice Queen! Hmmmhmm! No one could get near me—I was very, very picky. I used to go to those house parties and I was the best dancer—*Eh he,* suwa. [*Gets up, begins to dance.*] Wonai, wonai—ha, I've still got it! Ah, Evermore! Do you remember this one? This one? It was big around '92, '93—I hated it but it was so popular I had to know how to do it—*well.* Do you remember what it was called—ABORTION!! Imagine! So nasty hey! And the men wanted to come from behind! Ha, no me I would say "Just look hey, don't touch!" But then along came Stamford Murambe—ah, with him I was like [*bending over*], "You can touch, please touch!" [*Laughing.*] Ya, ya he won me over, fair and square, but he had to persevere! With maletters, flowers! Me I didn't come easy ka! [*Sits back down.*] He wants to forget all of that.

He'll come around, he just needs another boy. A girl?! What am I going to do with a girl in this world? No, two boys that's perfect. And they're going to grow up in Chisipiti or Glen Lorne,—no we can't stay in Hatfield anymore, ahh, it's too filled with strong rural types, too many muboi! I am sick and tired of living next door to people who keep chickens and goats in their backyard, I want to be around the poshy!! Those who know how to eat with a knife and fork. And our new house will have a swimming pool, DSTV, maybe a tennis court. Stamford can drive the Pajero because I'll drive the Benz. And the kids will go to St John's prep or Hartman House and learn the best these whites can teach, and I have a good feeling about this one [*points at stomach*] he could become the next Kofi Anan, or Bill Gates—why not! And Stamford will love this one so much; hmmhmm, he will take one look at him and never forget where home is again. [*Phone rings.*] Oh, its me! I thought I turned it off! Oh, let me take this Evermore it's the clinic . . . Hello . . . yes . . . this is Mrs Abigail Murambe . . . [*Exiting.*]

## TWO: NIA'S DREAM

**NIA**: [*Looking behind emergency room curtains*] Trina . . . ?

Trina . . . oh, sorry! [*Sucking her teeth.*] My bad.

Trina? Hey. [*Entering into Trina's space.*] How you doin'? Good.

Did you do what I told you? Lemme see your wrist—

Why not?

I said don't give them your real information!

You did give them your real name! You such a scaredy cat. What they gon' do, spank you?

Cuz! Now they gonna call Good Shepherd and then everybody gon' be all up in our business. Has the doctor even come in here yet? Be right back? Please, if we was dyin' we'd already be dead. Lemme see it. [*She looks at Trina's wound.*]

At least it not bleedin' no more. [*Sitting.*] Me? I think I got to get some stitches. Yeah. No, wait, the doctor was like, *"How did you get glass stuck in your side?"* I was like, *"Duh! They was shootin', people was goin' crazy! You get knocked over and stomped on you while you lyin' on a floor full-a shot-up glass and see what happen to you!"* Yeah, you laughin' now, [*beat*] but you looked fucked up then. I ain't gon' lie—all I saw was blood, you know, and I got scared. I was like, [*like an exaggerated mother crying over a child's coffin à la* Boyz in the Hood.]

Oh, Lawdy, lawd, lawd!

Lawdy, Lawd, what I's gon' do!?!

[*In a Baptist Church breakdown.*] Don't let Trina die!

Please don't let Trina die!!!

[*Laughing.*] You shhh! *You* silly!

Okay, lemme see it again.

At least it's gonna make a cute scar.

I'm just glad *you* okay.

Nothin'. Okay. But if I tell you somethin' Trina, you promise not to go tellin' everybody? Okay. No, the doctor wanted to give me this x-ray to see if I like broke a rib or somethin', but she made me pee in this cup to see if I was pregnant first, and . . . I am.

I know they gon' kick me out.

I don't know what—

She just gave me all these pamphlets, she did all these tests. Now I'm supposed to come back tomorrow but—

Of course, I'm gonna tell Darnell!

Yes, I am!

I'ma go right up to his practice . . . and I'm gonna take his hand and put it on my stomach, look up at him and say, *"Darnell, I'm pregnant."* And he gon' look down at me and say, *"For real?"* and I'ma say, *"ummm, humm."* [*Laughing.*] Then, he gon' get on his knees and put his ear against my belly and listen. Umm, humm! And then he gon' look up at me and say, *"My son in there?"* and I'ma say, *"umm-humm."* Then, we're gonna get married. Umm-humm. And move into a big-ass house cuz he gon' play for the Lakers and I'll just be—Oooh, shut up! Oh, I'll be rich doin' somethin'. Watch! [*Getting her cell phone out of her purse.*] I'll call him right now. I will tell him! Just watch and learn. [*She dials.*] Voicemail? *Darnell! Where are you? It's Nia. We was at the club waitin' for you—you will not believe what happened. I'll tell you when you come pick us up—me and Trina at the hospital. We need a ride. And, uh . . .* [*to Trina*] Shut up, I am! [*into the phone again*] *I . . . I got somethin' to tell you. Just call me back. No! Why haven't you called me? That's what's more important! It's been like four hours—!*

### THREE: THE DIAGNOSIS

**NURSE MUGOBO**: [*Steps out banging clip board*] Please, this is a clinic.

**NIA**: [*As if the nurse has chastised her for her cell phone usage*] My bad. I just—

**NURSE**: Please, can you control your children, they can't run around like eh . . . monkeys!

**NIA**: I'm comin' back! Dag! I got to go, this lady trippin' talkin' 'bout I can't be on my cell phone. Call me when you get this message. I love you. [*Putting away her cell phone.*]

**NURSE**: [*Looks at clipboard, talking to Abigail*] Right, Mrs Choto? You are not Mrs Choto. Mrs Choto, Mrs Choto!!!!

**NIA**: That *is* my real name. Why would I—Can I go!

**NURSE**: Ha, and vanhu vatema vanonetsa. [*Flips to next chart.*] Mrs Murindi? Murambe, ya, sorry, Abigail? Right. [*Looks through chart.*] I have your chart here . . .

**NIA**: My chart? Ya'll gon' call—? [*Sucking her teeth.*]

**NURSE**: Everything looks fi—oh.

**NIA**: What?

**NURSE**: You have tested HIV positive. This means you have the virus that causes the Acquired Immune Deficiency syndrome . . .

**NIA**: I'm sorry what?

**NURSE**: There is no cure for AIDS, it is generally transmitted through unprotected penetrative sex, anal or vaginal // with a person infected with HIV. And unprotected sex means sex without a condom, male or female to protect the sexual organs and in Africa that is generally through heterosexual contact.

**NIA**: [*// = overlapping dialogue*] You trying say I'ma hoe? Do I look like a junkie? Do it look like I'm gay? Do I look like I'm from Africa? No! Every time we come in here ya'll try to make us feel like we're dirty or stupid or something. [*Pulling out her cell phone.*] You don't know what the fuck you're talkin' about—s'cuse you—no, *s'cuse you!* [*She exits.*]

**NURSE**: We therefore recommend that from now on [*eyes follow Nia, to passing orderly*] Ewe what are you doing? Yes I can see that—but can't you see those are dripping on the floor? Take them to the back, those are contaminated. Yes they are! You barance wemunhu. [*Eyes follow him out. Back to Abigail.*] We therefore strongly recommend you practice abstinence from now on; but if you must, please can you protect others, there are three condoms, sorry we have run out. If you want we can show you how to use them on a banana in the next room. [*Eyes wander.*] But then you will only have two. Excuse me. Eh, Sisi Getty, are you going to the shops? Please Sisi help me sha, I am so hungry can you just buy me a sweet bun ne a coke? Thank you Sisi. Aiwa, I have the money, mirai.

[*Looks over at Abigail.*] Ah Miss, Miss—[*looks at chart*] Miss Abigail, why are you crying? No, aiwa, you must think clearly mange. I see here you have a son? Bring him in we can test him also. [*Finds no money in bra.*] Ahh, sorry Sisi I forgot my money—Oh . . . Thank you Sisi you are a life saver—surely, every time! [*Looks after Sisi Getty smiling, returns to Abigail, smile fades.*] Right, so, we must see your husband in the next few days—he must be formally informed and tested. Ah, *ah* Miss, Miss Abigail—there are no exceptions for that—I know it can be dangerous to tell him, many women are scared he will beat them and take the children—what what, even though usually its coming from him, but, sorry you tested first. *So*—you must tell him and bring him for testing. Even with the risky business of it. And we must see him as soon as possible, nhasi riri Friday saka on Monday, latest; we can make the appointment right now.

[*Looks down at chart.*] Ah, [*stops, puts down pen*] you are pregnant?

Ah . . . you women. You go and get this HIV then you want to have a baby or two? It's not good, munoziwa, its not good.

[*Goes back to chart.*] Drugs? Ah we don't have them here, if you have money you can try to find them, they are very, very expensive. Otherwise, change your diet—eat greens, negrains, nemeat. And don't breastfeed. We will test the baby soon after it is born.

So we will see you and Mr Stamford Mirindi, sorry Murambe, on Monday, 10 A.M. Please amai, if you don't come I will be forced to call him. Right. [*Flips to next chart.*]

Mrs Choto, Mrs Cho— [*Nia rushes in, referring to her as though she is Mrs Choto*] there you are, you are late, can you sit down. Ha, and vanhu vatema vanonetsa.

### FOUR: NIA'S DENIAL

**NIA**: Trina, get your stuff. Let's go. Just get your stuff!

I called Patti, she gon' give us a ride, but leavin' right—

Yes, I called Probation Patti—to get us a ride, Trina. Who else was I gonna call?

My mama?

What for? She don't care about me. Why don't you call yo' mama?—forget Darnell. He not comin'—

Whatchu yellin' at me for?

How is any of this my fault? You the one said you could hang. You the one begged me to come—If you didn't go—get yourself shot we wouldn't have this problem.

Did I stutter? You was the only idiot walkin' around when people shootin'. Ain't you ever heard gunshots before? You supposta get down. Duck, stupid!

You messed everything up! We was supposed to sneak out, go to the Club, have some fun, sneak back in—nobody was gon' know. Now I gotta listen to Patti's bougie mouth, all for what? Yo' bullet scratch and a couple-a stitches that you won't even see after two months with some cocoa butter!? I'm the one brought you here and made sure you got taken care of. I shoulda left yo' stank ass there. And just went back by myself. Then I wouldn't be here. I ain't even supposed to be here—!

Nothin's wrong!

I'm pregnant stupid. Whatchu think?

I don't see what you so worried about, Trina. All they gon' tell you is not to sneak out no more. I'm the one who can't go back to Good Shepard. If anybody should be mad, it should be me. And I figured Patti was gon' find out anyway cuz you used your real name—

So if we gon' get caught, we might as well have a ride!

Just get your stuff. Let's go.

**FIVE: HAVE MERCY**

[*Abigail on the street, trying to flag down a ride.*]

**ABIGAIL**: [*To street kids.*]

Fotsek! You kids get away. *No* I don't have any money. Don't touch me! I'll beat you like your mother should have. [*Pause.*]. Just go away. Please. [*Phone rings.*]

Hello Stamfo—. Simbi. [*Laughs/cries—relieved.*] Hello my big boy. How are you—no mummy is just happy to hear from you that's all—but what did mama say to you about calling her cell phone from the landline? *No* I said it's very expensive so you mustn't. What's wrong my beby, why are you calling me? Is daddy home? No don't put him on. No no no no, mummy doesn't need to speak to him right now, just don't put him on. Don't. Okay. [*Trying to flag down omnibus taxi.*] No, I am catching a commuter omnibus, so let mummy go so that I can catch one okay. [*To street kids.*] Ewe fotsek, I said I don't have any money. No, no not you baby. What? What did you put in my handbag? Simbi, I don't have time for thi—okay, okay, okay [*finds folded paper in handbag*] what is this Simbi? This is beautiful, did you draw it yourself? Okay, so who is the first person? Quickly, quickly. That's deddy, okay. And who is this one in the middle?! That's mummy? Okay! And who is the last one? That's you? Simbi you are funny! Why are you bigger than everyone else Simbi? But Simbi this is beautiful, we will to put it on the fridge when I get home. But

Simbi, next time you draw mummy don't draw her with hair that's going all over the place like that! Mummy's hair doesn't do that beby. Just draw me with simple hair, one, two, three, four, five neat little strokes that's all. But beby this is beautiful. [*To pestering street kids.*] Fotsek, go away, you kids, where are your parents . . . [*Slowly turns back around to street kids.*] Fotsek, go away, please, get away, just go. [*Flagging down ride.*] Simbi, Mama has to go now, okay, now you go to eat; see I just stopped one, I have to go. Mommy's coming.

### SIX: CHATTER HEADS

**PATTI**: Gosh! I cannot believe, at the peak of rush hour I had to—

Nia!

**PETRONELLA**: Abigail!

**PATTI**: Not you Trina, you wait inside!

**PETRONELLA**: Abigail Moyo!

**PATTI**: Nia, you get in!

**PETRONELLA**: Get in, get in! It's me, Petronella Siyanyarambazinyika!

**PATTI**: [*To driver.*] The 105 [*one o five*] to the 110 [*one ten*] 405 [*four o five*] to Beach Avenue and Centinela, please. Yeah.

**PETRONELLA**: How are you my dear??? I haven't seen you since—is it high school? Oh, my gosh its been too long! *Ah,* but you're looking well, kept that figure. Just tell Lovemore where you want to go. The city centre? Is that safe Lovemore? Okay. Good.

**PATTI**: I am not angry, Nia. Did you think I was angry? 'Cause I'm not.

I'm dumfounded, I'm worried, I'm completely devastated! We've been through Independent Living Classes, Life Skills Assessment, Job Readiness Training—we were getting somewhere, Nia! What was so important at this club that it was worth giving up everything we've worked for? And I tell you, if I miss my flight to Milwaukee for the second part of the Journey toward Self Discovery Conference I'll—

**PETRONELLA**: And did I hear correctly that you married Stamford Murambe? *Haa* well done my dear, he was gorgeous!! What a bloody catch! Oh, you still have him right? Whew! But good work my dear everyone wanted a piece of him!!! I too have officially joined the married club! Mmmhmm, just two years ago, do you remember Farai Mungoshi? Prince Edward, headboy, captain of the rugby team, a real feast for the eyes? No, I married his younger brother Richard.

**PATTI**: . . . Yes, but you tell the universe exactly what you want to experience by the choices you make every moment. And I know we don't always make the best choices, but—

Yes, even me, I don't always—Okay. Like yesterday, I was having lunch in the cafeteria and I had not one, but two helpings of macaroni and cheese. Not the best choice, no, but not going to drastically change my life.

You take the good job I found you at Nordstrom and chose to get fired by stealing—again. I've given you the easiest course curriculum developed for continuing education yet you throw away your chance at a diploma by ditching. You take the free housing in Westwood I gave you, and was asked to leave because you wouldn't keep curfew. I've even violated the state's abstinence only policy and given you condoms! Now you're telling me that one night of hangin' wit the homies, rockin' your phat gear and sportin' your big chain with the medallion of the mother land and shakin' your booty with some boy at some club is worth getting shot at? [*Beat.*] Okay. Good answer. So: With my choices, *I'm* telling the universe that I . . . want . . . to be fat. But, so what, big deal, we're talking about you! *You're* telling the universe that you want to be an uneducated, unemployed, homeless, kleptomaniac, soul train dancer. Is that what you want? If you were in my shoes, what would you do?

**PETRONELLA**: . . . oh you got those here? They look just look just like my Stella McCartney pumps. I know her personally actually, she gave me a pair—she couldn't give them to her step mother—she's only got one leg! Did you say you worked ZBC? Oh, [*laughs*] no, I am sorry, I just got back home so I am still adjusting to all the lingo, and someone the other day called it Dead BC. Good for you though hey! You were always a great public speaker! Me, oh, well . . . I went abroad soon after high school, to study at London School of Economics, I was there for both my undergrad and my master's, International Relations with a focus on Human Rights and Gender Development, and I am still there mostly, I work as a consultant for big organizations, the UN, OXFAM, stuff like that. Right now, I have been really focused on HIV and Southern African women and of course all the big organizations abroad are going to hire me right? I am like this perfect poster child—but I can't complain, I've been working with DATA—oh come on you know—Debt, AIDS, Trade, Africa—Bono—he's a rock star—he has an organization. [*Car swerves.*] Careful Lovemore!

**PATTI**: Ah, pardon, sir—

**PETRONELLA**: God, the way people drive in this country!

**PATTI**: Yes, but that clearly said, "no left turn"—

**PETRONELLA:** In England he would have been arrested on the spot!

**PATTI:** It is illegal!—I should write down your number and report—

It's just that it's a very risky turn, sir, and we have precious cargo.

Yeah! Thanks.

[*To Nia.*] Perfect example: There are many ways to get to Inglewood, but making an illegal short cut turn here is not one of them. There are no shortcuts in life, Nia! The laws are designed to keep us safe. And I hate to burst your bubble, but, no matter where you go there will be rules. On this road there are rules, gangs have rules, even in the wilderness there are rules. And there are consequences in choosing to violate the rules. Are you listening to me? Nia!

**PETRONELLA:** . . . there's not even any bloody petrol! This is not the country we grew up in. How do you survive? Anyway, concerning the whole AIDS issue—I was actually trying to get some statistics—that's why I was at the clinic—naturally the head nurse was on a two hour lunch or something! Zimboes! And of course you have to get the highest statistics possible in order to get them to do anything. That's when they get all aghast and say, "Oh those poor Africans who can't help themselves—lets bring them our great answers"—which are *what*? Okay—they are manufacturing some drugs here, but believe me they aren't the best kind and how is anyone supposed to be able to afford them long term in this economy? It's a bloody mess! And you want to know why? You want to know why? I'll tell you why. It's because we've been programmed. Yes! Because we look to them as our source of hope and redemption. Meanwhile we have the answers and we don't know it. I have been thinking a lot about our own traditional *African* healing and I—No! I am not saying they have the cure or whatever, but there is something in it, you can't argue that. Do you remember Sisi Thembi?

**PATTI:** . . . the value is not in material things. Nia, I don't know what I can give you that's more important than the opportunity to lift yourself up. That's what I did. Yeah. It may not look like it, but I'm from the 'hood—well, Ladera Heights—but I drove down Crenshaw every day—It doesn't matter! It doesn't matter your race or your gender or where you're from, it's where you're going. But I think you want to stay in the ghetto because no matter what I show you, no matter where I put you, you carry it with you in your mind.

Now, you can either take that Emergency Services number, call, and stay in a shelter tonight; or you can pick yourself up, march yourself in there and patch things up with your mother. A girl needs her mother, Nia. You know, my mother and I never got along either—well . . . it's 'cause she never really cultivated my garden of talents, it was either her way or no way, and I know you and your mother are experiencing a rift, that's the connection—okay, okay! I know, I know! I'm all in the kool-aid—

**PETRONELLA**: . . . remember when we caught her talking to trees?

**PATTI**: —my bad . . .

**PETRONELLA**: And she used to roast grasshoppers!

**PATTI**: . . . I learned that yesterday. Did I say it right?

**BOTH**: hahahahahhahahahahahaha . . . hheee . . . heee . . .

**PATTI**: Nia?

**PETRONELLA**: Abi?

**PATTI**: Are you alright?

Okay.

You know, I was online yesterday, surfing the web, and I saw that the city is looking for poetry to display on the MTA trains. I think you're work is perfect. Go online, download an application and submit some of your work. If you win, it's more scholarship money for when you—decide to go to community college. And your poems won at the Success Is Our Future Ceremony, now that's something! Believe you me there are plenty of opportunities out there for a girl like you!! You can still be anything you want to be!!! [*Light bulb.*] Change the course of history. Don't let yesterday's bad choices keep you from making good choices today. Huh!?! But I know you. I can tell, you're gonna do the right thing! Hey, there's no place for you to go but up, *huh*!!??—

Huh?

Well, you could go down and spiral . . .

**PETRONELLA**: . . . she was such a mad, mad, *mad,* woman—Sisi Thembi! I can't believe she is in the church now! Like every day that sort of thing? Oh what a shame hey—remember how she swore by witchdoctors? Remember how her . . . daughter, her daughter—had some sickness no one could figure out—she said her witchdoctor—sorry—traditional healer—fixed it! She had to do some strange things but it worked and nothing else did. There is something to it I tell you. What? You want to get out here? Abi there is nothing—*Abigail—* What are you doing the car is still moving. Lovemore stop the car! [*Getting out of car, yelling.*]

**PATTI**: Bye, Nia!

**PETRONELLA**: Abigail, wait!!!!

**PATTI**: [*Getting out of car, yelling*] Nia, wait!

**PETRONELLA**: You work for ZBC—do you host that show Breaking New Ground?

**PATTI**: Tell you mother I said hello!

**PETRONELLA**: No . . . well I really want to be on it, I think I have a lot to say this the country needs to hear, I am breaking new bloody ground. . . .

**PATTI**: I'm an Audi.

**PETRONELLA**: How do you say "bye" again Lovemore? Oh—*chisarai*!!!

**PATTI**: Five Thousand!

**PETRONELLA**: NO, what's the other one—*tichamboona*!!!

**PATTI**: No, Audi, like the car, but "*out of here!*" [*Makes the sound of a car speeding by.*] Nevermind . . . just go, go, go . . .

[*Her laughing at herself turns into . . .* ]

## SEVEN: MAMA

[*Friday morning. Mama's porch. She's calming her crying baby throughout the scene.*]

[* = *Imani, a six-month-old baby, crying.*]

**MAMA**: * Hey! Hey!! Get offa my grass! Get offa my grass and take your Funyion bag with you. [*To herself*] Bad ass kids. [*Beat.*] * Well, well, well. I knew you'd come back. Lemme guess: They didn't believe your lies at the Good Shepard either, huh? You thought it was gon' be easy as that. Well, life is not easy, guess you have to learn the hard way. And now you wanna come back. I'm still goin' to family court off of the shit you pulled; anger management, freakin' parenting classes like I don't know what the hell I'm doin', and you wanna come back just like that? No apology, no nothin'? And then you got the nerve to ask me for $400! I tell you—how you gon' pay me back? You got a job? You lookin' like a damn prostitute, what are you wearin'? It's nine o'clock in the morning, walkin' 'round like you been walkin' the streets. [*Baby talk to Imani.*] She walkin' the streets, ain't she? Ain't she?

[*Seriously.*] Is you walkin' the streets, Nia?

Don't get smart with me!

Then what you need $400 for, huh? Probably some Guess jeans. What happened to the money from that poetry contest? Ain't nobody payin' you to put'ch'a little rhymes together no more? Ain't got no job, no place to live, but spend all yo' time writin' poetry and shoppin'—for $400 Guess jeans. Are they self-cleaning? Do they pay rent? If anybody's getting $400 'round here, "*guess*" who it's gonna be—*me*. I'm tired of comin' second to ya'll. I can't remember the last time I had me some lotion or some new panties. Besides, you grown, remember? And us grown folk, we pay for our own shit. You old enough. Hell, when I was 19 I was *—And don't think you slick goin' behind my back askin' Marvin for the money. I thought you didn't like him. He ain'tchya daddy, so stop askin' him fo' shit. [*To Imani*] Huh? He's yo' daddy, huh? Yo' daddy! Who's yo' daddy? That's yo' daddy! [*To Nia*] I don't know. You should ask that lil' boyfriend of yours, Darnell, for $400. He'll buy them pants for you . . . since he the one like to get in 'em so often. Don't think I didn't usta hear your little narrow behind climbin' out the window to go oochie coochie with that boy. Like you the first one discovered how to sneak out the house? I invented that shit. I already been everywhere you been, Nia. I was just tryin' to keep your fast ass from goin' to half of them places. *Oh!* But you "grown"! Well, I'ma tell yo' grown ass this: I know you like him, and he look like he goin' places,* but don't you end up pregnant, Nia. Cuz once you turn this switch on, you can't turn it off, and I'ma be damned if I end up raisin' your kids cuz you couldn't use a condom. Oh, *Oh*! [*To Imani*] She woman enough to do the do, but she can't talk the talk. [*To Nia*] What would you rather I say, Ms. Nia? Look at me. Strap on the jimmy? Pull the balloon over the sausage? I wish somebody had told me about this shit, half-a ya'll wouldn't be here. And now days, you can catch all kinda stuff. Stuff you can't get rid of cuz it gets in your blood. Trust me: three minutes of slappin' bellies ain't worth death. And that's what it is, death. * Because it's a government experiment, it was designed—They've done it before and will do it again. You think it's consequential that we the ones got it the most out of everybody. They been tryin' to get rid of us since the Emancipation Proclamation. First they lynched us, then they got us high so they could put us in prison. Then they got the ones that ain't incarcerated to shoot up each other and now they brought this hopin' that we fuck ourselves to death. And you know they got a cure. What you think the whole civilian rights was about? That's why they really assassinated Martin: to distract us from the monkey fuckers that brought it back from Africa to kill us. And they killed Malcolm cuz, on his pilgrimage, he found out who the monkey fuckers were. You got to know your history. That's what's wrong with ya'll—

I know, I know, you love Darnell. Darnell love you. Ya'll invincible in love. Yes, I know. I was in love too, okay. Five times. Remember that. All I had to worry about was gettin' pregnant, but ya'll got a whole slew of other stuff you got to think about. Real love lasts forever, but so do real mistakes.

[*To Imani*] Yes, they do, huh? Yes they do! And I'ma tell you, just like I tol' them, yes I am, yes I am! You only got me 'til you're 18. That's it! Count down!

* [*To Nia*] That's it. Now you can go on in the back and get $60 outta my purse so that you can get you a room to rent for the night, cuz you can't stay here. I ain't gonna let ya'll run my world forever. And, uh, you grown, remember? And I ain't gonna let you scare this man away. Shiiit. One down four to go.

Look at them. That's exactly what I'm—Hey! *Hey!* Well, stop sprayin' paint on them walls, that shit ain't art! * [*She exits.*]

## EIGHT: THE CHURCH

[*"Akuna wakaita saJesu" is being sung by the congregation, Abigail rushes in, trying to look normal, greets people and sing and dances along as she searches for SisiThembi.*]

**ABIGAIL:** [*Singing along*] Hallo auntie! Muri right? Ya, Stamford is fine thanks!

Hi Pastor Manyika! How are you? No, we have had trouble with transport, no petrol ka! Otherwise twice a week I would come to worship!!

Shit.

[*Sees SisiThembi.*]

SisiThembi—SisiThembi wuya! Ahh.

[*makes her way through the pews.*]

Excuse me, sorry, pamsoroi! Sorry baby, don't cry. Excuse me please . . . [*Manoeuvres around a rather large man.*]

[*Reaches SisiThembi, tries to sing and look natural.*]

SisiThembi, I need the address of the, eh, [*looks up at large man*] remember that man you said helped you when your daughter was sick?

*Noo!* The man with the eh eh—herbs—

Come on. Okay look at me—the— [*Imitates a witchdoctor possessed.*]

THE WITCHDOCTOR MAN!!!!

[*Everyone stops, music stops.*]

He is the devil! Praise *God!!!*

[*Raises arms in the air dancing, after awkward pause, music resumes.*]

Come on Sisi—please!

121? Oh I know it, ya, I know it.

Thanks Sisi—Thank you.

[*Makes her way back through the pews.*]

Excuse me, sorry, pamsoroi, sorry baby, pamsoroi . . .

[*To congregation member*] Ha? Oh I am fine, I just felt the spirit telling me to go see a friend in need—but praise God, He is from where all blessings flow! [*Rushes out.*]

### NINE: KEYSHA (SHORT FOR KEYSHAWN)

**MISS KEYSHA**: [*To the waiter*] No, the water is fine. But could you bring some lemon. And sugar. No, I don't want lemonade. Did I ask for lemonade? If I wanted lemonade I would order lemonade. Thank you. [*To Nia*] Okay. So, should you have his baby? Should you have his baby? Should a dope fiend in a crack house run from the police? Hell yeah, you should have his baby. [*To the waiter*] Waiter! [*To Nia*] No, I don't, Nia. I really don't see what the dilemma is. It's not like you got pregnant by some ole, dirty, jerry curl juicy, gold-tooth pimp. We talkin' Darnell Smith. Dar-nell Smith. The crem de la crem. Do you know how many girls pokin' needles in condoms tryin'ta have his baby. And here you sit, on the come-up like Mary pregnant with Jesus, talkin' 'bout should you have his baby. Have Miss Keysha taught you nothin'? What else you gonna do? That's Darnell Smith's baby and everybody know Darnell Smith. And these recruiters is lickin' his anus tryin' to get him to go to they school. I'm talking UCLA, Notre Damé. Indian-I-A, all of 'em. And you know what's gonna happen when he get outta school. He goin' straight to the NBA. Do you know what that mean? Do you know what that mean? That mean yo . . . *we* about to be set for life. For *life*. I'm talkin' Malibu mansion. Mercedes Benz. SL class on Sprewells! I'm talkin' Louis Vetton luggage . . . no, no, no. Real Louis Vetton luggage. VIP parties, backstage passes . . . hold on. [*He has an orgasm.*] Ooooo! I can't believe I gave him to you. He was right on the line, he coulda went either way, either way. I was the one introduced ya'll when you was eight cuz I was tired of you followin' me around. Uhh huh. Those were my dark days of darkness—before I became the fine specimen you see before you. We was all staying' wit Auntie Gina—all of us up in that one room; and her makin' me take you with me when I went out, knowin' you would tell if I did somethin' wrong. Why you think I'd have you to go play with Darnell? To get yo' nosey ass out my business. Who knew Darnell would end up a damn star? He about to be so rich. I shoulda went ahead and did him then, with his little eight year old pee pee. [*Acting out what that might look and sound like.*] Speakin' of pee-pee. I gotta go tinkle. [*Laughing, he exits.*]

**WITCHDOCTOR**: [*Sings and dances complete with fly whisk and headress.*]

Mhondoro dzinomwa muna Save. Mhondoro dzinomwa muna Zambezi [×*2*]. [*Sits.*]

Don't mind all this [*indicating traditional attire*]. I had some whites, matourist, they wanted to see the witchdoctor like the one they see on TV. I didn't know I could do those dances, hey! [*Dances from a seated position a bit.*] But it was good, my daughter, I gave them a show, they give me some money, everyone was happy!

But, the spirits are happy to see you my daughter. They were angry at you—because—you have been running to these other cultures for your answers; but now you have returned they are happy. But you must know that this is from where all answers flow. These are your roots. So what's the problem here, eh, don't say anything, the ancestors will speak it to me. [*Throws bones.*]

Mmmm, you are a professional woman, very well dressed what what. I see you are married, ya. Not enough children, not enough children from you yah. But you're hips are looking like you could have some more if you wanted. Don't tell me you are pregnant—I knew that, I was going to say it! Don't anger the ancestors. [*Whisks himself angrily with whisk. Throws bones, sniffs the air, rubs nose.*] I'm smelling fear, fear of the husband, fear of the husband, fear of the husband—but why? [*Silences her with his hand, throws bones again, looks at them, then at her.*] Why are you so sad, you are pregnant, but you are sad, scared, and sad, scared and sad—but you are pregnant—he doesn't know eh? Yah! But what are you scared of? . . . Why are you telling me? You are going to bring on the wrath of the ancestors. [*Whisks himself with whisk.*]

So you are sick, ahh . . . its The Sickness.

Okay, okay, okay, okay [*gathers bones*], we don't cure that.

No one can heal that. There was a time, we thought it was a joke, we would call it American Ideas for Discouraging Sex. But now, now ahh, what we have seen, we know better.

But you can come back to me when the illnesses start, I can help you with those symptoms.

You can bring your husband to me too, if you tell him, I have a couples' discount.

[*Claps his hands.*] Hey! Stop crying! Usacheme mwanawangu!

You think you are the only one dealing with this problem?

If you go outside you can count, one, two, three—he has it.

One, two, three—she has it.

You are not special, there are many people who have this thing and still live their lives!

As for the other problems I've seen here [*indicating bones*], I can help you with those today.

For the fear of your husband beating you or leaving you, there is a love potion a muti. *Ah*—it is very popular these days I am running low.

Rub it on his penis thrice a day. He will never leave you or forsake you.

Don't ask the great ones how to do it!

That is your concern.

But, you women know how to get it when you want it, he he hehehehehe.

That one will allow the baby to die before it is born.

That way it won't have to suffer.

But don't confuse the two or your husband's penis will look like a piece of tree bark by morning. [*Winces continually at the thought and whisks himself.*]

[*Starts singing again.*]

That is all. And don't be so afraid my daughter, you are not alone.

[*Holds out hand while singing, gets $, looks, holds out hand again, looks satisfied.*] [*Keysha reenters.*] Sharp. Be gone. [*Keeps singing.*]

**KEYSHA**: Where is the complimentary bread. I tell you, that waiter got three mo' minutes—

[*To Nia*] Stop lookin' so sad. You not dyin', the world ain't over. You ain't the first one to end up pregnant. You should be happy! 'Cuz, you rollin' in the game with the big dogs now *Woof, Woof!* But let me warn you: this is not high school—these girls will be after Darnell and these bitches is ruthless. Don't trust none of 'em. They would fuck yo' man and yo' daddy in the same day. I've seen it happen: sports will turn these men into fools, but it'll turn women into . . . —Halle Berry in "Jungle Fever": [*Mocking*] *"Can I suck yo' dick? No? Uh, can I suck yo' dick? Anybody dick? Everybody dick?"* Just wait 'til he get a little money, a little more fame—I already see that nigga every weekend with his hand indiscriminately placed between somebody's legs. And them girls! Please! They love it. Well, they may cum, but they will go cuz they ain't shit to him. You got his baby. You stayin'. But it won't be easy. 'Cuz he'll be out with two, three of 'em at the same time every night and won't think nothin' of it. Then he'll bring you back some nastiness, his PR person will get involved and the next thing you know, you readin' about how you tried to give it to him to bribe him outta some money or somethin'. Hell yeah, we want to be paid and pampered, but not enough to be catchin' no STD. You remember my roommate Monica?

Monica. You know, [*imitates Monica sucking her thumb*]

Yeah her.

[*With discretion*] She had Chlamydia. Girl, yes! Walkin' around with it, thought it was a damn yeast infection. By the time she asked me to help her to the clinic, she couldn't even walk. And when she got there they said she had waited so long it turned into P-I-D—Pussy in Distress, yes. She got that shit from Jerry—that muthafucka didn't even know he had it. He coulda been walkin' around with herpes, shit, AIDS and not even know it. Of course she was afraid to tell him! I had to confront his punk ass and you know what he said? He said, *"I don't know whatchu talkin' 'bout. That's on her,"* like she gave it to herself. That nigga was on the DL, had Chla-my-di-a and he was still tryin' to make it seem like it was all on her. Like she did it like all by herself. How you even do that? What, you be like [*he imitates what giving herself a sexually transmitted disease would look like*]—Okay, okay, okay. The point is this: These men don't give a fuck about you. All you are to them is a piece of ass. And I'ma be damned if I'ma let my cousin get used up and then end up with nothin'. If you're givin' it up, then you best believe he givin' it up too. And you sho' ain't havin' no babies for free. That is not prostitution, that's called takin' care-a you. I mean, look-atcha mama! She dated some first class Negroes, had they baby, but still couldn't pay her rent. The last thing you wanna be is some hood-rat, baby-mama, walkin' around with cold sores and house shoes; buyin' government cheese with food stamps when yo' baby daddy in the N-B fuckin' A, and playin' husband to some other bitch and her kids. Then who the one lookin' stupid? Now, at least if you his wife, you get half, even if he divorce your ass; even if you do get Chlamydia. Then, whatever way it go, you won't never have to worry about money, and can do whatever the fuck you wanna do. Write your poetry, be Maya Angelou, whatever.

Listen to me: Don't let that boy out your sight. Remind him that you was the one at his games before anybody knew his name. Tell his mama you carrying his baby. Mmm-hum. Naw, go 'head, make it a family affair. Didn't you say you met her at they family picnic?

See! She probably already like you! And once you have her, it don't matter what he say. Don't stop 'til you get keys to the crib and a ring on that finger! Should you have his baby . . . how else you gon' pay me back for all the shit I did for you? Nia, havin' a baby is a blessing. I mean, think about it. I look better than all ya'll heifers put together, but I cannot have a baby out my ding-a-ling.

Whatever you do, I'ma always be your cousin, but remember, we already live in hell. Don't make it so you have to spend eternity there too. God gave you that baby. That baby is yo' ticket out. [*He exits.*]

### TEN: SEX WORKER

**SEX WORKER**: [*Enters smoking*] Dahling, dahling, dahling. How the bloody hell am I supposed to know how to make a man fall asleep so you can put love potion on his penis? Don't believe those stories about us sex workers stealing the penises of men who don't pay. That's all bullshit! [*Starts to sit, gets back up.*] Just give me a second my dahling. [*Takes out cloth tucked in side of pants, wipes between her legs.*] What a messy bastard . . . that's better.

[*Sits.*] Right, shit, you've got yourself into a pot of poo my girl!

Who would have thought Miss Priss Abigail would get herself in such a bind!

But, let me help you out my sister, since you have come to your old high school chum for advice.

You have to face the truth.

Your marriage is ova.

You think you can make him stay?

You know how these men are!

He will blame you for everything, even though you got it from him.

And the in laws!! Do you remember Elizabeth Chidzero?

It happened to her! Sent back to her village, penniless, the kids taken by the bastard and his family, even though she got it from him! Now she is waking up to the cockrels singing "kokoriko"—dancing at those fucking village pungwes for those old farts and she bathes in a filthy river, even though she's as sick as a bloody dog hey! You think it won't happen to you? You'll find yourself back in your village, grinding corn singing dum dum duri, dum dum duri.

Ha, and you were always the one who was going to go to America or something and become rich and famous.

What did you say your man's name was again? *Ahhhh.* [*Deep in thought, then looks back at Abigail.*] All I'll say is I am not suprised.

Shame.

The best thing I can offer you, my sister. Is a new lifestyle. Leave the bastard. Because he gave you AIDS! I can hook you up with a nice beneficiary

Who will take such good care of you

My love,

You will never need that man of yours again.

He will give you enough doughs to get the medicine and save that baby!

You can take your son, get your own place—you take care of the man every now and then.

*But*—you get the doughs, buy the drugs.

And you will live so much longer futi.

And no bullshit in law stress.

What have you got to loose my dahling. I don't understand the prob—

Ohh, ha! You think this lifestyle is planned or something?

The economy is shit my dear. In case you haven't noticed.

I was a secretary, couldn't pay for my rent,

Couldn't pay for my electric, I couldn't pay for my fucking DSTV!

And I was *not* going back to watching Dead BC.

No offense.

So I did it once, did it twice, next thing you know I had a business.

Listen, there is *nothing* wrong with being a kept woman. It's the least these bastards can do for us.

And it's a fair trade, almost like going back to the barter system.

And these African men, they love to flex their dollars, makes their dicks hard.

So, its there for the taking.

You have to decide what's more important to you

Remain Miss Priss Abigail, or become a survivor.

Because, you can't save both your marriage and that baby.

You can keep quiet about it, act as if nothing is wrong and

die horribly—watching your kid die too, all because you

Wanted to remain the perfect little Shona, Zimbabwean wifey.

Which many have done.

Or you can take care of yourself and your children.

Personally, I want to be a mother.

I have this one guy; he's a client, a really nice guy hey! He wants me to have his baby.

He says, no condoms.

Saka, me, I say, why not!

It's important to be a mother, it's the one thing we can do that these bastards can't!

This is just a hope for me, but you, you have children, So be a mother.

And forget about that potion girlie

Those n'angas are mad.

If they had anything that worked

Africa wouldn't even have AIDS. [*Looks outside.*]

Shit! Sorry dahling, it's another customer—and this one needs a little bit more time.

He's one of those old government chef bastards.

The machinery takes so much longer to oil. I can't even get into it.

Abi, Abigail—think about what I said, you have to do something, you can't keep running around like Speedy Gonzales! This is the best answer you are going to get!

[*Puts out cigarette, straightens out wig and shirt, looks over at client approaching.*]

Hi, howzit!?

[Ad-libs and overlaps with the Gail: "Hi, howzit . . . I'm fine." "Just don't be rough today, Chef!!"]

**ELEVEN: GAIL**

**GAIL**: Just be quiet, please! Shhh!

Damn it, Darnell! I said to take your medication and use a condom. Use a condom. I told him to—You kids don't think. You don't think beyond your own little circle of existence. You think this is a video game? This is life. You don't get to start over!

'Cause he's just a boy, he's a baby, how is he supposed to know how to—when you all just keep tossin' yourselves at him!

Don't give me that look. I see the way you look at him. Salavatin' with dollar signs in your eyes. You probably thought that if you latched onto him you could ride him all the way to the top. You think you the first one to try to lock him down? Ask his agent: he's already had two paternity claims.

Sit down. Sit back down! Why should I have told you anything, Nia? This is a private family matter. You should have kept your legs closed. And I warned Darnell about ya'll. I said, *"Darnell, baby, stay focused. You can't afford to get caught up."* And I made sure he played in all the right districts, with all the right coaches, he was seen by the recruiters! Look at his trophies. Look at them! Does this look like AIDS to you? Do you think he would be being recruited if anybody knew? Do you think he would be getting a scholarship? That's right! A scholarship for outstanding athletic achievement—to my son. So, no, nobody knows. It's none of they damn business. You consider what people will think about you if they knew. You think they gon' treat you the same? When you mention it, even the people you thought loved you will have you eatin' outta paper plates. Everybody turns on you; little kids say nasty things to you. Even the people at church! They gon' whisper behind your back; point at you in the pew, sayin', *"That's what happens to people who sin with the devil."* Think it won't happen.

Now, I'm trying to help you, Nia, but you have got to promise me—

Is this about money? Huh? Cuz I can get you money, Nia. Give me a couple of hours and I'll get you . . . $5,000. [*Maid enters, singing, starts cleaning.*] How's that sound? That'll be enough to get you a place, have some money left over to do what you got to do. That's what we'll do: I'll get you $5,000 for now, and we can worry about later, later.

### TWELVE: MAID

[*Maid, on hands and knees, cleaning the floor, singing "Tauya naye nemagumbezi."*]

**MAID**: Oh . . . Miss Abigail, Masikati, maskwera sei? Ndaskwera. I have put out the chicken and samoosas for Simbi's party, and the man is here with the jumping castles, but he wants to know if you want the jumping castle, kana the jumping giraffe. And that crazy little friend of Simbi's Fungai Mparaza he had to come early—and he has already broken two plates Miss Abi! And Bhudi Gilbert called, he said he was coming with the braaai stand—MissAbi are you okay? My husband? I don't have a husband MissAbigail. No, ya, of course, my family wants me to have one but I don't want. Anyway my family now its just my brother and aunts and uncles. My mother and father—they died kuma 1998 and 1999, then my sister kuma 2001. They had a long illness. Anyway, me I said, it's better to be alone, love between a man and a woman seems to end in death around here. And people say stupid things to me, but I don't care. Oh, they say things like—"eh, she thinks she is too good to get married, maybe she thinks she's a man. Eh, you don't want us—you are ugly anyway." [*Talks to imaginary men.*] I would like to say to them: *You are ugly anyway and you probably have something then you will beat me and leave me to suffer when I get it from you!!! No thanks.* But I just keep quiet. Saka, I am alone. I work here and go to night classes—I want to get a degree. Like you Miss Abi, you work, you went to school, and you are a wife and a mother futi—I don't want that part but I admire that—then I know I can do it too zvangu. People say, you can't do anything without a husband in Zimbabwe—but I will try anyway. At least like this I can say, Ini I know who I am, where I am going—I know what I am working for. And I am moving [*gestures*] forward, forward, forward, not this way or that way but forward. Maybe I stand alone, but I know who I am—Mary Chigwada—not Mrs So and So with the in laws and brideprice, and going to his village to cook at the funerals chi chi—*no*—just me Mary Chigwada.

*Ahh,* Miss Abi,—your mother and father are coming through the gate—ah, your mother looks so pretty! [*Straightening up.*] I am so glad you are back Miss Abi, there is so much to do, I haven't even put out the drinks yet and . . . Miss Abi—Miss Abi? Oh, maiwee! [*Rushes out.*]

## THIRTEEN: THE PRAYER—BILLS, BILLS, BILLS

**NIA**: It smell like booty

I wish I could fly away

Dirty ass motel.

Guess what, baby. Guess what? [*Dumping her purse.*] Today your mommy opened her purse to see how much money she had and she had a five dollar bill and a $5,000 check. $5,000. [*Folding up the check and putting it aside.*] But you know what? We don't need his money. No, we don't! Cuz mommy will go tomorrow and see if they still want her at Nordstrom. What was they talkin' 'bout payin'? Five dollars. But no, baby, no, we can do it. We just got to budget.

[*Tearing a piece of the five dollar bill with each item.*]

See this, this right here is for my retirement fund. Cuz Oprah says you should pay yourself first.

This, this is for your college fund, cuz you going to college.

This is for rent . . . on our mansion in Malibu.

And my Mercedes.

What else? What else you want, baby? You can have anything you want.

Oh wait! [*Tearing the last piece in three.*] Gas, water, and lights.

What! That's the life right there, baby. You got, retirement, college, mansion, Mercedes, gas, water, lights. What!

Ooooo! Mommy forgot to put food in the budget! How mommy forget to put food in the budget? But there's no more money.

There's $5,000.

[*She breaks down in tears.*] Because he knew. He knew. He knew the whole time—And he knows you're his baby cuz he the one made me pregnant. And now she thinks she can just throw $5,000 at me and I'ma just be quiet?

$5,000 dollars. I sold myself for $5,000. Nope, baby, that's how much I cost. That's how much you cost.

[*Balling up the check and throwing it down.*] No, no, we don't need his money. This is what we gonna do. [*Picking up the pieces of the five dollar bill.*] I'ma take the light money and make it the food money. Cuz we gotta eat.

But we don't need no lights.

[*À la "The Roof Is on Fire"*] We don't need no lights let the muthafuckas burn!

[*She b-boxes and makes a beat on the furniture.*]

Come on, baby.

*Cuz we got, huh? / What we got, huh?* What we got?!? We got, we got
*Sunlight*
*Insight*
*Out of sight—out of mind.*
*Full-time*
*Lifetime*
*Out-of-time*
*I'm outta my mind.*
*We gon'*
*Re-define*
*Discipline*
*Undermine that bottom line* [*Applying perfume.*]
*Drench myself in Vaseline*
*Make myself look feminine*
*I'll be dressed and drapped in Calvin Klein*
*And he'll come home at dinnertime*
*My womb is free of guilt and grime*
*Before this change, before this crime*
*Before the fall, before the climb* [*She begins to pray.*]
*Please keep me from this constant grind*
*Help me see, although I'm blind*
*Help me breathe despite the slime*
*Help me live if you're inclined*
*Please don't decline my prayer.*
*I know it's nobody's fault but mine*
*I won't bitch, complain or whine*
*If you help me out, one more time*
*I will not let you down.*
*I'll give up sex, weed, and wine. Everything. Everything.*
*Just plant my feet on solid ground.*

[*She sobs*] No. No! This what we gon' do. [*Picks up the check.*] Tomorrow we're going to go up to that scholarship ceremony. And I'm gonna make Darnell look me in the face and tell me I'm only worth $5,000. Then, I'm going to stand there in front of all those recruiters, in front of the whole world and I'ma just say it. And then all the girls he been with's gon' know. And all the girls he was thinking about doin's gon' know. And then everybody will know. [*Balling the check up and throwing it down again.*] I'm worth more than this money. [*She begins to exit. She doubles back for the check.*] Tomorrow.

**FOURTEEN: ABIGAIL'S PRAYER**

**ABIGAIL**: [*Enters, reading an old certificate.*]

Huh, I won that thing! I won that thing! [*Reading.*] This is to award Abigail Moyo of Malbereign Girls High as the winner of the National Interschools Public Speaking Championship, 1994, Harare, Zimbabwe.

I won that thing. What was my speech again? Oh, oh! Of course! [*Steps up on bed.*]

The New African Woman—Modernizing and Post Colonizing.

I was once number three of four wives—yet I chose to rise.

I was once denied usage of the same toilet as you [*laughs*] —I always had to look for a white—yet I chose to rise.

In me is the blood of the great Mbuya Nehanda—the spiritual medium who fought and died for this land.

In me is the pride of Winnie Mandela who marched the streets of Soweto singing "Free Nelson Mandela" until they did.

In me is the ferocity of the woman freedom fighter who let go of the milk of human kindness to fight for a free Zimbabwe!

I am no longer the third of four wives, but the first of the first.

And I can become whatever I please.

Because my dreams can be a reality . . .

[*She breaks.*]

He knew, he knew, that bastard. [*Steps down.*]

. . . how long . . . how long have you been bringing your hures into my house?

Have you been sleeping with them in my Woolworths sheets from Joburg?

But I knew it, I knew it all along, with the late nights and the way he was smelling . . .

but what could I have done Baba?

You are the one who said two become one, two flesh become one—and thats what I did—

So how did you allow one flesh to rot into the other when I lived according to your word?

And how can this be your plan for my life?

You want me to die like a prostitute?

That's your plan?

That's what you have been building me up to?

And don't give me that trial and tribulation bullshit!

I have come too far,

I have done everything the right way.

What more did you want from me? You've got to help me Baba, you've got to help me, you've got to help—

[*Stops to catch her breath, goes silent, drops to her knees.*]

Okay, okay, I will tell them.

But this is what I ask:

*Don't* you let them blame me.

You make them stand by me.

And support me.

And you make Stamford stay put.

You make him still love me and take care of me.

Because he's still mine and I am not giving up everything I worked for.

And I want my baby, so don't you let it have this illness.

[*Grips belly.*] You have to fight this baby with whatever you have. You just have to fight it okay. And if I must die—don't let me die like SisiStella who was convulsing in so much pain they had to strap her to a bed. And don't let me die like Sekuru Lovemore who was covered in so many sores they couldn't even show him at the funeral. And if I must die let my chil— [*Knock on the door—Abigail starts, sits on chair and composes herself.*]

[*Cheerily*] Come in. [*Enter Simbi.*]

Hello my big boy. Are you enjoying your party? You look so smart, is this the outfit daddy bought you? It's very nice . . . huh? They want to sing Happy

Birthday already. Okay, tell them I am coming—tell them Mummy spilt something on her dress and I have to change it. Okay . . . okay so you go ahead baby . . .

Simbi, dzoka mwanawangu, dzoka. [*Calls him back.*] Unoziwa kuti mummy loves you? Okay, saka iti "mummy loves me." Good boy. Ita futi, "mummy loves me." Good, okay, okay, you go ahead . . . mummy's coming.

## FIFTEEN: THE END

**ABIGAIL**: [*Singing "Watinti bafadzi" with Nia; both clear stage of stools.*]

*Watinta wafadzi watinti mbogoto uzagofa* [×*2*]

"Pamsoroi, Baba naAmai, na babamukuru, naBhudiGilgert, navatete. Tafara, we are happy you have come to celebrate Simbi's seventh birthday with us.

In our culture I know the family shares everything, and takes good, good care of one another. So I know I can share this with you and get your support. Stamford, I am telling you this here so we can find a harmony okay. Stamford, we have to go to the clinic tomorrow morning because I— . . . you . . . you and therefore we have acquired the acquired immune deficiency syndrome virus HIV and I am pregnant."

**NIA**: *"Good evening ladies and gentlemen. My name is Nia James, and I'm here to say that Darnell Smith gave me AIDS!"* // Then I'ma rip up the check. No, I can't say that . . .

**ABIGAIL**: // No—that acquired acquired thing is stupid . . . No, no this is good, he can't beat me or throw me out with my parents and Bhudi Gilbert there at his son's birthday futi . . .

**NIA**: . . . no, it's the right thing. Everybody should know . . .

**ABIGAIL**: He will have to beg my forgiveness. "Okay, okay, I forgive you—but you can't cheat anymore."—

**NIA**: *"He could be giving it to everybody. If I had know, I would have never"*—

**ABIGAIL**: "Now we must plan ahead for us and the children."

**NIA**: *"I'm not a hoe. Everybody has sex."*

**ABIGAIL**: "Yes I forgive you—no, no—don't hit him Bhudi Gilbert."

**NIA**: *"I didn't make this disease. I didn't give this to myself."*

**ABIGAIL**: "I choose to stay with you but you must find the money for treatments,"

**NIA**: *I should have protected myself, but he—*

**ABIGAIL**: "Because you got us into this trouble. Okay!"

**NIA**: I just wanted him to . . .

[*Abigail and Nia face each other in a mirror, but remain in opposite worlds.*]

**ABIGAIL**: "And you must look at me and see me, Abigail Moyo Murambe."

**NIA**: *"There's no amount you can pay me to take this away."*

**ABIGAIL**: "You must treat me like a wife you respect"—

**NIA**: *"Naw, I don't want yo' apology!"*

**ABIGAIL**: "Because I know who I am!"

**NIA**: *"I'm changing the course of history!"*

**ABIGAIL**: "And I am moving [*gestures*] forward, forward, forward—not this way or that. Okay!"

**NIA**: That's fine.

**ABIGAIL**: That's good.

**ABIGAIL/NIA**: So help me God. Let's go.

**ABIGAIL**: Okay kids, go play on the jumping castle!

**NIA**: [*To herself*] Damn, it's a lot of people . . .

**ABIGAIL**: [*Faces family*] Pamsoroi Baba, naAmai na babamukuru, navatetete naBhudiGilbert.

**NIA**: [*To herself*] There he is . . .

**ABIGAIL**: Tafara, we are happy you have come to celebrate Simbi's seventh birthday with us . . . eh . . .

**NIA**: [*To herself*] Just say it . . .

**ABIGAIL**: In our culture, we . . . move forward, forward, forward . . .

**NIA**: [*To the crowd*] Hey! I have . . . something I want to say . . .

**ABIGAIL**: No, no, I mean . . . with a family . . . eh . . .

**NIA**: [*To the crowd*] My name is Nia James . . .

**ABIGAIL**: We share everything . . .

**NIA**: [*To the crowd*] And I just came to say . . .

**ABIGAIL**: And that's why I know I can say what is happening between me . . . and Stamford . . . here . . .

**ABIGAIL/NIA**: eh . . . eh . . .

**ABIGAIL**: Stamford and I are having another baby!!! // Pururdza [*ululates*]!!! Eh, suwa, tinofara!! Ha? Ya, that was the news, that was it! Another boy ya that's what I was saying Tete! Another boy ya! Well, you were saying Simbi is getting lonely! So its time, ya, it's time. Sure ya. Maita! Tinofara . . . hehe.

**NIA**: Congratulations! // Oooa, Oooa! Oooa, Oooa! Huh? No, no that's what I came to say. Congratulations. Yeah. His mom's probably real proud, huh?! Hey! Can I get tickets to the games? Just two tickets? One ticket? I'ma get me a ticket, watch! You crazy! Heeee . . .

[*Both characters laugh in synchronicity into a blackout.*]

### Shona/Zimbabwe Glossary

**Aiwa:** no.
**Amai naba vako nevese nemumhuri menyu:** your mother and father and your family.
**Amai:** mother; also used as a sign of respect to a woman.
**Baba:** father; also used to substitute as Lord, God.
**Babamukuru:** older father; usually refers to an older uncle.
**Barance wemunhu:** idiot of a person.
**Beby:** baby.
**Bhudi:** brother.
**Chef:** a term used to describe men of power and influence in Zimbabwe.
**Chi chi:** etcetera, etcetera.
**Chisarai:** goodbye.
**Chisipiti:** an affluent suburb of Harare.
**Commuter omnibus:** a van used as a form of public transport.
**Dahling:** darling.
**Deddy:** daddy.
**DSTV:** equivalent of digital cable.
**Dum dum duri:** a song traditionally sung while grinding corn into flour with a large pestle and mortar.
**Dzoka mwana:** come back child, come back.
**Edgars:** major clothing chain around Southern Africa.
**Ewe:** you.

**Fotsek:** an expletive originally used to address dogs.
**Futi:** again, also.
**Glen Lorne:** an affluent suburb of Harare.
**Guyana ramwari munobvisa, matadzo epasi tinzireiwo tsitsi, ndipeyeiwo rugare:** lamb of God you take away the sins of the world, have mercy on us, grant us peace.
**Hartman House:** one of the most affluent boys prep schools in Harare.
**Head boy:** the top position a student can obtain in their final year of high school. A position of authority—from the British schooling system model—used in Zimbabwe as a result of colonization.
**Here:** converts a statement into a question.
**Howzit:** how is it going?
**Ini:** me.
**Ita futi:** say again.
**Iti:** say.
**Iwe waka pusa newewo uri HIV, futi Amai vako vane maronda panapa:** you are stupid and you have HIV, and your mother has sores here.
**Ka:** a Zimbabwean exclamation, often used for emphasis.
**Kana:** or.
**Kokoriko:** sound used to depict cockerels crowing.
**Kuma:** in.
**Kumusha:** a person's rural homeland.
**Kwete:** no.
**Maita:** thank you.
**Maiwee:** an exclamation or expression of distress.
**Marara:** bullshit, garbage.
**Masikati:** good afternoon.
**Maskwera sei:** how are you?
**Mati amaivangu vane AIDS:** did you say my mother has AIDS?
**Mbuya Nehanda:** legendary female spiritual medium who stood up against the British when they first invaded Zimbabwe in the 1890s. They executed her.
**Mhondoro dzinomwa muna Save, Mhondoro dzinomwa munaZambezi:** a song describing a lion drinking from the Save and Zambezi rivers.
**Mirai:** wait.
**Muboi:** derogatory term that black people use to describe lower-classed black people.
**MunomuZimbabwe:** here in Zimbabwe.
**Munoziwa kuti:** do you know that?
**Muri right:** how are you (are you "right")?
**Mwanawangu:** my child.

**Na:** and.
**Ndapota:** please.
**Ndibatsirewo:** help me out.
**Ne:** and.
**Nhasi ririFriday:** today is Friday.
**Nodo:** a children's game involving throwing a stone in the air and trying to move other stones out and inside of a circle while the stone is still in the air.
**N'yanga:** witchdoctor, traditional healer.
**Pajero:** prestigious Mitsubishi SUV in Zimbabwe.
**Pamsoroi:** excuse me.
**Paroadside:** at the side of the road.
**Pururudza:** a celebrative expression; often called ululating.
**Richiri jana rangu:** its still my turn.
**SABC:** South African Broadcasting Corporation.
**Sadza:** a staple Zimbabwean starch dish made from cormmeal, often used to reference food in general.
**Saka:** so.
**Saka hapana achatamba, hapana achatamba:** nobody's going to play, nobody's going to play.
**Saka wati Amai vangu vari HIV?:** so you said my mother is HIV?
**Sekuru:** grandfather/older uncle.
**Sha:** exclamation substituted for "man"; for example "come on *man,*" "come on *sha.*" Also short for *Shamwari.*
**Shamwari:** friend. Also used as an exclamation.
**Sisi:** sister.
**Suwa:** sure.
**Tafara:** we are happy.
**Tete:** aunt; specifically on one's father's side.
**Tichaboona:** see you.
**Tinofara:** we can all be happy.
**Tomato sauce:** children's play song.
**Totamba chi:** what should we play?
**Totanga:** let's start.
**Truworths:** major clothing chain around Southern Africa.
**Usacheme mwanawangu:** don't cry my child.
**Vako ndivo vari HIV:** they are the ones who have HIV.
**Vanhu vatema vanonetsa:** black people are a pain.
**Village pungwe:** traditional village meetings conducted in the rural areas.
**Watinta wafadzi wantinti mbogoto uzagofa:** you strike a woman you strike a rock and you will die. A South African Zulu song made famous by a musical production in the 1970s by the same name.

**Wonai:** look.
**Wuya:** come here.
**ZBC:** Zimbabwe Broadcasting Corporation (*Z* is pronounced "Zed").
**Zimboes:** a term used to describe Zimbabweans.
**Zvangu:** myself; used as an emphasis.

# SELECTED READINGS AND PLAYS

## Selected Readings


Banham, Martin, James Gibbs, Femi Osofisan, and Jane Plastow, eds. *African Theatre Women.* Oxford: James Curry, 2002.

Banham, Martin, Errol Hill, and George Woodyard, eds. *The Cambridge Guide to African and Caribbean Theatre.* Cambridge: Cambridge University Press, 1994.

Breitinger, Eckhard, ed. *Theatre for Development.* Rossdorf, Germany: TZ-Verlagsgesellschaft mbH, 1994.

———, ed. *Uganda: The Cultural Landscape.* Bayreuth, Germany: Bayreuth University, 1999.

Daymond, M. J., Dorothy Driver, Sheila Meintjes, et al. *Women Writing Africa: The Southern Region.* New York: The Feminist Press at the City University of New York, 2003.

James, Adeola, ed. *In Their Own Voices: African Women Writers Talk.* London: James Currey, 1990.

*Lihamba,* Amandina, *Fulata L. Moyo,* and *Mugaybuso M. Mulokozi,* eds. *Women Writing Africa: The Eastern Region.* New York: The Feminist Press at the City University of New York, 2007.

Mda, Zakes. *When People Play People: Development Communication through Theatre.* Johannesburg, South Africa: Witwatersrand University Press, 1993.

Nnaemeka, Obioma. *Sisterhood, Feminisms and Power: From Africa to the Diaspora.* Trenton, N.J.: Africa World Press, 1998.

Rubin, Don, ed. *The World Encyclopedia of Contemporary Theatre.* Vol. 3, *Africa.* London: Routledge, 1997.

Sall, Ebrima, ed. *Women in Academia: Gender and Academic Freedom in Africa.* Dakar, Senegal: Council for the Development of Social Science Research in Africa, 2000.
Sutherland-Addy, Esi, and Aminata Diaw, eds. *Women Writing Africa: West Africa and the Sahel.* New York: The Feminist Press at the City University of New York, 2005.
Taiwo, Oladele. *Female Novelists of Modern Africa.* London: Macmillan, 1984.

**Selected Plays by African Women (Published and Unpublished)**

Acholonu, Catherine. *In the Heart of Biafra.* Owerri, Nigeria: Totan, 1970.
———. *Trial of the Beautiful Ones.* Owerri, Nigeria: Totan, 1985.
Adichie, Amanda N. *For Love of Biafra.* Ibadan, Nigeria: Spectrum Books, 1998.
Aidoo, Ama Ata. *Anowa.* White Plains, N.Y.: Longman, 1985.
———. *Anowa.* In *Contemporary African Plays,* ed. Martin Banham and Jane Plastow, 137–206. London: Methuen Drama, 1999.
———. *Anowa.* In *Postcolonial Plays: An Anthology,* ed. Helen Gilbert, 97–127. London: Routledge, 2001.
———. *The Dilemma of a Ghost.* Accra, Ghana: Longman, 1965.
———. *The Dilemma of a Ghost.* White Plains, N.Y.: Longman, 1985.
Aimuwu, Agharese. *The Landlady.* Ibadan, Nigeria: Onibonoje, 1987.
Akinwumi, Isola. *Madam Tinubu: The Terror in Lagos.* Lagos, Nigeria: Heinemann, 1998.
Barungi, Violet. "Award Winner." Manuscript, 2000.
Chere, Julia. "Money Is Sweeter than Love." Unpublished play.
———. "Rise and Shine." Unpublished play.
Dangarembga, Tsitsi. *She No Longer Weeps.* Harare, Zimbabwe: College Press, 1987.
Dike, Fatima. *Glass House.* In *African Theatre Women,* ed. Martin Banham, James Gibbs, Femi Osofisan, and Jane Plastow, 132–53. Oxford: James Currey, 2002.
———. *So What's New?* In *Black South African Women: An Anthology of Plays,* ed. Kathy A. Perkins, 23–46. New York: Routledge, 1998.
———. "The Crafty Tortoise." Manuscript.
———. *The First South African.* Johannesburg, South Africa: Ravan Press, 1979.
———. "The Middle Passage." Manuscript, 2003.
———. "The Sacrifice of Kreli." Johannesburg, South Africa: Donker, 1976.
Essa, Saira, and Charles Pillai. *Steve Biko: The Inquest.* Durban, South Africa: Upstairs Theatre, 1985.
Klotz, Phyllis, Thobeka Maqhutyana, Nomvula Qsoba, Xolani September, Poppy Tsira, and Itemuleng Wa-Lehulere. *You Strike the Woman, You Strike the Rock.* Johannesburg, South Africa: Donker, 1994.
Lihamba, Amandina. *Hawala ya Fedha.* Dar es Salaam, Tanzania, 1980.
Liking, Werewere. *La puissance de Um.* Abidjan, Ivory Coast: Ceda, 1979.
———. "La Queue du Diable." In *Du Rituel à la scène.* Paris: Nizet, 1979.
———. "Les mains veulent dire." In *Spectacles rituels.* Dakar, Senegal: N.E.A., 1987.
———. *The Power of Um and A New Earth.* Trans. Siga Asanga, Jeanne N. Dingome, Innocent Futcha, and Nalova P. Lyonga. Bethesda, Md.: International Scholars, 1996.
———. *Singuè Mura.* Abidjan, Ivory Coast: Eyo Ki-Yi Editions, 1990.
———. *Un Touareg s'est marié à une Pygmée.* Brussels, Belgium: Lansman, 1992.

———. *Une Nouvelle Terre, suivi de Du Sommeil d'Injuste.* Dakar, Senegal: N.E.A., 1980.
———. *The Widow Dylemma.* Trans. Judith G. Miller. In *Plays by Women Book II,* ed. Françoise Kourilsky and Catherine Temerson, 87–111. New York: Ubu Repertory Theater Publications, 1994.
Magona, Sindiwe. *House-Hunting unlike Soweto.* In *Black South African Women: An Anthology of Plays,* ed. Kathy A. Perkins, 47–53. New York: Routledge, 1998.
Mcbagonluri, Diana Bamford. *Boomerang.* Accra, Ghana: Excellent Publishing and Printing, 2003.
Meer, Fatima. "Ahimsa-Ubuntu." Manuscript.
Mhlophe Gcina, Maralin Vanrenen, and Thembi Mtshali. *Have You Seen Zandile?* Braamfontein, South Africa: Skotaville, 1988.
———. *Have You Seen Zandile?* In *Black South African Women: An Anthology of Plays,* ed. Kathy A. Perkins, 80–101. New York: Routledge, 1998.
Mpesha, Nyambura. *Mugasha: Epic of the Bahaya.* Nairobi, Kenya: East African Education, 2000.
Msora, Bertha. *I Will Wait.* Harare: Zimbabwe Publishing House, 1984.
Mugo, Micere Githae. *The Long Illness of Ex-Chief Kiti.* Nairobi, Kenya: East African Literature Bureau, 1976.
Mugo, Micere Githae, and Ngugi wa Thiongo. *The Trial of Dedan Kimathi.* Oxford: Heinemann, 1977.
Naidoo, Muthal. *Flight from the Mahabarath.* In *Black South African Women: An Anthology of Plays,* ed. Kathy A. Perkins, 113–41. New York: Routledge, 1998.
———. *We Three Kings.* Durban, South Africa: Asoka Theatre Publications, 1992.
Ndlovu, Lueen Conning. *A Coloured Place.* In *Black South African Women: An Anthology of Plays,* ed. Kathy A. Perkins, 6–22. New York: Routledge, 1998.
———. "Sister Breyani." Manuscript, 2006.
———. "U-Voice." Manuscript, 1995.
Ntangaare, Mercy Mirembe. *Lady, Will You Marry Me?* Kampala, Uganda: MPK Graphics, 2002.
Ntangaare, Mercy Mirembe, and Dan Isiko Kisense. *Dustbin Nations and the Chief of Shumankuzi.* Kampala, Uganda: MPK Graphics, 2002.
Nwapa, Flora. *The First Lady.* Enugu, Nigeria: Tana Press, 1993.
———. *Sycophants.* Enugu, Nigeria: Tana Press, 1993.
———. *Two Women in Conversation.* Enugu, Nigeria: Tana Press, 1993.
Okoh, Julie. *Aisha.* Port Harcourt, Nigeria: Pearl, 2005.
———. *Edewede.* Owerri, Nigeria: Totan, 2000.
———. *In the Fullness of Time.* Owerri, Nigeria: Totan, 2000.
———. *Who Can Fight the Gods?* Port Harcourt, Nigeria: Pearl, 2002.
Okurut, Mary. *The Curse of the Sacred Cow.* Kampala, Uganda: Fountain, 1994.
Onwueme, Osonye Tess. *The Missing Face.* Lagos, Nigeria: Africana Legacy Press, 1997.
———. *Shakara Dance-Hall Queen.* San Francisco: African Heritage Press, 2000.
———. *Tell It to Women: An Epic Drama for Women.* Detroit: Wayne State University Press, 1994.
———. *Three Plays: The Broken Calabash, Parables for a Season, and The Reign of Wazobia.* Detroit: Wayne State University Press, 1993.
Phillips, Nerissa, and Gcina Mhlophe. *African Story Theatre: A Collection of Dramatized*

*Folk-Tales*. Stories as told by Thomas A. Nevin. Johannesburg, South Africa: Heinemann, 1996.
Sofola, Zulu. "The Adventures of Chike: Episode One, Chike on the High Sea." Manuscript.
———. "The Adventures of Chike: Synopsis of 13 Episodes." Manuscript.
———. "A Heart's Desire." Manuscript.
———. *The Disturbed Peace of Christmas*. Ibadan, Nigeria: Daystar Press, 1971.
———. *King Emene: Tragedy of a Rebellion*. Ibadan, Nigeria: Heinemann, 1974.
———. *Lost Dreams*. Ibadan, Nigeria: Heinemann, 1982.
———. *Memories in the Moonlight*. Ibadan, Nigeria: Evans Brothers, 1986.
———. *Old Wines Are Tasty: A Play*. Ibadan, Nigeria: University Press, 1979.
———. "Omu Ako of Isele Oligbo." Manuscript, 1989.
———. *Song of a Maiden: A Play*. Ibadan, Nigeria: University Press, 1991.
———. *The Sweet Trap*. Ibadan, Nigeria: University Press, 1977.
———. *Wedlock of the Gods*. Ibadan, Nigeria: Evans Brothers, 1972.
———. *The Wizard of Law*. Ibadan, Nigeria: Evans Brothers, 1972.
Sutherland, Efua T. *Edufa*. In *Crosswinds: An Anthology of Black Dramatists in the Diaspora*, ed. and intro. William B. Branch, 54–95. Bloomington: Indiana University Press, 1993.
———. *Foriwa: A Play*. Accra, Ghana: State Publishing, 1967.
———. *The Marriage of Anansewa: A Storytelling Drama*. Accra, Ghana: Sedco, 1998.
———. *Tahinta: A Rhythm Play for Children*. Accra: Ghana Publishing House, 1968.
———. *Vulture! Vulture! Two Rhythm Plays*. Accra: Ghana Publishing House, 1968.
Williams, Magi. *Kwa-Landlady*. In *Black South African Women: An Anthology of Plays*, ed. Kathy A. Perkins, 159–76. New York: Routledge, 1998.
———. "Noninzi." Manuscript.

# CONTRIBUTORS

**AMANDINA LIHAMBA** is a professor in theatre arts and has recently completed her tenure as the dean of the Faculty of Arts and Social Sciences of the University of Dar es Salaam. In addition to her academic and creative writings, she has also worked as a performer and director for the stage and screen. Her research interests, for which she has also written, include culture, politics, communication, the arts, gender studies, and education. She has been one of the pioneers of initiatives for gender equity and equality in education and the arts, including the Tuseme programme, which has received international and regional attention. A recipient of Rockefeller, Fulbright, and other fellowship awards, she has also been the chair and a member of numerous regional and national organizations of theatre, culture, media, gender, and governance.

**KATHY A. PERKINS** is professor and chair of lighting design in the Department of Theatre at the University of Illinois, Urbana-Champaign. She is the editor of *Black South African Women: An Anthology of Plays* and coeditor of *Strange Fruit: Plays on Lynching by American Women*, *Contemporary Plays by Women of Color*, and *Black Female Playwrights: An Anthology of Plays before 1950*. She is also a fellow in the College of Fellows in the American Theatre.

The University of Illinois Press
is a founding member of the
Association of American University Presses.

University of Illinois Press
1325 South Oak Street
Champaign, IL 61820-6903
www.press.uillinois.edu